Sr. Ann Laforest, ocd
Telephone: 914 424 4726
914 831 5572

1999 address: Carmelite Sisters
Graymoor PO Box 300
Garrison NY 10524

2000 on: Carmelite Monastery
139 De Peyster Ave
Beacon NY 12508

THE EUCHARIST IN THE WEST

Edward J. Kilmartin, S.J.

THE EUCHARIST IN THE WEST

History and Theology

For Ann:
May you continue to grow
more fully into the
Eucharistic life of our
Lord!

Edited by Robert J. Daly, S.J.

Bob Daly, S.J.

A PUEBLO BOOK

THE LITURGICAL PRESS COLLEGEVILLE, MINNESOTA

A Pueblo Book published by The Liturgical Press

Design by Frank Kacmarcik, Obl.S.B.

Library of Congress Cataloging-in-Publication Data

Kilmartin, Edward J.
The Eucharist in the West : history and theology / Edward J. Kilmartin ; edited by Robert J. Daly.
p. cm.
"A Pueblo book."
Includes bibliographical references and indexes.
ISBN 0-8146-6172-6 (alk. paper)
1. Lord's Supper—Catholic Church. 2. Catholic Church—Doctrines. 3. Lord's Supper—History. I. Daly, Robert J., 1933– . II. Title.
BX2215.2.K56 1998 98-24489
234'.163'09—dc21 CIP

Contents

PART TWO: THEOLOGY

Editor's Foreword

Edward J. Kilmartin, S.J., Professor Ordinarius of liturgical theology at the Pontificio Istituto Orientale, died in Boston, Massachusetts on June 16, 1994.[1] Among his papers left behind with the Jesuit Community at Boston College, which had been his home in his last illness, was the manuscript of this book in electronic form. That Kilmartin had been working on this book was widely known. It was generally assumed that it was the continuation of his earlier *Christian Liturgy*.[2] But when one examines the two works, this one seems to be less of a continuation than his final word, hastily entered into his laptop in that final period when he knew that his time was short.[3]

Most of the text was on the hard drive of his laptop computer. Some gaps could be filled in from the set of backup diskettes he carefully maintained. What emerged was the draft of a book in eleven chapters of diverse length. Although conceptually complete, the book was, technically and stylistically, in very rough condition. It was filled with typographical errors, stylistic inconsistencies, and numerous inexact or garbled references. It was also generously sprinkled with passages that could be deciphered only with great effort. But shining through I recognized an exciting statement which, properly edited, could become one of the most important books on the Eucharist to appear in the twentieth century. My high estimation of the value of this book has been amply confirmed when, over the past three and

[1] See Michael A. Fahey, S.J., "In Memoriam: Edward J. Kilmartin, S.J. (1923–1994)," *Orientalia christiana periodica* 61 (1995) 5–18, and "Bibliography of Publications of Edward J. Kilmartin, S.J.," ibid., 19–35.

[2] Edward J. Kilmartin, S.J., *Christian Liturgy: Theology and Practice*. Part I. *Systematic Theology of Liturgy* (Kansas City: Sheed & Ward, 1988).

[3] In January 1994, Kilmartin had summarized the main thesis of the book in his Berakah Award address to the North American Academy of Liturgy. At the time of his death, an expanded version of that summary was in the press as "The Catholic Tradition of Eucharistic Theology: Towards the Third Millennium," *Theological Studies* 55 (1994) 405–57.

one-half years, I have presented this project, or a part of it, on twelve different occasions to eight different groups, patristic, liturgical, and theological, in the United states and in Europe. Upon completion of this editing, and after publication of whatever else of publishable value can be found in Kilmartin's *Nachlaß*,[4] all his papers along with the essential record of my editing will be deposited in the Burns Library (archives) of Boston College.

THE EDITORIAL WORK

I have devoted most of a sabbatical year (1996–1997) to this task. The first major task has been stylistic. Frequent instances of hasty composition and inconsistent style had to be smoothed out. In addition, numerous passages and sentences had to be "decompressed" in order to make Kilmartin's meaning comfortably accessible. This will be no surprise to readers already familiar with Kilmartin's writings. Once something was clear in his own mind, he tended to move on quickly to the next point, often inattentive to the fact that his readers would still be struggling to grasp what went before. This was compounded by the fact that Kilmartin's thought ranged broadly across the biblical, patristic, historical, theological (both scholastic and modern), and liturgical disciplines. Not many readers can "fly" comfortably with him across all these disciplines. In the course of my various presentations and discussions of this material, I became deeply aware of the need to decompress Kilmartin's prose.

Decompression, however, does not mean altering or significantly adding to what Kilmartin wrote. This book is written in Kilmartin's voice, not mine. In the few instances where I was not sure that my decompressing and clarifying was precisely according to Kilmartin's mind, I have indicated this by the use of brackets and my initials [RJD].

The second major editorial task has been in the documentation. Since Kilmartin was not physically able to check and verify his sources, there were scores—perhaps hundreds—of instances of inexact or incomplete references and some instances of badly garbled references. In the course of this year's work, and with the assistance of the superb

[4] An in-principle decision has also been made to collect and publish Kilmartin's scattered articles and shorter essays. However, a publisher and publication timetable for this has not yet been arranged.

library of the Philosophisch-theologische Hochschule Sankt Georgen, Frankfurt am Main, I have been able to verify, and in many cases make more exact, all but one of Kilmartin's references to primary sources and secondary literature. However, the documentation had not only to be verified; it also had to be brought into the footnotes. In most cases Kilmartin had provided only the bare reference. In order to make the book more useful, I not only verified the sources and secondary literature; I also studied them enough to bring into the footnotes a sufficient selection of the texts and key secondary literature to enable careful scholars to verify for themselves the validity of Kilmartin's analyses. The material gathered in the footnotes, therefore, while faithfully following Kilmartin's often cryptic directions, and very rarely adding something he did not specifically point to [and these cases always editorially indicated] represent largely the work of the editor.

KILMARTIN'S METHOD

At one point in chapter ten, Kilmartin refers the reader to "observations made on the subject of the 'methodological approach to the theology of the Eucharist' contained in the introduction to this book."[5] I have not been able to find these observations; it is quite possible that Kilmartin never got around to writing them. Although there is a conceptual integrity to this book, it is clearly a work still in progress. What Kilmartin is doing is further complicated by the fact, which is also the book's great strength, that he is not talking simply about theological and/or dogmatic texts. The meanings he wants to discuss are partly mediated by doctrines, but also, and crucially, by liturgy as "done." He does not merely give an account of eucharistic teaching (what systematic theologians do), nor merely give an account of eucharistic practice (what most "liturgiologists" do). Since he wants to bring these back together where they belong, his method, especially since he was not given the time to reflect on it, will necessarily be messy.[6] What follows in this foreword, therefore, is my attempt, as editor, to fill this gap.

[5] Chapter ten, n. 22 (p. 282). This comes at the end of a section, "Constructive Theology" which, for information about Kilmartin's method, should be read along with my remarks here. See also the opening pages of chapter eleven.

[6] For these comments, as well as for the accuracy of what I say below about the relationship of Kilmartin's work to the Lonerganian functional specialties, I am indebted to my Boston College colleague, Charles C. Hefling, Jr.

First of all, is there a central vision, are there some dominant hermeneutical principles that guide Kilmartin in his work? The force and, indeed, the bluntness of many of his analyses and judgments lead one to assume that he must have had some central, guiding vision, or at least some clear sense of how things should be or must be. If we take this book manuscript, his final work, as our source, three figures stand out as foundational pillars of his method: (1) the Italian Jesuit liturgical scholar Cesare Giraudo, (2) the Irish theologian Brian McNamara, S.J. (and behind him Lonergan [implicitly] and Aquinas), and (3) Kilmartin himself.[7]

(1) When painting with his broad brush, Kilmartin frequently insisted that the major liturgical theological task before us is the reintegration of *lex orandi* in a proper balance with *lex credendi* as a privileged source of theology, and that the achievement of this integration will be the work of the third theological millennium. This terminology and this vision are from Giraudo. The frequency of Kilmartin's references to Giraudo's *Eucaristia per la chiesa* suggest that the opening methodological chapter of that book, "From a Present Static Theology to a Recovery of a Dynamic Theology," is a key source for Kilmartin's historical and liturgical-theological method. In addition, Kilmartin seems to owe much to Giraudo for his conviction about the basically bipartite internal structure of the classical Eucharistic Prayers of both East and West, and that those prayers, thus structured, provide a critically central source for the theology of the Eucharist.

(2) Brian McNamara, a systematic theologian, provides Kilmartin with the terminology and conceptuality of "higher perspectives." The search for a higher perspective from which to systematize more adequately the varied and often seemingly conflicting data from the different sources of liturgical theology is a central and recurring theme in Kilmartin's journey toward that better, i.e., more authentically systematic theology of the liturgy and of the Eucharist which he predicts will be the achievement of the third theological millennium. McNamara acknowledges his debt to the Canadian theologian Bernard J. F. Lonergan. Like Lonergan, McNamara saw himself as continuing the work of Aquinas in seeking a "higher intelligibility." I have found no indi-

[7] Cesare Giraudo, *Eucaristia per la chiesa: Prospettive teologiche sull'eucaristia a partire dalla "lex orandi"* (Rome: Gregorian University/Brescia: Morcelliana, 1989); Brian McNamara, "Christus Patiens in Mass and Sacraments: Higher Perspectives," *Irish Theological Quarterly* 42 (1975) 17–35; Edward J. Kilmartin, S.J., *Christian Liturgy: Theology and Practice.*

cation that Kilmartin saw himself as a follower of Lonergan. If he had so seen himself, he surely would have referred, not just to some of Lonergan's earlier works,[8] but also to his 1972 *Method in Theology.* Nevertheless, I find that reading Kilmartin from the background of Lonergan's eight functional specialties helps me to understand what he is doing, as well as to explain why he is often so hard to understand. For Kilmartin's work, unlike much modern scholarship, is not narrowly specialized; it ranges broadly across at least five of the eight functional specialties. The functional specialties of "interpretation." and "history" are central to Kilmartin's work, especially to Part One of this book. The functional specialty of "dialectic" pervades the entire book, for he is constantly sorting out the valid and the central from the inauthentic and the marginal. The specialties of "doctrines" and "systematics" are also central, especially to Part Two of this book where he works from the background of and towards the articulation of his central theological vision. Even though much of what he does here is report *in oratione obliqua* what other theologians have been saying, he is constantly trying to clarify precisely what the doctrines were and are (as well as what they were not and are not), and he is constantly seeking that "higher perspective" which will enable him to systematize them in relation to each other and to the experience of the Christian faith as a whole.[9]

(3) Kilmartin's own earlier work, specifically concerning trinitarian theology and the role of the Holy Spirit in the liturgy, provides the third foundational pillar for understanding his methodology. The Austrian theologian, H. B. Meyer, reviewing *Christian Liturgy I,* wrote: "To our knowledge, there has been no other book before this one which, on the basis of an extensive appropriation of the theological traditions of the East and the West, offers such a systematic and consistently trinitarian theology of Christian worship and sacraments."[10]

These three points help explain why Kilmartin could be so confidently blunt in pointing out the weaknesses of the "average modern

[8] The index to Kilmartin's *Christian Liturgy I* contains ten references to the earlier works of Lonergan.

[9] I cannot refrain from observing that the fact that there is little in Kilmartin's work that seems to correspond to the eighth functional specialty, "communications," may help explain why he is often so hard to understand. A major editorial concern has been to supply somewhat for this lack.

[10] Hans Bernhard Meyer, "Eine trinitarische Theologie der Liturgie und der Sakramente," *Zeitschrift für katholische Theologie* 113 (1991) 24–38, at 37.

Catholic theology of the Eucharist" and of its various antecedent developments in the scholasticism of the second theological millennium. He knew that the eucharistic theology of the future had to (1) reintegrate *lex orandi* as a privileged *locus theologicus,* (2) bring liturgical theology into systematic consistency with the rest of theology and Christian faith experience, and (3) be genuinely trinitarian and, especially in the Eucharist, highlight the (in the West) neglected role of the Holy Spirit. When he saw that a theological position failed in one or more of these points, he did not hesitate to dismiss it as inadequate.

Looking more closely, we can identify three more methodological principles at work in this book. The first is the concept of "models." Kilmartin distinguishes between "exogenous" models that come from outside the material being studied, and "endogenous" models that come from within that material. Of course, he favors the latter. In the history of Western eucharistic theology, this distinction is illuminating. In the first theological millennium, the endogenous model of the Incarnation was dominant, or at least remained prominent, in attempts to understand the mystery of the Eucharist. In the second theological millennium, the exogenous model of change in physical beings dominated. This helps explain Kilmartin's emphasis that one of the major tasks of the third theological millennium will be not just to identify and appropriate the valid achievements of the second millennium, but also, and especially, to reappropriate the theological insights of the first.

Next, I find the concepts "synchronic" and "diachronic" helpful in understanding what Kilmartin is about. Synchronically, Kilmartin attempts to appropriate and make sense of all that is going forward in contemporary Christian theology both in the West and in the East. From the point of view of Western theology, a touchstone of the adequacy of a particular aspect of eucharistic theology is its systematic consistency with other doctrines and theological areas such as the theology of grace, of prayer, of redemption, to say nothing of trinitarian theology, Christology, pneumatology, and ecclesiology. From the point of view of Eastern theology, the major contribution has been the recognition of the role of the Holy Spirit. Diachronically, Kilmartin's appropriation of the history of the liturgy is one of the sources of the richness as well as of the occasionally forbidding density of his writing.

Finally, an at least implicit part of Kilmartin's method was his commitment to consider the teaching of the ecclesiastical magisterium as well as the work of other theologians as important theological sources. It is humbly refreshing to see that someone who could be so blunt about the deficiencies of the "average modern Catholic theology of the Eucharist" was also someone who devoted great time and energy to study the teaching of the Church. This enabled him to point out not only where that teaching needs to become a better teaching, but also where it has already made major contributions towards that better theology that he hopes will be the achievement of the third millennium. His major instance of this positive contribution of the ecclesiastical magisterium is the recognition of the central role of the Holy Spirit in the postconciliar liturgical reforms and the new Roman Eucharistic Prayers introduced under Pope Paul VI.

Kilmartin's reliance on certain other contemporary theologians is extensive. When they produce something that helps him move towards a more adequate, more systematic theology of the Eucharist, he simply takes it over, makes it his own, and moves on. His appropriation of the work of Giraudo and McNamara are examples of this. But it is on this point that Kilmartin has also been criticized, and not totally without reason. He makes no attempt to provide even a selective *Literaturbericht,* or to be evenhanded in his use of contemporary theology. What he finds useful for his purposes, he uses; what he does not, he simply ignores. This means that some of the most accomplished of contemporary liturgical theologians, for example, David N. Power and Louis-Marie Chauvet, go unmentioned, even though the basic findings of their work seem to be quite congenial to those of his. Whether this single-mindedness will turn out to have been a narrow-mindedness, or perhaps simply one of the conditions which enabled Kilmartin to keep pushing ahead and thus to bring us significantly closer to a more adequate, more systematic theology of the Eucharist will be, in the years to come, for the readers of this book to judge.

ACKNOWLEDGMENTS

In the three and one-half years that this book has been entrusted to my care, hundreds of people have encouraged or assisted me in various ways. The Jesuit Community at Boston College, which was Ed Kilmartin's final home on earth, carefully preserved all his books, papers, and electronic records until they could be handed on to me; the New England Province of the Society of Jesus appointed me as Kilmartin's literary executor; and the staff of the Burns Library Archives at Boston College, where this material will eventually be stored, helped with technical advice. Then, when I began the editing task, my colleague, Harvey Egan, S.J., the staff of the Information Technology Services at Boston College, and a graduate assistant, Thomas Kelly, helped to upgrade and transfer the electronic data to forms accessible to me.

Between June 1995 and August 1997 I have made presentations of this material, or selected parts of it, to the following groups in the U.S. and in Europe: The Catholic Theological Society of America (in 1995 and 1997), the Boston Theological Society, the North American Academy of Literature (in 1996, 1997, and 1998), the North American Patristic Society (in 1996 and 1997), the Societas Liturgica (in 1995 and 1997), the Boston Area Patristics Group, the Jesuit faculty and the students of Sankt Georgen, Frankfurt am Main, and the Seventh International Congress on Origen Studies. These were mostly presentations of various parts of this book, but in some cases they consisted of additional contributions of my own, heavily based on Kilmartin's work. The accompanying reactions and discussions invariably confirmed my convictions about the importance of this work and my determination to prepare it for publication as faithfully as possible.

In the early stages of the work, a meeting with some dozen former students of Kilmartin helped shape the guidelines for my editorial work. This group also identified The Liturgical Press as the preferred publisher of the book. From this group, Mary M. Schaefer was particularly helpful in my work on chapter four where Kilmartin relied heavily on her doctoral research. In the final stages, Francis A. Sullivan, S.J., Gerard Sloyan, Charles C. Hefling, Jr., and John Boyd Turner made suggestions which have helped me to reduce the errors and increase the readability of the book. As we go to press, four graduate students, Stefanos Alexopoulos, David E. Drury, Juliann Heller, and Christopher J. Pedley have been reading the manuscript with me as the basis of a course on the Eucharist. Their suggestions have been a help, and their enthusiasm has brought joy to my work.

Robert J. Daly, S.J.
Boston College

Introduction

The theme of this book is the eucharistic theology of the Latin Church as distinguished from that of the traditions of the Eastern churches. Part One summarizes the history of this theology which begins in the third-century North African Church and carries through to modern times.

Our analysis of the history of eucharistic theology of the first millennium up through the period of early scholasticism reveals that the theology of eucharistic sacrifice, however unsatisfactory, did not prove to be a subject of serious debate. What was seriously debated, however, was the manner of conceiving the eucharistic sacraments of the body and blood. This oscillated between the more realistic theology of somatic real presence characteristic of the fourth-century School of Antioch exemplified by St. John Chrysostom, and the more symbolic theology of St. Augustine whose Neoplatonic philosophy prevented him from interpreting the sacraments as more than signs pointing to a spiritual reality.

Chapter one describes the characteristics of the eucharistic theology of the Western Latin Fathers. This includes brief accounts of the contributions of those individual theologians who not only serve as witnesses of their own churches but who also exercised significant influence over succeeding generations. Chapter two identifies the more important orientations and developments of the Catholic tradition from early medieval scholasticism up to the first part of the twelfth century. Chapter three singles out the special contribution of early scholasticism to Latin eucharistic theology. This proved to be a cornerstone of the school theology that has dominated Latin eucharistic theology from the thirteenth century to the present. Chapter four functions as a bridge from early scholasticism to High Scholasticism by outlining the general approach to a synthetic theology of the Eucharist which obtained at the beginning of the thirteenth century. Chapter five treats eucharistic theology from High Scholasticism to the Council of Trent. Chapter six summarizes the dogmatic teaching of the Council of Trent. This is followed, in chapter seven, by a treatment of salient features of post-Tridentine eucharistic theology. This focuses especially on the formulation of the average modern Catholic theology of eucharistic sacrifice and the official modern Catholic position on this subject. Part One closes, in chapter eight, with an analysis of the practice and theology of Mass stipends. The history of this was already discussed in the particular contexts of chapters two and five; here the current official teaching of the Roman magisterium is described and evaluated.

The question of eucharistic realism was officially settled for the Latin Church in the period of early scholasticism and subsequently confirmed by the Council of Trent. In contrast, the theology of eucharistic sacrifice remained in an embryonic state up through the thirteenth century. The closest one came to a systematic presentation of eucharistic sacrifice which showed some originality was the systematic approach of John Duns Scotus at the close of the period of High Scholasticism. Although Scotus's systematic eucharistic theology was not treated at length in the next two centuries, his conclusions did exercise considerable influence. Beyond that, as received and developed at the close of the scholasticism period by the Tübingen professor Gabriel Biel, Scotus's systematic approach became the preferred explanation of many Catholic apologists in their debate with the sixteenth-century Reformers. Moreover, Trent's formulation of the dogmatic content of the sacrificial aspect of the Mass left untouched, at least as regards the intention of the fathers of the council, the Scotus–Biel theology of eucharistic sacrifice.

Nevertheless the history of the postconciliar reception of the Thomistic and Scotistic theologies of eucharistic sacrifice reveals a development in the direction of the Thomistic synthesis. This emerged shortly after the Council of Trent. We illustrate how this Thomistic tradition—not to be simply identified with the actual teaching of Aquinas—has influenced the twentieth-century Roman Catholic magisterium. We do this by summarizing the major official documents which have dealt with this Thomistic tradition over the last five decades. But this treatment takes up the teaching of Aquinas himself only in passing, and mainly insofar as "received" by the post-Tridentine Thomists and the Roman magisterium.

In our own day, at the close of the second millennium, the situation which has obtained from the thirteenth to the twentieth century in the matter of the theology of eucharistic sacrifice remains unresolved.

The purpose of Part Two of this book is to provide information about the work of some twentieth-century Catholic theologians which can contribute to the recovery of the more authentic, whole tradition of the eucharistic sacrifice. We begin this, in chapter nine, with a detailed analysis of Aquinas's theology of the eucharistic sacrifice. Our purpose is not so much to make up for the omission of a detailed treatment of Thomas in Part One as to highlight certain aspects of his thought which continue to contribute to a better understanding of the mystery of the sacrifice of the Mass. This is followed in chapter ten by an account of some recent contributions to the formulation of a theology of the eucharistic sacrifice which have contributed to the average modern Roman Catholic synthesis. The material presented in the latter half of this chapter is increasingly critical of this synthesis, and increasingly suggestive of directions towards a new, more adequate synthesis. The final chapter, chapter eleven, consists of our attempt at a systematic elaboration. This builds on the data supplied by the previous chapter by highlighting important aspects of a truly systematic theology of eucharistic sacrifice which are generally omitted, or only marginally integrated, in the so-called average Catholic synthesis. We hope in this way to bring the typically modern Catholic approach a step further on the way to a new and more adequate systematic theology of eucharistic sacrifice.

Part One

History

Chapter One

Eucharistic Sacrifice: The Western Patristic Tradition

This chapter is designed as an introduction to the eucharistic theology of the Latin Church of the patristic age. We begin by describing the traits of the characteristic eucharistic theology of the Latin Church of the first seven hundred years. We then provide brief outlines of the eucharistic theology of Latin patristic writers. We have selected for special attention those authors who not only greatly influenced their contemporaries, but who also significantly determined the shape of development of the later Western tradition.

I. LATIN PATRISTIC EUCHARISTIC THEOLOGY: COMMON TRAITS

The earliest sources of the eucharistic doctrine and practice of the North African church show two important characteristics that mark the later Latin patristic tradition. The first of these characteristics is that the celebration is viewed above all as a sacrificial act of the Church made in union with Christ the High Priest who draws his disciples into his own worship of the Father. He does this by faith and within the context of the ritual memorial of the "death of Lord." Eventually the emphasis is reversed so that the attention becomes focused on the role of Christ as both the offerer and offered, the source of the possibility of the acceptable worship of the Church. In connection with this, the efficacy of the sacrificial activity of the Church and of the participation in the sacraments of the body and blood is regarded especially as a means of expressing and deepening the unity of the Church. The Eucharist, however, was not considered to be precisely the ground of membership in the Church; rather, it was seen as the chief source of the actualization and deepening of one's belonging to the social body of Christ.

In this North African milieu, the ritual activity of the Eucharist was understood to consist of a constellation of prayers and actions carried out under the presidency of a bishop or presbyter. These offices were regarded as essential substructures of the hierarchically ordered Church, and therefore altogether necessary for the realization of the manifestation and the realization of the mystery of the worshiping Church.

The co-offering of the faithful with the presiding ordained minister was expressed in two ways: First, the faithful brought bread and wine to the altar in a ceremonial procession as the visible manifestation of their active role in a sacrificial activity wherein they, in union with Christ, function as both priest and victim. Then, corresponding to this symbolic action, the president verbally proclaimed the sacrificial sentiments of the assembly in the Eucharistic Prayer.

The Eucharistic Prayer itself expressed the belief that the sacrificial act of the Church is made in union with Christ who is likewise, along with the faithful, acting as both (primordial) priest and victim. In this milieu, the liturgical prayer, as well as other theological sources, relate the liturgical activity of Christ to the once-for-all-sacrifice of the cross. Beyond that, however, a consistent common systematic understanding or explanation of this basic relationship is lacking. However, an early tendency toward establishing a real distinction between the sacrificial action of Christ in each eucharistic celebration and his historical redemptive self-offering on the cross is discernible, and this can be traced back to the third century. From the end of the sixth century it becomes a characteristic trait in Latin Church theology.

However this Western Latin theological tradition remained essentially unaffected by that early Greek patristic theology which was inclined to view the eucharistic celebration as a means of sacramental representation of the mystery of the historical redemptive work of Jesus Christ. In our day, many Catholic theologians of the Latin tradition favor the notion of the objective sacramental representation of the historical redemptive work of Christ "on the altar." In other words priority is awarded to the notion that the eucharistic liturgy is the means by which the historical redemptive sacrifice of Christ is represented sacramentally so as to become available to be encountered by faith. The advocates of this average modern Catholic position have attempted to support their position especially by an appeal to Greek patristic theology. However the ambiguity of the precise meaning of the Greek speculation on the link between the historical self-offering of Christ and the eucharistic sacrifice provides a major obstacle to this argument from the authority of tradition. Moreover, in contrast to this modern average Catholic position which tries to make the historical self-offering of Christ somehow "objectively" present, and on the grounds of more carefully thought through systematic theological principles, the understanding of the eucharistic liturgy as a means by which the liturgical assembly is represented to the mystery of the once-for-all sacrifice of Christ is gaining acceptance. We will discuss this important subject at length below in part two of this work. For the moment, we turn to the other important characteristic of the North African Church.

Within the Latin patristic tradition the specific grace of the sacraments of the body and blood of Christ is identified as a corporate grace: the grace of unity by which the believers are integrated more deeply into the body of Christ, which is the Church. However it remained somewhat of an open question how this ecclesiological grace is related to the sacraments, and how they, in turn, are to be regarded precisely as sacraments of the body and blood of Christ. In this milieu there is little evidence of any theological development along the lines of the fourth-century Antiochene doctrine of the somatic real presence—which implies the notion of a conversion of the being of the material elements—of Christ under forms of bread and wine.

The understanding of the Eucharist as celebration of the unity of the Church implied a relationship of dependence of the Eucharist on the existence of the one Church of Jesus Christ. In other words, the unity of the Church was not considered primarily as a fruit of the Eucharist, but this was seen as a means of deepening the unity that already exists. This outlook was consistently affirmed in the theological tradition of the North African Church. However, different conclusions were drawn by its most influential theologians. St. Cyprian, bishop of Carthage, taught that the celebration of the Eucharist is not possible outside the true Church. St. Augustine of Hippo did not agree with Cyprian's corollary. Nevertheless, in the controversy with the churches of the Donatists, while recognizing the existence of sacraments outside the true church, Augustine did not admit their fruitfulness.

On the subject of the reception of the sacraments of the body and blood, Augustine describes the gift that is bestowed on the communicant as a *virtus, unitas, caritas,* by which one is integrated more deeply into the "society of the predestined, called, justified, and glorified saints and faithful."[1] Augustine views the grace of the Eucharist as that which unites the believers to Christ and to one another. He describes this grace as grace of the Spirit of Christ, signified by the sacrament, and bestowed on believers on the occasion of their participation in the sacrament. The grace is not conceived as though contained, as it were, in the external sacrament. Much less does Augustine teach that the body and blood of Christ are "contained" under the forms of bread and wine. The theology of the fourth-century Antiochene School concerning the somatic real presence of Christ under forms of bread and wine is definitely not that of the bishop of Hippo.

On the other hand, the Eastern theology of the fourth-century Antiochene tradition, as exemplified in the writings of St. John Chrysostom, was clearly and strongly reflected in the writings of St. Ambrose of Milan. Ambrose confessed the somatic real presence of Christ under forms of bread and wine, effected through conversion of the elements into the body and blood of Christ. In his catechetical instructions Ambrose identifies the content of the sacraments as the reality of the body and blood of Christ, and therefore the whole "Christ": "Christ is in that sacrament, because it is the body of Christ."[2]

Between these two extremes of the Latin tradition regarding the nature of the sacraments of the body and blood, exemplified by the contrasting positions of Ambrose and Augustine, an important speculative consideration eventually had to be introduced. It is the matter of the distinction between the historical body and the eucharistic body of the incarnate Word, and the relation of the one to the other. St. Jerome (d. 419), in his commentary on Ephesians 1:7, makes the following observation:

"Indeed the blood of Christ and body are understood in a twofold sense, either that spiritual and divine, about which he himself said: 'My flesh is truly food . . .' [John 6:55]; and 'Unless you eat my flesh and drink my blood . . .' [John 6:53]; or the flesh and blood which

[1] "Hunc itaque cibum et potum societatem uult intellegi corporis et membrorum suorum, quod est sancta ecclesia in praedestinatis et uocatis, et iustificatis, et glorificatis sanctis, et fidelibus eius"—Augustine, *In Ioannis evangelium tractatus* 26.15 (Corpus Christianorum, series latina [CC] 36.267.27–30).

[2] "In illo sacramento Christus est, quia corpus est Christi"—Ambrose, *De mysteriis* 9.58 (Corpus scriptorum ecclesiasticorum Latinorum [CSEL] 73.115.97–98).

was crucified, and which was shed by the lance of the soldier [John 19:34]."[3]

Jerome does not explain more precisely the relationship between the two. But he appears to acknowledge a certain level of being of the historical body of Christ in the sacrament. This theological problem remained alive throughout the period of the first millennium. It was inherited by early scholasticism and became a primary subject of theological reflection in the wake of the controversy over the somatic real presence of Christ under forms of bread and wine, occasioned by the theological speculation of the eleventh-century Berengar of Tours.

During the early scholastic period the theology of the sacraments of the body and blood underwent a significant development. On the other hand, the theology of the eucharistic sacrifice of the Latin tradition, which had developed during the latter part of the first millennium, remained essentially intact. Concretely, this Latin theology of eucharistic sacrifice was based on a sharp distinction between the efficacy of the historical sacrifice of the cross with respect to the victory over original sin, and the efficacy of the sacramental repetition of the sacrifice of Christ in the Mass with respect to the victory over daily sins—with the emphasis on the propitiatory effect for the souls in purgatory. In addition, this inherited Latin theology of the eucharistic sacrifice of Christ and the Church featured two other effects which result from the efficacious liturgical petition for the divine acceptance expressed in the Eucharistic Prayer. These effects are the sanctification of the sacraments of the body and blood of Christ, and, along with that sanctification, the proleptic deepening of the unity of the liturgical assembly with the risen Lord and, in him, with the eschatological community of the blessed.[4]

II. EUCHARISTIC THEOLOGY: THE LATIN FATHERS

The Latin Fathers show less concern for the speculative aspects of eucharistic theology than the Greek Fathers. Their interest is geared

[3] "Dupliciter vero sanguis Christi, et caro intelligitur, vel spiritualis illa atque divina, de qua ipse dixit: *Caro mea vere est cibus* . . . (Joan. VI, 56); et: *Nisi manducaveritis carnem meam et sanguinem meam biberitis* . . . (ibid., 54); vel caro et sanguis quae crucifixa est, et qui militis effusa est lancea [John 19:30]"—Jerome, *Commentariorum in epistolam ad Ephesios* 1, on Eph 1:7 (Migne, PL 26.451A).

[4] See, for example, the *Supplices* prayer of the Roman Canon.

more to the pastoral and practical side of the efficacy of the eucharistic sacrifice and Holy Communion. Also, although acquainted with a Platonic way of thinking about reality, they were less consistent about its application to the Eucharist. Tertullian's understanding of the eucharistic food as "figure of the body of Christ" *(figura corporis Christi)* stands in the Christian Platonic tradition.[5] Other Latin Fathers who exercised significant influence on later Western eucharistic theology, such as St. Cyprian, St. Ambrose, and St. Augustine, do not fully carry through the type of Platonism that characterizes the Greek Fathers before the council of Ephesus (431). This holds for the application of the prototype–image concept to the theology of the sacraments of the body and blood as well as to the theology of the relationship of the sacrifice of the cross to the eucharistic sacrifice.

A. TERTULLIAN OF CARTHAGE (CA. 160–230)

In the text of Tertullian referred to above we read:

"Having taken bread, and having distributed it to his disciples, he made it his body, saying: 'This is my body,' that is, figure of my body. However it would not be figure unless the body were true. Moreover an empty thing, which is a phantasm, cannot take a figure, as if he made bread a body for himself because, lacking the truth of a body, he ought to hand over bread 'for us.'"

Here Tertullian rejects a gnostic thesis concerning the reality of Christ's historical body. The image character of the Eucharist guarantees the reality of the prototype.[6] Marcion ascribes to Christ the appearance of a body in accord with his dualistic view of reality: of flesh and spirit. Tertullian opposes him: the sacrament of the bread and cup witness the truth of the body and blood of Christ. "Whence by the sacrament of the bread and cup already in the Gospel we have proved the truth of the dominical body and blood, against the phantasm of Marcion."[7] If Marcion was correct one could not speak of a

[5] "Marcion . . . non intellegens ueterem fuisse istam figuram corporis Christi . . ." —Tertullian, *Adversus Marcionem* 4.40.2–4 (CC 1.656–57), at 4.40.3 (CC 1.656.7–8).

[6] Johannes Betz, *Die Eucharistie in der Zeit der griechischen Väter* I/1 (Freiburg: Herder, 1955) 222–23.

[7] "Proinde panis et calicis sacramento iam in euangelio probauimus corporis et sanguinis dominici ueritatem aduersus phantasma Marcionis"—Tertullian, *Adversus Marcionem* 58.3 (CC 1.686.21–23).

figure in the eucharistic forms; the sacrament would be a *vanitas* because what is pointed to would be itself only a phantasm. The *figura,* the *corpus Christi in pane* is contrasted with the historical Christ graspable through the senses, understood under the title *veritas corporis.*[8]

The appeal to the sacrament of the body and blood of Christ to support the mystery of the Incarnation of the Word of God is explainable solely on the grounds that the sacrament participates in the mystery to the extent that the mystery is rendered present in the image. There are many other examples of this mode of argumentation employed in patristic literature to explain and confirm various aspects of the theology of the Incarnation of the Word. This explains in part why the eucharistic sacrament is called *mysterium,* namely, because it is understood to participate in the great mystery of the Incarnation.

Tertullian initially applied the Greek idea of image of the prototype, the historical Incarnation of the Word, to the sacraments of the body and blood. However, in the end, after he became a Montanist, the eucharistic sacraments were valued less as means of salutary contact with the mystery of the Incarnation and more as pure signs of belonging to the Church. This latter outlook lies at the basis of the references to the Eucharist attributed to Novatian, rival of Bishop Cornelius at Rome in the third century.[9]

Regarding the nature of the eucharistic liturgy, Tertullian provides some examples which seem to suggest the practice of a ritual presentation of the eucharistic elements of bread and wine by the laity.[10] This kind of activity within the scope of the liturgical celebration signified

[8] On the opposition between *figura* as *corpus Christi in pane* and the *veritas corporis* of the historical Christ, confer Karl Adam, *Die Eucharistielehre des hl. Augustinus* (Paderborn: Ferdinand Schöningh, 1908) 21. Also, as we shall see below (pp. 38–41, 50–51, 58), the same argument used by Tertullian to refute the Marcionite teaching about the Incarnation is employed by the orthodox partner of the dialogue with the monophysite in the *Eranistes* authored by Theodoret of Cyrus.

[9] Hermann Josef Vogt discusses this development of Tertullian's theology of the Eucharist and also observes how Tertullian's later position corresponds to Novatian's understanding of the function of the sacraments of the Eucharist *(Coetus sanctorum. Der Kirchenbegriff des Novatian und die Geschichte seiner Sonderkirche.* Theophaneia 20 [Bonn: Peter Hanstein, 1968] 115).

[10] See, for example, *De oratione* 19 (CC 1.267–68); *De cultu feminarum* 2.1 (CC 1.366); *De corona militum* 3 (CC 2.1043); *Ad uxorem* 2.8 (CC 1.393). [EJK's manuscript reads: "Tertullian provides many examples of the practice . . ." Unable to verify so strong a claim in the texts listed, or elsewhere in Tertullian, I have somewhat qualified EJK's statement—RJD.]

the active participation of the laity in the corporate action of the ecclesial assembly which signifies the spiritual self-offering of the believers.

B. ST. CYPRIAN, BISHOP OF CARTHAGE (CA. 200–258)

Cyprian stresses the ecclesiological aspect of the Eucharist, a characteristic of the North African church. The eucharistic worship and reception of the sacraments of the body and blood are valued as a means of the manifestation and realization of the unity of the members of the Church with one another and with Christ. Cyprian also refers frequently, in the context of the persecution of the Church, to eucharistic sacramental communion as a source of strengthening the faith to live the ethical demands of the gospel.

Cyprian supplies the earliest witness from the Latin writers concerning the common belief of his Church that Christ offers his body and blood in the Eucharist of the Church. However, in contrast to the later representative of the fourth-century Antiochene tradition, St. John Chrysostom, he does not employ in this context the concept of commemorative actual presence of the once-for-all historical sacrifice of the cross. Instead he speaks of a kind of gradation between the sacrifice of Christ and that of Melchizedech:

"Who is more priest of the highest God than our Lord Jesus Christ, who offers a sacrifice to God the Father! And indeed he offers the same as Melchizedech, namely bread and wine, namely his body and blood."[11]

Although Cyprian does not develop a systematic theology of eucharistic sacrifice, he shows the tendency to individualize the eucharistic activity of Christ the High Priest related to the new sacrificial act on the part of the Church.[12]

Cyprian's concept of the sacraments of the body and blood of Christ remains obscure. He uses the language of prototype-image philosophy. But there is a tendency to a view that goes against the image-thinking of the Greek Fathers, as the theology of sacrifice shows. On the pastoral side Cyprian sees the sacraments of the body and blood of Christ as a means of strengthening Christians for mar-

[11] "Nam qui magis sacerdos Dei summi quam Dominus noster Iesus Christus, qui sacrificium Deo patri optulit et optulit hoc idem quod Melchisedech optulerat id est panem et uinum, suum scilicet corpus et sanguinem"—Cyprian, *Epistula* 63.4 (CSEL 3.703.11–15).

[12] Alexander Gerken, *Theologie der Eucharistie* (Munich: Kösel, 1973) 86.

tyrdom in time of persecution.[13] At the same time he opposes church leaders who reconcile the lapsed immediately after persecution and so allow easy access to the Eucharist. In his opinion the external sharing is meaningless without inward conversion. It deepens the separation from God and therefore is a hindrance to salvation.[14]

Between whom is peace established through reconciliation? What fellowship is granted again by access to the Eucharist? Cyprian typically responds that it is a matter of establishing peace with the Church and fellowship with the Church. Through participation in the Eucharist the unity with the Church is confirmed and strengthened. Through fellowship with the Church the fellowship with Christ and God is deepened. Access to eucharistic worship, including participation in Holy Communion, is the liturgical consequence of reconciliation with the Church. Since the Church is the outward sign of inner fellowship with God, the bishop must refuse the Eucharist to the lapsed who have not undergone the conversion process.

C. ST. HILARY, BISHOP OF POITIERS (310–367)

Hilary is especially noteworthy for his teaching concerning the eucharistic somatic presence of the risen Lord. His teaching on this subject was undoubtedly influenced by his contact with the Antiochene tradition during the period of his exile in the East. He also devoted considerable attention to the relation of Eucharist to the Church.[15] His starting point for the grounding of the mystery of the Trinity is the reality of the Eucharist in the life of the Church. He develops this in a commentary on chapters 6–17 of the Fourth Gospel. For, according to him, the Eucharist flows into the mystery of the Trinity in whose life it enables us to share.

In his work *De Trinitate* 8.17 Hilary treats the problem that derives from the Arian teaching about the correspondence of the nature of the unity between the Father and Son, and between believers and Christ. Hilary grants the link between the two relations. But on the basis of the Fourth Gospel he concludes that the unity between believers and

[13] Cyprian, *Epistula* 57.2 (CSEL 3.651–52); e.g., 652.2–5: ". . . protectione sanguinis et corporis Christi muniamus, et cum ad hoc fiat eucharistia ut possit accipientibus esse tutela, quos tutos esse contra aduersarium uolumus, munimento dominicae saturitatis armemus."

[14] *De lapsis* 15–16 (CSEL 3.1.247–49).

[15] Michael Figura, *Das Kirchenverständnis des Hilarius von Poitiers.* Freiburger theologische Studien 127 (Freiburg: Herder, 1984).

Christ is of the order of being. Hence believers really become sons in the Son. Correspondingly the unity between Father and Son pertains not only to the unity of wills, but also to the order of being.

The argument of Hilary is based on the eucharistic food. In *De Trinitate* 8.13, he quotes John 17:22-23. But the problem is this: In what sense is Christ united to the Father in a way that corresponds to our unity with him? The Arian position is shown to be untenable on the basis of John 1:14 and John 6:56. The fact that we really receive the Word made flesh in the "dominical food" means that we are united to Christ in a way that pertains to the order of being. Corresponding to this, the unity of Father and Son is of the same order.[16]

Hilary's next step is to prove what he has stated about the eucharistic food from the literal interpretation of John 6:56-57. He quotes these verses, which leave no doubt about

"the truth of his body and blood. . . . And having received this and drunk that, they effect that both we are in Christ and Christ is in us. . . . Therefore he is in us through the flesh, and we are in him: What we are, is, namely, with him in God."[17]

The difference between our being in Christ "through the sacrament *(sacramentum)* of the communicated flesh and blood" and Christ's being in the Father "by the nature of divinity" is explained with the help of John 14:19-20. Since Christ is in the Father, and believers are in Christ, and Christ in them, believers arrive at union with the Father.[18] Finally John 6:57-58 is introduced to witness to the fact that

[16] The chapter concludes with the words: "Ita enim omnes unum, sumus, quia et in Christo Pater est et Christus in nobis est. Quisquis ergo naturaliter Patrem in Christo negabit, neget prius non naturaliter uel se in Christo uel Christum sibi inesse: quia in Christo Pater et Christus in nobis, unum in his esse nos faciunt. Si uere igitur carnem corporis nostri Christus adsumpsit, et uere homo ille qui ex Maria natus fuit Christus est, nosque uere sub mysterio carnem corporis sui sumimus, et per hoc unum erimus, quia Pater in eo est et ille in nobis, quomodo uoluntatis unitas adseritur, cum naturalis per sacramentum proprietas perfectae sacramentum sit unitatis?"—Hilary of Poitiers, *De trinitate* 8.13 (CS 62A.325.13–326.14).

[17] "De ueritate carnis et sanguinis non relictus est ambigendi locus. . . . Et haec accepta adque hausta id efficiunt, ut et nos in Christo et Christus in nobis sit. . . . Est ergo ipse in nobis per carnem et sumus in eo, dum secum hoc quod nos sumus in Deum est"—Hilary of Poitiers, *De trinitate* 8.14 (CS 62A.326.11–327.18).

[18] "Quam autem in eo per sacramentum communicatae carnis et sanguinis simus, . . . Nisi ut cum illo in Patre per naturam diuinitatis esset, nos contra in eo

we live in the same way through the flesh of Christ, as he lives through the Father.[19] *De Trinitate* 8.17 summarizes the Arian position and the argument against it from the eucharistic food.[20]

While Hilary's theology of the eucharistic sacraments stands in the fourth-century Antiochene tradition, his ecclesiology is situated between that of Cyprian of Carthage and Optatus of Mileve. Optatus worked out a systematic ecclesiology which focused on the relation between Church and sacraments, and holiness in the Church. The mystery of the Church and the binding of Christ and the Church is not featured. Hilary, however, focuses on the mysterious identification of Christ and the Church. He finds this identification on the basis of the relation of unity between believers and Christ through the Incarnation, specifically on the basis of the Eucharist and insertion into the risen body of Christ: "For he himself (Christ) is the Church, because he contains her completely in himself through the mystery of his body."[21]

Hilary's ecclesiology is centered on the relationship between Christ and Church. The concept of Church as body of Christ is fundamental. "Body of Christ" has a field of meaning that includes: (1.) body which the Word assumed; (2.) eucharistic body, left as his legacy; (3.) the glorified body of Christ, which he possesses at the right hand of the Father. This threefold body effects the binding between Christ and humankind. This binding finds its visible expression in the Church which is placed in a living communion with the natural, sacramental, and, above all, glorified body of Christ.

The Church is already the body of the risen Lord and, as such, the Church cannot lose its communion with Christ. The binding of the earthly and heavenly Church holds for the totality of redeemed humanity.[22] But what is the inner basis of the linking between Christ and

---

per corporalem eius natiuitatem, et ille rursum in nobis per sacramentum inesse mysterium crederetur; ac si perfecta per mediatorem unitas doceretur, cum nobis in se manentibus ipse maneret in Patre, et in Patre manens maneret in nobis; et ita ad unitatem Patris proficeremus, cum qui in eo naturaliter secundum natiuitatem inest, nos quoque in eo naturaliter inessemus, ipso in nobis naturaliter permanente?"—Hilary of Poitiers, *De trinitate* 8.15 (CS 62A.327.1–15).

[19] "Viuit ergo per Patrem, et quo modo per Patrem uiuit, eodem modo nos per carnem eius uiuemus"—ibid., 8.16 (327.1–328.22, at 328.8–9).

[20] Ibid., 8.17 (328.1–329.10).

[21] "Ipse est enim ecclesia, per sacramentum corporis sui in se uniuersam eam continens"—Hilary of Poitiers, *Tractatus in psalmum* 125.6 (CSEL 22.609.19–20); Figura, *Das Kirchenverständnis*, 57, 363.

[22] Ibid., 50–59.

Church? The Church is the body of Christ because the Word of God assumed all humanity's flesh in the Incarnation, through the acceptance of an individual human nature. This is the presupposition for the ability to assume the whole humanity according to nature. But the assumption of the flesh of the whole human race means that something is changed in human beings as such. The divinization of humanity is bound up with it.

Christ is united to humankind in a threefold way. He assumed all in the Incarnation. Thereby the divinization of the human being is given in principle. But the application of the assumption of humanity happens first, especially in the Eucharist, in the time of the Church. The Eucharist is the means that enables believers to share truly and corporeally in the divinization already bestowed in the Incarnation of the Word. Through the Eucharist they live now from and in that divinization that Christ brought to every human being in the Incarnation.[23] The conditions for the participation in the mystery of the assumption of the flesh by Christ are conversion, baptism, and the practice of the new life corresponding to one's new being in Christ.[24]

The physical binding between Christ and humanity that occurs through the Incarnation opens for believers the way to the possibility of belonging to the glorified body of Christ.[25] This latter possibility happens in the Church. For Christ himself is the Church, since he holds it in himself through the mystery of his body.[26]

Concerning the liturgy of the eucharistic sacrifice, Hilary reflects the theology conformed to the Eastern tradition where he refers to the presbyters who suffered in the Arian persecution. He speaks of the "consecrated body of the Lord" which results from the liturgical sacrificial action of orthodox priests, as opposed to heretical ones.[27]

D. ST. AMBROSE, BISHOP OF MILAN

On the whole, Ambrose is concerned primarily with the ethical-pastoral aspect of the Eucharist. His dogmatic teaching is always em-

[23] Hilary of Poitiers, *De trinitate* 8.13–16 (CS 62A.325.1–328.22); see the passages quoted above in nn. 16–19 and 21.

[24] Figura, *Das Kirchenverständnis*, 59–70.

[25] Ibid., 70–76.

[26] Ibid., 77–80.

[27] The *consecratum Domini corpus* is identified as resulting from the *sacrificium a sanctis et integris sacerdotibus confectum* (Collectanea Antiariania Parisina, Series A IV 1.9 [CSEL 65.55]).

bedded in the context of an exhortation to the ethically unobjectionable life.[28] He was directly influenced by the eucharistic theology of the Greek Fathers whom he studied after his episcopal consecration. But his reception of this theology was only partial.

He affirms the common fourth-century Antiochene doctrine of the somatic real presence, that is, the doctrine of the change of the nature (essence) of the bread and wine that comes about "by the blessing." This teaching is found in *De mysteriis* 9.50. Moreover, in language reminiscent of John Chrysostom, he attributes the change to the creative word of Christ,[29] and introduces terms to express the notion of change which correspond to the Greek verbs used by Chrysostom: *mutare, convertere, transfigurare.*[30]

Although Ambrose speaks of the change of the "nature" of bread and wine "by the blessing" *(benedictio),*[31] it is not clear exactly how Ambrose conceives the liturgical process of the sanctification of the eucharistic elements. According to J. R. Geiselmann, Ambrose considers the words of institution as a factor in the event of the consecration, that is, an indispensable element of the whole process of the ritual consecration which is not limited to the recitation of the narrative of

[28] Ernst Dassmann, *Die Frömmigkeit des Kirchenväters Ambrosius von Meiland.* Münsterische Beiträge zur Theologie 29 (Münster: Aschendorff, 1965) 170. See, e.g., *De patriarchis* 9.39 where, after quoting John 6:51, he writes: "ille enim accipit qui se ipsum probat" (CSEL 32/2.147.11).

[29] "Quod si tantum valuit humana benedictio, ut naturam converteret, quid dicimus de ipsa consecratione divina, ubi verba ipsa domini salvatoris operantur? Nam sacramentum istud, quod accipis, Christi sermone conficitur. Quod si tantum valuit sermo Heliae, ut ignem de caelo deposceret, non valebit Christi sermo, ut species mutet elementorum? De totius mundi operibus legisti: Quia ipse dixit et facta sunt, ipse mandavit et creata sunt [Psalm 148:5]. Sermo ergo Christi, qui potuit ex nihilo facere quod non erat, non potest ea, quae sunt, in id mutare, quod non erant? Non enim minus est novas rebus dare quam mutare naturas"—Ambrose, *De mysteriis* 9.52 (CSEL 73.112.34–44). ". . . de sermone Christi qui operatur, ut possit mutare et convertere genera instituta naturae"—Ambrose, *De sacramentis* 6.1.3 (CSEL 73.72–73).

[30] For *mutare* and *convertere,* see, in addition to the passages just quoted in n. 29, *De sacramentis* 4.15–17 (CSEL 73.52–53). For *transfigurare,* see *De fide* 4.10.124 "Nos autem quotiescumque sacramenta sumimus, quae per sacrae orationis mysterium in carnem transfigurantur et sanguinem, *'mortem domini adnuntiamus'*" (CSEL 78.201.46–49); cf. *De incarnationis dominicae sacramento* 4.23: ". . . transfigurandum corpus altaribus . . ." (PL 16.824C).

[31] See, e.g., *De mysteriis* 9.50 (quoted below in n. 37) and 9.52 (quoted above in n. 29).

institution. In this connection he cites a text of Ambrose's *De fide:* "However as often as we receive the sacraments, which are transfigured by the mystery of the holy prayer into the flesh and blood, we proclaim the death of the Lord."[32]

Among the contemporary modern commentators on the subject of Ambrose's view of the liturgical time of the transformation of the eucharistic elements, Raymond Johanny argues that the *Fac nobis* section of the fourth-century Milanese eucharistic prayer "accomplishes the mystery."[33] In a still more recent discussion of this subject contained in his study of the ancient liturgy of Milan,[34] Josef Schmitz concurs with Johanny that the canon of Ambrose does not have an epiclesis of consecration. He bases this conclusion on the fact that Ambrose explicitly attributes the consecration to the words of Jesus.[35]

In one passage of *De mysteriis,* Ambrose's commentary on the nature of the presence of Christ in the eucharistic sacraments makes it unclear whether he affirms the somatic presence of Christ. He could be interpreted as confessing a presence of the Lord in the Pneuma, or a presence of the divine Spirit:

"Christ is in this sacrament, because it is the body of Christ. Therefore it is not corporeal, but a spiritual food. . . . The body of God is, namely, a spiritual body, the body of Christ is the body of the divine Spirit, because Christ is Spirit."[36]

[32] "Nos autem quotiescumque sacramenta sumimus, quae per sacrae orationis mysterium in carnem transfigurantur et sanguinem, mortem Domini annunciamus"—Ambrose, *De fide* 4.10.124 (CSEL 78.201). Cf. Josef Rupert Geiselmann, *Die Abendmahlslehre an der Wende der christlichen Spätantike zum Frühmittelalter* (Munich: Max Hueber, 1933) 200–1.

[33] Raymond Johanny provides a survey of the various opinions on the subject of the liturgical time of the transformation of the eucharistic elements in *L'Eucharistie centre de l'histoire de salut chez saint Ambrose de Milan. Théologie historique* 9 (Paris: Beauchesne, 1968) 104–24. Johanny himself prefers the theory that the *"Fac nobis* . . . accomplishes the mystery" (124). He argues that an epiclesis of sanctifiction of the eucharistic gifts was lacking in the Eucharistic Prayer of Milan (125–34).

[34] Josef Schmitz, *Gottesdienst im altchristlichen Meiland. Eine liturgiewissenschaftliche Untersuchung über Initiation und Messfeier während des Jahres der Zeit des Bishofs Ambrosius (d.397).* Theophaneia 25 (Cologne–Bonn: Peter Hanstein, 1975).

[35] Ibid., 403. He refers to *De sacramentis* 4.4.14 and 4.5.23 (CSEL 73.52 and 56). Cf. also Schmitz's bibliographical notes on the literature about the teaching of Ambrose on this unresolved debate (pp. 408–10).

[36] "In illo sacramento Christus est, quia corpus est Christi. Non ergo corporalis esca, sed spiritalis est. . . . corpus enim dei corpus est spiritale, corpus Christi

In any case, Ambrose proves the presence of Christ by contrasting the power of the blessing with the power of nature.

"Perhaps you say: 'But I see something other (than the body of Christ)! Why then do you think I receive the body of Christ?' And truly it remains that we prove it. How many examples therefore ought we to draw on in order to prove that it is not a question of what nature forms but what the word of blessing consecrates, and that the power of blessing is greater than the power of nature. For the nature itself is changed by the blessing."[37]

When he asks about the possibility of the somatic real presence, he cannot simply refer to a cosmic law to clarify the possibility as a Platonist might do. He must refer to the creative will of God and Christ: "If the word of Elisha was so powerful that he brought fire from heaven, cannot the word of Christ change the *species elementorum* . . ."[38] In this passage Ambrose has in mind the divine act of Christ: "He spoke and it became. . . . Therefore the word of Christ, which could create from nothing what was not, can he not change that which already is, into that which it was not?"[39] Here he recalls the scriptural idea about Christ, insofar as divine intervening in special ways in history. He compares the divine action of Christ in creation with the making of the sacraments of his body and blood: What Christ did in creation, he does in the Eucharist.

Ambrose stresses the personal encounter with Christ in the sacrament as no other Father of the Church: "See, no longer in shadows, no more in symbol *(figura)*, no more in image, but in truth radiating light . . . face to face . . . I find you in your sacraments."[40] This point

corpus est divini spiritus, quia spiritus Christus"—Ambrose, *De mysteriis* 9.58 (CSEL 73.115.97–102).

[37] "Forte dicas: 'Aliud video; quomodo tu mihi adseris, quod Christi corpus accipiam?' Et hoc nobis adhuc superest, ut probemus. Quantis igitur utimur exemplis, ut probemus non hoc esse, quod natura formavit, sed quod benedictio consecravit, maioremque vim esse benedictionis quam naturae, quia benedictione etiam natura ipsa mutatur"—Ambrose, *De mysteriis* 9.50 (CSEL 73.110.1–6).

[38] Ibid., 9.52 (quoted above in n. 29).

[39] Ibid.

[40] The full text of this powerful passage reads: "Quod enim *oculus non uidit nec auris audiuit nec in cor hominis ascendit, hoc praeparauit deus diligentibus eum* [1 Cor 2:9]. Uidens igitur ea dicit: ecce iam non in umbra nec in figura, non in typo, sed in ueritate lux aperta resplendet: ecce nunc ueritatem aspicio, splendorem ueritatis agnosco, nunc te maiore, domine deus noster ueneror adfectu. *Ecce enim ueritatem*

of view is foreign to the prototype–image theology where truth and image are made opposites, and where the notion of participation of the one in the other is decisive.

At times, however, Ambrose also expresses an alternate approach to eucharistic doctrine, namely in the language of Greek image theology. In his *De fide,* the word *transfigurare* is used: "as often as we receive the holy signs . . . which are transformed *(transfigurantur)* through the mystery of the blessing prayer into the flesh and blood."[41] This manner of conceiving the process of conversion of the eucharistic elements, namely, as the *elevation* of the nature of the elements (rather than their conversion) to serve as sacraments of the body and blood, is at variance with that proper to the metabolic understanding of the change of the nature of the eucharistic elements. This metabolic understanding of the change is a new concept which goes beyond what would develop from an image theology. Hence, at least in the early Middle Ages, Ambrose's teaching also provided the basis for an alternative to the traditional fourth-century (realistic, metabolic-conversion) Antiochene explanation of the process of eucharistic conversion.

On the question of the sacrificial character of the Eucharist, Ambrose provides an example of the difference of the orientation between the Eastern and Western traditions. The Greek Fathers of the fourth-century Antiochene tradition base the sacrificial character of the Eucharist on the concept of *anamnesis:* the commemorative actual presence of the one and unique sacrifice of Christ on the cross. The third-century bishop of Carthage, Cyprian, as was noted above, did not follow this interpretation. Ambrose also omits the Greek concept of commemorative sacrifice. Rather, he views Melchizedech in his priestly activity as identified with Christ in the sense of type of the priesthood of Christ.[42] The members of the Church co-share in this activity of Christ the High Priest in the eucharistic sacrifice:

"We see the high priest among us. We see and hear him offer his blood for us. We, the priests . . . present the sacrifice for the people.

---

dilexisti: non per speculum, non in aenigmate, sed facie ad faciem [1 Cor 13:12; Deut 34:10] te mihi, Christe, demonstrasti; in tuis te inuenio sacramentis"—Ambrose, *De apologia prophetae David* 1.12.58 (CSEL 32/2.339.18–340.5).

[41] Ambrose, *De fide* 4.10.124 (quoted above in n. 30).

[42] Ambrose, *De mysteriis* 8.44–46 (CSEL 73.107.15–109.43); *De sacramentis* 4.3.10–12 (CSEL 73.49.6–51.40).

. . . If Christ now appears not to offer, nevertheless he himself is offered on earth because the body of Christ is offered. Indeed it witnesses itself that he offers in us, whose words consecrate the sacrifice that is offered."[43]

In his *De officiis ministrorum* Ambrose states the following:

"Christ is offered today . . . and he offers himself as priest in order that he may remit our sins: here in image, there in truth where, as our advocate, he intercedes for us before the Father."[44]

Elsewhere in the *De sacramentis*, the *Ergo memores* section of the Milanese Eucharistic Prayer explains the matter in this way:

"Therefore we recall his most glorious passion and resurrection from the lower world, and ascension into heaven. We offer to you this immaculate victim, unbloody victim, this holy bread and cup of eternal life. And we ask and entreat that you receive this offering at your altar on high through the hands of your holy angels. As you deigned to receive the gifts of your just servant Abel and the sacrifice of our patriarch Abraham, and what the high priest Melchizedech offered to you."[45]

Ambrose teaches that it is precisely the liturgical assembly that is the subject of the offering of the eucharistic sacrifice. He distinguishes between the oblation and the proclamation of the Eucharistic

[43] ". . . uidimus principem sacerdotum ad nos uenientem, uidimus et audiuimus offerentem pro nobis sanguinem suum. Sequimur ut possumus sacerdotes, ut offeramus pro populo sacrificium etsi infirmi merito, tamen honorabiles sacrificio, quia, etsi nunc Christus non uidetur offerre, tamen ipse offertur in terris, quia Christi corpus offertur, immo ipse offerre manifestatur in nobis, cuius sermo sanctificat sacrificium quod offertur"—Ambrose, *Explanatio psalmi* 38.25 (CSEL 64.203.19–25).

[44] "Ante agnus offerebatur, offerebatur et vitulus, nunc Christus offertur . . . et offert se ipse quasi sacerdos, ut peccata nostra dimittat: hic in imagine, ibi in veritate, ubi apud patrem pro nobis quasi advocatus intervenit"—Ambrose, *De officiis ministrorum* 1.48 (PL 16.94AB).

[45] "Ergo memores gloriosissime eius passionis et ab inferis resurrectionis et in caelum ascensionis offerimus tibi hanc immaculatam hostiam, rationabilem hostiam, incruentam hostiam, hunc panem sanctum et calicem vitae aeternae. Et petimus et precamur, uti hanc oblationem suscipias in sublime altare tuum per manus angelorum tuorum, sicut suscipere dignatus es munera pueri tui iusti Abel et sacrificium patriarchae nostri Abrahae et quod tibi obtulit summus sacerdos Melchisedech"—Ambrose, *De sacramentis* 4.6.27 (CSEL 73.57.4–12).

Prayer.[46] The fact that the laity are active participants of the eucharistic sacrifice (oblation) is expressed by the presentation of the eucharistic gifts at the altar.[47] While recognizing that the one who presides at the Eucharist represents Christ,[48] Ambrose can say to the Emperor Theodosius in effect: "I am worthy to be heard by you, because I am worthy to offer for you."[49] Therefore in carrying out his role as liturgical leader, the minister is related to members of the Church in such a way that these co-share in his sacrificial offering, for all are the "chosen race, royal priesthood, holy nation (1 Peter 2:9)." All are anointed for kingship and priesthood.[50]

All are included in the words of the anaphora: "We offer to you the immaculate victim."[51] Ambrose does not dare to offer on behalf of Theodosius if the latter does not repent of the massacre at Thessalonica.[52] He must free himself from the crime. Then, not merely the outward gift but the meaning is altered.[53] For according to Ambrose

[46] On the subject of the presentation of the eucharistic gifts, in *De Cain et Abel* 26, Ambrose makes an important observation: "The oblation and oration ought not to be confused, but distinguished—*Oblationem autem atque orationem oportet non confusam esse, sed competenti divisione distinctam*" (PL 14.351B).

[47] In the prologue to *Expositio psalmi* 118, Ambrose explains that neophytes offer gifts at the altar only after the eighth day because they must first be instructed, lest the ignorance of the offerers impair the mystery of the oblation (CSEL 62.4). In *Explanatio psalmi* 38.25, as we have seen (text in n. 43), Christ himself is offerer and gift.

[48] ". . . iam non suis sermonibus utitur sacerdos, sed utitur sermonibus Christi" —Ambrose, *De sacramentis* 4.14 (CSEL 73.52.14–15).

[49] "Nam si indignus sum, qui a te audiar, indignus sum, qui pro te offeram"—Ambrose, *Epistola* 40.1 (PL 16.1101).

[50] "Populus ipse quid est nisi sacerdotalis? Quibus dictum est: *Vos autem genus electum, regale sacerdotium, gens sancta* [1 Peter 2:9], ut ait apostolus Petrus? Unusquisque unguitur in sacerdotium, unguitur in regnum, sed spiritale regnum est et sacerdotium spiritale"—Ambrose, *De sacramentis* 4.13 (CSEL 73.47.15–19).

[51] Ibid., 4.6.27 (text above in n. 45).

[52] "Ego certe in omnibus aliis licet debitor pietati tuae, cui ingratus esse non possum, quam pietatem multis imperatoribus praeferebam, uni adaequabam: ego, inquam, causam in te contumaciae nullam habeo, sed habeo timoris: offerre non audeo sacrificium, si volueris assistere. An quod in unius innocentis sanguine non licet, in multorum licet? Non puto"—Ambrose, *Epistola* 51.13 (PL 16.1163A).

[53] "Nihil invenio quod in specie munerum repraehendam, nisi quod et Cain munera sua displicuisse cognovit et dominus dixit: *Si recte offeras, recte autem non dividas, peccasti* [Gen 4:7 *Vetus Lat.*]. Ubi igitur est crimen, ubi culpa? Non in oblatione muneris, sed in oblationis adfectu. Sunt quidem qui 'recte' arbitrentur, quia alius, quae offeret, elegerat, alius, quae viliora habuit, offerebat; sed non est ita

the Church in its members is not only the subject of the offering but also that which is offered to God. Here the text of Romans 12:1-2 is applied to the communal act of worship of the eucharistic assembly.[54]

Ambrose's theology of eucharistic sacrifice which stresses the active presence of Christ as High Priest as well as the active co-offering of the liturgical assembly under the leadership of the presiding priest adheres to the Western theological tradition. An individualistic concept of eucharistic sacrifice is discernible not only for the ecclesial aspect but also for the Christological dimension of the sacrificial act. The idea that each individual Mass has a value in itself as a kind of new act of Christ performed in and through the sacrificial offering of the Church derives from the experience of the mystery of the Eucharist. It is fostered by the *lex orandi,* the literal meaning of the Eucharistic Prayer. It is nourished by the typical Western way of thinking which is focused on the individual and concrete event, and disinclined to speculate about the relationship of the once-for-all historical sacrifice of Christ to the eucharistic sacrifice.

Ambrose's doctrine of the somatic presence of Christ under forms of bread and wine was borrowed from the fourth-century Antiochene tradition. But, as we have noted above, it was not "received" within the Platonic horizon of thought of the Greek theologians. However, his teaching on this subject, thus separated from its natural Platonic horizon, became the viable—and eventually triumphant—option in the Latin Church of the early Middle Ages over against the "spiritualized" interpretation of the content of the sacraments of the body and blood linked to the Augustinian tradition. Likewise Ambrose's teaching about the Christological aspect of the eucharistic sacrifice shows no signs of the influence of the Greek notion of commemorative

---

inops spiritalium sensus in nobis, ut putemus quia dominus corporale sacrificium, non spiritale quaerebat. Et ideo addidit: *Quiesce* [Gen 4:7 *Vetus Lat.*] tolerabilius significans abstinere a muneribus deferendis, quam infideli studio munus offerre. Qui enim nescit dividere, nescit iudicare, *spiritalis autem diiudicat omnia"* [1 Cor 2:15 *Vetus Lat.*]—Ambrose, *De incarnationis dominicae sacramento* 1.2–3 (CSEL 79.225.7–226.19).

[54] "Novato quoque et Donato et omnibus, qui sundere corpus ecclesiae gestierunt, viritim dicitur: *Si recte offeras, recte autem non dividas, peccasti* [Gen 4:7 *Vetus Lat.*]. Ecclesia enim sacrificium est, quod offertur deo, ad quam Paulus dixit: *Obsecro autem vos, fratres, per misericordiam dei exhibere corpora vestra hostiam vivam, sanctam deo* [Rom 12:1 *Vetus Lat.*]. Male ergo sacrificium diviserunt, ecclesiae membra lacerando"—Ambrose, *De incarnationis dominicae sacramento* 2.10 (CSEL 79.228.20–229.26).

sacrifice. This fact, which proves that Ambrose's "reception" of Greek eucharistic theology was only partial, is indicative of the difficulty which the Western theological mindset has traditionally experienced in its attempts to grasp the Greek notion of commemorative sacrifice.

By the end of the sixth century this Greek concept, which could have served the interests of a more balanced theology of the eucharistic sacrifice, was no longer present to the Western tradition. At the same time the tendency of the Western theology of eucharistic sacrifice toward postulating a complete disjunction between the historical sacrifice of the cross and the eucharistic sacrifice received additional support from Pope Gregory the Great's saying that "(Christ) in the mystery of the holy sacrifice is offered for us again *(iterum)*."[55] This text is one of the earliest that refers to Christ being "newly" offered. Supported by the authority of Gregory it became an important proof text for the notion that the sacrifice of Christ is repeated in each Mass in an "unbloody way."

At the same time this perception of the eucharistic sacrifice as first and foremost a liturgical repetition of the once-for-all sacrifice of the cross also had the unfortunate effect of obscuring the notion of the active participation of the faithful in the sacrificial activity. The earlier Latin theology, as noted above, viewed the eucharistic liturgy as a constellation of gestures and prayers in which the liturgical activity of the faithful constituted an essential ingredient for the realization of the eucharistic sacrifice. In the later development, however, the eucharistic sacrifice was more narrowly defined as the offering of the one victim through the ministry of the priest. Therefore the laity were understood to participate, not in their own right, but through the ministerial service of the presiding minister.

This new theology of the eucharistic sacrifice provided a building block for the practice of the private Mass which came about due to a number of pastoral and devotional concerns. The transference of the system of stational churches from Rome to the regions beyond the

[55] "Debemus itaque praesens saeculum velquia jam conspicimus defluxisse, tota mente contemnere, quotidiana Deo lacrymarum sacrificia, quotidianas carnis ejus et sanguinis hostias immolare. Haec namque singulariter victima (*Grat., de consecrat.*, dist. 2, § 1) ab aeterno interitu animam salvat, quae illam nobis mortem Unigeniti per mysterium reparat, qui licet resurgens a mortuis jam non moritur, et mors ei ultra non dominabitur (*Rom.* VI, 9), tamen in semetipso immortaliter atque incorruptibiliter vivens, pro nobis iterum in hoc mysterio sacrae oblationis immolatur"—Gregory the Great, *Dialogorum libri iv* 4.58 (PL 77.425CD).

Alps necessitated the confinement of altars honoring martyrs to just one church. The Eucharist was celebrated on these altars in accord with the axiom: martyrs are honored by being buried under altars; altars are places for celebrating the eucharistic sacrifice. Initially the simultaneous celebration of Masses on these altars together with the Mass at the high altar was practiced. But in view of the understanding of the eucharistic sacrifice as a new offering of Christ, the celebration of such Masses on these altars gradually became more frequent. Also, the practice of Irish missionaries of privately celebrating Mass on their missionary excursions in the Frankish lands exercised considerable influence on the development of the private Mass. It was justified on the ground that where the priest is there Mass can be celebrated. Also, in the Frankish milieu the question of exchange of material goods for spiritual goods, monastery lands and other foundations for spiritual blessing, led to the employment of the Mass as the most favored spiritual good to be involved in the "holy commerce."

E. ST. AUGUSTINE, BISHOP OF HIPPO

In Augustine's eucharistic theology three basic perspectives come to the foreground: (1.) sacrifice, (2.) the unity of Christ and Church (eucharistic food), and (3.) Neoplatonic philosophy.

1. Sacrifice

According to Augustine the eucharistic celebration is the memorial of the sacrifice of the cross. As such the Eucharist is this sacrifice in a certain sense. Hence, in the memorial of the once-for-all sacrifice of the cross, Christ offers himself to the Father as priest and victim. Because the one mediator is present and active in the celebration, Christians are brought near to the redemptive sacrifice of Christ and are enabled to offer themselves to God as the body of Christ through the one High Priest, Christ.

The whole Christ offers the eucharistic sacrifice: head and body. The visible sacrifice is sign of the invisible one: "This is the sacrifice of Christians: the many one body in Christ."[56] At its depth this sacrifice

[56] *De civitate dei* 10.6, a key text for Augustine's concept of Christian sacrifice, is mostly an exposition of the practical, ethical nature of Christian sacrificial activity based on Romans 12:1-3. It concludes with the words quoted here: "Hoc est sacrificium christianorum: *multi unum corpus in Christo.* Quod etiam sacramento altaris fidelibus noto frequentat ecclesia, ubi ei demonstratur, quod in ea re, quam offert, ipsa offeratur" (CSEL 47.278–79, at 279.52–55).

is the love of the holy ones grounded in the Spirit of Christ who animates the ecclesial body. In the Eucharist the community offers, as community, the love of Christ *(caritas Christi)*, that flows through the community to the Father. Every act of Christian love is, in a true sense, the Christian sacrifice.[57] These personal sacrifices have their altar: the heart. They are the content *(res)* of the eucharistic sacrifice! Consequently the eucharistic liturgy can be called the sacrament of the true sacrifice of Christians. In the celebration the community offers as community, the *caritas Christi* that flows through it to the Father.

In Augustine's theology the essence of the Church's sacrifice is found in its being one in Christ. The sacrifice of the Church is that of the whole Christ *(totus Christus)*: "This one is the priest, himself offering, himself also that which is offered, the daily sacrament of which he wished to be the sacrifice of the Church, which since it is the body of the head himself, he teaches it to offer through himself."[58] The fire that transports the Church to the heavenly places is the *caritas Christi* in all the saints. The altar on which the sacrifice takes place is the heart: "On the altar of our hearts, we offer to him a sacrifice of humility and praise, aglow with the fire of love *(caritas)*."[59] The core of the eucharistic liturgy is love: unity of Christians in Christ and with one another in the Spirit of Christ who is the soul of the Church. This unity is the essential presupposition of the possibility of the authentic eucharistic celebration and not merely an effect of the reception of the eucharistic flesh and blood.

2. *Eucharistic Food*

Augustine frequently refers to 1 Corinthians 10:17 ("Because there is one bread, we who are many are one body, for we all partake of the one bread") and links it with the formula of the institution of the Eucharist. Hence he emphasizes the relation of this mystery to the unity of the whole Christ. For him the content *(res)* of the sacrament is Christ and the Church. However the Church is the *res*, the content of the sacrament, only insofar as it is holy, that is, according to its invisible being. Since the eucharistic food is symbol of the whole Christ,

[57] Augustine, *De civitate dei* 10.6.

[58] "Per hoc et sacerdos est, ipse offerens, ipse et oblatio. Cuius rei sacramentum cotidianum esse uoluit ecclesiae sacrificium, quae cum ipsius capitis corpus sit, se ipsam per ipsum discit offerre"—*De civitate dei* 10.20 (CSEL 47.294.6–9).

[59] "Ei sacrificamus hostiam humilitatis et laudis in ara cordis igne feruidam caritatis"—*De civitate dei* 10.3 (CSEL 47.275.22–23).

head and body, it is dispensed to those who live the full life of the Church. Those separated from the Church do not really receive (i.e., not spiritually) the eucharistic food.

In *Sermon* 227, on the subject of the Pauline saying: "We the many are one bread, one body" (1 Cor 10:17), Augustine states: "You become the bread, that is the body of Christ."[60] The consequence of this for the eucharistic sacrament is expressed in *Sermon* 272: "Therefore if you yourselves are the body of Christ and his members, then your own mystery lies on the altar. . . . Be what you see, and receive what you are."[61]

Here the Pauline thought of the relation of eucharistic body and ecclesial body is deepened and made the principle of the doctrine of the eucharistic sacrament. Augustine understands that the eucharistic elements, especially the bread, are images of the whole Christ: head and body. The baptized, who live by faith and love, are the body of Christ and participate more deeply in what they are through the symbolic realities of the eucharistic sacraments. Therefore the Eucharist does not afford, precisely, an "encounter" with Christ, as in the case of Ambrose's teaching, but a deepening of one's being in Christ. In the Eucharist we do not so much receive Christ; rather, he receives us and grafts us more deeply into his body.[62]

Recent Catholic scholarship seems to favor the traditional assumption of scholastic theology that Augustine maintained the fourth-century Antiochene belief, exemplified by St. John Chrysostom, that Christ the Head of the Church is really mediated through the symbol of his body and blood. This would indeed be in harmony with Greek Platonic thinking, and it was in fact supported at Antioch by the influence of the Aristotelian concept of change. However, Augustine's Neoplatonic theology led him to downplay the tension between the corporeal and the invisible, when speaking of the visible sacrament.

In this (Augustine's) Neoplatonic thinking, the image does not exercise more than the function of pointing to the properly spiritual reality. Signs relate to what is signified as concrete things to ideas.[63]

[60] ". . . efficimini panis quod est corpus Christi" *Sermo* 227 (Sources Chrétiennes 116.238.40–41).

[61] "Si ergo vos estis corpus Christi et membra, mysterium vestrum in mensa Domini positum est . . . . Estote quod videtis, et accipite quod estis" *Sermo* 272 (PL 38.1247–48).

[62] See *Sermo* 272 (PL 38.1246–48) and *Sermo* 227, 40 (SC 116.234–42).

[63] Augustine, *Principia dialecticae* 5 (PL 32.1410–11); *De doctrina christiana* 2.1.1 (CC 32.32.5–7).

The visible in the sacrament is the expression and possibility of encounter with the invisible, i.e., Christ and the invisible Church: "These things, brothers, are called sacraments, because in them something is seen, [but] something else is understood."[64]

Scripture expresses the tension between the "already" and "not yet" of salvation history. However, Augustine interprets this in a timeless, Neoplatonic way, as the relation between the visible and the invisible. Sacraments are possible because the Son became incarnate. The Incarnation and passion are themselves symbolic events. Behind this thought stands Augustine's concept of time as sign and vestige of eternity *(vestigium aeternitatis).* The corporeal, visible sign of the sacrament is a necessary step to attain the invisible in the economy. In it the lordship of Christ works commensurate to the dispensation of his *sacramentum.*[65]

For Augustine, the material elements of the Lord's Supper are images of the body and blood. Decisive in all this is the spiritual appropriation by the faithful of what is signified: abiding in Christ, and love for the brethren in the Johannine sense.[66] In the phrase "Believe and eat" *(Crede et manducasti)*[67] Augustine accentuates the *Crede;* the eucharistic elements are somewhat played down, just as the material substance of water in baptism. The corporeal visible sign in the sacrament loses something of its importance. It is only a necessary step to attain the invisible, the eternal.

Augustine agrees with the faith of the Church in the matter of a real dynamic presence of Christ in the context of the eucharistic celebration. However, Augustine agrees in all respects neither with the Greek Fathers nor with the later doctrinal position of the West. A careful analysis of Augustine's treatment of John 6, clearly shows that he does not teach the eucharistic realism of Chrysostom or Hilary of Poitiers.[68] Later on, the early medieval interpretation of Augustine

[64] "Ista, fratres, ideo dicuntur Sacramenta, quia in eis aliud videtur, aliud intelligitur"—Augustine, *Sermo* 272 (PL 38.1247); cf. *Principia dialecticae* 5 (PL 32.1410–11).

[65] Augustine, *De diversis quaestionibus* 83, quaestio 69.9 (PL 40.78–79).

[66] See esp. *In Ioannis evangelium tractatus* 26.12–18 (CC 36.265–68). Cf. also *De civitate dei* 21.25 (CC 48.794–96).

[67] *In Ioannis evangelium tractatus* 25.12 (CC 36.254.9).

[68] Ibid., 25–27 (CC 36.248–77). See Edward J. Kilmartin, "The Eucharistic Gift: Augustine of Hippo's Tractate XXVII on Jn 6:60–72," in David G. Hunter, *Preaching in the Patristic Age: Studies in Honor of Walter J. Burghardt, S.J.* (New York: Paulist, 1989) 162–82.

progressively downplays his eucharistic spiritual interpretation of the sacraments of the body and blood. That Augustine's eucharistic theology could be interpreted spiritually is obvious from such texts as *Enarrationes in Ps* 98:9 which reads:

"Understand spiritually what I have spoken. It is not the body, which you see, that you will eat, nor drink that blood which is shed . . . I have commended to you a sacrament; understood spiritually, it will make you live."[69]

Texts of this kind occasioned the tradition of a "merely" symbolic concept of the sacraments of the body and blood as opposed to a realistic concept of the sacramental objective presence of the historical and glorified body and blood of Christ. To some extent these two tendencies lay at the basis of the theological interpretations of the content of the eucharistic sacraments that surfaced in the ninth-century writings of Paschasius Radbertus, abbot of Corbie, whose realist view of the Eucharist was attacked by Ratramnus, a monk of the same monastery.

The tendency to interpret Augustine "symbolically" in the early Middle Ages can be shown from the fact that the realists did not content themselves with quoting; they also paraphrased passages of Augustine to support their position on the authority of the bishop of Hippo. For example, Augustine says:

"The one who does not abide in Christ and in whom Christ does not abide, doubtless neither eats his flesh nor drinks his blood."[70]

The venerable Bede and Alcuin render the text this way:

"The one who does not abide in Christ and in whom Christ does not abide, doubtless neither eats his flesh nor drinks his blood in a spiritual way, although he chews in a corporeal way and in visible form the sacrament of the body and blood of Christ with his teeth."[71]

[69] "Spiritualiter intellegite quod locutus sum: non hoc corpus quod uidetis, manducaturi estis, et bibituri illum sanguinem, quem fusuri sunt . . . Sacramentum aliquod uobis commendaui; spiritaliter intellectum uiuificabit uos"—Augustine, *Ennarationes in psalmos* 98.9 (CC 39.1386.57–61).

[70] ". . . qui non manet in Christo et in quo non manet Christus, procul dubio nec manducat carnem eius, nec bibit eius sanguinem"—Augustine, *In Ioannis evangelium tractatus* 26.18 (CC 36.268.6–8).

[71] ". . . qui non manet in Christo et in quo non manet Christus procul dubio nec manducat *spiritualiter* carnem eius nec bibit eius sanguinem *licet carnaliter et visi-*

In short, Augustine teaches that the Church is the true body of Christ *(verum corpus Christi)* while the eucharistic elements are the sacrament of the body of Christ *(sacramentum corporis Christi)*. Hence the sacrament of the body of Christ is received in the true body of Christ.[72] And the sacrament of the body of Christ is the sacrifice of the true body of Christ. Nevertheless the belonging to the sign does not include, by itself, the belonging to the reality of the Church. For where one has the Spirit of Christ, he is in the body of Christ. Where the body of Christ is, there is also the Spirit of Christ. The Church is not immediately attainable. It lies in the realm of the invisible-spiritual. But the Church has its sign. The sacrament of the body of Christ corresponds to the body of Christ. Therefore the visible Church and the Eucharist have a like meaning. The sign shares in the inaccessibility of the reality signified. This means that the belonging to the sign is a condition for belonging to the "true body of Christ," just as the belonging to the body of Christ is a condition of being one with the Spirit of Christ. But this also means that the belonging to the sign does not include by itself belonging to the reality. If one takes seriously the Augustinian concept of the relation of the historical and pneumatic Christ, a relation of the sacramental forms to the historical Christ as conceived in the fourth-century Antiochene tradition is not indicated.

3. Neoplatonic Philosophy

In order to understand Augustine's eucharistic theology, one must have a grasp of his view of the relation between ecclesial sanctifying activity and divine sanctifying activity. Augustine's theology of grace always emphasizes the distinction between the sphere of God's activity and that of the activity of the *ecclesia catholica*. Thus in the anti-Manichean period he distinguishes what the Church does in word and sacrament from what God does. The former is meaningful but does not penetrate to the inner sphere of the *anima rationalis*. Rather, God directly bestows grace on the soul; as teacher, he makes his internal word audible, and as inward light bestows the illumination necessary to understand it.

---

biliter premat dentibus sacramentum corporis et sanguinis Christi . . ." The italicized words are the apparent additions/changes which are found in Bede and Alcuin, and are not found in any known manuscript of Augustine—see Fritz Hofmann, *Der Kirchenbegriff des hl. Augustinus in seiner Grundlagen und in seiner Entwicklung* (Munich: Max Hueber, 1933) 411, n. 217.

[72] Augustine, *De civitate dei* 21.25 (CSEL 48.794–96).

These earlier writings reflect Augustine's Neoplatonic concern to maintain a clear line of demarcation between the spiritual-intelligible and the material-sensible world. The soul encounters the spiritual by means of a spiritual reality. From this point of view Augustine developed his theory of sign. Signs are ontologically inferior to the realities of the spiritual world. They allude to something that is graspable only by immediate spiritual appropriation. The *res spiritualis* signified by the sign is attained only by the spiritual soul through spiritual contact. Words and signs do not cause the spiritual reality to be appropriated by the soul: "For what are certain corporeal sacraments except certain *quasi verba visibilia,* indeed holy, nevertheless changeable and temporal?"[73]

In the subsequent controversy with the Donatists, Augustine's Neoplatonic concerns entered a new phase. The Donatists held for the identification of the spiritual with the empirical Church, of the holiness of sacraments with the holiness of the priest who administers them. Augustine, by contrast, distinguishes between the validity of a sacrament and the effect of sanctification. He concedes to schismatics a validity reduced to purely formal holiness. The schismatics have a *forma pietatis,* but not the *virtus pietatis invisibilis.*[74] Neoplatonic ontology enabled Augustine to use the idea of a two-dimensional sacrament. But the two dimensions are not always present at the same time. Since the priest is only the "minister," the fact of the celebration of baptism does not of itself include the communication of grace; God alone sanctifies. Schismatic churches can administer valid sacraments. They have one dimension of Church but they lack the internal dimension of the power of the Spirit.

In his final anti-Pelagian period, Augustine developed a doctrine of grace that places the relation between the activity of Church and divine saving activity in a new light. He modifies his Neoplatonic approach to a certain degree. But he still retains a two-dimensional ecclesiology. Augustine is convinced that the human being is so

[73] "Quid enim sunt aliud quaeque corporalia sacramenta nisi quaedam quasi uerba uisibilia, sacrosancta quidem, uerum tamen mutabilia et temporalia?"—Augustine, *Contra Faustum Manichaeum* 19.16 (CSEL 25/1.513 [PL 42.356–57]).

[74] "Proinde corporalia Sacramenta, quae portant et celebrant etiam segregati ab unitate corporis Christi, formam possunt exhibere pietatis: virtus vero pietatis invisibilis et spiritualis ita in eis non potest esse, quemadmodum sensus non sequitur hominis membrum, quando amputatur a corpore"—Augustine, *Sermo* 71.19 (PL 38.463).

steeped in sin that one can be enlightened only from the outside. The light of grace must come from God; no creaturely mediation is possible. Preaching and the biblical word point to the reality known only from the internal word *(verbum internum);* the same holds for sacraments.

This structure carries over to the Church. There is the external community and the community of saints. There is no salvation outside the *ecclesia catholica.* But what is the relation between the immediacy of the saving activity and the ecclesial mediation of salvation? Augustine bases the necessity of the external Church and its institutions on the divine will. God wills to order the sanctifying work and the ecclesial event one to the other. God does not bestow grace without the ministry of human beings. Augustine holds that God could indeed lead humankind to salvation without word and sacrament, but God does not choose to do so after the passion of Christ.

Augustine also establishes an inner connection between the essence of the invisible Church of the Spirit and the visible Church. There is the matter of the *condicio humana* mentioned in the prologue to the *De doctrina christiana.* There is the matter of the *admonitio* function of word and sacrament. Moreover, there is the matter of Augustine's concept of *caritas.* In his thought, the love of the saints is the fruit of the work of the Spirit of Christ. This *caritas* is always related to the visible fellowship of the *ecclesia catholica,* to unity and peace in the Church. It belongs to the essence of *caritas* that it be maintained in the historical sphere of human relations. This love has as object the Church, Scripture, preaching, and sacraments. Whoever has contempt for sacraments cannot be saved. The Church is both object of love and sphere of love. The fact of predestination is indicated by the way in which the Christian is adjusted in his whole inner striving to the visible Church. The fact that Christ has grounded his Church as external institution is not only the expression of his will, but corresponds to the being of human beings: it corresponds to their corporeal-sensible nature, and to their task: their determination to love.[75]

[75] See Berndt Hamm, "Unmittelbarkeit des göttlichen Gnadenwirkens und kirchliche Heilsvermittlung bei Augustin," *Zeitschrift für Theologie und Kirche* 78 (1981) 409–41. This nuanced article argues that there is in Augustine no contradiction between the immediacy of the work of divine grace and the necessity of an ecclesial mediation of salvation, and that there is in Augustine a correlation between the inner working of the Spirit and the external institution of Church.

F. FAUSTUS OF RIEZ (FL. 455–488)

The *Homily on the Body and Blood of Christ* attributed to an unknown author of Provence, and dependent on Faustus of Riez, borrows from the theology of the sacraments of the Eucharist taught by Ambrose. The author equates the notion of consecration with that of conversion. He mentions that at the Last Supper "Christ was about to consecrate the sacrament of his body and blood."[76] How this takes place is clarified by the explanation of the nature of the ministerial action of the priest who presides at the Eucharist: "For the visible priest, through a secret power, converts by the word the visible creatures into the substance of his body and blood speaking thus . . ."[77] Finally, the author attributes the consecration of the bread and wine to the invocation of the name of Christ: "Before the substances of the bread and wine are consecrated by the invocation of his name . . ."[78]

G. POPE GELASIUS I (492–496)

The theology of the sacraments of the body and blood taught by Pope Gelasius is reminiscent of the Augustinian point of view. However, it is in fact borrowed from the Antiochene theology of the fifth century which had abandoned the more realistic fourth-century teaching of that tradition. To this extent it differs from the Ambrosian eucharistic doctrine of the somatic real presence which is dependent on the earlier, fourth-century Antiochene version. Gelasius's theology of the sacraments of the Eucharist reflects the actual situation of the official Roman theology of the Eucharist at the end of the fifth century. However, scholars have paid little attention to it until now. That is why we give so much more attention to it than to the teaching of the other authors discussed in this chapter.

Gelasius was a Roman citizen by birth, possibly born in North Africa. As a member of the Roman clergy he became special assistant to Pope Felix II (483–492). After the death of Felix II he was elected

[76] "Et quia corpus assumptum ablaturus erat ab oculis nostris, et sideribus illaturus, necessarium erat, ut nobis in hac die sacramentum corporis et sanguinis sui consecraret, . . ." Pseudo Faustus, *Homilia de corpore et sanguine Christi* 1 (PL 30.272A).

[77] "Nam visibilis sacerdos, visibiles creaturas in substantiam corporis et sanguinis sui, verbo secreta potestate convertit ita dicens: *Accipite et comedite, hoc est corpus meum* (Matt XXVI, 26)"—ibid., 2 (PL 30.272B).

[78] ". . . antequam invocatione sui nominis consecrantur, substantia illic est panis et vini, post verba autem corpus et sanguis est Christi"—ibid., 12 (PL 30.275D).

Bishop of Rome and held the post with distinction for almost five years. He is usually reckoned as the most outstanding fifth-century Roman bishop after Pope Leo I. Gelasius is well known for his efforts to cope with the problem of the thirty-four years of schism between Rome and Constantinople, and for his contribution to the enrichment and reform of the Roman liturgy of the Mass which was undertaken at the end of the fifth century.

The extant works of Gelasius contain numerous references to the subject of eucharistic liturgical practice and theology.[79] They supply valuable information concerning the order of celebration of the Roman Mass as well as contemporary approaches of various sects to eucharistic theology. As might be suspected, Gelasius maintains a typical Latin approach to the theology of sacramental worship in general, and to the eucharistic celebration in particular. Above all, his writings on these themes betray the influence of St. Augustine of Hippo.

Gelasius instinctively understands that the unity of the Church is not primarily a fruit of the Eucharist, but its presupposition. As we have already seen, this point of view, characteristic of the North African Church, was developed by Augustine. On the subject of the full restoration of sinners to the life of the Church upon the completion of public penance, Gelasius says that it entails "communion, that is, integration with the rest of the faithful and the reception of the holy body and blood."[80]

Concerning the necessity of reception of the sacrament of the Eucharist for salvation, Gelasius follows the traditional doctrine of the Latin Church originating in the North African exegesis of the Fourth Gospel. In this case his dependence on Augustine's treatment of the subject is unmistakable. In the context of his refutation of the Pelagian doctrine of original sin and baptism, this Pope introduces the literal interpretation of John 3:5 and John 6:53 to prove that the reception of both baptism and the sacrament of the Eucharist is necessary for salvation. The connection between the two sacraments is explained as follows: Baptism is the "salutary sacrament" by which

[79] See Eligius Dekkers, *Clavis Patrum Latinorum*, 3rd ed. (Turnhout, Belgium: Brepols, 1995) nos. 1667–76, pp. 543–45. In this work we have used the collection of Gelasius's writings in Andreas Thiel, ed., *Epistolae romanorum pontificium genuinae et quae ad eos scriptae sunt a S. Hilaro usque ad Pelagium II*, vol. 1: *a S. Hilaro usque ad S. Hormisdam, ann. 461–523* (Brunsberg: in aedibus Eduardi Peter, 1868) 285–613.

[80] ". . . communionem, id est consortium ceterorum fidelium et perceptionis sacri corporis et sanguinis Christi"—Gelasius, *Fragment* 49 (Thiel 510).

participation in the body and blood of Christ is made possible. On the other hand, participation in eternal life is dependent on the reception of Holy Communion. The relationship of dependence of salvation on the reception of the two sacraments admits of no exception.[81] The teaching of John 3:5 and 6:53 is applicable also to dying infants: "without baptism they (infants) are able neither to eat nor drink the body and blood of Christ. However without this (Eucharist) they cannot 'have life in themselves.'"[82]

In this case Gelasius simply repeats the rigid doctrine of Augustine. He does not reckon with the logical consequences of traditional doctrine about the ecclesiological effect of baptism, namely the belonging to the body of Christ, the Church. However, the contemporary of Gelasius, and faithful disciple of Augustine, Fulgentius of Ruspe (462–527), does not overlook the implication of this ecclesiological effect of Christian initiation. His teaching is discussed below.

Gelasius's understanding of the relationship of the unity of the Church to the Eucharist, as explained above, leads logically to the conclusion of Fulgentius on the subject of the necessity of eucharistic communion for salvation. Moreover, as we shall see, Gelasius's theology of eucharistic consecration is almost identifiable with that of Augustine and Fulgentius. The difference lies in the differentiated understanding of the nature of the relationship of the eucharistic grace to the external sacraments.

Gelasius always remained under the spell of Augustine's theology of the sacraments in general, and of the Eucharist in particular. However, an important exception is Gelasius's theology of the sacraments of the body and blood of Christ contained in no. 14 of his *Tractatus III seu De duabus naturis in Christo adversus Eutychem et Nestorium.*[83] It

[81] ". . . ubi utique neminem videmus exceptum, nec ausus est aliquis dicere, parvulum sine hoc sacramento salutari ad aeternam vitam posse perduci"—Gelasius, *Epistola* 6.5 (Thiel 329).

[82] ". . . dum sine baptismate corpus et sanguinem Christi nec edere valeant nec potare, sine autem hoc vitam in semetipso habere non possint"—Gelasius, *Epistola* 6.6 (Thiel 331). Augustine consistently held this rigid doctrine concerning the necessity of eucharistic communion for the salvation of infants. For example, *De peccatorum meritis et remissione* 1.20.27 (CSEL 60.26–27).

[83] Thiel 530–44, at 541–42. The most recent critical edition of this work is in E. Schwartz, *Publizistische Sammlungen zum Acacianischen Schisma.* Abhandlungen der Bayerischen Akademie der Wissenschaften, Philosophisch-historische Abteilung, Neue Folge, Heft 10 (Munich: Bayerische Akademie der Wissenschaften, 1934) 85.23–95.33, at 94.23–34.

should be noted that the main purpose of this treatise was to be a defense of Catholic doctrine concerning the permanence in the hypostatic union of the human and divine natures of Christ. In doing this, Gelasius, as others had done before him, makes use of the mystery of the Eucharist to confirm this Christological teaching.

Since the second century, the similarities between the event of the Incarnation of Christ and the sanctification of the eucharistic elements had been seen as grounding the notion of eucharistic incarnation. In other words, it was the Incarnation that provided the conceptual model for thinking about the sacraments of the body and blood of Christ, especially in Eastern theology. Consequently, it was also possible to reverse the process and argue not just from the Incarnation to the Eucharist, but also, as Gelasius does, from the theology of eucharistic consecration to the theological implications of the Incarnation of Christ.

The explanation of the eucharistic sanctification from the event of the Incarnation was determined, from an early date in the life of the Church, by the Logos Christology of John 1:14: "The Word became flesh." Just as the Logos assumed the humanity of Jesus from the moment of its conception in the womb of Mary, so the elements of bread and wine are taken up by the Logos who makes them sacraments of his body and blood. Later on in the East, with the development of the theology of the Holy Spirit, the implications of the Spirit Christology of Luke 1:34-35 were integrated into the event of the Incarnation itself. The Spirit was understood to have exercised a special personal role in the event of the Incarnation itself as divine agent of the sanctification of the human nature created by the Trinity as such and assumed by the Word. Hence one could now say that in the act of creation of the humanity of Jesus, accomplished by the Trinity as such, the Spirit sanctified the humanity that was assumed by the Word. Here the activity of the Spirit is viewed as prior to the assumption of the humanity of Jesus by the Word, not in a temporal sense, but in the sense of priority of nature. Correspondingly, in the case of the eucharistic sanctification, the Holy Spirit was assigned the role of sanctifier of the elements of bread and wine: the divine agent by whom the earthly elements are elevated to unity of being with the risen Lord. In short, given the correspondence between the two Incarnations, the way was open to the employment of the theology of the liturgical Incarnation to shed light on the mystery of the historical Incarnation of the Son of God, or vice versa.

The introduction of the theology of the Eucharist to support a theology of the Incarnation is exemplified in the context of the fifth-century Christological controversy. That situation pitted Alexandrian theology against that of the Antiochene school. For at Antioch, preoccupation with defending the dogma of the unity of the human nature with the divine nature, unconfused and unseparated, against what appeared to the Antiocheans to be a monophysitic tendency of Egypt, brought into play a more symbolic theology of eucharistic consecration that markedly differed from the older, more realistic Antiochene tradition.

The typical fifth-century Antiochene argument which looked to the theology of the Eucharist in order to refute monophysitic Christology was introduced by the Patriarch of Constantinople, Nestorius, and fully developed by Theodoret of Cyrus. The surprising thing about Nestorius's theology of the sacraments of the Eucharist is its denial of a change of the nature or substance of the elements. This explicit doctrine regarding eucharistic conversion (in which real conversion is denied by Nestorius and Theodoret) was a special development away from the earlier, fourth-century Antiochene school. As we have already indicated above, this fourth-century Antiochene theology of the Eucharist, as exemplified by John Chrysostom and Theodore of Mopsuestia, maintained as axiomatic the doctrine of a change of being by which the bread and wine become the sacraments of body and blood of Christ. But the conclusion was not drawn (at least not at that time) that this concept of change is applicable to the humanity of Jesus. Rather, this humanity remains united to the divine Word, unconfused and unseparated also after the glorification of the incarnate Word. Hence, according to traditional Antiochene theology, although there exists a *correspondence* between the eucharistic and historical Incarnation, a *strict parallel* between the historical Incarnation and the eucharistic Incarnation is *denied.*

Nestorius's new theology of the eucharistic sacraments of the body and blood, which runs contrary to the venerable (fourth-century) Antiochene tradition, has not always been recognized by scholars. Henry Chadwick, for example, writing on the occasion of the fifteen-hundredth anniversary of the Council of Chalcedon, dealt with the theme of the role played by the doctrine of the Eucharist in the Nestorian controversy.[84] He attempted to prove that the "nerve center of Cyril's

[84] Henry Chadwick, "Eucharist and Christology in the Nestorian Controversy," *Journal of Theological Studies* n. s. 2 (1951) 145–64. Even before the controversy with

objection to Antiochene doctrine" was the negative consequences for the theology of the eucharist.[85] In brief, Cyril of Alexandria judged that the Antiochene description of the "conjunction" between the humanity and divinity in Christ did not suffice to account for the efficacy of the Eucharist. According to this Alexandrian theologian, the flesh of Christ is so united to the Logos that it is endowed with the *energeia* of the divinity and, therefore, by participation in the sacrament, the believer receives the life-giving power of the divinity.

Chadwick compares the eucharistic theology of Cyril with that of Nestorius, relying on the dialogue with "Sophronius" found as an addition to Nestorius's *Book of Heraclides*.[86] Here he does not find a difference between the two theologians on the subject of conversion of the eucharistic gifts. "Nestorius evidently shares with Cyril the belief in a conversionist doctrine of the Eucharist. Neither defines how he conceives of the manner of the change, and it is dangerous to attempt to label them with the names of later orthodoxies or heresies."[87] However, a closer reading of this passage of *Heraclides* 1.1[88] analyzed by Chadwick yields a different view.

The representative of Cyril's theology urges the argument that the Alexandrian Christology is proved by eucharistic belief. But this is followed by a Nestorian *argumentum ad absurdum:* "If the essence *(ousia)* of the body of Christ is changed into the divinity, are we now changed into the *ousia* of the God–Logos?"[89] Moreover, in *Heraclides* 2.1, Nestorius is clear enough about the fact that the eucharistic bread remains bread. This meant for him that a change in the nature *(physis)* of the elements has no place. On the other hand, he affirmed that a change of meaning of the elements occurs in and through the celebration of the divine liturgy in such a way that they become the body and blood

---

Nestorius began, Cyril had already begun his anti-Antiochene polemic on the grounds of the threat it posed for eucharistic belief.

[85] Ibid., 152.

[86] The genuinity of this dialogue is challenged. Cf. Luise Abramowski, *Untersuchungen zum Liber Heraclidis des Nestorius.* Corpus Scriptorum Christianorum Orientalium 242, Subsidia Tome 22 (Louvain: Secretariat du Corpus SCO, 1963) 114–17, 132–34. It seems to have been composed after Chalcedon, possibly influenced by Philoxenus of Mabbug. Cf. L. Abramowski, *Zeitschrift für Kirchengeschichte* 77 (1966) 122–25.

[87] Chadwick, "Eucharist and Christology" 157, n. 1.

[88] *Heraclides* 1.1.39–40 (Paul Bedjan, *Nestorius, Le livre d'Heraclide de Damas* [Paris: rue de Sèvres, 95/Leipzig: Otto Harrassowitz, 1910] 45–47).

[89] *Heraclides* 1.1.41 (Bedjan 48).

of Christ for the liturgical assembly of believers. Still this observation leaves unresolved the question whether the elements serve as a kind of objective vehicle of grace or merely as a symbol of what happens in the believing conscience through the exercise of faith alone.[90]

Theodoret of Cyrus (d. ca. 466), the most outstanding theologian of the School of Antioch after Theodore of Mopsuestia, provided a development of Nestorius's position in a treatise in which a particular version of a monophysitic Christology and eucharistic doctrine is contrasted with a contemporary orthodox treatment of the same themes.

Theodoret's *Eranistes,*[91] is a work that records the basic dogmatic elements of the controversy at the Synod of Constantinople of 448. It is in the form of a dialogue between a monophysite theologian and his orthodox opponent. Theodoret attributes to the monophysite a concept of change of the nature of the humanity of Jesus which is linked to his ascension and which amounts to the absorption of the humanity by the divinity. Correspondingly, the same monophysite also affirms that the effect of the sanctification of the eucharistic elements which follows the epiclesis entails the change of the elements into something else, that is, they are similarly swallowed up by the divinity.

The monophysite establishes a strict parallel between the eucharistic sanctification and the resurrection–ascension of Jesus:

"Just as the symbols are one thing before the invocation (ἐπίκλησις) of the priest, and after the invocation are changed and become another thing, so the body of the Lord is changed after the ascension into a divine substance."[92]

[90] Bedjan 49. Cf. Johannes Betz, *Eucharistie in der Schrift und Patristik.* Handbuch der Dogmengeschichte IV/4a (Freiburg: Herder, 1979) 118–19.

[91] Gerard H. Ettlinger, *Theodoret of Cyrus, Eranistes* (Oxford: Clarendon, 1975). The *Eranistes* was written in 447 or 448, probably against Eutyches. In the year 449, at the synod of Ephesus, Theodoret was deposed from office, while Eutyches was approved by Dioscorus of Alexandria. Theodoret appealed to Pope Leo I who declared the decision of Ephesus to be null and void. At the Council of Chalcedon Theodoret was admitted as an orthodox father.

[92] "Ὥσπερ τοίνυν τὰ σύμβολα τοῦ δεσποτικοῦ σώματός τε καὶ αἵματος ἄλλα μέν εἰσι πρὸ τῆς ἱερατικῆς ἐπικλήσεως, μετὰ δέ γε τὴν ἐπίκλησιν μεταβάλλεται καὶ ἕτερα γίνεται, οὕτω τὸ δεσποτικὸν σῶμα μετὰ τὴν ἀνάληψιν εἰς τὴν θείαν μετεβλήθη οὐσίαν"—Theodoret, *Eranistes,* Dialogue 2 (Ettlinger 152.9–12).

Thus, on the one hand the monophysite employs the idea of eucharistic change that first gained prominence at Antioch in the fourth century, and on the other hand deviates from the old Antiochene Christology by identifying the change of the humanity of Jesus after the ascension with the notion of absorption by the Divinity.

It is not possible from the evidence at hand to identify individuals or a particular branch of monophysites who championed this theology. We only have the witness of the Patriarch Michael I (1166–1199), quoting Timothy Aelurus, that two Eutychians held for such a eucharistic change.[93] Moreover, following the definition of the Council of Chalcedon (451) a new phase of monophysitism began with those who rejected the Christological formulation of this council. While the theologians of this later movement emphasize the mysterious unity between the divinity and the humanity of Christ, none of the later representatives of the monophysite theology of the Eucharist employ the traditional terminology of change of the nature or essence of the material elements when speaking of the way in which the sacrament of the body and blood comes into being. This holds for Jacob of Sarug (451–521); Severus, Patriarch of Antioch (512–518); and Philoxenus of Mabbug (d. 523). Quite possibly, Theodoret is referring to a popular monophysitic view.

The identification of the source of the "orthodox" theology of the *Eranistes* is another matter. It is clearly in line with the teaching of Patriarch Nestorius. The orthodox partner of the dialogue with the monophysite denies the monophysitic claim that the humanity of Jesus undergoes a change in the event of the resurrection-ascension and likewise the monophysitic claim of the change of the substance or nature of the eucharistic bread and wine. Concerning the sacraments of the body and blood, the orthodox theologian states in *Dialogue* 2: "For neither do the mystical symbols recede from their proper nature *(physis)* after the sanctification. Rather they remain in the previous essence *(ousia)* . . . figure, form, are visible and tangible as before."[94]

Here and elsewhere in his writings Theodoret favors the Nestorian position although he was acquainted with the older Antiochene eu-

[93] *Chronique de Michel le Syrien, Patriarche jacobite d'Antioche* (Paris, 1900–1910) II. 128.

[94] "Οὐδὲ γὰρ μετὰ τὸν ἁγιασμὸν τὰ μυστικὰ σύμβολα τῆς οἰκείας ἐξίσταται φύσεως μένει γὰρ ἐπὶ τῆς προτέρας οὐσίας, καὶ τοῦ σχήματος καὶ τοῦ εἴδους, καὶ ὁρατά ἐστι, καὶ ἁπτά, οἷα καὶ πρότερον ἦν"—Theodoret, *Eranistes,* Dialogue 2 (Ettlinger 152.13–16).

charistic theology. Theodoret knew the teaching of Theodore of Mopsuestia on the subject of eucharistic realism, an exposition that corresponds essentially to that of John Chrysostom. But he consciously disassociated himself from it. A comparison between a passage of Theodore on the subject of the Eucharist of the Last Supper and one of Theodoret on the same subject can exemplify the difference.

In *Fragmentum in Matt 26:26,* Theodore of Mopsuestia writes:

"He (Jesus) did not say: 'This is the symbol of my body and blood,' but: 'This is my body and blood.' In this way he taught us not to look at the nature (φύσις) of what lies before us, but that this is changed (μεταβάλλειν) into the body and blood through the accomplishment of the thanksgiving (εὐχαριστία)."[95]

A somewhat similar statement is made by Theodoret in *Eranistes, Dialogue* 2, where he comments on the fact that at the Last Supper Jesus called the bread and wine his body and blood. According to Theodoret, by changing the name of the symbols he, Jesus, disclosed a change in the gifts.

"For he wished the participants in the mysteries not to give heed to the nature (φύσις) of what is seen, but through the alteration of the names to believe the change (μεταβολή) happening on the ground of the grace (χάρις). For he who called the natural body bread (reference to: bread of life) and described himself as a vine, has honored the visible symbols by the term 'body and blood,' not because he changed (μεταβάλλειν) their nature but because he added to their nature (φύσις) the grace (χάρις)."[96]

[95] "Οὐκ εἶπε, Τουτό ἐστι τὸ σύμβολον τοῦ σώματος μου καὶ τοῦτο τοῦ αἵματος μου, ἀλλά, Τουτό ἐστι τὸ σῶμα μου καὶ τὸ αἷμα μου, διδάσκων ἡμᾶς μὴ πρὸς τὴν φύσιν ὁρᾶν τοῦ προκειμένου, ἀλλὰ διὰ τῆς γενομένης εὐχαριστίας εις σάρκα καὶ αἷμα μεταβάλλεσθαι"—Theodore of Mopsuestia, *In Evangelium Matthaie,* Fragment 26 (On Matt 26:26 [PL 66.713B]).

[96] "Ἠβουλήθη γὰρ τοὺς τῶν θείων μυστηρίων μεταλαγχάνοντας μὴ τῇ φύσει τῶν προκειμένων προσέχειν, ἀλλὰ διὰ τὴς τῶν ὀνομάτων ἐναλλαγὴς πιοτεύειν τῇ ἐκ τὴς χάριτις γεγενημένῃ μεταβολῇ. Ὁ γὰρ δὴ τὸ φύσει σῶμα σίτον καὶ ἄρτον προσαγορεύσας, καὶ αὖ πάλιν ἄμπελον ὀνομάσας, οὗτος τὰ ὁρώμενα ούμβολα τῇ τοῦ σώματος καὶ αἵματος προσηγορίᾳ τετίμηκεν, οὐ τὴν φύσιν μεταβαλῶν, ἀλλὰ τὴν χάριν τῇ φύσει προστεθεικώς"—Theodoret, *Eranistes,* Dialogue 1 (Ettlinger 78.27–79.2). Elsewhere in Tractate 3.10 (Thiel 538–39) Gelasius asks about the application of the term *nature* in Christology. He argues that every *res* has a proper substance, which is called a nature. He finds special significance in the fact that the "blessed apostle

Theodore's text is interpreted by Theodoret in such a way that the change taking place through the liturgical action does not involve a change of being of the elements. Rather, the addition of the *charis* is identified as that which constitutes the change. Still, Theodoret can employ the terminology of change that approaches in its meaning that of Theodore. It is a general concept of a change that is rooted in the ancient understanding that the essence of a thing is ultimately to be defined by the power by which it is possessed. Change of relation of possession constitutes a change of essence. Change of essence is the effect of the altering of the relation of possession occurring with the thing.[97] The difference between the two theologies lies in the fact that one, the fifth-century Antiochene version, attributes to the visible elements an intrinsic relation to the divine grace in which the distance between sign and symbolized is not overcome. The other, the older fourth-century Antiochene tradition, describes the consecrated elements as symbols in which the distance between the sign and symbolized is overcome not only ontologically (a change of meaning), but in the sense of realization of the unity of being of the sign with the signified. However it must be said that, on this subject, Theodoret still employs the traditional language of fourth-century Antioch. This implies a deeper level of eucharistic realism than that expressed in his speculative thought. Sharing in the eucharistic mysteries is described as "sharing in the Lord himself."[98] Again he affirms that the "mystical symbols . . . are understood to be what they have become, and believed and adored as that which they are believed to be."[99]

Peter" did not hesitate to use this term for "God himself" when he preached the "mystery of Christ the Lord" in 2 Peter 1:4. In general Gelasius uses the terms nature and substance interchangeably.

[97] See Johannes Betz, *Die Eucharistie in der Zeit der griechischen Väter.* Band I/1, *Die Aktualpräsenz der Person und des Heilswerkes Jesu im Abendmahl nach der vorephesinischen griechischen Patristik* (Freiburg: Herder, 1955) 309, 317.

[98] After quoting 1 Cor 10:17, "Because there is one bread, we who are many are one body, for we all partake of the one bread," Theodoret continues: "Τῶν ἱερῶν ἀπαλαύοντες μυστηρίων, οὐκ αὐτῷ κοινωνοῦμεν τῷ Δεσπότῃ οὐ καὶ τὸ σῶμα εἶναι καὶ τὸ αἷμά φαμεν, ἐπειδὴ πάντες ἐκ τοῦ ἑνὸς ἄρτου μεταλαγχάνομεν"—Theodoret, *Interpretatio primae epistolae ad Corinthios* 10:16 (PG 82.305B).

[99] The full sentence reads: "Οὐδὲ γὰρ μετὰ τὸν ἁγιαστικὰ σύμβολα τῆς οἰκίας ἐξίσταται φύσεως μένει γὰρ ἐπὶ τῆς προτέρας οὐσίας καὶ τοῦ σχήματος καὶ τοῦ εἴδους, καὶ ὁρατά ἐστι, καί ἁπτά, οἷα καὶ πρότερον ἦν νοεῖται δὲ ἅπερ ἐγένετο, καὶ πιστεύεται καὶ προσκυνεῖται, ὡς ἐκεῖνα ὄντα ἅπερ πιστεύεται"—Theodoret, *Eranistes,* Dialogue 2 (Ettlinger 152.14–17).

The theology of the sacraments of the body and blood attributed to the orthodox partner of *Eranistes* resembles that employed by Pope Gelasius in *Tractate 3, De duabus naturis* 14, to confirm the Catholic doctrine of the hypostatic union. Whether Gelasius actually used the *Eranistes* remains an open question. In any case it is certain that Gelasius's formulation of the theology of the eucharistic transformation of the symbols of the body and blood is dependent on the typical fifth-century Antiochene model. What follows here is a translation of the relevant passage of Gelasius's *De duabus naturis,* divided into six numbered sections (numbering ours) and a commentary on the content of each section. The text reads as follows in English:

"[1] Holy Scripture witnesses that this mystery began from the outset of the blessed conception by saying: 'Wisdom built herself a house' (Proverbs 9:1a), propped under by the solidity of the septiform Spirit (Proverbs 9:1b), that would provide the nourishment of the Incarnation of Christ by which 'we are made partakers of the divine nature' (2 Peter 1:4).

"[2] Certainly the sacraments of the body and blood of Christ, which we receive, is a divine thing. On account of this and through the same 'we are made partakers of the divine nature' (2 Peter 1:4). And yet the substance or nature of the bread and wine does not cease to exist.

"[3] And certainly the image and likeness of the body and blood of Christ are celebrated in the action of the mysteries.

"[4] Therefore it is shown clearly enough to us that we ought to think about Christ the Lord himself what we confess, celebrate and receive in his image:

"[5] that just as they pass over into this, namely, into the divine substance by the working of the Holy Spirit, yet remaining in the peculiarity of their nature;

"[6] so they demonstrate, by remaining in the proper sense those things which they are, that the principal mystery itself, whose efficacy and power they truly represent to us, remains the one Christ, integral and true."[100]

[100] [1] Quod mysterium a beatae conceptionis exordio sic coepisse sacra scriptura testatur dicendo: *Sapientia aedificavit sibi domum,* septiformis Spiritus soliditate subnixam, quae incarnationis Christi, per quam *efficimur divinae consortes naturae,* ministraret alimoniam. [2] Certe sacramenta, quae sumimus, corporis et

COMMENTARY

(1.) Gelasius begins by affirming the dogma of the coincidence of the mystery of the Incarnation and the conception of Jesus in the womb of the Virgin Mary. Gelasius has repeatedly affirmed that the mystery of the unity of the two natures in Christ coincides with the moment of conception: "the outset of the blessed conception." It is the reason why Jesus will be called Son of God from the outset, according to Luke 1:35.[101]

Gelasius favors Luke 1:34–35 as chief witness to the Incarnation. The other classical Scriptural text, John 1:14, is said to have been inspired by the "Spirit of God" to affirm that the Word was not "converted into flesh."[102] Elsewhere Gelasius paraphrases Luke 1:35 as follows: "The flesh . . . was united to the deity by the coming over of the Holy Spirit and the overshadowing power of the Most High."[103] However, neither here nor elsewhere does the Pope supply a more precise description of the role of the Holy Spirit in the event of the Incarnation.

Still, this role should be interpreted in the light of what Pope Leo maintains as axiomatic: "In this ineffable unity of the Trinity . . . works are common in all things."[104] The fifth-century Roman trinitar-

---

sanguinis Christi divina res est, propter quod et per eadem *divinae efficimur consortes naturae;* et tamen esse non desinit substantia vel natura panis et vini. [3] Et certe imago et similitudo corporis et sanguinis Christi in actione mysteriorum [Schwartz: mystica] celebrantur. [4] Satis ergo nobis evidenter ostenditur hoc nobis in ipso Christo Domino sentiendum, quod in ejus imagine profitemur, celebramus et sumimus: [5] ut sicut in hanc, scilicet in divinam, transeant sancto Spiritu perficiente substantiam permanentes tamen in suae proprietate naturae; [Schwartz: ut sicut haec licet in diuinam transeant sancto spiritu perficiente substantiam, permanent tamen in suae proprietate naturae] [6] sic illud ipsum mysterium principale, cujus nobis efficientiam virtutemque veraciter repraesentant, ex quibus constat proprie permanentibus, unum Christum, quia integrum verumque, permanere demonstrant—Gelasius, *Tractate* 3 *De duabus naturis in Christo adversus Eutychem et Nestorium* 14 (Thiel 541–42 [Schwartz: see above in n. 83]).

[101] *De duabus naturis* 2 (Thiel 531). Cf. *De duabus naturis* 7: "in the commencement itself of the conception" (Thiel 535). Along the same line, Leo I quotes Augustine: "our nature was . . . created in the assumption—*natura quippe nostra non sic assumpta est ut prius creata, post assumeretur, sed ut ipsa assumptione crearetur*"—Leo the Great, *Epistola* 35.3 (PL 54.807C).

[102] Gelasius, *De duabus naturis* 2 (Thiel 531).

[103] ". . . et caro nonnisi in iisdem visceribus sancto Spiritu superveniente et Altissimi obumbrante virtute est unita deitati"—Gelasius, *De duabus naturis* 10 (Thiel 539).

[104] "In hac autem ineffabili unitate Trinitatis, cujus in omnibus communia sunt opera . . ."—Leo the Great, *Sermo* 64.2 (PL 54.358C). Confer *Sermo* 75.4: "in these

ian theology maintained the Augustinian view which affirmed the principle that, relative to creation, the Father, Son, and Spirit are "one principle, as one creator and one Lord."[105] Gelasius may be presumed to have held the same doctrine.

Gelasius's theology of the Incarnation allows us to conclude that the humanity of Jesus, created by the Godhead as such, was united to the Word of God by the action of the triune God which is "appropriated" to the Holy Spirit.

Turning again to the content of this first section of the text, one meets a passage of the Old Testament, Proverbs 9:1a-b, that was widely applied to the mystery of the Incarnation in the Eastern and Western theological traditions.

The version of Proverbs 9:1b that follows: "Wisdom built herself a house . . ." is unique. The Vulgate has: "cut out *(excidit)* seven columns." Gelasius uses "propped under" *(subnixam)*, a concept that corresponds to Augustine's version which uses *subfulsit*.[106] The substitution of "septiform Spirit" for "seven columns" relates to the version of the *Homily on the Body and Blood of Christ* found in a collection of sermons of the second half of the fifth century made by an anonymous author of Provence, and which stem from Faustus of Riez (d. ca. 495). The homily is found in the appendix to the writings of Jerome.[107] Here, the version of Proverbs 9:1a-b reads as follows:

"But in Solomon, announced by God himself, we read: 'Wisdom,' he said, 'built herself a house, that is, assumed the body of a man, in which dwells the fullness of the divinity (Col 2:9). She cut out seven columns because the blessing of the septiform grace filled it . . .'"

It is not unlikely that Gelasius had at hand a version of Proverbs 9:1a-b similar to that used in the *Homily on the Body and Blood of*

---

three persons there is no distinction of substance, power, will, or operation—*in his tribus personis nec substantiae, nec potentiae, nec voluntatis, nec operationis est ulla diversitas*" (PL 54.402C).

[105] ". . . ad creaturam uero pater et filius et spiritus sanctus unum principium sicut unus creator et unus dominus"—Augustine, *De trinitate* 5.14[15] (CC 50.223.35–37).

[106] *De civitate dei* 17.20 (CSEL 40/2.260.4).

[107] This homily is listed as: Jerome, *Epistola* 38 seu *Homilia de corpore et sanguine Christi* (PL 30.271D–276A). The Latin text of this passage reads: "Sed in Salomone de ipso deo praedictum legimus: *Sapientia,* inquit, *aedificavit sibi domum* (Prov. IX, 1) id est, corpus hominis assumpsit: in quo habitat plenitudo divinitatis: *Excidit* columnas septem: quia illum benedictio gratiae septiformis implevit" (PL 30.274C).

Christ. For the content of the one version parallels closely that of the other. But whereas the homily explains the meaning of "Wisdom built herself a house" after citing the text, Gelasius gives the meaning beforehand. The homily introduces Colossians 2:9 to affirm the mystery of the indwelling of the Word, and follows by interpreting the seven columns as referring to the "septiform grace," another term for the divine Logos. Gelasius telescopes the two notions by employing the term "septiform Spirit." Elsewhere Gelasius uses Colossians 2:9 to affirm the divinity of Jesus Christ, "in whom all fullness of divinity dwells corporeally."[108]

The second half of the first sentence: ". . . that would provide the nourishment of the Incarnation . . ." has a meaning determined by the adaptation of Proverbs 2:5-6 to the institutional aspect of the mystery of the Incarnation. The Vulgate version reads: "She slaughtered her victims, mixed wine and prepared her table (v. 2). . . . Come, eat my bread and drink the wine I have mixed for you (v. 5). Forsake infancy and live, and walk in the ways of prudence" (v. 6). The traditional spiritual exegesis of the Latin tradition views the preparation of the banquet of Wisdom as a foreshadowing of the institution of the Eucharist by the Word. The invitation of Wisdom to participate in the banquet as a condition for life is understood to signify the invitation given to believers to share in the true life through eucharistic communion. Augustine's exegesis of Proverbs 9:1-6 can serve as an example:

"Here certainly we recognize that the Wisdom of God, the eternal Word of the Father, built a house for himself in the virginal womb, a human body, and to this joined the Church as members to the head, that he immolated victims, the martyrs, that he prepared the table with wine and bread, where also the priesthood according to the order of Melchizedek appears, that he called the foolish and those devoid of sense, because as the apostle says, 'He chose the weak of this world to confound the strong' (1 Cor 1:27). However he says to these infirm: 'Forsake foolishness, that you may live, and seek prudence, that you may have life.' Yet to be made participant of this table is to begin to have life."[109]

[108] Gelasius, *De duabus naturis* 8 (Thiel 536).

[109] "Hic certe agnoscimus Dei sapientiam, hoc est Verbum Patri coaeternum, in utero uirginali domum sibi aedificasse corpus humanum et huic, tamquam capiti membra, ecclesiam subiunxisse, martyrum uictimas immolasse, mensam in uino et panibus praeparasse, ubi apparet etiam sacerdotium secundum ordinem

Gelasius follows this tradition. The Logos prepares the nourishment of the Incarnation; the effect of participation in this nourishment is sharing in divine nature, the true life.

The *alimonium . . . incarnationis Christi* means nourishment originating from the Incarnation. Since it is the cause of divinization, it can be called spiritual nourishment, a qualification given by Pope Leo I:

"In that mystical distribution of the *spiritualis alimonia,* the command is given that it be taken in order that receiving the power *(virtus)* of the heavenly food we pass over into the flesh of the one who was made our flesh."[110]

Here *virtus* refers to the essence of a thing. Evidently Gelasius is thinking along the lines of Leo I. However, he does not explicitly say that the effect of this "divine thing," or "power," is to unite the communicant to the glorified flesh of the risen Lord.

But what exactly is this divine thing that constitutes nourishment originating from the Incarnation of Christ? Perhaps a clue to what Gelasius means is given in the florilegium that forms an appendix to *De duabus naturis,* and which seems to have originated from that of Theodoret of Cyrus's lost work *Pentalogos.*[111] Here the commentary on John 7:39 from Athanasius's *De incarnatione et contra Arianos* 3–4 reads as follows:

"When the evangelist says: 'As yet there was no Holy Spirit, because Jesus was not yet glorified,' he said that his flesh was not yet glorified. For the Lord of glory was not glorified, but the flesh of the Lord accepts this glory coascending to him in heaven. Whence both the Holy Spirit of adoption was not yet in men, and that first fruits assumed from us had not yet ascended into heaven."[112]

Melchisedech, insipientes et inopes sensu uocasse, quia, sicut dicit apostolus, *infirma huius mundi elegit, ut confunderet fortia* [1 Cor 1:27–28]. Quibus tamen infirmis quod sequitur dicit: *Derelinquite insipientiam, ut uiuatis, et quaerite prudentiam, ut habeatis uitam* [Prov 9:6]. Participem autem fieri mensae illius, ipsum est incipere habere uitam"—Augustine, *De civitate dei* 17.20 (CSEL 40/2.260.10–20).

[110] "Quia in illa mystica distributione spiritalis alimoniae hoc impartitur, hoc sumitur: ut accipientes virtutem coelestis cibi, in carnem ipsius qui caro nostra factus est transeamus"—Leo the Great, *Sermo* 59.2 (PL 54.868B).

[111] Ettlinger, op. cit., 28.

[112] "Καὶ ὅτε λέγει Οὔπω ἦν Πνεῦμα ἅγιον, ὅτι 'Ιησοὺς οὐδέπω ἐδοξάσθη [John 8:39], τήν σάρκα αὐτοῦ λέγει μήπω δοξασθεῖσαν. Οὐ γαρ ὁ Κύριος τὴς δόξης δοξάζεται, ἀλλ' ἡ σὰρξ τοῦ Κυρίου τὴς δόξης αὔτη λαμβάνει δόξαν συναναβαίνουσα αὐτῷ εἰς οὐρανόν.

In the background of the relation between the glorification of the flesh of Christ and the sending of the Spirit of adoption lies the following patristic axiom: The Incarnation of Christ grounds the divinization of all humanity because, by assuming a human nature from us and for us, the Word of God obtained fellowship with us. Therefore, it could be said that Christ died in order to destroy death through his Resurrection or, put more precisely, in order to destroy death through the permanent effect of the Resurrection, that is, through the glorification of his human nature.

Through this glorification, the humanity of Christ became immortal and the cause of the immortality of others. As first fruits of the resurrection-glorification among humankind, Christ is the guarantee of the resurrection of others: the *causa exemplaris,* so to speak, of the fate of humanity.[113] Beyond this, according to Scripture, the glorified Lord is the divine-human source of the sending of the Holy Spirit from the Father. By a theandric act, the risen Lord sends the Holy Spirit to establish the Church and to sanctify the members of the Church.

The saying of Gelasius about the "nourishment of the Incarnation of Christ" seems to be based on the idea of the solidarity of Jesus Christ with humanity, and the working of the Holy Spirit consequent upon the glorification of the human nature of Jesus. The content of this sanctification is traditionally described as "divine adoption," "divinization," the "true life," etc. The principle of this sanctification is identified in both Greek and Latin theology as the Holy Spirit. Gelasius provides no exception to this rule. Hence it can be taken for granted that what he describes as the "nourishment of the Incarnation" is ultimately the Holy Spirit of adoption, or the gift of the Holy Spirit. For the effect of this nourishment is divinization.

But where do the sacraments of the body and blood of Christ fit into this outlook? A partial answer to this question is given in the next sentence of the text.

"Ὅθεν καὶ Πνεῦμα υἱοθεσίας οὔπω ἦν ἐν ἀνθρώποις, διότι ἡ ληφθεῖσα ἀπαρχὴ ἐξ ἡγῶν οὔπω ἦν ἀνελθοῦσα εἰς οὐρανόν"—Athanasius, *De incarnatione et contra Arianos* 3 (PG 26.989B). This text, as it appears in Theodoret's florilegium, can be found in Ettlinger 161.4–9. This is the apparent source for Gelasius when (in his florilegium to *De duabus naturis*) he writes: "Dum dicit evangelista: *nondum erat Spiritus sanctus, quia Jesus nondum fuerat glorificatus,* carnem ejus dicit nondum glorificatam. Non enim Dominus gloriae glorificatur, sed caro Domini hanc gloriam accepit coascendens ei in coelum, unde et Spiritus sanctus adoptionis nondum erat in hominibus, et quod assumptae ex nobis primitiae in coelum nondum ascenderant" (Thiel 554).

[113] *Confer* Augustine, *Enarrationes in psalmos* 101.2.14 (CC 40.1448–49).

(2.) Here Gelasius continues the theme of the efficacy of participation in the sacraments. He appeals to this efficacy to prove that the *sacrament* "is a divine thing." The use of the term *divina res* recalls Augustine's employment of *res* where he speaks about the mystery signified by sacraments of the New Law: ". . . concerning the variety of signs, which since they pertain to *res divinas,* are called sacraments."[114] In particular Augustine also uses the term *res* to designate the mystery signified by the eucharistic elements.[115] However, Augustine regards the holy signs as indicators of the *res* and an occasion for the bestowal of the grace of the Eucharist. Gelasius, to the contrary, considers the *res* as intrinsically related to the sign, or added to it in such a way that the sacrament can be identified as a divine thing. Hence he is convinced that "because of this and through the same" the communicant is divinized. On the other hand he insists that the nature of the eucharistic elements does not change from what it was before becoming the visible sacrament.

This aspect of Gelasius's eucharistic theology evokes the Augustinian distinction between *sacramentum et res* as applied to the eucharistic nourishment. Augustine establishes a sharp contrast between the visible eucharistic food and the signified invisible grace: "The sacrament is one thing, the power *(virtus)* is another."[116] A distinction of this sort can be explained in such a way that it is applicable to the eucharistic sacramental realism of the fourth-century Antiochene school. But it would not be conformed to the meaning intended by Augustine.

A typical Augustinian statement about the mystery of the eucharistic sacraments always displays hesitancy concerning the old Antiochene eucharistic sacramental realism. For example: "In a certain way the sacrament of the body of Christ is the body of Christ, and the

[114] "Nimis autem longum et conuenienter disputare de varietate signorum, quae cum ad res diuinas pertinent, sacramenta appellantur"—Augustine, *Epistula* 138.7 (CSEL 44.131.9–11).

[115] *Res ipsa:* "Sed non quaerant spiritum sanctum nisi in Christi corpore, cuius habent foris sacramentum, sed rem ipsam non tenent intus, cuius illud est sacramentum, et ideo sibi iudicium manducant et bibunt"—Augustine, *Epistula* 185. 11.50 (CSEL 57.43.19–22). *Res vera:* "Ostendit quid sit non sacramento tenus, sed re uera corpus Christi manducare et eius sanguinem bibere; hoc est enim in Christo manere, ut in illo maneat et Christus"—Augustine, *De civitate dei* 21.25 (CC 48.795.79–796.82).

[116] "Nam et nos hodie accipimus uisibilem cibum; sed aliud est sacramentum aliud uirtus sacramenti"—Augustine, *In Ioannis evangelium tractatus* 26.11 (CC 36.265.18–20).

sacrament of the blood of Christ the blood of Christ . . ."[117] The qualification "in a certain way" implies that to receive the sacrament does not necessarily mean to receive the *res* signified. For the spiritual reality happens inwardly in the communicant. Evil persons and heretics have the "sacrament only outwardly, but they do not have the reality itself *(res ipsa).*"[118] Catholics, on the contrary, "eat not only in the sacrament, but in reality *(re ipsa)* the body of Christ, since they themselves are constituted in this his body."[119]

Gelasius agrees with Augustine to the extent that he eschews the concept of change of the nature of the eucharistic elements. But he differs from Augustine by not assigning a rigid separation of the grace of the sacrament from the visible symbols, which reduces the latter merely to liturgical signposts. Gelasius, on the contrary, teaches that the divine thing is communicated by the sacrament: "because of it and through the same we are made partakers of the divine nature." He would probably agree more readily with a formulation of the following saying of a disciple of Augustine, Facundus of Hermiane (fl. ca. 550), which does not seem to imply the Augustinian radical separation of the sign from the *res:*

"We call the sacrament of the body and blood (of Christ), which consists in the consecrated bread and cup, his body and his blood, not because the bread is his body and the cup his blood in the proper sense *(proprie),* but because they contain in themselves the mystery of his body and blood."[120]

Gelasius has identified the *sacramenta* as a *divina res.* This way of speaking is traditional since sacraments are defined by their essence,

[117] "Sicut ergo secundum quendam modum sacramentum corporis Christi corpus Christi est, sacramentum sanguinis Christi sanguis Christi est, ita sacramentum fidei fides est"—Augustine, *Epistula* 98.9 (CSEL 34.531.6–9).

[118] ". . . cuius habent foris sacramentum, sed rem ipsam non tenent intus . . ."—Augustine, *Epistula* 185.11.50 (CSEL 57.43.18–44.12, at 43.20–21).

[119] ". . . non solo . . . sacramento, sed re ipsa manducauerunt corpus Christi, in ipso scilicet eius corpore constituti . . ."—Augustine, *De civitate dei* 21.25 (CC 48.794.28–30).

[120] ". . . sicut sacramentum corporis et sanguinis eius, quod est in pane et poculo consecrato, corpus eius et sanguinem dicimus, non quod proprie corpus eius sit panis et poculum sanguis, sed quod in se mysterium corporis eius sanguinisque contineant"—Facundus of Hermiane, *Pro defensione trium capitulorum* 9.5.25 (CC 90A.290.196–200). Cf. Johannes Betz, *Eucharistie in der Schrift und Patristik.* Handbuch der Dogmengeschichte IV/4a.157.

and the essence by the change of meaning which the material components undergo in becoming visible symbols of divine realities. The divine thing, so qualified, pertains to the deity. It is a power *(virtus)* of the deity by which a communication of the divinity itself is extended to the communicant of the sacraments "of the body and blood." In short, what is effected is a participation in God, for it is a participation in the "divine nature."

(3.) What takes place in the eucharistic liturgy, that is, "in the action of the mysteries," is described as celebration of the "image and likeness of the body and blood of Christ." This rather obscure and concise sentence needs to be unraveled. Its meaning can be formulated in the following way: The bread and wine become image and likeness of the body and blood of Christ, that is, the visible sacrament in virtue of the ritual action accomplished *(celebrare)* in the liturgy of the Eucharist *(actio mysteriorum).*

Gelasius uses *actio* as a designation for the celebration of the Mass as such where he confirms older legislation that a presbyter may not undertake the *sacra actio* without authorization of the bishop.[121] The ritual accomplishment within the *actio* by which the elements become "image and likeness" is undoubtedly what Gelasius calls the "consecration of the mysteries" where, in a letter to *Coelestino episcopo,* he lifts the ban on the celebration of Mass in a basilica dedicated without proper authorization, "in order that the place of procession might lack neither priest nor minister *ad mysteriorum consecrationem.*"[122] It is the moment of the epiclesis of the Spirit in the liturgy when "the invoked Spirit descends *ad mysterii consecrationem.*"[123]

Gelasius's use of the notion of "consecration" raises two questions: First, under what formality does the Holy Spirit merit the special title

[121] "Nec minus etiam presbyteros ultra modum suum tendere prohibemus, nec episcopali fastigio debita sibimet audacter assumere: non conficiendi chrismatis, non consignationis pontificalis adhibendae sibimet arripere facultatem. Non praesente quolibet antistite, nisi fortasse jubeatur, vel orationis vel actionis sacrae suppetere sibi praesumat esse licentiam; neque sub ejus adspectu, nisi jubeatur, aut sedere praesumat aut venerabilia tractare mysteris"—Gelasius, *Epistola* 14.6 (Thiel 365).

[122] ". . . ut locus processionis celeberrimus ad mysteriorum consecrationem nec sacerdote indigeat nec ministro"—Gelasius, *Epistola* fragm. 5 (Thiel 486).

[123] "Nam quomodo ad divini mysterii consecrationem coelestis Spiritus invocatus adveniet, si sacerdos, et qui eum adesse deprecatur, criminosis plenus actionibus reprobetur?"—Gelasius, *Epistola* fragm. 7.2 (Thiel 486).

of "consecrator" of the "mysteries" as opposed to the other members of the Trinity? Second, what is the precise content of the consecratory act? The first question can be answered easily. The second requires more attention since the textual evidence is ambiguous.

A clue to the meaning of "consecrator" as applied to the Holy Spirit can be found in Gelasius's understanding of the role exercised by the Holy Spirit in the realization of the historical Incarnation. This role, as we have seen, amounts to an action performed by the Godhead as such but "appropriated" to the Holy Spirit. However, the Latin tradition also affirms that the Word incarnate was filled with the Holy Spirit. Augustine, for example, teaches that the incarnate Word bestowed the Spirit as God, and received the Spirit as man.[124] There is no evidence in Gelasius's writings that he did not favor the same understanding. Correspondingly, in the event of the "consecration" of the eucharistic gifts, which remain what they were after the consecration, Gelasius is thinking about the *addition* of the grace of the Spirit to the elements.

This theological outlook corresponds to the interpretation of the epiclesis of the Spirit given by the disciple of Augustine, Fulgentius of Ruspe, where he responds to the question: Why is the Spirit alone invoked as though the Father and Son do not exercise a sanctifying activity? He answers: "It seems to me that nothing else is petitioned except that the unity of love be preserved continually uninterrupted in the body of Christ (which is the Church) through spiritual grace."[125]

Gelasius's qualification of the consecrated bread and wine as "image and likeness" has a meaning that does not correspond exactly to the fourth-century Antiochene notion of "real symbols" of the body and blood of Christ, i.e., sacrament of the somatic presence of the body and blood. Rather, the clue to its meaning can be found in Theodoret's *Eranistes,* where the monophysite asks about the meaning of the "mystical symbols offered by the priest."[126] When the or-

[124] "Accepit quippe ut homo, effudit ut deus"—Augustine, *De trinitate* 15.26.46 (CC 50A.527.72).

[125] "Cum ergo sancti Spiritus ad sanctificandum totius Ecclesiae sacrificium postulatur aduentus, nihil aliud postulari mihi uidetur nisi ut per gratiam spiritalem in corpore Christi (quod est Ecclesia) caritatis unitas iugiter indisrupta seruetur"—Fulgentius of Ruspe, *Ad Monimum* 2.11.1 (CC 91.43.391–95).

[126] "τὰ μυστικὰ σύμβολα παρὰ τῶν ἱερωμένων τῷ προσφερομένα, τίνων ἐστὶ σύμβολα"—Theodoret, *Eranistes,* Dialogue 2 (Ettlinger 151.14–15).

thodox dialogue partner responds that they are "symbols of the real body and blood,"[127] he adds by way of explanation the following: "For it is necessary that the archetype of the image *(eikôn)* exist . . . as a divine and lordly body, not changed into the nature of the Divinity, but filled with divine glory."[128] Regarding the sense in which the consecrated elements are to be described as "images" or "antitypes" of the real body, the orthodox partner explains:

"Place now . . . the image alongside the archetype and you will see the likeness *(homoioêta)*. For the type *(typos)* must be like the truth. Then also the body (resurrected) has . . . in short, the previous essence *(ousia)*."[129]

Gelasius's use of "image and likeness" is not precisely an example of hendiadys, but is inspired by a point of view similar to that of Theodoret. The sacraments are an "image and likeness" of Christ in that the material elements, in virtue of the consecration, contain a *divina res,* and yet remain what they were before the consecration. But being the image and likeness of Christ himself in this sense, means that Christ himself remains always the same: the body remains united with the Divinity unconfused and unseparated. Since the sacrament is such an image, it both signifies and contains a divine thing, a grace of divinization.

Gelasius, generally so dependent on Augustine for much of his theological discourse, does not introduce here the ecclesiological aspect of the Eucharist. Augustine says "the bread that one sees on the altar [that is sanctified by the Word of God] . . . is the body of Christ."[130] The grace related to the Eucharist is almost always described by Augustine as a power *(virtus)*. This corresponds to the *divina res* of Gelasius. But Augustine defines this *virtus,* above all, in relation to the ecclesial body of Christ: "The power itself . . . is *unitas,* in order that, brought into his body and made his members, we may

[127] Ibid., 151.14–19.

[128] "Χρὴ γὰρ εἶναι τὸ τῆς εἰκόνος ἀρχέτυπον. . . . θεῖον μέντοι καὶ δεσποτικὸν σῶμα, οὐκ εἰς θεότητος φύσιν μεταβληθέν, ἀλλά θείας δόξης ἀναπλησθέν" (ibid., 151.19–26).

[129] "Παράθες τοίνυν τῷ ἀρχετύπῳ τὴν εἰκόνα, καὶ ὄψει τὴν ὁμοιότητα. Χρὴ γὰρ ἐοικέναι τῇ ἀληθείᾳ τὸν τύπον. Καὶ γὰρ ἐκεῖνο τὸ σῶμα τὸ πρότερον εἶδος ἔχει, καὶ σχῆμα καὶ περιγραφήν, καὶ ἁπαξαπλῶς, τὴν τοῦ σώματος οὐσίαν" (ibid., 152.17–21).

[130] "Hoc quod videtis in altari Dei . . . panis est corpus Christi"—Augustine, *Sermo* 272 (PL 38.1246).

be what we receive."[131] Since the Spirit is bestowed in the context of the Eucharist, the grace of the Spirit builds up the body of Christ.

Gelasius bypasses the ecclesiological aspect and simply speaks of the grace of divine adoption. In this regard his exposition reflects the emphasis characteristic of Eastern eucharistic theology. However this is not to say that Gelasius in another context would not stress the ecclesiological aspect of the eucharistic grace as does Augustine.

Up to this point Gelasius has established three things concerning the sacraments of the body and blood. They have (1.) a divine component; (2.) in virtue of which the reception of the earthly component affords a participation in the divine nature; (3.) the material component, remaining unchanged in nature, becomes the "image and likeness " of the body and blood of Christ in virtue of the ritual consecration within the liturgy of the Mass. In the subsequent sentence Gelasius draws a conclusion about the meaning of all this for the understanding of the mystery of Christ.

But before taking up this subject, there still remains the second problem concerning the precise content of the consecratory act mentioned in the phrase of *Epistola* fragm. 7.2: "For how shall the celestial Spirit, invoked for the consecration of the divine mystery, descend . . . ?"

The *Letter of Gelasius to Elpidius of Volterra,* an ancient city of Etruria, exists in two fragments.[132] The first fragment, which begins with *Quo ausu,* deals with the initiative of the young bishop of Volterra who had recourse to Ravenna, the seat of the government of the emperor Theodoric, without first consulting Gelasius. Such an action ran contrary to the canons and made the offender liable to deposition from office. Gelasius asks: ". . . are you in a hurry to be deprived from this office of which you show yourself unworthy by these excesses?"[133]

It is not clear how the second fragment relates to the first. It contains two sentences: the first affirms a general principle; the second applies the principle to the Eucharist. The text reads as follows:

"The holy service of God, which observes the Catholic teaching and practice, claims for itself so much respect that no one would venture to engage in it except with a pure conscience. For how shall the celes-

[131] "Virtus enim ipsa . . . unitas est, ut redacti in corpus ejus, effecti membra ejus, simus quod accipimus"—Augustine, *Sermo* 57.7 (PL 38.389).

[132] *Gelasius [epistola] Elpidio episcopo Volterrano,* fragm. 7 (Thiel 486).

[133] Ibid. Evidently Elpidius weathered the storm, for he attended the synod of Rome in the year 502.

tial Spirit, invoked for the consecration of the divine mystery, descend, if the priest *et qui* petitions him to be at hand, stands condemned as full of wicked deeds."[134]

The general principle underscores the importance of holiness on the part of those engaged in the service of God. The second sentence asks about the implications of this principle in the instance where the spiritual condition of the priest does not conform to his service at the very heart of the eucharistic celebration: the invocation for the coming of the Spirit.

There are two major difficulties related to this text. One concerns the translation of the *et qui;* the other concerning the effect of the spiritual state of the minister who presides at the eucharistic celebration.

The meaning of the phrase *si sacerdos et qui* is disputed. J. R. Geiselmann takes it to be the introduction to a relative clause. Hence it is equivalent to *et is qui* (and this one too who). The third person singular of "stands condemned," namely, *reprobetur,* shows that one subject is meant.[135] J. Brinktrine rejects this interpretation on grammatical grounds. A relative clause intended to explain more precisely a substantive, and which is joined to the substantive by *et,* is foreign to the Latin language. A relative clause added to an attributive adjective or appositive by the copulative conjunction *et* is common. But this is not applicable here. Second, the use of the third person plural for two subjects is the rule. But exceptions are found where different subjects are felt together as constituting a whole. The singular may be used, for example, where the linking together is conditioned by a leading concept. In our case this would be *sacerdos.*[136]

[134] "Sacrosancta religio, quae catholicam tenet disciplinam, tantam sibi reverentiam vindicat, ut ad eam quilibet nisi pura conscientia non audeat pervenire. Nam quomodo ad divini mysterii consecrationem coelestis Spiritus invocatus adveniet, si sacerdos, et qui eum adesse deprecatur, criminosis plenus actionibus reprobetur?" (ibid.). The term *Sacrosancta religio* refers to the forms of active service of God. Confer, e.g., Fulgentius of Ruspe (A.D. 468-533): *Epistola* 8.4.10: "Vera enim religio in unius constat veri Dei servitio" (PL 65.365A).

[135] Geiselmann, *Die Abendmahlslehre,* 220.

[136] Johannes Brinktrine, "Der Vollzieher der Eucharistie nach dem Brief des Papstes Gelasius (†496) an den Bischof Elpidius von Volterra," *Miscellanea Liturgica in honorem L. Cuniberti Mohlberg,* vol. 2 (Rome: Edizioni liturgiche, 1949) 61–69, at 62–64. See also "Neue Beiträge zur Epiklesenfrage," *Theologie und Glaube* 21 (1929) 446–50.

Geiselmann's solution avoids the problem posed by the introduction of someone other than the *sacerdos*, as capable of invoking liturgically the descent of the Holy Spirit. Brinktrine solves the problem by showing that Gelasius normally uses *sacerdos* for a bishop and not for a presbyter.[137] Since the only other cleric qualified to lead the eucharistic liturgy is the presbyter, it follows that the phrase should read: "the priest (bishop) and he who (presbyter)."

If one excludes the argument of Brinktrine, made on grammatical grounds, the solution of Geiselmann is more satisfactory. For the context offers no reason why Gelasius should be talking about two subjects. Furthermore *sacerdos* is also used for presbyter when such a one is placed in the context of the ministry of the Eucharist.[138] Finally if the *et qui* is understood in the sense of "the priest, and 'this one too who,'" the emphasis falls more emphatically on the relationship between the worthiness of the priest and his active service of God: a relationship that is the theme of the first sentence which states the general principle.

The literal reading of the text concerning the effect of the sinfulness of the presiding minister of the divine liturgy offers several possible interpretations: (1.) The holiness of the priest is a condition of the advent of the Spirit for the consecration of the divine mystery. (2.) The holiness of the priest is a condition of the advent of the Spirit for an additional blessing accruing to the sacraments already consecrated by the application of the *verba Christi.* (3.) The holiness of the minister is a condition for his fruitful participation in the "grace of the mysteries."[139]

The first interpretation is excluded. Gelasius holds that the administration of true sacraments does not depend on the holiness of the priest. He states this explicitly with regard to baptism and ordination.[140] Also there is no reason to think that Gelasius would follow a different path from that of Augustine regarding the sinful priest's ability to conduct the celebration of the Eucharist in the Church.

The second interpretation (favored by Brinktrine) is excluded. We have already seen in Gelasius's *Tractate* 3.14 that the consecration of the elements is a work attributed to the Holy Spirit which does not

[137] Brinktrine, "Der Vollzieher," 62–64.

[138] Gelasius, *Epistola* fragm. 5 (Thiel 486).

[139] "mysteriorum gratia" in Gelasius, *Epistola* 25 (Thiel 392).

[140] Gelasius, *Epistola* 3.6 (Thiel 315).

involve a change of being of the material elements. Moreover, there is no indication that the teaching of St. Ambrose on the subject of the eucharistic consecration by the *verba Domini* is presupposed by Gelasius. Hence it seems that we are left with the final option. Gelasius's question implies that the sinful priest does not profit from his role in the celebration of the Eucharist.

(4.) In the next sentence, Gelasius begins his conclusion by summarizing three things affirmed previously about the sacraments of the body and blood. He does this with three key words: what we *believe (confess)* about the sacraments; what we ritually *accomplish (celebrate)* in the consecration of the elements; what we *receive* in Holy Communion. In order to explain what this is, Gelasius describes what happens as the divine response to the epiclesis of the Holy Spirit:

(5.) "that just as they pass over into this, namely, into the divine substance by the working of the Holy Spirit, yet remaining in the peculiarity of their nature; . . ."

Here Gelasius employs the verb *transire* to describe the movement of the earthly elements from the sphere of this world to the sphere of the divine. This verb is commonly used in the fifth-century Latin Church to express an activity that is the effect of a divine action: the anabatic movement that is the effect of a divine katabatic movement.

In the florilegium of patristic texts added to *Tractate* 3, a text of John Chrysostom's commentary on the Fourth Gospel interprets John 1:14 to mean: "The substance (of the Word) did not pass over *(transiit)* . . . and remaining what it is, assumed the *forma servi*."[141] As employed by Gelasius, *transire* conveys the idea of exchange of location but also something more.[142] The cause of the passing over of the elements into the sphere of the divine substance is identified as the action of the Holy Spirit. It is the descent of the Holy Spirit that effects the ascent of the elements by which they are taken into possession by God and so filled with divine power. In the *transitus* they remain what they always were according to their nature. However, they gain a grace, that is, the grace of divine adoption is added to the visible

[141] Thiel 553.

[142] On the other hand, Gaudentius of Brescia (d. ca. 410) uses the term in the sense of change of location when interpreting eucharistically the "passover of the Lord": "For it is the passover of the Lord [Exod 12:11]. . . . this is the *transitus domini* . . . who *transiit* in that and made that his body and blood.—*Pascha est enim domini . . . . hoc est transitus domini . . . qui transiit in illud et fecit illud suum corpus et sanguinem*"—*Tractatus 2 in Exodum* 25 (CSEL 68.29.161–64).

species, intrinsically related to them. This process is said to manifest how we should think about Christ:

(6.) "so they demonstrate, by remaining in the proper sense those things which they are, that the principal mystery itself, whose efficacy and power they truly represent to us, remains the one Christ, integral and true."

The principal mystery is that in which the mysteries of the Church participate. The cultic celebrations of the Church, especially baptism and Eucharist, are obscure manifestations of the divine economy of salvation in Christ, which have meaning for the sanctification of believers. According to Gelasius the sacraments of the Eucharist communicate the grace of the principal mystery. Hence he says: ". . . they truly represent to us the efficacy and power . . . of the principle mystery itself."

But the main concern of Gelasius is to stress the fact that after the consecration the elements remain what they were before the consecration. Given the rigid parallel between the eucharistic Incarnation and the historical Incarnation of Christ, this proves that Christ's human nature was assumed by the Word at the outset of the "blessed conception," and given the fact that the eucharistic Incarnation is the sacramental representation of the mystery of Christ as it was then and now, it is shown that the principal mystery in which the eucharistic mystery shares, "remains the one Christ, integral and true."

GELASIUS—CONCLUSION

There is no serious reason to deny that Gelasius makes his own a theology of the eucharistic consecration that originates in the fifth-century Antiochene context. Catholic scholars have recognized the obvious similarities between the teaching of Theodoret of Cyrus and Gelasius. Nevertheless, traditionally, they have generally presumed that Gelasius did not exclude the notion of conversion of the eucharistic elements. The reason for this is not difficult to discover. It was commonly taken for granted that the "whole orthodox Church" explicitly professed this conversion in the fifth century. Consequently, the attempt was made, in one way or another, to demonstrate how Gelasius's explanation could be harmonized with the dogma of eucharistic conversion and the doctrine of transubstantiation. For example, it was frequently argued that Gelasius affirms the permanence only of the qualities of bread and wine.[143]

[143] Thiel 542, n. 28 favors this solution.

However, modern critical scholarship has displayed somewhat less confidence in the "orthodoxy" of this Pope's eucharistic theology. For example, in the collection of eucharistic texts published in 1954 by Jesus Solano, an editorial comment notes the obscurity of the pericope in question. On the one hand,

"it affirms that the nature of the bread and of the wine remains, which amounts to the negation of transubstantiation; but, on the other hand, says that it passes into the divine substance, or, into the body and blood of Christ which is the body and blood of God in virtue of the hypostatic union."[144]

Nevertheless, Solano himself evidently favors the traditional interpretation held by Catholic theologians. This can be shown from the fact that he accepts Johannes Brinktrine's explanation of the term *consecratio* used in Gelasius's letter to Elpidius, bishop of Volterra.[145] As we have already seen, Brinktrine presumes that Gelasius maintains the dogma of eucharistic conversion.

More recently the late Professor of Würzburg, Johannes Betz, situating the theology of Gelasius in the context of fifth-century Latin theology, has little difficulty in admitting that Gelasius's theological interpretation of the transformation of the eucharistic elements is not essentially different from that found in Theodoret's *Eranistes*. Betz suggests that the position of Gelasius is best explained in connection with the remark he makes in fragment 7.2 of his letter to Elpidius, bishop of Volterra, concerning the descent of the Holy Spirit who is invoked for the consecration of the divine mystery.[146] According to Betz this implies that "through the consecration (the elements) receive a divine power."[147] In my opinion, the conclusion drawn by Betz is correct.

For the rest, Gelasius's theological outlook is similar to that of Theodoret of Cyrus as developed in the *Eranistes*. His explicit denial of the change of the substance or nature of the bread and wine

[144] Jesús Solano, *Textos eucaristicos primitivos II* (Madrid: Biblioteca de autores cristianos, 1954) 558, n. 176.

[145] Solano, 558–59. The term *consecratio,* found in Gelasius's letter to Elpidius, fragm. 7.2 (Thiel 486) is understood by Brinktrine to refer to a consecration that presupposes a conversion of the elements in the strict sense, and which is dependent on the acceptance of the spiritual sacrifice of the Church ("Der Vollzieher," 66–69).

[146] Thiel 486.

[147] *Eucharistie in der Schrift und Patristik.* Handbuch der Dogmengeschichte IV/4a.155–56.

corresponds to the latter's version of the orthodox position expressed in *Eranistes*, Dialogue 2, and quoted above."[148] Both Gelasius and Theodoret appeal to the experience of the senses to prove that the nature of the bread and wine remains unchanged, and yet these elements function as holy symbols in virtue of a divine sanctifying activity by which they gain a real relation to a divine reality. The motivation is the same in both cases: to refute the monophysite thesis that the body of Christ is changed into the divine essence in virtue of the glorification. Both theologians argue from the correspondence, which amounts to a strict parallel, between a theology of the Eucharist and the hypostatic union, in order to confirm the dogma of the Council of Chalcedon.

Without doubt, the theologies of eucharistic consecration of Gelasius and Theodoret are in substantial agreement. Still, minor differences in the presentations prevent us from concluding to a direct borrowing of the orthodox exposition of the *Eranistes* by Gelasius. For example, the difference in the liturgical interpretation of the meaning of the eucharistic transformation is significant. Gelasius considers this to be the sacramental representation of the mystery of the Incarnation. On this basis he attributes to participation in the consecrated elements an efficacy analogous to that of the historical Incarnation: divinization. Theodoret, on the other hand, in the *Eranistes* views the eucharistic transformation as the sacramental representation of the resurrection of Christ. This orientation serves to highlight the fact that participation in the eucharistic body and blood has an efficacy analogous to that of the resurrection of the earthly body of Jesus Christ from the dead. Hence, in this case, we have an argument against a direct dependence of Gelasius on Theodoret's *Eranistes*.

There are significant points of contact between the theology of eucharistic consecration of Augustine of Hippo and Gelasius. Above all, neither one teaches the fourth-century Antiochene theology of realistic eucharistic conversion. Rather, they both relate a grace of the Spirit to the reception of the body and blood. However, they differ as to how the grace relates to the sacramental sign. Gelasius may have been influenced by Augustine's "spiritualizing" of the content of the sacraments of the body and blood. It supplied a point of view that could easily be adjusted to the new fifth-century Antiochene theology once the requirements of Augustine's Neoplatonic philosophy were overcome.

[148] Ettlinger, 152.13–14.

H. FULGENTIUS OF RUSPE (462–527)

We have seen how Pope Gelasius simply repeats the rigid doctrine of Augustine concerning the necessity of the reception of Holy Communion in order to share in divine life. He does not reckon with the logical consequences of traditional doctrine about the ecclesiological effect of baptism, namely the belonging to the body of Christ, the Church. However the contemporary of Gelasius, and faithful disciple of Augustine, Fulgentius of Ruspe does not overlook the implication of this ecclesiological effect of Christian initiation.[149] According to Fulgentius the teaching of John 6:53 should not cause the faithful to be anxious about the salvation of those who "even if they are legitimately baptized in sound mind, anticipating death soon, are not allowed to eat the body of the Lord and drink his blood." "For," he argues, "in the sacrament of baptism believers are made members of Christ." In this connection he quotes 1 Corinthians 12:27: "You are the body of Christ and individually members of it." This implies that the baptized are not only participants in Christ's sacrifice but are also the holy sacrifice itself *(ipsum sanctum sacrificium)*,[150] the "true bread and true body *(verum panem verumque corpus)*.[151] The baptized persons are participants of the one bread from the moment when they begin to be members of the body, and so a "living victim" *(viva hostia)*.[152] Fulgentius interprets sermon 272 of Augustine in this direction: The baptized are participants of the "body and blood of the Lord" even if they die before eating and drinking the bread and cup.[153]

The teaching of Fulgentius on the subject of the ecclesial effect of baptism also has something to say about his theology of the sacraments of the body and blood. Fulgentius is able to equate the effect of baptism with the effect symbolized by the participation of the sacraments of the body and blood because he follows the teaching of Augustine on this subject, namely, that the eucharistic sacraments signal the effect of unity of the Church which accrues to the worthy participants of Holy Communion.

[149] Fulgentius of Ruspe, *Epistula 12 ad Ferrandum* 24 (XI) (CC 91.377.507–378.560).

[150] Ibid. (CC 91.377.520).

[151] Ibid. (CC 91.377.530–31).

[152] Ibid. (CC 91.378.543–48).

[153] "Sacramenti quippe illius participatio ac beneficio non privatur, quando ipse hoc quod illud sacramentum significat invenitur"—ibid., 26 (CC 91.380.608–381.618, at 381.615–17).

This theological outlook corresponds to Fulgentius's interpretation of the efficacy of the liturgical epiclesis of the Spirit where he responds to the question: Why is the Spirit alone invoked as though the Father and Son do not exercise a sanctifying activity? He answers: "It seems to me that nothing else is petitioned except that the unity of love be preserved continually uninterrupted in the body of Christ (which is the Church) through spiritual grace."[154]

Fulgentius's interpretation of the relationship of the grace of the Eucharist to the sacraments of the body and blood does not seem to agree with that of Gelasius. Rather, he follows Augustine. He would probably not want to make his own the saying of Facundus of Hermiane, another disciple of Augustine, quoted above, which does not seem to imply the Augustinian radical separation of the sign from the *res*.

I. ISIDORE OF SEVILLE (D. 636)

Toward the end of the Western patristic epoch Isidore of Seville developed a theology of the Eucharist, influenced by Augustine and Ambrose. Following Augustine, he teaches that the Eucharist is a sacrifice of Christ and the Church. His teaching on the sacraments of the Eucharist is in line with that of Ambrose.

According to Isidore, the eucharistic celebration is the sacrifice of Christ and of the Church, in which the whole community offers in union with Christ through the ministry of the presiding priest. Isidore's commentary on the Mass, together with the contemporary Spanish liturgical textual evidence, makes clear that the eucharistic sacrifice is conceived as an activity in which the whole congregation participates in and through the ministry of the presiding priest who acts as representative of the Church.[155] As for participation in the celebration of the Eucharist, it is open only to the baptized who can participate actively.[156]

[154] "Cum ergo sancti Spiritus ad sanctificandum totius Ecclesiae sacrificium postulatur aduentus, nihil aliud postulari mihi uidetur nisi ut per gratiam spiritalem in corpore Christi (quod est Ecclesia) caritatis unitas iugiter indisrupta seruetur"—Fulgentius of Ruspe, *Ad Monimum* 2.11.1 (CC 91.43.391–95).

[155] See the detailed treatment of Isidore's teaching on the sacrifice of the Mass in Raphael Schulte, *Die Messe als Opfer der Kirche. Die Lehre frühmittelalterlichen Autoren über das eucharistische Opfer.* Liturgiewissenschaftliche Quellen und Forschungen 35 (Münster: Aschendorff, 1959) 13-54.

[156] The following instruction is given in Isidore, *Etymologies* 6.19.4 (PL 82.252): "Missa, tempore sacrificii, est quando catechumeni foras mittuntur, clamante

The form of the consecration of the eucharistic elements, writes Isidore, includes the words of Christ:

"The words of God spoken by the priest in the sacred ministry pertain to the substance of the sacrament, namely: 'This is my body,' bread of wheat and wine, to which water is wont to be added."[157]

Elsewhere, the consecration is attributed to the mystical prayer:

"It is called sacrifice, made holy as it were, because it is consecrated by the mystical prayer in memory of the passion of the Lord for us; whence we call this, by his command, the body of Christ and blood; which, while it is from the fruits of the earth, it is sanctified, and made sacrament by the Spirit of God working [in]visibly. The sacrament of the bread and cup which the Greeks call Eucharist is interpreted in Latin as good grace. And what is better than the body and blood of Christ?"[158]

III. ESCHATOLOGICAL DEPTH OF THE EUCHARISTIC LITURGY

At the outset of this chapter, reference was made to the distinction between the historical flesh and blood of Christ and the eucharistic "spiritual and divine" flesh and blood as formulated by St. Jerome. Jerome does not explain the relationship between the two bodies. But he seems to acknowledge a level of being of the historical body of Christ in the sacrament.

---

levita: *Si quis catechumenus remansit, exeat foras,* et inde missa, quia sacramentis altaris interesse non possunt qui nondum regenerati noscuntur.—The Mass, at the time of sacrifice, is when the catechumens are sent out at the cry of the levite: 'If there are any catechumens left, let them depart'; then the Mass begins, because those who have not yet been reborn cannot be present at the sacraments of the altar" (PL 82.252B).

[157] "De substantia sacramenti sunt verba Dei a sacerdote in sacro prolata ministerio, scilicet: *Hoc est corpus meum,* panisque frumenti et vinum, cui consuevit aqua adhiberi"—Isidore, *Epistola ad Redemptum Archdiaconum* 7.2 (PL 83.905D–906A).

[158] "Sacrificum dictum, *quasi sacrum factum,* quia prece mystica consecratur in memoriam pro nobis dominicae passionis; unde hoc eo iubente corpus Christi et sanguinem dicimus; quod, dum sit ex fructibus terrae, sanctificatur, et fit sacramentum, operante visibiliter Spiritu Dei, cujus panis et calicis sacramentum Graeci Eucharistiam dicunt, quod Latine bona gratia interpretatur. Et quid melius corpore et sanguine Christi?"—Isidore, *Etymologies* 6.19.38 (PL 82.255B-C).

This distinction is related somehow to the distinction implied in the *Supplices* prayer of the old Roman Canon which reads: "Almighty God, we pray that your angel may take this sacrifice to your altar in heaven. Then as we receive from this altar the sacred body and blood of your Son, let us be filled with every grace and blessing."

A. ITS RECEPTION IN EARLY SCHOLASTIC THEOLOGY

The theological problem raised by the twofold body of Christ remained alive throughout the period of the first millennium. It was inherited by early scholasticism and served as the basis for the initial expansion of the Augustinian concept of the composition of a sacrament. The more original version of the anonymous early scholastic tractate *De corpore igitur Domini sic opportune videtur agendum*, used the simple Augustinian schema *sacramentum et res* for the analysis of the composition of the sacrament of the Eucharist. However, the tractate was an open book that invited additional theological reflection. In time, the Augustinian schema was expanded in the following way. The *sacramentum*, or visible species, signifies the eucharistic body. The eucharistic body, on the other hand, is the sacrament of the historical body of Christ. For the historical body actualizes and presents itself in the eucharistic body as spiritual, divine flesh: bread from heaven. Moreover, insofar as the eucharistic spiritual flesh effects the unity of the body of Christ, it is sacrament of the unity of the Church, which is ordered to it.[159]

In this analysis there is a twofold sacrament, and a twofold thing is signified. The visible sacrament signifies the invisible *res*: the eucharistic body and blood; the invisible eucharistic body and blood signify the visible historical and glorified body of Christ. However, the invis-

[159] Confer Ludwig Hödl, "Sacramentum et res—Zeichen und Bezeichnetes," *Scholastik* 38 (1963) 161–82, on the history of *sacramentum et res* in the early scholastic tracts on the Eucharist. Hödl points out that the tractate *De corpore igitur Domini sic opportune videtur agendum* existed in numerous and quite diverse forms, and has survived in many manuscripts (he lists eight). In other words, "the early scholastic *Liber de corpore et sanguine Domini* is an open book, capable of being added to at any time" (Hödl, 163). An extended form of the text (Munich Clm 2598, fol.68^{v}–73^{r}; Fulda, cod.theol. 4° Aa 36 fol.42ra–47rb) has worked in the brief systematic tract *In sacramento altaris septem sunt attendenda* known from the edition of the *Sententiae Ps. Anselmi* (Hödl,163). In the shorter, more original version of the tract *De corpore igitur . . .* , the question: What is the *res* of the sacrament? is answered pointedly: "Res hujus sacramenti Christus est—the *res* (reality) of this sacrament is Christ" (Cod. lat. Aa 36, Fulda, fol. 43rb; Cod. lat theol. 4° 253, Stuttgart, fol. 17va [Hödl,

ible eucharistic body also signifies the unity of the Church, insofar as this unity is ordered to it.

This approach to the understanding of the *res* signified by the sacrament gave a reasonable account of the relationship between the historical body of Christ, the eucharistic body, and the ecclesial body. But it proved to be too complicated for everyday use in systematic theology. In the course of the twelfth century the composition of the sacrament of the Eucharist was reduced to the ternar: *sacramentum—sacramentum et res—res;* and in the definitive form, achieved in the thirteenth century, the middle term was reversed to *res et sacramentum.*

It is not necessary to trace the process of development of the classical scholastic schemas concerning the composition of the sacraments of the body and blood. It suffices here to note that for the first half of the twelfth century the grace of eucharistic Communion is conceived as "contained" in the sacrament. A new stage of development in the analysis of the composition of the sacraments of the Eucharist was introduced by Peter Lombard. His commentary on 1 Corinthians 11: 24 in *Collectanea super b. Pauli epistolas* (ca. 1142–1143),[160] seems to be the first scholastic source to situate the grace signified by the eucharistic sacrament outside the sacrament itself. He uses the ternar: *sacramentum—res contenta et significata—res signficata et non contenta,* to which corresponds: *species—caro et sanguis—unitas ecclesiae.*

Subsequent to P. Lombard's analysis, the grace of the sacrament of the Eucharist, with few exceptions, was placed outside the sacrament itself as the "thing signified but not contained in the sacrament." This

---

167]). Stress is placed on the somatic real presence of Christ. Nevertheless, insofar as the spiritual, divine flesh of the eucharistic bread brings about the new life of the predestined, the body of the Lord is identified as *sacramentum unionis.* It is a sign of the reality of the union ordered to it. Thus a distinction is made between a twofold *res* and a twofold sacrament. The body of Christ is the *res* of the sacrament, and at the same time, sacrament of another res (Cod. lat. 4° Aa 36, Fulda, fol. 43va [Hödl, 169]). The body of Christ is *sacramentum, id est sacrae rei signum,* of the union that is conferred in the sacrament for the life of the predestined. At the same time it is sacrament of the body of the cross, the crucified and glorified body which actualizes the sacrament, and through and in this the union of the predestined. It is both sacrament and *unio* (Hödl, 169).

The analysis of *sacramentum et res* in the parallel tract, *In sacramento altaris,* taken over and enlarged in the tract *De corpore igitur . . . ,* comes to the same conclusion. The body of the Lord, present in the species, makes available to men the kingdom of God, and the kingdom of God is enclosed in the eucharistic body of Christ (Hödl, 169–70).

[160] PL 191.1642A-B.

analysis had the advantage of highlighting belief in the somatic real presence of the body of Christ himself, which implies the idea of conversion of the elements into the body and blood of Christ. But the idea that the body of Christ is contained in the sacrament needed further clarification. For, as Ambrose had said: If the body of Christ is present, then Christ is present. The solution to the problem of the presence of the whole Christ, or the total presence of Christ, was resolved for Western scholastic theology through the development of the doctrine of transubstantiation. This doctrinal theory is not intended to be a defense of the old (fourth-century) Antiochene theology of conversion of the being of the eucharistic elements. Rather, it supplies a philosophical explanation for a change of the act of being of the elements of bread and wine by which they not only pass over into the body and blood of Christ but become sacraments of the presence of the whole Christ.

While P. Lombard's analysis of the composition of the sacrament of the Eucharist had the effect of supporting the theology of the eucharistic somatic real presence of Christ, it obscured the eschatological dimension of the actual event of the reception of the sacraments of the body and blood. Without doubt, comprehensive body-fellowship with Christ remained the fixed horizon of the eucharistic world of grace in the scholastic perspective. Lombard himself explicitly taught that the grace of unity was available to the worthy communicant as fulfillment of what the sacrament signifies according to the divine intention. However, the growing fascination with the somatic presence of the body and blood of Christ, which was encouraged by the Lombardian explanation of the ternar, had the effect of obscuring the vision of what is ultimately signified by the sacrament, i.e., the eschatological dimension, namely, Christ in heavenly glory, in the midst of the holy ones, as fulfillment of the eucharistic celebration.

As long as the *res* ultimately signified by the sacrament was identified as the inner-power of the eucharistic body, the saving effect of the reception of Holy Communion was described as a grace radiating from the eucharistic body, which enables spiritual communion with the glorified flesh of the risen Lord. Pope Leo I pays special attention to this aspect: ". . . having received the power *(virtus)* of the heavenly food we pass over into the flesh of the one who was made flesh for us."[161] But to be in communion with the glorified flesh of Christ

[161] ". . . ut accipientes virtutem coelestis cibi, in carnem ipsius qui caro nostra factus est transeamus"—Leo the Great, *Sermo* 59.2 (PL 54.868B).

necessarily includes being present to the risen Lord in the midst of the heavenly Church. Early scholastics valued the sacramental body of Christ as a means of access to the heavenly reality of the eschatological kingdom of God. The ultimate purpose of Holy Communion was identified with the proleptic participation of the earthly Church in the fellowship of the risen Lord surrounded by the blessed in the kingdom of heaven.

This theology of the eschatological effect of participation of the sacraments of the body and blood was also applied to the Eucharistic Prayer and accompanying action, which were valued as a sacrificial means of "consecration of the sacraments of the body and blood of Christ." In short, early Scholasticism understood that the proclamation of the Eucharistic Prayer attains at the level of prayer the eschatological effect which is attained at the level of sacramental participation of the body and blood of Christ. In this connection a text of Gregory the Great was often quoted:

"Then let us ponder what this sacrifice is for us, which for our pardon continually imitates *(imitatur)* the passion of the only begotten Son. For who of the faithful could harbor doubt that in the hour of the immolation at the voice of the priest the heavens open, that the choirs of angels are present in that mystery of Jesus Christ, the lowly associate with the highest, the earthly are joined to the heavenly, and from the visible and invisible are formed one."[162]

The meaning which early scholasticism attached to the notion of eucharistic consecration was not restricted to the divine activity by which bread and wine are converted into the eucharistic flesh and blood of Christ, nor even to the additional sanctification of the sacramental body and blood effected through the co-mingling at the rite of fraction of the Roman Canon, which was conceived as a "consecration of the body and blood." Rather, the term has a field of meaning that embraces (1.) the *transitus* of the elements into the eucharistic flesh and blood, (2.) the *transitus* of the consecrated flesh and blood

[162] "Hinc ergo pensemus quale sit pro nobis hoc sacrificium, quod pro absolutione nostra passionem unigeniti Filii semper imitatur. Quis enim fidelium habere dubium possit, in ipsa immolationis hora ad sacerdotis vocem coelos aperiri, in illo Jesu Christi mysterio angelorum choros adesse, summis ima sociari, terrena coelestibus jungi, unumque ex visibilibus atque invisibilibus fieri?"—Gregory the Great, *Dialogues* 4.48 (PL 77.425D–428A).

into the heavenly body of Christ, and (3.) the purpose of the twofold *transitus,* namely, the integration of the liturgical community into this single *transitus* of Christ from suffering to glory in virtue of its self-offering made in union with Christ in the power of the Holy Spirit.

From the eleventh to the middle of the twelfth century, during the earliest period of early scholasticism, the phrase "consecration of the body and blood" continued to be used without difficulty alongside the notion of "consecration of the bread and wine." However, from the middle of the twelfth century, as the focus of attention turned to the problem of working out a systematic explanation of the mystery of the somatic real presence of Christ under forms of bread and wine, the difficulty created by the distinction between the two bodies of Christ faded into the background. Now the question of the formulation of a doctrine about the somatic presence of the whole Christ became acute. At the same time, and understandably, a narrowing of the concept of consecration began to take hold.

Gradually the term consecration came to be employed exclusively to express the idea of the conversion of the bread and wine. By the latter part of the twelfth century it was no longer correct to speak of the "consecration of the body and blood of Christ" in systematic theological discourse. The transition from the older usage to the newer one is illustrated in the *Summa Bambergensis.* There, the older point of view is handed on in its commentary on the presence of angels at the liturgy:

"For we believe that the angels assist the priest when he consecrates. Whence it is read in the *Sententiae:* 'In an instant the body of Christ is consecrated and taken up into heaven by the ministry of angels in order to be united with the (heavenly) body of Christ.'"

But now the author quickly adds a correction for the contemporary period when consecration simply refers to the conversion of bread and wine:

"However there are three verbs here, which are to be referred to three things. For *consecrari* applies to the bread, *rapi* to the form, *consociari* indeed to the body of the Lord."[163]

[163] *"Credimus enim angelos assistere sacerdoti quando consecrat. Unde legitur super Sententias: 'In momento consecratur corpus Christi et in coelum rapitur ministerio angelorum consociandum corpori Christi.'* Sint autem hic tria verba quae ad tria sunt

The *Summa quaestionum* of the Codex Harley 1762 in the British Museum of London objects to the saying that the body and blood of Christ are consecrated. For the body and blood need no consecration. Rather, it is theologically correct to affirm that it is the bread and wine that are consecrated, that is, are converted into the body and blood.[164]

The phrase "consecration of the body and blood" has a long history. It was inherited from the Latin theological tradition of the first millennium. Likewise, the content of the process of consecration of the eucharistic elements (which includes the making of the sacrament, the *transitus* of the sacrament to union with the body of the risen Lord, and the *transitus* of the liturgical assembly to union with the Lord and the heavenly Church) derives from the same theological tradition. The phrase was used by early scholastics without difficulty because of their broader understanding of the concept of "eucharistic consecration" which was inherited from the Latin theological tradition of the first millennium.

However, the *terminus a quo* of this development cannot be established with any precision. It remains doubtful whether, and to what extent, the Latin patristic sources employed the term "consecration of the body and blood" to express the broader field of meaning connected with the notion of sanctification, namely the conversion of bread and wine, the elevation of the sacrament to unity with the body of the risen Lord, and the elevation of the liturgical community to union with the risen Lord through participation in the eucharistic liturgy.

B. PATRISTIC SOURCES OF THE TWOFOLD NOTION OF CONSECRATION

In Latin patristic sources, the term consecration is applied to the eucharistic elements of bread and wine as well as to the "body and blood of Christ." More commonly, the notion of the "consecration of

---

referenda, nam consecrari ad panem, rapi ad formam, consociari vero ad corpus Domini retorquetur" (Cod. Misc. Patr. 136, Staatl. Bibliothek, Bamberg, fol.67vb). Confer: Ludwig Hödl, "Die Transsubstantiationsbegriff in der scholastischen Theologie des 12. Jahrhunderts," *Recherches de théologie ancienne et médiévale* 31 (1964) 232. The Summa Bambergensis witnesses to the old terminology and the effort to attribute to it the current theological understanding of consecration as applied to the mystery of the Eucharist.

[164] "Consecrantur autem panis et vinum, non corpus Christi vel sanguis, sed illa in corpus Christi et sanguinem" (fol. 101ra; cf. Hödl, "Der Transsubstantiationsbegriff," 231–32).

bread and wine" is encountered in these same sources. At times, moreover, the meaning intended by the "consecration of the body and blood" seems to be the same. Nevertheless, certain patristic sources seem to employ the more inclusive notion of eucharistic consecration which is suggested by the latter formula and actually found in some of the writings of early scholastic theologians.

What is the proof that the phrase "consecration of the body and blood" reflects a Latin patristic concept of sanctification which is not confined to the meaning expressed by "consecration of the bread and wine"? Does "consecration of the body and blood" place the accent on a sanctifying action that presupposes the making of the sacraments of the body and blood from the eucharistic elements? In other words does it refer more precisely to the process of unification of the sacraments of the body and blood with the risen and glorified Lord?

1. Consecration of the Bread and Wine

Only rarely in the patristic period is the role of "consecrator" or "sanctifier" of the eucharist applied to human agency. And where this notion is found, the dominant idea is that of consecration of the eucharistic gifts of the Church through ritual offering. It is in this sense that Irenaeus of Lyons says: "Now we make offerings to him . . . thus sanctifying what has been created."[165] The ritual ecclesial act of sanctification is clearly distinguished from the divine acceptance through which the eucharistic elements become sacraments of the body and blood. It is this latter meaning (divine acceptance) that is primarily intended by the phrase "consecration of the bread and wine."

Within the scope of the eucharistic theologies of Ambrose of Milan (d. 397) and Augustine of Hippo (d. 430) and their disciples, the meaning of consecration of the bread and wine differs. In the Ambrosian tradition[166] the term consecration of the eucharistic bread and wine implies the peculiar concrete effect by which the elements of

[165] "Offerimus enim ei, (non quasi indigenti, sed gratias agentes donationi ejus et) sanctificantes creaturam"—Irenaeus, *Adversus haereses* 4.18.6 (SC 100/2.612. 123–25 [Harvey 2.209]).

[166] Ambrose employs the term consecration where he identifies the liturgical blessing as means of the sanctification of the elements of bread and wine. Also, as is well known, Ambrose highlights the consecratory role of the eucharistic words of Christ contained in the accounts of institution. He also explicitly describes the ministerial action of the priest associated with the recitation of the words of Christ contained in the liturgical account of the institution of the eucharist as a consecratory activity. For example, he identifies the "rich food" *(pinguis panis)* of Genesis

bread and wine are sanctified, namely, the conversion of the eucharistic elements, which is ultimately attributed to the divine action.[167] Hence the term consecration could be, and was, used by Ambrose as a synonym for the effect of conversion. Within this tradition special mention must be made of *The Homily on the Body and Blood of Christ* attributed to an unknown author of Provence, and dependent on Faustus of Riez (fl. 455–480). The author of this work equates the notion of consecration with that of conversion.[168]

Augustine applies the term consecration to the subjects of baptism and orders, and is not uneasy about the use of the term in the context of his understanding of the subjective sanctification of believers associated with participation in the eucharistic celebration. Also, he refers to the gifts "consecrated by mystical prayer . . . sanctified by the Spirit of God working invisibly" *(operante invisibiliter Spiritu Dei),* since all these things that are done in that work by corporeal movement, God works."[169] Still, consecration is not the term usually employed by him for the sanctification of the eucharistic elements, or for the sanctification of the sacrifice of the Church, or for the sanctification of the sacraments of the body and blood of Christ.

Among those influenced by the eucharistic theology of Augustine are Gelasius I (pope 492–496), Fulgentius of Ruspe (467–532) and Facundus of Hermiane (fl. 550). Gelasius, as we have seen, employs the term *consecratio* where he refers to the requirement of the ministry

---

49:20 as that which the priest himself consecrates in his own words—*consecrat suis verbis* (i.e., by the words of Christ).

In addition, Ambrose hands on the tradition according to which the deacon St. Lawrence exercised the ministry of consecration, or sanctification, of the wine of the communion cup for the faithful by adding to it a portion of the wine consecrated in the cup used by the priest.

[167] "De ipsa consecratione divina"—Ambrose, *De mysteriis* 9.52 (CSEL 73.111).

[168] Referring to the Last Supper of Jesus with his disciples, he says: "Christ was about to consecrate the sacrament of his body and blood." Here the term "consecrate" serves as a synonymn for "make." What this "making" entails is clarified by the explanation of the nature of the ministerial action of the priest who presides at the eucharist: "For the visible priest, through a secret power, converts by the word the visible creatures into the substance of his body and blood speaking thus . . ." Finally the author attributes the consecration of the bread and wine to the invocation of the name of Christ: "Before the substances of the bread and wine are consecrated by the invocation of his name" (texts quoted above in nn. 76–78).

[169] ". . . prece mystica consecratum . . . non sanctificatur . . . nisi operante inuisibiliter spiritu dei, cum haec omnia quae per corporales motus in illo opere fiunt deus operetur . . ."—Augustine, *De trinitate* 3.4.10 (CC 50.136.41–47).

of the ordained priest for the consecration of the mysteries.[170] Likewise he attributes to the invoked Spirit the consecration of the divine mystery.[171] This consecratory activity of the liturgical leader and the Holy Spirit presumably take place within the *sacra actio*, or comprehensive eucharistic liturgy in connection with the epiclesis: "(When) the invoked Spirit descends for the consecration of the divine mystery."[172]

As was explained above, Gelasius attributes the role of "consecrator" to the Holy Spirit. But, in accordance with the prevailing fifth-century Latin theology, it amounts to an action performed by the Godhead as such. Regarding the content of the "consecratory act," Gelasius, as described above, excludes the idea of a conversion of the elements of bread and wine. Rather, they remain what they were, while receiving an added grace, the grace of the Spirit.

Gelasius differs from Augustine by identifying a special grace intrinsically related to the sacraments of the body and blood. His teaching on this subject, as we demonstrated above, is reminiscent of the position attributed to the orthodox theologian in the *Eranistes* of Theodoret of Cyrus, who explicitly rejects the fourth-century Antiochene conversionist doctrine of the Eucharist and maintains the idea of a grace added to the eucharistic elements which otherwise remain unchanged.[173]

Pope Gelasius's understanding of the meaning of consecration corresponds in part to the saying of Facundus of Hermiane, which was mentioned above. It is not completely clear from that text what meaning is to be attached to the verb *consecrare*. However, it seems probable that, as consecrated, the eucharistic species are understood by Facundus to contain the added grace which is communicated to the worthy participant of the sacrament.[174]

The meaning of *consecratio* in Gelasius's *Epistola* fragm. 7.2, as observed above, is disputed. We took the position that it refers to the

[170] ". . . ut . . . ad mysteriorum consecrationem nec sacerdote indigeat nec ministro"—Gelasius, *Epistola* fragm. 5 (Thiel 486).

[171] "Nam quomodo ad divini mysterii consecrationem coelestis Spiritus invocatus adveniet . . ." (ibid.).

[172] Ibid., fragm. 7.2.

[173] As described earlier in this chapter (p. 36), Theodoret's teaching on this subject represents a development of the position of the Patriarch Nestorius in his work *The Book of Heraclides* 2.1.

[174] On the contrary, the question of the *caro Christi* in itself does not attract the attention of Augustine. For, in accord with his Neoplatonic ontology, there is no place

consecration of the eucharistic elements, while the question: "How shall the celestial Spirit . . . descend?" refers to the problem of the manner of the coming of the Spirit to the sinful priest who invokes the coming of the Spirit.

The key to the interpretation of this passage seems to be the epiclesis of the liturgy. This epiclesis traditionally has two dimensions. There is, first, the petition for the sanctification of the gifts of the Church, and, second, the petition for the sanctification of the communicants of the sacraments of the body and blood of Christ. While the first petition is always heard, the second is conditioned by the proper disposition of the communicants. From this perspective it appears probable that Gelasius's use of *consecratio mysterii divini* refers to the sanctification of the eucharistic elements, while under the theme of the descent of the Spirit is included the second aspect of the liturgical epiclesis. Gelasius explicitly mentions an invocation of the Spirit that is related to the consecration of the eucharistic gifts. Whether he also witnesses to a liturgical epiclesis for the coming of the Spirit is a matter of conjecture. Such a petitionary prayer might have been inserted into the *Quam oblationem* prayer of the Roman Canon.[175] In any case,

---

for thinking about the communication of a divine *res per signa*. Confer Augustine's exegesis of John 6:57 which is found in only one place in his extant writings. In his *In Iohannis evangelium tractatus* 26.19, Augustine comments on the phrase: "he will live because of me." He writes: "by participation in the Son, through the unity of his body and blood, which this eating signifies, we are made better. Therefore we live because of him, that is, accepting eternal life" (CC 36.269.6–11). The central idea is repeated at the end of this tractate: "Who eats Christ, lives forever, because Christ is eternal life"—ibid., 26.20 (CC 36.269.7–8). In this pericope "unity of the body and blood" refers to the unity of the Church. The being in the body of Christ is the condition for eating the Son. The eating and drinking of the sacraments of the eucharist "signify" the participation of "eternal life."

[175] Ludwig Eisenhofer suggests that the Roman Canon, with such an insertion, could have read: *Quam oblationem tu, Deus, in omnibus benedictam etc. facere digneris, eique virtutem Sancti Spiritus infundere digneris, ut nobis corpus et sanguis fiat dilectissimi filii tui Domini nostri Jesu Christi—Handbuch der katholischen Liturgik*, 2 vols. (Freiburg: Herder, 1933) 2.169. On this, see Josef A. Jungmann, *Missarum Sollemnia* 2.4.2.11 *Quam oblationem*, n. 37 (Vienna: Herder, 1952) vol. 2, p. 242. Jungmann suggests that Gelasius may have understood the whole canon as a general epiclesis. But this is doubtful. He already knew of a liturgical epiclesis from contacts with the East. Also it is to be noted that Fulgentius of Ruspe knows of an epiclesis of the Holy Spirit. He asks: "Why is it, if the sacrifice is offered to the whole Trinity, for the sanctification of the gift of our oblation, only the sending down of the Holy Spirit is requested?—*cur scilicet si omni Trinitati sacrificium offertur, ad sanctifi-*

Gelasius witnesses to the role of the Spirit in the consecration of the eucharistic elements. It can be presumed that the understanding of the sanctifying action of the Spirit corresponds to that expressed in *Tractate* 3.14. It is a question of the divine action "appropriated" to the Spirit by which the elements are elevated to the sphere of the divine by being endowed with an added divine power of sanctification.

On the other hand, there is also the question of the subjective appropriation of the offer of grace signified by the active participation in the eucharistic celebration. On this point, Gelasius clearly followed the teaching of Augustine. The bishop of Hippo taught that the Holy Spirit works through the worthy minister of the sacraments, sanctifying both him and those who are consecrated by him. He taught the same for the unworthy priest, except that the unworthy priest does not reap the reward of grace for his work.[176] Again, commenting on 1 Corinthians 3:6–7, the bishop of Hippo insists that the minister of Christ is *aliquid* in the sense that he is dispenser of the sacrament; but he is not *aliquid* in the sense that he is able to effect the interior sanctification of the sacrament.[177] This is the context of his remark that [even] the murderer is heard [when, as priest, he exercises his office of] petitioning "over the eucharist—*super eucharistiam").*[178]

If Gelasius's question were put to Augustine and Gelasius's contemporaries: Will the petition for the coming of the Holy Spirit be heard, if the priest who petitions is a grave sinner?, the answer would be no, insofar as he is a sinner; yes, insofar as he is an authorized minister of the Church. Actually, Gelasius seems to have two things in mind. First of all, there is the question of the sanctification of the elements of bread and wine. Secondly, there is the matter of the *goal* of the consecration of the elements, namely the sanctification of the participants of the liturgy. The question: How will the Spirit descend? has reference to the sinful priest. In what manner will the Spirit come to the sinful priest? The question is not focused on the matter of the sanctification of the elements as such, but on the sanctification of the communicants. The question as to how the Spirit will descend for the consecration of the bread and wine is answered by the reference to the liturgical invocation. There is the petition for the sanctification of

---

candum oblationis nostrae munus, sancti Spiritus tantum missio postuletur?"—Ad Monimum 2.6.1 (CC 91.39.242–44); see also ibid., 2.9.1 (CC 91.43.391–92).

[176] Augustine, *Contra epistulam Parmeniani* 2.10.21 (CSEL 51.68.21–70.6).

[177] Augustine, *Contra litteras Petiliani* 3.54.66 (CSEL 52.220.22–32).

[178] Augustine, *De baptismo* 5.20.28 (CSEL 51.285.10–286.9, at 286.3).

the eucharistic elements, a petition which is always heard. In contrast, the petition for the sanctification of the participants of the eucharistic worship and receivers of Holy Communion is conditioned by their proper dispositions.

Fulgentius of Ruspe attributes the consecration of the sacrifice of the Church to the sending of the Holy Spirit.[179] In this case his theological perspective corresponds in part to the interpretation of the epiclesis of the Spirit given by Pope Gelasius. In his commentary on petitioning the Holy Spirit for the sanctification of the "gift of our oblation" Fulgentius explicitly rejects the notion of a sanctifying activity confined only to the work of the Holy Spirit.[180]

According to Fulgentius, the "grace of the Holy Spirit" is the grace that enables the Church to offer the sacrifice pleasing to God. It is the *unitas spiritalis* that enables the offering of true sacrifice to God.[181] Hence to the question raised about singling out the sanctifying activity of the Holy Spirit, this anticipated response was already given:

"When therefore the advent of the Holy Spirit is petitioned to sanctify the sacrifice of the whole Church, it seems to me that nothing else is petitioned except that the unity of charity in the body of Christ (which is the Church) be maintained perpetually uninterrupted through spiritual grace."[182]

Isidore of Seville (560–636), toward the end of the Western patristic tradition, developed a theology of the Eucharist which was influenced by Augustine and Ambrose. In fact, he is the inaugurator of the typically early medieval linking of Ambrosian metabolism and Augustinian symbolism.[183] Following Augustine, he accentuates the ecclesial dimension of the Eucharist: sacrifice of Christ and the Church, in which the liturgical community offers in union with Christ.[184] His teaching on the sacraments of the body and blood is in line with the

[179] "Spiritus sanctus ad consecrationem ecclesiae sacrificii mittendus . . ."—Fulgentius of Ruspe, *Ad Monimum* 2.6.1 (CC 91.39.250–51).

[180] Ibid., 241–51.

[181] Ibid., 2.11.6 (CC 91.47.572–80).

[182] "Cum ergo sancti Spiritus ad sanctificandum totius Ecclesiae sacrificium postulatur aduentus, nihil aliud postulari mihi uidetur nisi ut per gratiam spiritalem in corpore Christi (quod est Ecclesia) caritatis unitas iugiter indisrupta seruetur"—ibid., 2.11.1 (CC 91.43.391–95).

[183] Geiselmann, *Die Abendmahlslehre*, 241.

[184] Cf. R. Schulte, *Die Messe als Opfer der Kirche*, 13–54.

realistic metabolism of Ambrose. From this point of view he is able to interpret many of Augustine's statements about the sacraments of the body and blood in a realistic sense that goes beyond the Augustinian sacramental symbolism.[185] Also in keeping with the eucharistic doctrine of Ambrose, Isidore describes the words of Christ found in the account of institution of the Eucharist as pertaining to the substance of the sacrament of the Eucharist.[186]

He refers to the order of Mass and prayers by which the sacrifices are consecrated.[187] The word "sacrifice" means "made holy." It is explained as applicable to the sacrament of the Eucharist which is "made holy, because it is consecrated by the mystical prayer, in memory of the Lord's passion for us." To this observation Isidore adds that "We call this . . . the body of Christ and blood" which, derived from the "fruits of the earth, is sanctified, and made sacrament by the Spirit of God working visibly."[188] It is clear that Isidore uses the word *consecrare* in the sense employed by Ambrose.

2. *Consecration of the Body and Blood*

The phrase "consecration of the body and blood" can take on various meanings. Where the eucharistic elements are designated by anticipation as the "body and blood of Christ" before they become the sacraments through the divine action, the term consecration can signify the liturgical action through which the sacraments of the body and blood are made in virtue of the divine activity.

In this instance consecration includes the reference to the priestly activity of the liturgical assembly which sanctifies the eucharistic gifts through the sacrificial offering.

The terms "body and blood" can also refer to the historical body and blood of Christ, which is the content of the sacraments of the somatic real presence of Christ. In this case consecration can refer to the action by which the sacramentally present Christ liturgically offers himself to the Father in union with the self-offering of the Church.

[185] See, for example, *Etymologies* 6.19 (PL 82.252A–260B); *De ecclesiasticis officiis* 1.15 and 18 (CC 113.16–23); *De fide catholica contra Judaeos* 2.27 (PL 83.535B–536C).

[186] "De substantia sacramenti sunt verba Dei a sacerdote in sacro prolata ministerio, scilicet: *Hoc est corpus meum,* panisque frumenti et vinum, cui consuevit aqua adhiberi"—Isidore, *Epistola* 7 *Ad Redemptum Archdiaconum* 2 (PL 83.905D–906A).

[187] "Ordo autem missae uel orationum, quibus oblata deo sacrificia consecrantur"—*De ecclesiasticis officiis* 1.15 (1) (CC 113.16.2–3).

[188] Isidore, *Etymologies* 6.19.38 (PL 82.255B-C) text above in n. 158.

Also the term consecration can take on a more comprehensive meaning. It can include a threefold process: [1] the sanctification of the eucharistic elements whereby they become sacraments of the historical body of the cross, [2] the elevation of the sacramental body and blood to union with the body of the risen and glorified Lord, [3] the inclusion of the body of Christ, the Church, in the sacramental ascension. Hilary of Poitiers refers to the "consecrated body of the Lord" which results from the liturgical, sacrificial action of orthodox priests, as opposed to heretical ones.[189] In this case we have a good example of the use of consecration as applied to the priestly activity of the liturgical offering. It corresponds to the usage of Irenaeus of Lyons cited above.

The presbyter Sedulius (fl. 425–450), referring to the event of the Last Supper, says that Jesus "consecrated the two gifts of life of his body and blood."[190] He certainly has in mind the idea of the sacrificial dedication of Christ himself to the work of redemption which is symbolically expressed in the New Testament accounts of the institution of the Eucharist.

Caesarius of Arles (470–542), among the Latin fathers, is especially favorable to the concept of "consecration of the body and blood of Christ." He observes that the liturgical assembly hears and sees "the consecration of the body and blood."[191] Hence he is referring to the liturgical symbolic verbal and gestural language which expresses the sacrificial action accomplished over the eucharistic gifts. He also employs the phrases: "the spiritual sacraments are consecrated,"[192] and "the divine sacrifices are consecrated."[193] At the Last Supper Christ is said to have "consecrated the mysteries of the salutary consolation."[194] In the usage of Caesarius, "body and blood," "spiritual sacraments," and "divine sacrifices" seem to be almost equivalent terms. This also holds for "mysteries of the salutary consolation."

[189] The *consecratum Domini corpus* is identified as resulting from the *sacrificium a sanctis et integris sacerdotibus confectum*—Hilary of Poitiers (Collectanea Antiariania Parisina, Series A IV 1.9 [CSEL 65.55].

[190] ". . . corporis sui . . . et sanguinis duo uitae munera consecrauit"—Sedulius, *Paschale opus* 5.3 (CSEL 10.275.10–11).

[191] ". . . consecrationem vero corporis et sanguinis Christi non alibi nisi in domo dei audire et videre poteritis"—Caesarius of Arles, *Sermo* 73.2 (CC 103.307). Cf. also ". . . corpus vel sanguis domini consecratur" (ibid.).

[192] ". . . sacramenta spiritalia consecrantur" *Sermo* 74.2 (CC 103.311).

[193] ". . . divina sacrificia consecrantur"—*Sermo* 228.1 (CC 104.91).

[194] ". . . salutiferae consolationis mysteria consecravit"—*Sermo* 202.2 (CC 104.815).

Here the notion of "consecration of the body and blood" probably refers to the liturgical offering of the eucharistic elements identified proleptically as the body and blood of Christ to which the worshiping community's self-offering is associated. The point of view expressed in these texts does not presuppose a consecratory activity prior in time to the sacrificial consecration of the sacraments of the body and blood of Christ. Nowhere in the extant writings of Caesarius does one find any hint of a distinction of this sort.

Still, it remains an open question whether Caesarius has in mind a comprehensive notion of consecration that includes not just the aspects of sanctification of the offering of the elements of bread and wine designated as body and blood, but also the following aspects: the process by which the elements become sacraments of the historical body and blood of Christ; the *transitus* of the sacramental body and blood by which they are united to the risen and glorified body of Christ; and the process by which the liturgical community is elevated to communion with the risen Lord through participation in the eucharistic sacrificial offering in union with Christ, the High Priest and victim.

Gregory the Great (540–604) attributes to the apostles the custom of consecrating the victim *(hostia)* at the prayer of the oblation.[195] He uses the term consecration to refer to the Church's liturgical offering of the eucharistic elements designated by anticipation as the victim of the sacrifice of the cross. This consecratory action of the Church performed by the presiding priest is understood to serve as transparency for the mystery of the holy sacrifice of the Church, namely, that "(Christ) in the mystery of the holy sacrifice is offered for us again *(iterum)*."[196] Moreover, he also includes in the sacramental event of the consecration the special presence of the heavenly Church to which the earthly Church is united.[197]

IV. SUMMARY

The Ambrosian tradition, which draws on the fourth-century Antiochene doctrine of the somatic real presence of Christ under the forms of bread and wine, is exemplified by Ambrose of Milan and Ps.

[195] ". . . mos apostolorum fuit ut ad ipsam solum modo orationem oblationis hostiam consecraret"—Gregory the Great, *Epistula* 9.26 (CC 140A.587.30–31).

[196] Gregory the Great, *Dialogues* 4.58 (PL 77.425D). Text above in n. 55.

[197] Ibid., 428A.

Faustus of Riez. They employ a notion of consecration of the bread and wine, which corresponds to "conversion" of bread and wine into the body and blood of Christ. Also Isidore of Seville employs consecration in the sense of the conversionist theology of the Eucharist favored by Ambrose.

The followers of the Augustinian tradition concerning the composition of the sacraments of the body and blood favor a theology which is more at home with the fifth-century Antiochene doctrine, favored by the Patriarch Nestorius and Theodoret of Cyrus. They employ a concept of consecration which places in the foreground the idea of sanctification of the eucharistic elements through a divine action by which a grace is added to the eucharistic elements which otherwise remain unchanged. While Augustine himself views the grace as related to the eucharistic sacrament by extrinsic denomination and offered only to members of the Church, others understand the grace to be contained in the sacrament.

Fulgentius of Ruspe probably follows Augustine's teaching regarding the sanctification of the eucharistic elements. But he refers the term explicitly to the sanctification of the liturgical assembly by which it is enabled to offer the acceptable sacrifice to God. Facundus of Hermiane seems to opt for the idea that consecration identifies the divine action by which the eucharistic grace is added to the eucharistic elements and thereby qualifies them as sacraments of the body and blood of Christ.

Pope Gelasius's use of consecration includes the meaning attributed above to Facundus of Hermiane. In the reference to consecration of the "divine mystery" in *Epistle* 7.2, it seems that Gelasius has in mind the theological outlook of Theodoret of Cyrus: the sanctification of the elements of bread and wine, and the goal of the consecration of the elements, namely, the sanctification of the participants of the divine liturgy.

The phrase "consecration of the body and blood" is used by Hilary of Poitiers, the presbyter Sedulius, and Caesarius of Arles. To this group can be added Pope Gregory the Great who introduces a similar saying. For *hostia* means, in some sense, the body and blood of Christ.

Hilary refers to the historical body of Christ which has been consecrated by the sacrificial act of approved priests and, therefore, which exists under the formality of sacrament of the historical body: the eucharistic body of Christ which is qualified as consecrated body, because it is the body liturgically sacrificed. Sedulius refers to the action of Christ at the Last Supper when he dedicated himself, his life, through the ritual offering of his body and blood. Here consecration has the meaning of sacrificial action.

Caesarius of Arles says that the liturgical assembly both "sees and hears" the consecration of the body and blood. Hence he is referring to the liturgical symbolic verbal and gestural language which expresses the sacrificial action of the Church in union with Christ accomplished over the eucharistic gifts, and in virtue of which the elements become the "body and blood," "spiritual sacraments," "divine sacrifices."

Among the examples cited, Pope Gregory the Great projects the concept of consecration which unambiguously includes that of making the sacrament of the body and blood, the elevation of the sacrament to unity with the risen and glorified Lord, and the elevation of the earthly Church to unity with the heavenly Church. But it remains doubtful whether for him the phrase "consecration of the body and blood" bears the technical meaning of the inclusive notion that is clearly discernible in some early scholastic sources.

CONCLUSION

It seems probable that the explicit formulation of the distinction between two interpretations of the meaning of "consecration," as applied to the eucharistic gifts, is a contribution of early scholasticism. Before the middle of the twelfth century the term could bear the meaning of ritual expression of the mystery of conversion of the eucharistic elements of bread and wine, or include also the *transitus* of the eucharistic flesh to the heavenly realm in order to be united to the glorified body of the Lord.

The early scholastic theological analysis of the composition of the sacraments of the Eucharist preceded in time the narrowing of the meaning of the term consecration to the ritual expression of the conversion of the bread and wine. Moreover, it made possible the rejection of the inclusive concept of "consecration of the body and blood." In the end the classical tripartite analysis of the composition of the sacraments of the body and blood limited the *sacramentum et res* to the true body and blood of Christ; and the grace of ecclesial unity, ultimately signified, was placed outside the sacrament. At the same time the term consecration defined the ritual activity which serves as the medium of the conversion of the bread and wine, and, therefore, by extension could serve also as a synonym for conversion.

Chapter Two

Eucharistic Theology in the West: Early Middle Ages

In the early Middle Ages Western theology came under the influence of the German worldview. Introduced into the new cultural and historical situation, the ancient patristic understanding of reality was naturally "received" in a differentiated new way. In this milieu, thingly realism was contrasted radically with the symbolic. Whereas the idea of participation of the image in the prototype was taken for granted in the ancient Greek worldview, the image now took on the role of signaling a reality to which it can be related only externally. This resulted in a basically different approach to the understanding of the eucharistic mystery.

The cause of this new worldview can be assigned in some measure to the unsettled situation of migratory peoples throughout northern Europe from the fourth to the ninth century. From the experience of constant social changes and insecurity of life, there seemed to develop a kind of practical positivism, or practical materialism. In such situations, the one stronghold often turns out to be what is accessible, what can be concretely grasped. But in this particular situation, a deeply religious thinking also went hand in hand with this "thingly realism": a vital and unique awareness of the divine presence that can be contrasted with that of Eastern Christians.

For example, the court chapel of Charlemagne at Aachen was modeled on St. Vitale, Ravenna. But it was, in fact, also a new creation. For the relatively unsophisticated theology of the Frankish people was unable to penetrate to the depth of the "image thinking" of the East. This inability was clearly brought to the light of day in the overly simplistic position taken by the Frankish theologians in the controversy over icon veneration.[1] Icon veneration in Byzantium derived from prototype-image thinking, something that was not part of the worldview of the Frankish theologians.

The Second Council of Nicea (787) defended the veneration of icons against the Synod of Hiereia (754). Decades of conflict followed. The dust did not begin to settle until the 842 Synod of Constantinople finally established the teaching of Second Nicea as the definitive position of the Orthodox Church. The source of Greek iconoclasm was probably linked in some way to the edict of Islam against making images. In any case, the concrete theological problem was this: In what way can the Christological formula of the Council of Chalcedon be applied to icons? The defenders of icons formulated a distinction between the unity of the divine–human in Christ and the "quasi-hypostatic union" in icons. Therefore, they argued, different kinds of veneration, and not just the absolute latreia owed to God, were possible. The arguments on both sides of the question were carried on at a high intellectual and theological level.

In its defense of icon veneration, the Second Council of Nicea excluded *latreia* and advocated veneration of what is depicted, basing its position on the implications of the ancient prototype-image thinking. The acts of the council were received and approved in Rome, and then sent on to Charlemagne, the emperor, in the form of an inept and at times totally misleading Latin translation.[2] Charlemagne assigned his theologian, Theodulph, a Visigoth of Catalonia who held the post of bishop of Orléans and abbot of St. Benoit-sur-Loire, to write a position paper on the decision of the council. The resulting work, *Capitulare de imaginibus,* disputed the simplistic position which it erroneously thought, on the basis of the faulty translation, was the teaching of the council. The Frankish theologians even ingenuously demanded that the pope reverse his approval of Second Nicea. How-

[1] See Herbert Schade, "Die Libri Carolini and ihre Stellung zum Bild," *Zeitschrift für katholische Theologie* 79 (1957) 69–78, and Ann Freeman, "Theodulph of Orleans and the Libri Carolini," *Speculum* 32 (1957) 663–705. [For a general update on this whole question (but without special attention to its reception in the West) and its contemporary ecumenical significance, see: Hans Georg Thümnel, "Der byzantinische Bilderstreit," *Theologische Rundsahau* 61 (1966) 355–71.]

[2] E.g., where one bishop at the council had said: "I accept and respectfully kiss images, but I give latreutic veneration only to the Trinity," the translation sent to Charlemagne had him saying: "I venerate images in the same way that I venerate the Trinity" (Schade, "Die Libri Carolini," 70).

ever, Pope Hadrian I defended Nicea II against the court of the Emperor. This papal position was countered by Theodulph who, together with the cooperation of other theologians of Charlemagne, composed the *Libri Carolini* (791) which incorporated without change the position taken in the original *Capitulare de imaginibus*.[3]

This debate over image veneration can possibly shed more light on the discussions of the doctrine of the somatic real presence of the body and blood of Christ than many of the writings concerned explicitly with this issue. For this early medieval debate reflects the different ways of thinking of the Greek and the German-Frankish worlds. The rejection of icons in the *Libri Carolini* is grounded on what the Frankish authors saw as the lack of spiritual quality in the (material) icons themselves. They argued that images, by which they meant primarily paintings, are something purely material, and so cannot contain a mystery. They can serve only as ornamentation, or to represent historical events, or as a help to the memory.[4] The Neoplatonic and Plotinian philosophical nuances which enabled the Greek venerators of images to see a range of acceptable and desirable positions beneath divine *latreia* but still above idolatry or superstition, were not available to the Frankish theologians who were also (for political reasons) delighted to be able to find something to correct in their Eastern counterparts.

The *Libri Carolini* recognizes the divine presence in the world only in the forms that are created by God. In the East, the opponents of icon veneration saw the particular mode of this presence as the image of the "invisible God" in Christ. In contrast, the Frankish opponents of icon veneration—actually, they were trying to establish a middle

[3] The best edition of the *Libri Carolini* is Hubertus Bastgen, ed., *Monumenta Germaniae Historica* [MGH]. Legum Sectio III. Concilia. Tomi II suppl. (Hannover and Leipzig: Impensis Bibliopolii Hahniani, 1924); also in PL 98.941–1350. Veneration of images was a major issue for the Frankish theologians at the end of the eighth and through much of the ninth century. See, e.g., the extensive documentation in MGH Legum Sectio III. Concilia. Tomi II. Pars I and II (Hannover and Leipzig: Impensis Bibliopolii Hahniani, 1906 and 1908) see index under "imago"; some typical texts: 87.9–27, 91.23–36, 487.28–35. There is some evidence to suggest that Alcuin rather than Theodulph might have been the principal author of the *Libri Carolini* (Schade, 70).

[4] The typically Western veneration of the cross is part of this picture. For Westerners did not look on the cross as an image; rather they saw in it—especially in its *relics*—the very wood of the cross on which hung the salvation of the world (see Schade, 71–75).

position between what they saw as the extremes of iconoclasm on the one hand and superstitious idolatry on the other—saw this divine presence (i.e., in the forms created by God) not in Christ, but in the *Ark of the Covenant.* This accounts for the mosaic in the apse of the church of Germigny-des-Prés, built by Theodulph and inaugurated in 806. The mosaic depicts the Ark of the Covenant as the central symbol of the mysterious divine presence. In other words, the central place in the apse is not awarded to the *Majestas Domini,* the enthroned Christ. Clearly Christ was, in this early German-Christian view, less the revealer of the Father veiled in the light, than the God walking the earth, directly accessible.

It was in this cultural and historical situation that the Franks "received" the traditional doctrine of the Eucharist from the Eastern and Western patristic sources.

I. PASCHASIUS AND RATRAMNUS OF CORBIE

The classical example in this period of two contrasting approaches to the mystery of the sacraments of the body and blood, in which the Emperor was also partially involved, is found in the works of two monks of the Abbey of Corbie in Northern France. The protagonists of this ninth-century exchange were the Abbot Paschasius Radbertus (d. 851 or 860), who wrote *De corpore et sanguine Domini,* and Ratramnus (d. 868), who wrote a tract with the same title on the basis of some questions addressed to him by the Emperor Charles the Bald and occasioned by the treatise of Paschasius. In general, Paschasius represents the more "realistic" line of thinking which eventually dominated in medieval theology, and Ratramnus the more symbolic or spiritualistic line of thinking which eventually suffered a great setback with the eleventh-century condemnations of Berengar of Tours.[5] The interpretation of both works is disputed today. This is understandable in the context of the transitional period in which they wrote. In the new cultural milieu, the ancient image thinking was not clearly understood.

In reading the treatise of Paschasius and the response of Ratramnus, one gets the distinct impression that neither of them had an ade-

[5] Paschasius Radbertus, *Liber de corpore et sanguine Domini* (CCCM 16; PL 120. 1267–1350); Ratramnus of Corbie, *Liber de corpore et sanguine Domini,* critical text: J. N. Bakhuizen van den Brink, ed., Verhandelingen der koninklyke nederlandse Akademie der Wetenschappen, AFD. Letterkunde, Nieuwe Reeks, Deel 61, no. 1 (Amsterdam: North Holland, 1954) also PL 121.1226–70.

quate appreciation of the dynamic character of the eucharistic mystery as understood in early Greek theology. One looks in vain for a significant appreciation of the Greek idea of the commemorative actual presence of the once-for-all redemptive work of Christ or the notion of somatic real presence conceived from the perspective of prototype-image thinking. Instead, the somatic real presence, which was originally embedded in the *anamnesis,* becomes isolated. The priest-celebrant becomes a ministerial means to the somatic real presence. The theological meaning of the *anamnesis,* as it was explained by the Greek Fathers (and which was, in fact, more in line with biblical thinking), is not understood by these Western theologians. This accounts in part for the tendency, in the effort to fill the void, to reduce the notion of *anamnesis* to allegory.

Paschasius composed the first extant systematic treatise on the Eucharist for young monks (831–833). This work concentrates on the relation of the sacramental body of Christ to the historical body of Christ. Paschasius is concerned with defending the unity of figure and thing *(figura et res).* Ratramnus, for his part, also does not neglect the problem raised by the levels of being in prototype and image. But both have the same problem: How can something be the reality if it is only an image of the reality? In their writings both theologians show that they have not truly grasped the content of the ancient understanding of religious images. On the other hand, within the new way of thinking, the tendencies of these two theologians differ. They begin at different starting points.

Paschasius begins from an understanding of image that does bear at least some traces of the ancient thinking: "Through the humanity of Christ one has access to the divinity of the Father, and so it is rightly called figure *(figura)* or character, or the substance of him."[6] But in this case, as in that of the Eucharist, Paschasius uses the relation prototype-image in a narrower sense than did the Greek Fathers. He calls the eucharistic body of Christ the truth *(veritas),* where truth includes both reality and image. What the sense perceives is image, but what is believed is not the image but the truth contained in the image. The criterion for the distinction between prototype and image is the sensible experience of believers. Thus the relation between prototype

[6] "Ex humanitate Christi ad diuinitatem Patris pervenitur et ideo iure figura uel character substantiae illius uocatur"—Paschasius, *De corpore* 4 (CCCM 16.29.60–62; PL 120.1279A).

and image—which, in the Greek perspective, was grounded on the real participation of the eucharistic elements in the reality of the crucified and risen Lord who has his natural mode of existence at the right hand of the Father—becomes conceived by Paschasius as a relation grounded simply on the *presence of the reality within the eucharistic food itself.* The all-important distinction between the natural mode of existence of the risen Lord in heaven and the sacramental mode of existence in the sacraments of the body and blood, as understood in Greek image theology, is not carried through.

Briefly, in Paschasius's theology the criterion of the distinction between reality and image comes from the sensible experience of the human being. It is the senses that perceive the image, but faith that knows the reality. This perspective has lost the possibility of seeing the reality of the image as a *reality of a particular kind.* The image, therefore, is not a lower form of a higher reality. The prototype is already fully present in the image. For Greek theology, on the contrary, the prototype is Christ and his saving work. The eucharistic celebration *is* a *reality of a particular kind:* participation in the prototype.

In Paschasius's elaboration of the notion of somatic real presence, the salvation-history trait of "already—not yet" is not expressed. For the prototype is conceived as already fully present, if invisibly present, in the sacraments of the body and blood. The eschatological depth of the mystery of the somatic real presence of Christ, as the real promise, or first fruits of definitive salvation, is obscured.

In his letter to Frudegard, Paschasius says: "We receive in the bread that which hung on the cross."[7] This statement reflects the conceptual identification of two levels of reality. Reality is seen on only the one level of the "thingly." This leads to the simplistic identification of the historical body of Christ with the eucharistic body of Christ. In contrast, the old prototype-image theology could not say this without further qualification. For the Greeks, the prototype is not present in the image in a univocal way; it has a sphere proper to it. Image is a special form of the reality and its presence; the prototype is present

[7] The passage from which this text [here italicized] comes, with important nuances, reads: "Ac per hoc, quia sic credidimus spiritaliter fieri, nec istud est sine ipso quod tunc gestum est sacramento, nec illud reiteratur in facto, ut moriatur Christus, sed immolatur pro nobis quotidie in mysterio, ut *percipiamus in pane quod pependit in cruce,* et bibimus in calice quod manauit de latere"—Paschasius, *Epistola ad Frudegardum* (CCCM 16.151.190–95; PL 120.1355A). This text is part of a quote which Paschasius attributes to Augustine.

through the image, but not in the image, univocally, as Paschasius seems to suggest. Paschasius has reduced image theology to the sensual sphere: What we see is the image; but the prototype is present in the same univocal sense. On the other hand, for the ancients, image cannot be *opposed* to the prototype, as was generally presupposed in this early medieval Western thought world, because image is a special form of the reality and presence of the prototype. Paschasius interprets the ancient image theology in the direction of realism. The symbolism is reduced to the relation of something that is visibly present (properties of bread) to something that is invisibly present (Christ).

Ratramnus of Corbie had a different starting point. He was much more concerned with securing the symbolism. Bread and wine are *figurae.* As such the bread and wine *veil* the presence of the body and blood. This was quite different from the ancient theology in which the figure does not veil but *reveals* the presence. While Paschasius conceives the visible as "figure" and seeks to identify the reality underlying it, Ratramnus does not seem to conceive reality as graded. For Ratramnus, the visible is *veritas;* the invisible is also *veritas.* Under the veil of the visible (the corporeal), the spiritual body exists and is known by faith. He does not, however, explain the nature of the unity between the two.

In Ratramnus's explanation the dynamic tension: "already—not yet" is also lacking. Instead, the tension is reinterpreted and *statically* conceived as the relation "corporeal—spiritual," whereby spiritual is present but hidden.

"Under the veil of the corporeal bread and the corporeal wine, the spiritual body and the spiritual blood exists. Not as though there are two things distinguished among themselves: body and spirit. Rather there is one and the same thing. According to one way, bread and wine; according to another way, body and blood of Christ."[8]

This text shows that reality is not seen as graded. The ontological categories of spirit-body are conceived as ontologically different, but also as becoming dialectically identified. Reality appears as one-dimensional and disconnected.

Paschasius wants to secure the reality of the sacrament and so uses the concept *veritas* for the *invisible* reality of salvation. Ratramnus, however, uses *veritas* for the reality which is *visible.* So he secures the

[8] Text below in n. 10.

symbolism. However, he ends up by a splitting of the sacramental reality into spirit and body. While Paschasius inclines to a simple identification of the historical and eucharistic body of Christ, Ratramnus inclines to a differentiation insofar as the historical body of Christ is invisible truth and the sacrament is a visible truth.

Paschasius says that the eucharistic elements are changed *(transferri; consecrari; commutari; confici)* through the word of Christ into the flesh and blood of Christ, and become identical with the body of Christ born of the Virgin, who suffered, died, and is now in heaven.[9] Ratramnus makes no remarks on the process of change. His sacramental realism is subdued by the influence of Augustine's thought. It ultimately comes to a spiritual reception through faith. A typical passage from Ratramnus reads:

"Because they are confessed to be the body and blood of Christ, and because this could not have come about except by a change into something better, and by a change not carried out in a bodily way but spiritually, it is now necessary that this be said to be done figuratively because under the veil of the corporeal bread and the corporeal wine the spiritual body and the spiritual blood exists. Not as though there are two things distinguished among themselves: body and spirit. Rather there is one and the same thing: according to one way, bread and wine; according to another way, body and blood of Christ. For according to what they are corporeally, they are corporeal creatures; but according to what they have been made spiritually, they are mysteries of the body and blood of Christ."[10]

A typical passage from Paschasius reads:

"But because it was fitting for him to penetrate the heavens according to the flesh, in order that those reborn in him might more confidently seek him there, he left to us this sacrament, the visible figure

[9] Paschasius, *De corpore* 2 (CCCM 16.22.64 [PL 120.1274B]); *De corpore* 4 (CCCM 16.28.20 [PL 120.1278A] and 30.84 and 89 [PL 120.1279B and C]).

[10] "At quia confitentur et corpus et sanguinem esse Christi nec hoc esse potuisse nisi facta in melius commutatione neque ista commutatio corporaliter sed spiritaliter facta sit, necesse est iam ut figurate facta esse dicatur quoniam sub uelamento corporei panis corporeique uini spiritale corpus Christi spiritalisque sanguis existit non quod duarum sint existentiae rerum inter se diuersarum, corporis uidelicet et spiritus, uerum una eademque res secundum aliud species panis et uini consistit, secundum aliud autem corpus est et sanguis Christi"—Ratramnus, *De corpore* 16 (Bakhuizen van den Brink 37; PL 121.134B–135A).

and character of flesh and blood, in order that through these our mind and our flesh might be nourished more richly through faith to grasp the invisible and spiritual. What is eternally perceived here is the figure or character, but it is the whole truth and not its shadow that is internally perceived; and through this is opened up the very truth and sacrament of [Christ's] very flesh. *It is indeed the true flesh of Christ which was crucified and buried, it is truly the sacrament of that flesh* (Ambrose) which, through the priest on the altar, is divinely consecrated by the Holy Spirit in the words of Christ. Hence, it is the Lord himself who cries out *This is my body.*"[11]

PASCHASIUS AND RATRAMNUS: SUMMARY

The question was posed: What is the relation between truth and figure in the mystery of the Eucharist? According to Paschasius, the figure is what is seen; it *contains* the truth fully present. As such, figure is not a lower form of a higher reality; it is something over against or opposed to truth. By contrast, according to the ancient view, the prototype, although it stands outside the image, actually bestows itself *in* the image. For Ratramnus, on the other hand, the sign *conceals* the reality. The Eucharist is *not simply two things:* body and spirit. But it is *two things from different points of view:* bread and wine; body and blood. They are ontologically different, but dialectically identified: two realities: one-dimensional and disconnected. There is no unbroken relation between symbol and mystery.

This difference of approach to the sacrament also holds for the relation between the eucharistic celebration and the sacrifice of the cross. Neither Paschasius nor Radbertus begins with the notion of the commemorative actual presence of the Christ-event. What is the relation

[11] "Sed quia illum secundum carnem caelos oportuit penetrare, ut per fidem illuc in illo renati confidentius appeterent, reliquid [sic] nobis hoc sacramentum uisibilem [uisibile in] figuram et caracterem carnis et sanguinis, ut per haec mens nostra et caro nostra ad inuisibilia et spiritalia capescenda per fidem uberius nutriatur. Est autem figura uel caracter hoc quod exterius sentitur, sed tantum ueritas et nulla adumbratio quod intrinsecus percipitur ac per hoc nihil aliud hinc inde quam ueritas et sacramentum ipsius carnis aperitur. *Vera utique caro Christi quae crucifixa est et sepulta, uere illius carnis sacramentum* (Ambrose) quod per sacerdotem super altare in uerbo Christi per Spiritum Sanctum diuinitus consecratur. Unde ipse Dominus clamat: *Hoc est corpus meum*"—Paschasius, *De corpore* 4 (CCCM 16.30.73–85; PL 120.1279A-B).

between the cross and Eucharist? According to Paschasius, the once-for-all sacrifice is *present in* the Eucharist. Christ died once but is immolated daily *in mysterio.* Here Paschasius is dependent on Gregory the Great, who teaches that Christ in the eucharistic sacrifice offers himself continually for the daily sins of the people.[12] According to Ratramnus, the Mass is the image of the passion; its function is to recall to believers the past historical sacrifice of Christ.

This classic ninth-century discussion raised the question which became a central theological issue two centuries later: How can one unite realism and symbolism in the understanding of the sacrament? How can this be done in a new form of thought? Before the task was to be completed, a long process was involved. However, between the ninth and eleventh centuries, the Church did not have the means of arriving at a correct theological expression for the reality of the Eucharist. In the theological position achieved in this period, a position which continues to influence Catholic theology to this day, the overcoming of the fatal opposition between symbolism and extreme realism was not achieved.

In Paschasius's day, his strongly realistic teaching was considered somewhat of a novelty in some of the more learned circles. Hrabanus Maurus, among others, did not approve of it.[13] Especially opposed to Paschasius was Ratramnus, as we have seen, in his response to the two questions of Charles the Bald (composed after 844).[14] While Paschasius Radbertus explained the Eucharist in the spirit of the Fathers of the Church, and was indeed fairly well versed in the writings of the patristic age, Ratramnus manifests a new theology in which symbol and reality are opposed in the liturgy. He is more a man of his culture; for in that culture symbol is understood as intimation, as

[12] See above, chapter one, p. 76.

[13] "Recently there have been some who, not thinking rightly about this sacrament of the body and blood of the Lord, have said: This same body and blood of the Lord, which was born of Mary, and in which the Lord suffered on the cross and rose from the tomb . . is the same that is received from the altar. Responding to this error as best we could in our letter to Abbot Egilus, we have expounded what is to be truly believed about this body"—Hrabanus Maurus, *Poenitentiale* 33 (PL 110.493A). The letter to Egilus to which Hrabanus refers can be found in PL 112.1507–1518, where it is accompanied by an informative introductory note by Mabillon (1509D–1512D).

[14] Confer J. F. Fahey, *Eucharistic Teaching of Ratramnus of Corbie* (Mundelein, Ill., 1951).

allegory, or example. By contrast, what is real must be something that is graspable, something physical.

The breakup of the unity between *figura* and *veritas* in the mystery not only excluded the presence of the reality of the sacrifice of the cross in the figure but also threatened the conviction of faith concerning the real presence of the body and blood of Christ in the eucharistic gifts. The formulation of the doctrine of transubstantiation, in the twelfth and thirteenth centuries, brought a halt not just to the "spiritualizing" tendency, but also to the reactionary, sensualistic view of sacramental real presence. However, the doctrine of transubstantiation did not remedy the fatal split that had already occurred between sacrifice and sacrament. Since the ninth century, the sacrament of the real presence of the body and blood of Christ was more commonly thought to be opposed to rather than supported by, a figurative representation of the once and for all sacrifice of the cross.

The crisis of the concept of the eucharistic sacrifice and sacrament is manifested in the works of other ninth-century writers. Especially interesting are the opposing positions of Amalar of Metz and Florus of Lyons, to which we now turn.

II. AMALAR OF METZ AND FLORUS OF LYONS

Amalar of Metz (d. 850 or 851) and Florus of Lyons (d. ca. 860) offer strikingly different views of the theology of the liturgy.[15] Amalar's method of rememorative allegory, a (sometimes seemingly arbitrary) subjective recall of different events of Christ's life, was similar, but only superficially, to the old allegorical method of the Church Fathers. Florus's theology was, by contrast, in significant continuity with that of the Fathers. Influenced by the old Platonic view, Florus could see that the sensible sign (or cultic mystery) did not merely point to or subjectively recall the salvation reality but some-

[15] Amalar of Metz: *Liber officialis,* Johannes M. Hanssens, ed., *Amalarii Episcopi opera liturgica omnia,* vol. 2, Studi e Testi 139 (Vatican City; Biblioteca Apostolica Vaticana, 1948) also in PL 105.985–1242. Florus of Lyons: *De expositione missae* (PL 119.15–72); *Opuscula adversus Amalarium* (PL 119.71–96); *Epistola Flori totius veritatis plena contra falsiloquas adinventiones Amalarii quondam Lugdunensis chorepiscopi* (MGH Epistolarum Tomus V. Karolini Aevi III. [Berlin: Apud Weidmannos, 1899] 267–73); *Oratio in Concilio Carisiacensi habita* (MGH Legum Sectio III. Concilia. Tomus II, Pars II [Hannover and Leipzig: Impensis Bibliopolii Hahniani, 1908] 768–78); *Relatio de Concilio Carisiacensi* (ibid., 778–82).

how actually communicated it. Understandably, then, Florus considered Amalar's method to be "laughable"[16] and a dangerous deviation from the ancient tradition. Amalar's commentary on the Mass was indeed reminiscent of the old patristic interpretation of the ritual of the eucharistic liturgy. But it was, in fact, a tributary more disconnected than connected with the earlier model which is grounded on a theology of the history of salvation.[17]

The concept "history of salvation," as this was generally understood in the world of the Fathers, contains the idea that God acts in and through history. Hence, what happens in the historical events of the life of individuals, or of a people, is not viewed as a matter of mere chance by those who have a deep and vital awareness of the "historically" acting God. The prophetic writers of the Old Testament fall into the class of those who experienced God's involvement in the history of his people. As a consequence, they reread the history of the chosen people as a series of events ordered to a fulfillment that was to be realized in God's own good time. The understanding that historical events held a spiritual meaning because God is acting in these events for his own good purpose, is also found in the New Testament. Here God's actions in the past are seen as ordered to a fulfillment that is concretized in Jesus' life and work. The full meaning of God's activity in history is revealed once for all in Jesus Christ.

The fact that Jesus was "saved from death" (Hebrews 5:7) is understood to have a profound significance for all humanity. Its deeper

[16] ". . . qui tantis vesaniis et erroribus confertus est, ut quibuslibet etiam imperitis palam ridendus conspuendusque videatur"—Florus, *Epistola . . . contra falsiloquas adinventiones Amalarii* (MGH Epistolarum Tomus V. Karolini Aevi III. 268.17–18).

[17] For general background, see Josef Andreas Jungmann, "Die Abwehr des germanischen Arianismus und der Umbruch des religiösen Kultur im frühen Mittelalter," *Zeitschrift für katholische Theologie* 69 (1947) 36–99, esp. 37–43, 94–99. For discussion of Amalar's method of commentary on the Mass, and the reaction to it by Florus and others, see A. Cabaniss, *Amalarius of Metz* (Amsterdam: North Holland, 1954); Raphael Schulte, *Die Messe als Opfer der Kirche: Die Lehre frühmittelalterlicher Autoren über das eucharistische Opfer,* Liturgiewissenschaftliche Quellen und Forschungen 35 (Münster: Aschendorff, 1959) esp. 146–68; Adolf Kolping, "Amalar von Metz und Florus von Lyon: Zeugen eines Wandels im liturgischen Mysterienverständnis in der Karolingerzeit." *ZKT* 73 (1951) 424–64. For background on the patristic allegorical method, see Jo Tigcheler, *Didyme L'Aveugle et l'exégèse allégorique,* Graecitas Christianorum Primaeva 6 (Nijmegen, Dekker & Van de Vegt, 1977).

meaning is "for us" the revelation that we, too, are saved, in principle, through the action of God in Jesus Christ. However, this happens only to the extent that we freely assent to have the Christ-event touch our lives. This happens concretely through our acceptance of the way of Christ's approach to God in the obedience of faith, hope, and love. In this way, the believer begins the ascent to God that is fulfilled at the end of earthly life by the faithful God.

In the third century, Origen, inspired by the Scriptures, systematized the various levels of spiritual meaning of the historical events of the people of God of the old and new covenant. The literal meaning of the Scriptures points to truths of faith about Jesus and the Church (allegory), and its consequences for the practice of Christian life (tropology), and the ultimate meaning of the economy of salvation (anagogy).

Then, in the fourth- and fifth-century mystagogical catecheses, this method was applied to the liturgy of the Church, especially to the sacraments of baptism and Eucharist. This patristic tradition supplied the basis for a method of explanation of the Mass that is now found in the ninth century. However, this early medieval method was only superficially similar to the old allegorical method employed by Cyril of Jerusalem, Theodore of Mopsuestia, and Ambrose of Milan. The new approach is often identified with Amalar of Metz, but he did not create it out of whole cloth. It seems that Amalar's visit to the East, bringing him into contact with the Eastern allegorical method of explaining the liturgy, served to encourage him in his efforts to work out a systematic explanation of the rites of the Mass. It is clear, in any case, that the main elements of these rites were already available in the Gallican tradition.[18]

It should be noted, however, that the method he developed was not accepted by many of his contemporaries. Agobard of Lyons, who had a profound knowledge of patristic literature, recognized the novelty of Amalar's teaching, as did his pupil Florus. So, too, did the fathers of the local synod of Quierzy (A.D. 838); they rejected the work of Amalar as not in keeping with the ancient tradition of the Church.

[18] See *Expositio brevis antiquae liturgiae gallicanae in duas epistolas digesta* (PL 72. 89–98). This document, attributed by some to Saint Germain, bishop of Paris (d. 576), probably originates somewhat later. See Robert Cabié, "Les lettres attribuées à saint Germain de Paris et les origines de la liturgie gallicane," *Bulletin de littérature ecclésiastique* 73 (1972) 183–92.

A. AMALAR OF METZ

Amalar's explanation of the liturgy begins with the principle that the individual liturgical rites have a meaning *(ratio)* that is intimated in the rites themselves.[19] He follows the old tradition superficially, i.e., to the extent that liturgical rites are understood to have a sign function, realized through the outward form of the rites. But in that venerable tradition, there is a strict ordering of the outward form of appearance of the rites to the inward salutary content. In other words, the Fathers of the Church saw that the content of salvation is expressed in the externals of the rite, and that it is mediated in such a way that not only knowledge of the reality but the saving reality itself is communicated in the rite.

Amalar, however, does not conceive the outward form of the rites as the way to the inward reality, to the sacramental content. He does not see the explanation of the meaning of the rites as being developed from the salvation reality communicated by the rite. Rather, he conceives the rite as a means of subjective recall that can bring to the memory a variety of things. Insofar as the meaning of the rites does not lie open to the light of day, Amalar speaks of a "mystery" hidden in the rite, a doctrine that is only discovered with difficulty from the intimation of the rite. Therefore he departs from the main line of the patristic tradition by perceiving cultic rites not so much as mysteries but as pointing to mysteries.

Amalar's method of "rememorative allegory" works with the idea that the individual rites of the liturgy correspond to the various stages of the life of Christ. He explains the rites not from their sacramental meaning and power but from their ability to intimate the instruction that is consistent with their external form of appearance. For example, the offertory procession of the Mass is explained as a reference to the offering of gifts of the law of the Old Covenant *(oblatio legalis)*, to the offering of Christ's sacrifice *([oblatio] Christi)*, and to the self-offering of the faithful *([oblatio] nostra)*.[20] In this, and other in-

[19] ". . . in which we may learn about the office of the Mass, what the reason is for the diversity of things performed there *(quid rationis in se contineat diversitas illa quae ibi agitur)*, since the mere blessing of the bishops and presbyters, without the singing and reading and the other things performed there, would suffice for blessing the bread and wine with which the people are nourished for the salvation of their souls"—Amalar, *Liber officialis* 3, praef. (Hanssens 21.256).

[20] *Liber officialis* 3.19.1 (Hanssens 2.311.19–20). This is developed in detail in the course of this chapter (3.19) which bears the title: *De officio quod vocatur offerenda*

stances, it is noteworthy how Amalar *reverses* the typological explanation of the Fathers. Whereas the Fathers see the Old Testament fulfilled in New Testament worship, Amalar finds in Christian worship, not a fulfillment of Old Testament worship, but allusions to it.

Amalar grounds rememorative allegory on an institution by Christ. Christ's words at the Last Supper, "Do this in memory of me," are referred not only to the central actions of the Last Supper but also to the individual events of the whole life of Christ.[21] Amalar locates the rememorative trait of the eucharistic celebration not in the sacramentality of the rite, as indicated by the eucharistic words of institution, but in externals of the rite and in the instructional possibility which these rites offer. The mystery contained in the rites is, therefore, identified with the meaning hidden in the rite itself, in the *medulla* of the external rite.[22]

Thus, according to Amalar, the cultic rites are not themselves mysteries. Hence the meaning of the rites is not sought in the sacramental efficacy of the rites but is seen in other relations. And, in fact, the question of sacramental efficacy does not hold the theological interest of Amalar. The high sacramental theology of the patristic period does not seem to have been accessible to him, any more than it was to many of his contemporaries. For example, Amalar explains the chrismation of episcopal ordination in this way: "All these things that are done exteriorly are signs of interior things. If one has these things in mind, he is a true priest."[23] The rite is described as pointing to the inner sentiment of *caritas.* It is not seen as the showing forth of what God does in the ordination rite.

Amalar's conception of the real presence of Christ in the sacrament of the body and blood is indicative of the change in thinking that characterizes the Carolingian age. No longer are the sacramental signs intimately related to the whole world of faith of the divine economy in Christ. He expresses the fundamental statement of faith about the eucharistic presence in this way: the "sensible nature of the bread and wine is changed *(verti)* into the rational nature, namely of the body and

---

(Hanssens 2.311.16–322.7).

[21] *Liber officialis,* prooemium 6–7 (Hanssens 2.14.40–15.15).

[22] ". . . ut sciam quid habeat in medulla res memorata"—*Liber officialis* 1 praef. 4 (Hanssens 2.26.33).

[23] "Omnia haec quae extrinsecus geruntur, signa sunt rerum intimarum Si quis in mente habuerit ipsas res, ipse est verus sacerdos"—*Liber officialis* 2.14.8 (Hanssens 2.235.8–9).

blood of Christ."[24] But he conceives the "conversion" so realistically that he says Christ remains in us and we in him "through the man received."[25] The sacrament is filled with the hidden reality. But from Amalar's perspective, the reality appearing to us is the proper reality, that with which we must reckon. Hence if the eucharistic elements are the body and blood of Christ, then the body of Christ must be present in accord with the manner of the physical reality appearing before us.

Amalar does not deny the relation of the Eucharist to the Church, an essential aspect of Augustine's theology of the Eucharist. The Eucharist is indeed administered by the Church, according to Amalar. But he sees the sacrament as more isolated, received for itself, and less in the (Augustinian) view that the Eucharist is made by the Church and makes the Church. The Eucharist is received so that the *sumptum corpus*[26] may be in us. As a consequence of this Amalar advises frequent Communion.[27]

On the subject of the sacrifice of the Mass, he states: "The immolation through the priest at the altar is, in a certain way, like the immolation of Christ on the cross."[28] He speaks of the sacrifice of Christ present on the altar in this fashion: the "one victim, Christ, was offered for the just and the unjust. The same sacrifice, which was placed [offered?] before, remains on the altar."[29]

Properly speaking, the sacrifice of the Mass is the sacrifice of the Church. In the preface, the priest offers his personal sacrifice; in the trisagion is found the sacrifice of the angels;[30] the sacrifice of the faith-

[24] "Hic credimus naturam simplicem panis et vini mixti verti in naturam rationabilem, scilicet corporis et sanguinis Christi"—*Liber officialis* 3.24.8 (Hanssens 2.339.30–32).

[25] "Per eucharistiam Christus in nobis manet, et nos in illo *per assumptum hominem*"—*Liber officialis* 3.34.1 (Hanssens 2.365.7).

[26] Amalar, *Liber officialis, Epistula* 6.15 (Hanssens 2.397.36).

[27] "Praecipitur in canonibus ut omnes ingredientes ecclesiam communicent . . . gustare et videre fas est quam dulcis sit Dominus. A tam dilecto hospite non oportet dilectores diu abesse, quem compulerunt secum hospitari in die resurrectionis eius duo ex discipulis in Emaus"—ibid., 6.16–18 (Hanssens 2.398.9–27).

[28] "Sic est immolatio sacerdotis in altari quodammodo ut Christi immolatio in cruce"—*Liber officialis,* prooemium 6 (Hanssens 2.14.9–10).

[29] ". . . una hostia, Christus, oblata est pro iustis et iniustis. Idem sacrificium permanet in altari, quod ante positum est"—*Liber officialis* 3.24.1 (Hanssens 2.337.27–29).

[30] "Quia enim de sacrificio agitur, restat ut sit et gratiarum actiones, quas sacerdos offert, pro sacrificio eius accipiamus, et ministeria angelorum, quae recolun-

ful takes place in the prayer *Te igitur* to *jubeas grege numerari.*[31] Following Cyprian, Amalar explains that the mixing of water and wine is a sign of the inclusion of the faithful in the sacrifice of Christ.[32]

Amalar teaches that Christ is present in the whole of the liturgy. He refers to the Lord's presence in the reading of Scripture.[33] The Lord is present subjectively in the believers when, in the *Unde et memores* prayer, his passion, death, and resurrection are recalled:

"In the sacrament of the bread and wine, and also in my memory, the passion of Christ is at hand . . . the body of Christ is alive in the sacrament of the bread and wine, and also in my memory, thus in the present he ascends on the cross."[34]

B. FLORUS OF LYONS

Florus, the severest critic of Amalar, bases his theology of the Eucharist on the conviction that the sacrament of the body and blood of Christ is the real and objective presence of Christ. While this is also true of Amalar, Florus has another experience of reality. He conceives the reality of the sacrament in other categories. His way of thinking is determined by the old Platonic view that sees the reality above the sensible becoming transparent in the physical world of appearances while remaining untouched by processes that occur in the sensible world. It is with the category of cultic mystery that he expresses this relation between the sensible world of appearance and the nonsensible world that exists in the sacraments. He holds that the reality above the sensible mediates itself somehow through the sensible signs. In other words, the sensible sign is so intimately bound to the salvation reality that this reality is communicated to believers through the cultic mystery.

---

tur in praesenti ymno [the Sanctus], pro eorum sacrificio"—*Liber officialis* 3.21.5 (Hanssens 2.325.16–19).

[31] "Nunc de 'Te igitur' dicendum est. Ab initio orationis usque ad locum ubi dicitur 'Et in electorum tuorum iubeas grege numerari per Christum Dominum nostrum' caelebratur sacrificium electorum"—*Liber officialis* 3.23.6 (Hanssens 2.331.22–25).

[32] *Liber officialis* 3.19.27–30 (Hanssens 2.319.9–321.40).

[33] Ibid., 3.18 (Hanssens 306.31–311.15).

[34] "In sacramento panis et vini, necnon etiam in memoria mea, passio Christi in promptu est. . . . Christi corpus est vivum in sacramento panis et vini, atque in memoria mea, ita in praesenti ascendit in crucem"—*Liber officialis* 3.25.1–2 (Hanssens 2.340.36–38).

The sacramental signs signify the historical cause of salvation. They also signify the consequences of the sacramentally mediated grace of Christ, namely, that the believing participants become the body of Christ. In contrast to Amalar, Florus holds that the significative function of the sacraments grows precisely out of the meaning that the sacrament has for salvation. Hence he finds Amalar's far-flung explanations of the rites of the Mass unacceptable.

Both Amalar and Florus conceive the Mass as mystery but in different ways. Florus views the Mass as an activity, a sacrifice, in which an acceptable cultic offering is made to God. This offering takes place through the priest in the name of the Church and is intimately related to the bread and wine. These gifts become the body and blood of Christ through the consecration by Christ, in the power of the Spirit. As a consequence the Church now offers the body and blood of the Lord. This offering is a real offering of the body and blood of the Lord present *in mysterio,* but really at hand. This real offering repeats mysteriously the death of the Lord, the bloody offering of the cross. It is from the historical reality of the sacrifice of the cross that the sacrifice of the Church unfolds.

"The Lord himself handed on to the apostles the command that the universal Church celebrate the memorial of her Redeemer. [The consecration of the bread and wine takes place] 'by the power and words of Christ . . . . He speaks daily in his priests. They function by office, he works by the majesty of divine power.'"[35]

"Jesus alone is mediator of God and man because the mediator is human divinity and divine humanity."[36] . . . "God above us, man for us; through the humanity he intercedes for us before the Father, through the divinity he hears . . . with the Father."[37] "In this mystery of the holy oblation, he is immolated again *(iterum)* for us."[38]

[35] "Christi ergo virtute et verbis semper consecratur et consecrabitur. Illius sermo est qui coelestis sacramenta sanctificat. Ille in suis sacerdotibus quotidie loquitur. Illi funguntur officio, ille majestate divinae potestatis operatur"—Florus of Lyons, *De expositione missae* 60 (PL 119.52C).

[36] "Inter solam divinitatem et humanitatem solam, mediatrix est humana divinitas, et divina humanitas Christi"—Florus, *De expositione missae* 22 (PL 119.33C).

[37] "Idem namque mediator Dei et hominum Deus super nos homo propter nos per humanitatem interpellat pro nobis apud Patrem, per divinitatem exaudit et praestat cum Patre"—ibid. (PL 119.33D–34A).

[38] "Pro nobis iterum in hoc mysterio sacrae oblationis immolatur"—Florus. *De*

For Florus, the Mass is a cultic mystery that celebrates the one mystery of salvation; for Amalar, the Mass contains many mysteries. Florus has no time for the subjective interpretations of Amalar. According to Florus the sacramental signs must represent an objective ontological relation to the salvation reality, and only this, according to the will of Christ. What they represent, they also contain, as God has determined.

III. BERENGAR OF TOURS (D. 1088)

There is a characteristic process that is recognizable in the history of dogma. When a new age breaks in with its particular forms of thought and language, it affects the traditional doctrine of the faith that had been handed down from another age clothed in another structure of thought and language. At first, this takes place in an unreflective way. Later on, formal theological reflection on the consequences of the new form of thought leads to a crisis. How can the new theology be reconciled with the old so that the gospel message is authentically expressed?

A good example of this process can be found in the eleventh-century debate over the eucharistic sacraments (i.e., sacrament of the body and sacrament of the blood). It was initiated by Berengar, rector of the Cathedral School of Tours. At the time, an extremely "thingly" concept of being held sway over the theological understanding of the eucharistic sacramental presence of Christ. It was inevitable that this extreme realism would produce a reaction in the direction of symbolic thinking. Within the thinking of the day, however—and this is what magnified the crisis—signs were accorded only a gnoseological character. Signs did not "contain," were not identified with, did not participate in, the reality they signified. Hence the question could be posed: Is Christ "really" present, or is he present only "symbolically"?

Berengar thought through philosophically the consequences of the thingly concept of being. He applied this to the Eucharist, and ended up by extending the ninth-century explanation of Ratramnus to its logical conclusion. Berengar is dependent in part on Ratramnus's theological reflection, whose work he attributed to John Scotus Erigena. In Berengar's systematic thinking, the opposition between *veritas* and *figura* play an important role. Bread and wine "are not the true body, nor the true blood, but a figure or likeness *(figura . . . similitudo).*" He

---

expositione missae 63 (PL 119.55C); reference to Gregory the Great *[iterum], Dialogues* 4.58 (PL 77.425 [see above, p. 76]).

distinguishes sharply between the sign and the *signatum*, between the body and blood of Christ, as *res sacramenti*, and the *sacramentum*.

Berengar's singular contribution to the development of Latin theology of the Eucharist is his analysis of the process of change whereby the elements of bread and wine become the sacrament of the body and blood of Christ. This involves a sensual concept of *substantia*, that is, where the substance or *forma* of a thing is the sum of sensible, perceptible properties. This led him to conclude that the "substance of bread does not change into the sacrament of the body of the Lord."[39] The process consists in this: the bread and wine become symbols of the body and blood; Christ works gracefully through these symbols in the spirit of the believers.

While Berengar placed *veritas* vis-à-vis *figura*, he actually analyzed the process of change! This is new. During the Carolingian period the question was posed: What are bread and wine? But in the instance of the eucharistic consecration, the basic question is really: What change takes place, and how is it to be conceived? Within the context of a way of thinking in which the real is opposed to the symbolic, questions eventually arise concerning the exact time of the change, and the exact instrumental cause of the change. When and by what means does the change take place?

Since the time of Berengar, and largely because of the controversy associated with his eucharistic teaching, the following questions have been explicitly asked by theologians: (1) What are bread and wine? (2) What change takes place with the bread and wine? (3) How is the change to be conceived? (4) When does the change take place? (5) By what instrumental cause does the change take place?

Berengar's response to some of these questions can be formulated in the following ways. *What are bread and wine?* The substance of bread and wine is the sum of sensible properties. *What kind of change takes place?* The sensible properties of bread and wine remain unchanged. Nothing happens to the substance, which is the *veritas* of the bread and wine, except that the bread and wine become symbols through which Christ works gracefully in the spirit of the faithful. The sphere of the symbol does not touch the reality, but the symbol is related to

[39] "Sapis enim contra omnis naturae rationes, contra evangelicam et apostolicam sententiam, si cum Paschasio sapis, in eo quod solus sibi confingit sacramento Dominici corporis decedere panis omnino substantiam"—Berengar of Tours, *Epistola ad Ascelinum* (PL 150.66B).

the grace of the Eucharist by extrinsic denomination in virtue of its institutional (i.e., by Christ) origin.

The reaction of so-called traditionalists to Berengar's eucharistic theology set in motion the official inquiry of the Roman magisterium. Berengar was invited to a synod in Rome, scheduled for April 1050, under Pope Leo IX. But apparently he was already excommunicated before his arrival.[40] In September 1050, he was newly judged in a synod convened at Vercelli, at which his opponent Lanfranc of Bec (1010–1089) was present. In 1051 Berengar had a public debate with Lanfranc at Brionne. Finally, in a Roman synod of 1059, under humiliating circumstances, Berengar had to burn his books before Pope Nicholas II and confess a formula that satisfied the contemporary Roman view of the essentials of the eucharistic somatic presence of the body and blood of Christ.[41] However, in 1076, Berengar renewed his previous teaching in *Rescriptum contra Lanfrancum*.[42] Afterward, in 1079, a synod under Gregory VII demanded from him an altered confession of faith concerning eucharistic realism.[43]

The oath required of Berengar at the Council of Rome of 1059, composed by Cardinal Humbertus a Silva Candida, states in part:

"I, Berengar, . . . anathematize all heresy, especially that . . . which attempts to restrict the bread and wine which are placed on the altar, to be, after the consecration, only the sacrament and not the true body and blood of our Lord Jesus Christ which are sensually touched or broken or torn apart by the teeth of the faithful. I consent, however, to the holy Roman Church and Apostolic See, and profess by mouth

[40] See Lanfranc, *De corpore et sanguine Domini* 4 (PL 150.413B): (addressing Berengar) ". . . promulgata est in te damnationis sententia, privans te communione sanctae Ecclesiae, quam tu privare sancta ejus communione satagebas."

[41] Ibid., 4 (PL 150.409B-C). For the profession of faith: DS 690.

[42] Berengar of Tours, *Rescriptum contra Lanfranum,* formerly known as *De sacra coena,* ed. R.B.C. Huygens, CCCM 84 (1988). The most complete modern edition of Berengar's works is by W. H. Beekenkamp, vol. 1: *De avondmalsleer van Berengarius van Tours;* vol. 2: *De Sacra Coena adversus Lanfrancum* (The Hague, 1941). For background and sequel to the Berengarian controversy, see Gary Macy, *The Theologies of the Eucharist in the Early Scholastic Period* (Oxford, 1984). For quick orientation and initial bibliography: O. Capitani, "Berengar v. Tours," *Lexikon des Mittelalters* 1 (1980) 1937–39, and Goeffrey Wainwright, "Berengar of Tours," *Encyclopedia of Religion* 2 (1987) 112–13.

[43] The article "Early Scholastic Contribution to Eucharistic Theology" in vol. 2 of Beekenkamp contains an extended treatment of the content of the two oaths which were forced on Berengar.

and heart concerning the sacrament of the Lord's table to hold that faith, which the Lord and venerable Pope Nicolaus and this holy synod handed on to be maintained by evangelical and apostolic authority: namely that the bread and wine which are placed on the altar, after the consecration, are not only the sacrament, but also the true body and blood of our Lord Jesus Christ, and sensually, not only by sacrament, but in truth, are touched, broken and torn apart by the teeth of the faithful."[44]

The oath distinguishes between two effects which obtain "after the consecration": the bread and wine become "sacrament," but also the "true body and blood of Jesus Christ our Lord." In the case of the second effect, the somatic presence of the true body and blood is explicitly affirmed in terms that are reminiscent of the theological outlook of Paschasius Radbertus.

At the Council of Rome of 1079, under Pope Gregory VII, Berengar was required to confess this alternative:

"I, Berengar, believe in the heart and confess by mouth, that the bread and wine, which are placed on the altar, through the mystery of the holy prayer and the words of our Redeemer, are converted substantially into the true and proper and vivifying flesh and blood of Jesus Christ our Lord. After the consecration they are the true body of Christ, which was born of the Virgin, and which hung on the cross as an offering for the salvation of the world, and which sits at the right hand of the Father, and the true blood of Christ which was poured forth from his side, and not merely by virtue of the sign and power of the sacrament but in the property of nature and truth of substance."[45]

[44] "Ego Berengarius . . . anathematizo omnem haeresim, praecipue eam . . . quae adstruere conatur, panem et vinum, quae in altari ponuntur, post consecrationem solummodo sacramentum, et non verum corpus et sanguinem Domini nostri Iesu Christi esse, nec posse sensualiter, nisi in solo sacramento, manibus sacerdotum tractari vel frangi vel fidelium dentibus atteri. Consentio autem sanctae Romanae Ecclesiae et Apostolicae Sedi, et ore et corde profiteor de sacramento dominicae mensae eam fidem me tenere, quam dominus et venerabilis papa Nicolaus et haec sancta Synodus auctoritate evangelica et apostolica tenendam tradidit mihique firmavit: scilicet panem et vinum, quae in altari ponuntur, post consecrationem non solum sacramentum, sed etiam verum corpus et sanguinem Domini nostri Iesu Christi esse, et sensualiter, non solum sacramento, sed in veritate, manibus sacerdotum tractari et frangi et fidelium dentibus atteri"—DS 690.

[45] "Ego Berengarius corde credo et ore confiteor, panem et vinum, quae ponuntur in altari, per mysterium sacrae orationis et verba nostri Redemptoris substan-

This oath identifies the source of the conversion of the bread and wine: "the mystery of the holy prayer and the words of our Redeemer." Through the conversion they are the "vivifying flesh and blood of Jesus Christ." As a consequence, "after the consecration" what was bread and wine are the body "born of the Virgin . . . which hung on the cross . . . and which sits at the right hand of the Father, and the true blood of Christ which was poured forth from his side and not merely by virtue of the sign and power of the sacrament." It is especially noteworthy that the second oath affirms the presence of the body born of the virgin, which hung on the cross and which sits at the "right hand of the Father."

The register of the Council of Rome of 1079 sheds some light on this latter confession. It is recorded that "the majority affirmed that the bread and wine, through the words of the sacred prayer and the consecration of the priest, the Holy Spirit working invisibly, are converted."[46] Here the "words of the sacred prayer and the consecration of the priest" are identified as the instrumental means by which the Holy Spirit converts the bread and wine.

In short, the first oath uses consecration to describe the action by which the bread and wine become sacraments and also the "body and blood of Christ." The second oath attributes the conversion of the bread and wine to the "mystery of the holy prayer and the words of the Redeemer." The register of the council supplies another formulation which unpacks the meaning intended by this concise expression. Putting the two formulations together the following result obtains:

"The bread and wine . . . are converted through the mystery (that is, through 'the Holy Spirit working invisibly') of the holy prayer and the words of the Redeemer (that is, 'through the consecration of the priest,' or through the words of consecration of the Redeemer spoken by the priest)."

---

tialiter converti in veram et propriam ac vivificatricem carnem et sanguinem Iesu Christi Domini nostri et post consecrationem esse verum Christi corpus, quod natum est de Virgine et quod pro salute mundi oblatum in cruce pependit, et quod sedet ad dexteram Patris, et verum sanguinem Christi, qui de latere eius effusus est, non tantum per signum et virtutem sacramenti, sed in proprietate naturae et veritate substantiae"—DS 700.

[46] "Maxima siquidem pars panem et vinum [per] sacrae orationis verba et sacerdotis consecrationem, Spiritu Sancto invisibiliter operante, converti substantialiter in corpus Dominicum de Virgine natum, quod et in cruce pependit, et in sanguinem qui de ejus latere militis effusus est lancea, asserebat"—PL 148.811A-B.

Moreover, in the second oath, the content of the sacrament is specified more exactly as the "vivifying flesh and blood" of Christ, or the historical and glorified body of Christ.

It should not be overlooked that the statement of the second oath concerning the presence of the "true body of Christ" identifies this body in terms reminiscent of the patristic distinction between the historical body of Christ and the body of the risen Lord in heaven. This formulation seems to have been influenced by the commonly held understanding of the process of sanctification as one in which the bread and wine become the sacrament of the body and blood of Christ and then are transferred to heaven to be united to the heavenly risen body of Christ. Regarding this subject, already discussed in part three of chapter one (above pp. 61, 65–66, 76, 78), it will suffice to recall the teaching of representative contemporary theologians, among whom Odo of Cambrai (ca. 1050–1113) and Honorius Augustodunensis (fl. ca. 1098–1130), can serve as examples.[47]

A. ODO OF CAMBRAI

In his *Expositio in canonem misssae,*[48] Odo comments on the *sanctificas* of the *Per quem haec omnia.* Here he says that "daily he [Deus] sanctifies by the prayer of the priest and the cooperation of the Holy Spirit."[49] The prayer of the priest is the section of the Eucharistic Prayer from the *Quam oblationem* through the *Supplices.* This prayer is said to be spoken by the priest as representative of the universal Church in the case of the private Mass. Otherwise Odo recognizes that the gathered community is first and foremost the celebrating Church. Hence Odo understands that the prayer of the priest is the prayer of the Church. This prayer can only be carried out fruitfully "with the cooperation of the Holy Spirit."[50] Since the Holy Spirit co-

[47] [This is a fine example of the need to be able to step out of one's own worldview. For if one assumes that consecration/sanctification refers only or primarily to the substantial transformation of the table gifts, one will not understand the rich meaning it had for these medieval theologians—RJD.]

[49] "Quotidie [Deus] sanctificat, oratione sacerdotis et cooperatione Spiritus sancti"—ibid. (PL 160.1069A).

[50] The phrase *cooperante Spiritu sancto* is found, in the Roman liturgy, in the second communion prayer of the priest *(Domine Iesu Christi),* where it refers to the cooperation of the Holy Spirit in the redemptive death of Jesus. It remains an optional prayer in the Missal of Paul VI. This prayer first appeared in the private

operates only within the Church in this activity, Odo concludes that the Eucharist can only be celebrated in the Church. "For outside the communion there is no place for offering to God true sacrifice."[51] And by this he means also that heretics cannot celebrate the Eucharist: The "for us" of the *Quam oblationem* "excludes pagans, it excludes Jews, it excludes heretics. . . . For there is no place of true sacrifice outside the Catholic Church."[52]

The attribution of the efficacy of the Eucharistic Prayer to the cooperation of the Holy Spirit working in and through the believing Church is an example of "appropriation" of an activity of the whole Trinity to one of the divine persons because it fits the traits of that person. This also holds for the attribution of the conversion of the bread and wine to the Holy Spirit which is frequently found in the writings of early scholastics. However, there is one exception to this rule, a contemporary of Odo, Rupert of Deutz. His teaching about the trinitarian missions of Word and Spirit, especially with reference to the Eucharist, can be quickly summarized.

Rupert of Deutz (1075–1129) follows the Western theological line concerning the procession of the Spirit from the Father and the Son. However, he also appears to teach a typical Eastern trinitarian theology concerning the personal and proper missions of the Holy Spirit, for, at least in his *Commentary on Exodus,* he assigns to the Holy Spirit the personal and proper role of sanctifier of the bread and wine.

Rupert does not refer to the role of the Spirit in his *De divinis officiis.*[53] However, he holds for an *actio propria* of each person of the Trinity in the work *ad extra.* All three divine persons act together in the world, but there is a proper action of each person. In his *De trinitate,* Rupert identifies the proper action of the Word as that of bestowing the *imago dei* on his humanity, while that of the Spirit consists in effecting the *similitudo dei,* the likeness of the common

---

prayer books of the late ninth century: the Prayer Book of Charles the Bald; the ninth-century mixed Gallican Sacramentary of Amiens. In the eleventh century it is found in a version of communion devotions of Monte Cassino as a prayer for communicants.

[51] "Extra communionem namque non est locus offerendi Deo veri sacrificii vel vota solvendi"—Odo of Cambrai, *Expositio in canonem missae* (PL 160.1058C).

[52] "*Nobis* exclusit paganos, exclusit Judaeos, exclusit haereticos . . . Non est enim locus veri sacrificii, extra catholicam Ecclesiam"—ibid. (PL 160.1061D).

[53] Rupert of Deutz, *De divinis officiis,* ed. Hrabanus Haacke, CCCM 7 (Turnhout: Brepols, 1967).

love of the Father and the Son.[54] In the mission of the Spirit, the Father and the Son are the sending principle, since the Spirit proceeds from the Father and the Son.[55] In the *De sandaliis* of the *De divinis officiis,* Rupert teaches that the Holy Spirit is the bond by which the Word unites himself to the flesh.[56] But only in his *Commentary on Exodus* (see below) does Rupert explicitly refer to the proper operation of the Spirit in the eucharistic conversion.

His *Commentary on the Fourth Gospel* explains that, in the eucharistic change, the bread and wine are taken up into the sphere of the divine: "And this the Word . . . is made visible bread by assimilating and transferring bread into the unity of his person."[57] In his *Commentary on Exodus,* however, the change is attributed to the Holy Spirit: "The Virgin conceived him by the Holy Spirit and through the same Spirit . . . this one offered himself a living victim to the living God."[58] Then he goes on to say: "For by the operation of the Holy Spirit, the bread is made the body and the wine the blood of Christ."[59] Rupert then goes on to develop the idea that both the Incarnation and the eucharistic conversion are attributed to the Holy Spirit.[60] Hence the Holy Spirit is now awarded a proper activity in the sanctification of the bread and wine.

[54] Rupert of Deutz, *De sancta trinitate et operibus eius,* ed. Hrabanus Haacke, CCCM 21–24 (Turnhout: Brepols, 1971–72), here: *De operibus Spiritus Sancti* 1.10 (CCCM 24.1831–32; PL 167.1579C-D).

[55] Ibid., 1.5 (CCCM 24.1826–27; PL 167.1574D–1575C).

[56] *De divinis officiis* 11.24 (CCCM 7.513–16).

[57] "Proinde sicut de carne nostra, quam Virgo Maria peperit, uere fatemur propter unitatem personae, quia Deus est, sic nihilominus de pane isto uisibili quem eiusdem Verbi inuisibilis diuinitas assumemus in carnem suam transfert"—Rupert of Deutz, *In Iohannis evangelium* 6:52 (CCCM 9.357.2218–21).

[58] "Virgo illum concepit, et ipse per eundem Spiritum sanctum, ut apostolus ait, obtulit semetipsum hostiam uiuam Deo uiuenti"—Rupert of Deutz, *De sancta trinitate,* here: *In Exodum* 2.10 (CCCM 22.646.443–45).

[59] "Operatione namque Spiritus sancti panis corpus et uinum fit sanguis Christi"—ibid., 446–47.

[60] "Sed comedetis, inquit assum tantum igni, id est, totum attribuetis operationi Spiritus sancti, cuius effectus non est destruere vel corrumpere substantiam, quamcumque suos in usus assumit, sed substantiae bono permanenti quod erat, inuisibiliter adicere quod non erat. Sicut humanam naturam non destruxit, cum illam operatione sua ex utero Virginis Deus Verbo in unitatem personae coniunxit, sic substantiam panis et uini, secundum exteriorem speciem quinque sensibus subiectam, non mutat aut destruit, cum eidem Verbo in unitatem corporis eiusdem quod in cruce pependit, et sanguinis eiusdem quem de latere suo fudit, ista con-

Odo himself understands that the Father creates the flesh and blood of Christ from bread and wine through Christ insofar as Word of God. Thus, for example, in the commentary on the *Per ipsum* he says:

"'Through whom (Christ) the Father creates flesh from bread . . .'[61] In the Mass Christ is acting as divine person: 'Truly your word is all-powerful . . . . Therefore the body and blood of Christ is made by the speech of Christ. As often as we receive these through the agency of the powerful word . . .'"[62]

But there is still the matter of the transfer of the gifts to the heavenly altar, expressed in the *Supplices.* Odo says that this transfer is not a transfer of place:

"In the same place what was bread becomes the flesh of the Word. It is not transferred from a place, in order that from bread flesh is made; nevertheless it is transferred from the altar to heaven, because it is transferred from bread to God. But because God is everywhere, it is not done by a change of place in order that flesh made from bread may be joined to God."[63]

From this analysis we can conclude that Odo attributes a special effect to the working of the Holy Spirit in the prayer of the Church, which is distinguished from the instrumental effect of the words of Christ contained in the account of institution of the Eucharist. While the Holy Spirit is the source of the acceptability of the eucharistic

iungit. Item quomodo Verbum a summo demissum caro factum est, non mutatum in carnem sed assumendo carnem, sic panis et uinum, utrumque ab imo subleuatum; fit corpus et sanguis Christi, non mutatum in carnis saporem siue in sanguinis horrorem, sed assumendo inuisibiliter utriusque diuinae scilicet et humanae, quae in Christo est, immortalis substantiae ueritatem. Proinde sicut hominem, qui de Virgine sumptus in cruce pependit, recte et catholice Deum confitemur, sic veraciter hoc quod sumimus de sancto altari, Christum dicimus, agnum Dei praedicamus"—ibid., 647.453–73.

[61] "Per quem Pater de pane carnem creat . . ."—Odo of Cambrai, *Expositio in canonem missae* (PL 160.1069B).

[62] "Etenim omnipotens sermo tuus, o Genitor. Fit ergo sermone Christi corpus et sanguis Christi. Quae quoties verbo potenti sumimus, mortem Domini, donec veniat, memoramus (1 Cor. II)"—ibid., 1063D.

[63] "Sed, sub eodem loco, qui panis erat fit Verbi caro. Non transfertur loco, ut de pane fiat caro; transfertur tamen ab altari ad coelum, quia transfertur de pane ad Deum. Sed quia Deus est ubique, non fit loci mutatione, ut conjungatur Deo de pane facta caro"—ibid., 1067A.

prayer of the Church, the creative power of Christ's divinity makes the sacrament of the body and blood from the eucharistic elements.

Furthermore, Odo distinguishes between the sacrament of the body and blood on the earthly altar and the transference of it to the realm of the divine to be joined to God, associated with the petition of the earthly Church expressed in the *Supplices* prayer. This implies that the notion of "sanctification" has a broader meaning than that of "conversion" of the bread and wine into the eucharistic flesh and blood. It includes the idea of transfer of the sacraments of the body and blood to the sphere of heaven and joined to the risen Lord.

Odo continues on this subject, explaining how the faithful are included in the process. Commenting on the *Supplices* prayer, the ecclesiological aspect of the petition is clarified with the help of the metaphor of shepherd and sheep. As the shepherd places the sheep on his shoulders when bearing it to the altar of sacrifice, so this prayer petitions that the *"homo assumptus a Verbo* be carried to the altar on high." Since the Word of God "is the sublime altar," the prayer asks that "the *hostia* be carried into the sight of God, . . . the Word of the Father," and that "through it we be introduced." It is in this way that "daily the Word of God assumes to himself the faithful, by the participation of this sacrifice." Odo concludes this pericope thus:

"Therefore to carry the victim to the sublime altar, to the sight of God, what is it, except that our oblation be joined to the Word, be united to the Word, be made God *(fieri Deum),* and through it we be assumed into God and our devotion accepted."[64]

[64] The full text without the ellipses, reads: "Quid est perferri hostiam in sublime altare, nisi ovem humeris Pastoris imponi? Et quid ovis humeris imposita, nisi homo assumptus a Verbo? Et quid est sublimius Verbo Dei? Quotidie assumit sibi fideles Verbum Dei, participatione hujus sacrificii. Verbum ergo Dei sublime altare est, ad quod oramus hostiam perferri in conspectu Dei, et per eam nos introduci. Conspectus Dei est Verbum Patris, in quo conspicit omne quod fecit. Nam omne quod agit Pater, in Verbo ejus est. Nam *quod factum est, in ipso vita erat* (Joan. I); et: *In principio creavit Deus caelum et terram* (*Gen.* I), id est in verbo, et: *Verbo Domini caeli firmati sunt* (*Psal.* XXXII); et: *Omnia in sapientia fecisti* (*Psal.* CIII). Quid rectius dicitur conspectus Dei quam Sapientia sua, in qua conspicit omne quod agit? Hostiam ergo perferri in sublime altare, in conspectu Dei, quid est, nisi oblationem nostram conjungi Verbo, uniri Verbo, fieri Deum, et per eam nos in Deum assumi, et vota nostra acceptari?"—ibid., 1067C-D).

B. HONORIUS AUGUSTODUNENSIS

Another contemporary, Honorius Augustodunensis (fl. ca. 1098–1130), in *Gemma animae*,[65] uses consecration when referring to the action by which the Holy Spirit makes the sacraments of the body and blood. He also states that the consecration "ought not to be celebrated without light, for light signifies the Holy Spirit, who consecrates the sacrament."[66] This means, as Honorius says elsewhere, that the "seven gifts of the Holy Spirit confect the sacraments of the Mass."[67]

In the *Eucharistion* he refers to the three bodies of Christ, the one born of the Virgin, the eucharistic body, and the body of Christ which is the Church. In regard to the second (the eucharistic) body he says:

"It is called the body of the Lord which, handed on as pledge of the Church by the consecrating Holy Spirit, is confected from the substance of bread and wine daily by the mystery of priests, and transferred into the said body by the divinity operating."[68]

The mystery of priests refers to the function of the priest to act as ambassador of Christ to the people (Christ being the ambassador of the Father) and as ambassador of the Church to the Lord.[69] The notion of the elevation of the sacrament of the body and blood is attributed to a divine action differentiated from that by which the sacrament is confected.

In his commentary on the *Qui pridie*, the consecration is attributed to the words of Christ:

[65] Honorius Augustodunensis, *Gemma animae sive de divinis officiis et antiquo ritu missarum, deque horis canonicis et totius annis solemnitatibus* (PL 172.543–738B).

[66] "Lumen Spiritum sanctum significat, ideo cum lumine missa celebratur, quia hoc sacramentum per Spiritum sanctum consecratur"—*Gemma animae* 1.118 (PL 172.583A).

[67] "Et quia septem dona Spiritus sancti sacramenta missae conficiunt"—*Gemma animae* 1.9 (PL 172.547B).

[68] "Secundo: Corpus Domini dicitur, quod ob pignus Ecclesiae traditum Spiritu sancto consecrante ex substantia panis et vini mysterio sacerdotum quotidie conficitur, ac Divinitate operante in praedictum corpus transfertur"—Honorius Augustodunensis, *Eucharisti[c]on, seu liber de corpore et sanguine Domini* (PL 172.1249–58) at chap. 1 (PL 172.1250A).

[69] "*Missa* quippe dicitur legatio: 1° Quia in ejus officio nobis legatio Christi repraesentatur, qua pro humano genere patris legatione fungebatur. 2° Item missa legatio dicitur, quia in ea sacerdos pro Ecclesia ad dominum legatione fungitur"—*Gemma animae* 1.2 (PL 172.543A).

"As the world was made from nothing by the word of the Lord, so through the words of the Lord the appearance of things is truly changed into the body of the Lord."[70]

In *Eucharisticon*, on this same subject, he writes:

"Christ . . . who had formed his body in the womb of the Virgin, is alone the one who consecrates this body through any catholic priest. . . . Outside the Church . . . this sacrifice is not accomplished by heretics . . . . However simonaics, who . . . are connected to Catholics by an integral faith, confect the body of Christ by trinitarian faith."[71]

In brief, Honorius teaches that Christ confects, i.e., consecrates, by his creative word. The Holy Spirit is a kind of divine agent of consecration. This activity is only appropriated to the Spirit because the whole Trinity is understood to operate the consecration. Finally "consecration" refers to the action of the Holy Spirit or Christ by which the bread and wine are converted into the eucharistic body of the Lord. This consecration is apparently *ordered to* the movement by which the sacrament of the body of Christ is transferred to the heavenly realm to be united to the heavenly glorified flesh of Christ. But it is not certain that the term actually implies the broader notion of "consecration" which includes not just the conversion of the bread and wine, but also the aspect of the transfer of the sacrament to the heavenly realm.

IV. THE RELATIONSHIP OF THE CROSS TO THE MASS

In the period of early scholasticism, there existed a fairly uniform understanding of the sacrificial aspect of the eucharistic liturgy. Alger of Liège (d. 1130) can serve as representative of the early scholastic understanding of the relationship of the cross to the Mass. He locates the identity of the sacrifice of the cross with that of the Mass in the reality of the eucharistic body and blood of Christ: "It is, therefore, to be noted that our daily sacrifice is the same as that wherein Christ offered

[70] "Sicut Verbo Domini ex nihilo factus est mundus, ita per verba Domini haec species rerum mutatur vere in Domini corpus"—*Gemma animae* 1.105 (PL 172.578C).

[71] "Christus . . . qui corpus suum in utero virginis formaverat, solus etiam per quemlibet catholicum sacerdotem hoc ipsum consecrat . . . . Extra ecclesiam autem, scilicet ab haereticis . . . nec hoc sacramento perficitur . . . Simoniaci tamen, qui . . . fide integerrima Catholicis admiscentur, per fidem Trinitatis Christi corpus conficiunt . . ."—*Eucharistion* 6 (PL 172.1253B-C).

himself once for all on the cross, insofar as here and there is the same true substance of the body of Christ."[72] He solves the question of the unique sacrifice of Christ and its sufficiency for all times in this way:

"Therefore because it is impossible to confer another salvation, the sacrifice that was offered once must be the same as our daily sacrifice, so that the same one be not superfluous, but the same always sufficient and always necessary."[73]

However correct this last statement may be, for Alger the real identity of the Mass and sacrifice of the cross is grounded only on the identity of the victim:

"Although the oblation of Christ once on the cross is true *(vera)*, although the daily one on the altar is figurative *(figurata)*, nevertheless, indeed, here and there is the grace of our salvation . . . because here and there the true Christ is *potens ad omnia*."[74]

A detailed explanation of how the eucharistic sacrifice was related to the cross in the period from the thirteenth century to the twentieth century will be provided in the following chapters. For now, at the end of chapter two, we turn to the problem of the origin of the Mass stipend practice which is rooted in the early Middle Ages. Following that, in chapter three we will focus our attention on the period at the close of early scholasticism, in order to note the changing orientation regarding eucharistic theology.

V. THE ORIGIN OF THE PRACTICE OF THE MASS STIPEND: FROM COMMUNAL TO INDIVIDUAL ACTIVITY

The practice by which the faithful make offerings in connection with the eucharistic celebration as a particular mode of active participation

[72] "Notandum ergo quia quotidianum nostrum sacrificium idem ipsum dicit cum eo, quo Christus semel oblatus est in cruce, quantum ad eandem veram hic et ibi corporis Christi substantiam"—Alger of Liège, *De sacramento corporis et sanguinis Domini libri tres* (PL 180.739–854).

[73] "Quia ergo impossibile est aliam conferri salutem, oportet eamdem esse illam semel oblatam, et nostram quotidianam oblationem, ut eadem sibi ipsi non sit superflua, sed eadem semper sufficiens et semper necessaria"—ibid., 786C.

[74] "Licet oblatio Christi semel in cruce sit vera, quotidiana autem in altari sit figurata; prorsus tamen eadem hic et ibi nostrae salutis est gratia . . quia hic et ibi idem verus Christus potens est ad omnia"—ibid., 787B-C.

in the eucharistic sacrifice has a long history. Such offerings are the symbolic expression not only of one's spiritual union with the sacrificial worship of Christ, but also of one's membership in the celebration of the faith of the hierarchically organized local Catholic community.

A uniquely Western Latin practice, as distinguished from that of the Eastern tradition, is generally acknowledged to have originated in the Roman provinces of Africa and taken the form of an offertory procession. This ritual act, which was an extension of the earlier practice by which the faithful brought bread and wine for use in the eucharistic celebration, was in vogue in third-century North Africa, and possibly at Rome. In the fourth century, it was in use at Milan, Aquileia, as well as in Spain. The custom was for the faithful to carry bread and mixed wine to the altar, and from these offerings the priest selected what was required for the eucharistic consecration, the rest being distributed in favor of the needy. These offerings by the faithful were conceived as the expression of their co-offering of the eucharistic sacrifice with and through the presiding bishop or presbyter. The meaning of this practice derives from the understanding of the celebration as a constellation of prayers and actions in which each participant had a role to play in the realization of the one sacrificial worship.

This ante-Nicene practice, received in other Western churches beginning in the fifth century, gradually took on a new meaning accompanied by corresponding external changes. In the new (Western) environment, alongside bread and wine, other gifts of value were added. Obviously the symbolism of the old offertory procession was no longer functioning undisturbed. Whereas the original communality of the gifts signaled a communal act in which the differentiation of the offerers is not expressed, the new practice of offering a variety of gifts underscored the individuality of the offerers. The theological outlook that exercised considerable influence on the development of the new practice was the understanding of the eucharistic worship as a unified sacrificial act performed by the priest on behalf of the community and in the name of Christ. The offering of gifts was considered to be the expression of the desire of the faithful to participate in the celebration—which in the West came to be seen increasingly, eventually even primarily, as an act of the priest—by adding a kind of sacrifice of their own.

In the fifth century this new practice of the offertory procession had already begun to penetrate the church of Rome. However the new meaning implied in this practice was not highlighted. Here, as in North Africa, the symbolism of the co-offering of the faithful was maintained. But the way was already opened to a more individualistic understanding of the offertory procession which emerged in the Roman Church before the end of the first millennium.

This adaptation of the old offertory procession eventually resulted in the loss of its original meaning. It no longer appeared to be an activity performed by members of a community which is owned in common, but rather as activities which belong to individual members as such. This tributary of the old offertory procession continued down to the age of early scholasticism. However, it was not the only one that existed in the latter part of the first millennium. Rather, a completely new form, which had roots in the seventh century, began to emerge in the eighth century in Gaul, Spain, the British Isles, and France. It was fairly widespread elsewhere in the West by the middle of the ninth century. It is this new form that eventually proved to be the forerunner of the practice of the Mass stipend, that was fully established by the thirteenth century.

The material gifts offered in the tributary of the offertory procession consisted of fruits of nature and money. But, in the process of the development, the preference for gifts of money or other valuables over the products of nature was already manifested at the end of the first millennium.

There is a certain continuity in discontinuity in the matter of the reasons and goal of the developments that took place in the custom of making offerings for the Eucharist. The original offertory procession furnished more bread and mixed wine than was required for the eucharistic consecration. What was left over contributed to the support of the needy. But the precise reason for the offering of bread and wine, as has been said, was the desire to be engaged in a corporate act as a member of the Church. No special divine consideration was expected. But then, with the more individualistic understanding of the act of offering gifts, the motivation shifted to a stress on the special interests of the offerer.

The practice of adding a gift during the eucharistic celebration, whether before or during Mass (and in addition to the later form of the offertory procession), is well attested in the eighth century. It has earlier roots than this, and in any case it took on the same meaning as individualized participation in the "offertory." Whether the gift was offered beforehand, or in the Mass itself, the donor could be understood as co-offering in the Mass in a special way through the gift, with and through the priest, even when the gift no longer served the communitarian function of the old offertory procession. The practice of placing one's gift before God in the Eucharist was an expression of one's devotion and a way of contributing to the needs of the Church and its ministers. Also, normally, it was motivated by the desire to have one's particular interests placed before God by the priest who would act as representative of the donor by making the donor's intention his own in the prayer of the Mass. However, an important distinction must be made between two first-millennium understandings of the practice of offering a gift to a priest in order that one's intention might be included explicitly in his intercessory prayer in the Mass.

One of these understandings is based on the old Roman notion of gift-giving which does not entail reciprocity. Gifts freely given are freely received without the obligation of recompense. From this point of view the priest who accepts the gift given in view of a special remembrance at Mass is considered to be bound in charity—but not, strictly, in justice—to remember the donor's intention. But there is another understanding of gift-giving which gave rise to a different understanding of the relationship of the priest to the donor of a gift. In this other understanding, the gift is made with the request for a special remembrance in the Mass. This fully new form took shape in the German milieu which was mentioned above.

A. THE GERMAN PRACTICE

When the tributary of the old offertory procession took hold in the Frankish territories, a new meaning accrued to the gift and, consequently, to the relationship between donor and priest. Here the gift was instinctively understood to imply *reciprocity* of gift-giving. In the legal system, the juridical overtones carried through: the gifts remained recoverable unless sealed with a comparable gift. The principle was applied to the exchange between material gifts offered by the laity and spiritual gifts offered by the Church in return. For example, Mass foundations were exchanged for gifts of land, monasteries, etc. Also, in the matter of gifts given to the priest for special remembrance in a Mass, the concept of a holy *commercium* was not absent.

This system appeared first in Gaul, West Gothic Spain, and the British Isles. By the middle of the ninth century it had become fairly widespread. It was found even in the environs of the church of Rome. A notable development of this new form was occasioned by the conviction of the importance of placing oneself on the side of the priest "mediator" in order to share more fully in the blessings of the Mass. This understanding of the priest's role in the Eucharist, as analogous to that of the Old Testament priest, led to the persuasion that one gains more blessings from the Mass if the priest agrees to celebrate the Mass for one donor only to the exclusion of other donors of gifts. This notion was also shared by priests and put into practice.

From the ninth to the twelfth centuries the old Roman notion of free gift and also free access of donors of offerings to the Mass remained alive despite the new development in Frankish lands and elsewhere. The reaction of the Synod of Rome of 826, under Pope Eugene, showed that the new practice had made inroads into the regions of the Roman church, but was considered unacceptable there. Against the Gallican custom the synod stressed that the priest should, under no circumstances, refuse the gifts of all who come to the Mass. For he must be there for all as "mediator of God and humanity," otherwise it might appear that the "Redeemer was not able to accept the prayers of all and loosen the bonds of all sins."[75] Nevertheless, during this same period, from the ninth to the close of the eleventh century, one can find only a few theologians who reject the Gallican practice.

In the end, and under very precise conditions for such transactions, including their juridical consequences, and with the full approval of ecclesiastical authorities, the practice of celebrating distinct Masses for distinct intentions of individual donors of offerings became the rule everywhere. Moreover this pastoral practice now served as a very important source of the theology of the efficacy of the Mass. The question to be addressed now was: What does this practice of the Church, based on the insight of faith, imply for the efficacy of the Mass?

[75] Canon 17 reads: "*De presbyteris, qui pro unius oblatione alterius recipere nolunt.* Presbyteri nullius blandiuntur aut suadeantur sermonibus, ut non omnium ad se concurrentium in quibuslibet sacris locis oblationes ad missarum solemnitatem recipiant, quia, cum mediatores Dei hominumque existunt, in exercendis votis relaxandisque peccatis largissimam debent orationem peragere. Si quis autem contra haec temerator extiterit, aut desinat aut doctoris proprii constringatur sententia. Redemptor etenim noster, cum sit omnipotens inmensaeque misericordiae plenus, quantorum populorum vota non recipit et vincula peccatorum unatenus non resolvit! *Forma minor.* XVII. Presbyter pro unius oblatione alterius non spernat"—"46. Concilium Romanum. 826. Nov. 14.15," canon 17 (MGH Legum Sectio III. Concilia. Tomi II. Pars I [1906] 575.1–9).

B. THEOLOGICAL BACKGROUND FOR FURTHER DEVELOPMENTS

In order to understand the response given by theologians to this question, it is necessary to backtrack historically and take account of certain other developments which began to emerge at the end of the first millennium and flowered in the period up to the close of early scholasticism.

In the first place, a new understanding of the role of the faithful as co-offerers of the eucharistic sacrifice gradually emerged. This was influenced by a theology of priesthood in which priests were not only conceived as mediators on analogy with the Old Testament priests, they were also seen as having been enabled by their ordination to preside at the eucharistic celebration with the power to offer sacrifice. This theology was already formulated by the end of the first millennium. Moreover, in the context of this theology, the gift-giving of the laity at the eucharistic celebration and in the ritual offertory procession was viewed, on analogy with the Old Testament practice, as a sacrifice of almsgiving.

A further important theological development was the determining of the essential form of the eucharistic sacrifice. This took place in the course of the twelfth century. A role for the words of institution of Christ in relation to the consecration of the elements of bread and wine had been recognized by classical theologians of both East and West since the fourth century. But there was no common agreement on the explanation of that role. Early scholasticism, however, drew out the conclusion that the words of Christ, found in the narrative of institution, were the form (indeed the *forma essentialis*) of consecration. Hence, it is precisely when they are spoken by the priest that the eucharistic transformation takes place.

At this moment the priest is said to be placed precisely *on the side of Christ vis-à-vis* the liturgical assembly and to act in the name of Christ. Moreover, it was also concluded that, in this role, he also acts in the name of the Church. The laity were understood to have a part to play in the Mass, and especially in the eucharistic prayer, in which the priest acted as their representative. But they were understood to act as "hearers" and to participate by reason of their spiritual devotion.

Another noteworthy development took place in this connection. In the first millennium the idea that the local church represents the universal Church in its eucharistic celebration was clearly recognized. This idea was an important principle for determining whether a eucharistic celebration could be recognized as such. But a new development gradually emerged as the distinction between priest and people became more sharply defined. The notion of the universal Church's involvement in the eucharistic sacrifice of the local church gradually gave way to the notion of the local community's involvement in the Eucharist of the universal Church because it is part of the mystical body of Christ. This development coincided with the understanding of the priest as representative of the hierarchical institutional church which serves the mystical body of Christ. Hence the conclusion was drawn that all the members of the mystical body of Christ, present or absent, stand in the same relation to the celebration of the Eucharist through their representative, the priest. They are all able *by their devotion* to contribute to the spiritual benefits that derive from the Mass.

C. FURTHER DEVELOPMENTS

With the foregoing background in mind, a number of things become understandable regarding thirteenth-century developments. First of all, since the people were no longer understood as active subjects of the offering of the eucharistic sacrifice, the gifts given for the celebration of Masses for special intentions were ranked in the category of a contribution to the livelihood of the priest and called "stipends" or "alms." At the same time the practice of celebrating a Mass for the intention of the donor of a stipend to the exclusion of other stipend donors and their intentions seemed to imply that there is a special propitiatory and impetratory value intrinsic to the Mass prior to any consideration of the devotion of those participating in the Mass, and that this value is extensively limited prior to any subjective dispositions of the offerers and those for whom the Mass is offered. Finally the fact that such Masses can be repeatedly offered for the same intentions seemed to imply that the special fruit derived from the application of the Mass is somehow limited.

Chapter Three

Early Scholastic Contribution to Eucharistic Theology

The theological problem raised by the threefold body of Christ[1] remained alive throughout the period of the first millennium. It was inherited by early scholasticism and became a primary subject of theological reflection in the wake of what has come to be known as the second classical controversy over the theology of the sacraments of the body and blood of Christ. This eleventh-century debate, as we have seen, was initiated by Berengar of Tours. It represents a continuation of an unresolved ninth-century discussion of the same theme undertaken by Paschasius and Ratramnus, monks of Corbie.

As a result of reflection on the threefold body of Christ, early scholasticism contributed to the formulation of the theology of the composition of the eucharistic sacraments of the body and blood of Christ which has been employed down to this century. However, this gain was partially offset by a negative effect. For the development of the analysis of the composition of the eucharistic sacraments had the effect not only of weakening the conscious awareness of the eschatological dimension of the eucharistic celebration, but also of contributing to a distorted systematic theology of the sacrificial and sacramental dimensions of the liturgy of the Eucharist.

I. COMPOSITION OF THE EUCHARISTIC SACRAMENTS

It will be recalled that scholastic theologians of the eleventh century had in hand the teaching of Augustine, Ambrose, and Jerome. From

[1] The body born of the Virgin, the eucharistic body, the body of Christ which is the Church (see above under Honorius Augustodunensis in chapter two, III B, pp. 107–8).

Augustine, they learned to identify the specific grace of the sacrament as the unity of the Church. The tradition of eucharistic realism handed down from Ambrose had taught them to link this grace with the somatic real presence of Christ. Jerome's distinction between the eucharistic body and the crucified and risen body of Christ required special attention.

Augustine taught that the thing *(res)* signified by the sacrament *(sacramentum)* is the grace of unity of the Church, the body of Christ. Early scholasticism employed this Augustinian schema: *sacramentum et res,* but it identified the *res* with Christ who is both signified and really contained in the sacrament. The orientation to the person of Christ naturally led to the question of the relation of the historical body of Christ in heaven (at the right hand of the Father), to the eucharistic body of Christ (the *caro spiritualis et divina*).

In chapter two we analyzed the content of the oaths prescribed for Berengar along with texts from Odo of Cambrai and Honorius Augustodunensis. In those sources, where the term *consecratio* is employed, it is used in the narrow sense to describe the activity by which the bread and wine are converted into the body and blood of Christ. Nevertheless it is evident that this concept of *consecratio* is understood to initiate a process by which the sacrament becomes the life-giving flesh and blood of the crucified and risen Lord. This second step is described as the movement by which the sacrament is transferred to the heavenly realm where it is united to the glorified body of the risen Lord. The distinction between two effects involved in the sanctification of the eucharistic elements was commonplace in the early scholastic eucharistic theology: (1) the making of the sacrament of the body and blood, and (2) the unification of it with the body of the risen Lord by which it becomes the "vivifying flesh and blood." This whole process could conceivably be described by a notion of consecration that goes beyond the idea of conversion of the elements into the body and blood. It suggests the broader notion of consecration that also includes the concept of the transfer of the sacraments to the heavenly realm to union with the glorified Lord.

Moreover, the different meanings attached to the term consecration, the narrower and broader meaning, seem to be found in early scholasticism, especially through the version of an anonymous tractate on the subject of the eucharistic body of Christ, to which we now turn.

A. THE EARLY SCHOLASTIC TRACTATE ON THE EUCHARIST: BEYOND THE AUGUSTINIAN DYAD

The content of the anonymous early scholastic tractate *De corpore igitur Domini sic opportune videtur agendum* was discussed in chapter one, part III (above pp. 62–63). There we pointed out how the more original version made use of the simple Augustinian schema *sacramentum et res* for the analysis of the composition of the sacrament of the Eucharist, and we noted how this schema was expanded to meet the needs of a systematic theology. The expansion consisted in a schema that postulated a twofold *sacramentum* and a twofold *res.* (1.) The visible sacrament signifies the invisible *res:* the eucharistic body and blood. (2.) The invisible eucharistic body and blood signify the visible historical and glorified body of Christ. (3.) The invisible eucharistic body also signifies the unity of the Church, which is ordered to it.[2]

This explanation of the *res* signified by the sacrament gave a reasonable account of the relationship between the historical body of Christ,

[2] Confer Ludwig Hödl, "Sacramentum et Res—Zeichen und Bezeichnetes: Eine begriffsgeschichtliche Arbeit zum frühscholastischen Eucharistietraktat," *Scholastik* 38 (1963) 161–82, on the subject of the history of *sacramentum et res* in the early scholastic tracts on the Eucharist. The tractate *De corpore igitur Domini sic opportune videtur agendum* is found in many manuscripts (Hödl, 162–63). An extended form of the text (Munich Clm 2598, fol. 68^{v}–73^{r}; Fulda, cod. theol. 4° Aa 36 fol. 42ra–47rb) has worked in the brief systematic tract *In sacramento altaris septem sunt attendenda,* known from the edition of the *Sententiae Ps. Anselmi* (Hödl, 163). On the theme of the *res sacramenti,* in the shorter version of the tract *De corpore igitur* . . . , the answer is given: *Res hujus sacramenti Christus est* (Fulda, cod. theol. 4° Aa 36 fol. 43rb; Stuttgart, cod. theol. 4° 253 fol. 17va). Stress is placed on the somatic real presence of Christ. Nevertheless insofar as the spiritual, divine flesh of the eucharistic bread brings about the new life of the predestined, the body of the Lord is regarded as enclosing the mystery of the fellowship of the elect. Hence the eucharistic body is identified as *sacramentum unionis.* It is sign of the reality of the union ordered to it. Thus a distinction is made between a twofold *res* and a twofold sacrament. The body of Christ is *res* of the sacrament and, at the same time, sacrament of another *res* (Fulda, cod theol. 4° Aa 36 fol. 43va). The body of Christ is *sacramentum, id est sacrae rei signum,* of the union that is conferred in the sacrament for the life in the predestined (Fulda, cod. theol. 4° Aa 36, Fulda fol. 43va). At the same time it is sacrament of the body of the cross, the crucified and glorified body which actualizes the sacrament, and through and in this, the union of the predestined. It is both sacrament and *unio.* The analysis of *sacramentum et res* in the parallel tract, *In sacramento altaris,* taken over and enlarged in the tract *De corpore igitur* . . . , comes to the same conclusion. The body of the Lord, present in the species, makes available to men the kingdom of God, and the kingdom of God is enclosed in the eucharistic body of Christ.

the eucharistic body, and the ecclesial body. But it proved to be too complicated for everyday use in systematic theology. This problem was resolved during the course of the twelfth century by reducing the composition of the sacrament of the Eucharist to the triad: *sacramentum—sacramentum et res—res.* In its definitive form, achieved in the thirteenth century, the middle term was reversed *(res et sacramentum).*

B. THE SCHOLASTIC TRIADIC SCHEMA OF THE COMPOSITION OF THE EUCHARISTIC SACRAMENTS

The salient features of the development of the classical scholastic schemas concerning the composition of the sacraments of the Eucharist can be quickly summarized. Early scholasticism's initial schema was borrowed from Augustine: *sacramentum* (= visible sign) signifies the *res* (= grace of unity). This was followed by the early development in the eleventh and twelfth centuries found in the anonymous tractate referred to above.[3] Here, as previously observed, the Augustinian schema *sacramentum et res* was expanded. The species signifies the eucharistic body of Christ; the eucharistic body signifies the glorified body as well as the unity of the ecclesial body which is ordered to it.

Alger of Liège (ca. 1110–1115) formulated this variation: the species signifies both Christ's body and blood and the risen body as well as the Church. Also the risen body on the altar signifies the historical body and the Church.[4]

Gerhoh of Reichersberg (ca. 1135) remains within the tradition which situates the grace of the Eucharist in the sacrament itself: The species (as such) signifies the unity of the Church; the consecrated species is *sacrificium* or body of Christ which effects the unity of the faithful.[5]

[3] Fulda, Hessische Landesbibl. cod. theol. 4° Aa 36 fol. 42ra–47rb (here: 43rb; 43va. Cf. Hödl, "Sacramentum et Res," 167–68).

[4] Alger of Liège, *De sacramento corporis et sanguinis Domini libri tres* (PL 180.739–854) here (with the PL chapter headings) 1.5 "Quod visibile sacramentum panis et vini, nuncupative dicatur corpus Christi" (PL 180.752B–754A); 1.17 "Quod dupliciter vel tripliciter dicitur corpus Christi" (PL 180.790B–791D); 1.18 "Quod invisibile corpus Christi in sacramento, sacramentum sit visibilis corporis Christi in humana forma, verum veri, idem ejusdem" (PL 180.792A–794A); 1.19 "Quod sacramentum duobus modis significat, vel sua ex se similitudine, vel alicujus actionis erga se" (PL 180.794A–797B).

[5] Gerhoh of Reichersberg, *Libellus de eo, quod princeps mundi huius iam iudicatus sit (Liber de simoniacis),* ed. Emil Sackur, MGH, *Libelli de Lite Imperatorum et Pontifi-*

Hugh of St.-Victor distinguishes between the visible species, the truth signified, and the power of the sacrament. He employs the triad: *species et veritas et virtus* to which corresponds: *visibilis imago, imago-res* (invisible body and blood), *gratia spiritualis.*[6]

Robertus Gauterius repeated the schema of Hugh of St.-Victor: *species et veritas et gratia,* to which correspond: elements, body and blood, spiritual grace. But he also was the first one to introduce an explanatory terminological distinction that would become normative: *sacramentum tantum, res et sacramentum, res tantum.*[7]

In the *Summa sententiarum,* Hugh developed the following distinction: *sacramentum tantum, sacramentum et res, res tantum sacramenti* to which correspond: species/actions, body and blood, unity of body of Christ, the Church. Here the species and action signify the symbolic reality of the body and blood as well as the inner power of the symbolic reality, namely the unity of the body of Christ, the Church.[8]

In all the above schemas the grace of the Eucharist is conceived as "contained" in the sacrament. A new stage of development of the analysis of the composition of the sacraments of the Eucharist was introduced by Peter Lombard. His commentary on 1 Corinthians 11:24 seems to be the first scholastic source to situate the grace signified by the eucharistic sacrament *outside* the sacrament itself. He uses the triad: *sacramentum, res contenta et significata, res significata et non contenta* to which correspond: *species, caro et sanguis, unitas ecclesiae.*[9]

---

cum Saeculis XI. et XII. Conscripti. Tomus III (Hannover: Impensis Bibliopolii Hahniani, 1897) 239–72, at 261–67.

[6] Hugh of St.-Victor, *De sacramentis christianae fidei,* lib 2, pars 8, cap. 7 (PL 176. 466C).

[7] Robertus Gauterius, *De sacramentis ecclesiasticis* (Cod lat. 219, Stadtbibl. Besançon, fol. 1ra–94^{v}, at fol. 42^{v} [Cod. lat. 142, Stadtbibl. Tours, fol. 127^{v}–173rb]). Cf. Hödl, "Sacramentum et Res," 171.

[8] "Itaque tria in hoc sacramento consideranda sunt: species visibiles, quae sacramentum sunt et non res, et verum corpus Christi quod sub specie est panis et vini, tertium ipsa efficacia sacramenti, quae spiritualis caro Christi et virtus sacramenti appellantur, ut diximus"—Hugh of St.-Victor, *Summa Sententiarum,* tract. 4, cap. 3 (PL 176.140D).

[9] ". . . in hac enim specie tradidit quia res hujus speciei expressam habet similitudinem cum utraque re hujus sacramenti, contenta scilicet et significata, et significata et non contenta. Res contenta et significata est caro Christi quam de Virgine traxit, et sanguis quem pro nobis fudit. Res autem significata, et non contenta est unitas Ecclesiae in praedestinatis vocatis, justificatis et glorificatis. Haec est duplex caro Christi. . . . Sunt itaque tria in hoc sacramento consideranda, unum quod tantum est sacramentum, alterum quod est sacramentum et res, tertium

Praepositinus follows the distinction found in Hugh of St. Victor's *Summa sententiarum,* and situates the grace of the sacrament in the sacrament: *tantum sacramentum, sacramentum et res, tantum res,* to which correspond: *species, corpus et sanguis, ecclesia.* Here the species signifies the body and blood and also the Church.[10]

Gaufred of Poitiers employed the following variation of the tripartite distinction: *tantum sacramentum, sacramentum et res, tantum res sacramenti et non sacramentum,* to which correspond: *species, corpus et sanguis, caro mystica.*[11] Innocent III, in a letter to Archbishop John of Lyons, describes the composition of the sacrament in this way: *sacramentum et non res, sacramentum et res, res et non sacramentum.*[12]

Stephen Langton repeats the distinction introduced by the *Summa sententiarum,* namely, *sacramentum tantum, sacramentum et res, res tantum,* to which correpond: *species, corpus et sanguis, unitas ecclesiae.*[13]

---

quod res et non sacramentum. Sacramentum et non res est species visibilis panis et vini. Sacramentum et res, caro Christi propria et sanguis. Res et non sacramentum est mystica Christi caro"—Peter Lombard, *Collectanea in omnes D. Pauli apostoli epistolas, In Ep. I ad Cor,* cap. 11, vv. 23–24 (PL 191.1642A-B).

[10] "Item dicitur quod in illo sacramento tria sunt, unum quod est tantum sacramentum, scilicet species panis et vini, unum quod est sacramentum et res, corpus Christi quod traxit de Virgine et sanguis, aliud quod est tantum res corpus Christi quod fit res Ecclesiae (Todi: quod est Ecclesia). Primum significat secundum et tertium, secundum significatur a primo et significat tertium, tertium significatur a primo et a secundo et nullum significat" (clm 9546, fol. 179va; Cod. lat. 71, Todi, fol. 134rb)—Praepositinus, *Summa quaestionum,* as cited in Hödl, "Sacramentum et Res," 175.

[11] "In hoc sacramento sunt tria, unum quod tantum est sacramentum ut panis, alterum quod est sacramentum et res sacramenti, scilicet illa caro Christi quae crucifixa est et sanguis qui de latere eius effluxit, et alterum quod tantum res sacramenti et non sacramentum mystica eius caro, quae est unitas fidelium. Panis sacramentum est verae carnis Christi et mysticae"—Gaufried of Poitiers, *Summa quaestionum,* Cod. lat. Paris. 15747, fol. 81rb (cited from Hödl, "Sacramentum et Res," 175, n. 37).

[12] "Distinguendum est tamen subtiliter inter tria, quae sunt in hoc sacramento discreta, videlicet formam visibilem, veritatem corporis et virtutem spiritualem. Forma est panis et vini, veritas carnis et sanguinis, virtus unitatis et caritatis. Primum est 'sacramentum et non res.' Secundum est 'sacramentum et res.' Tertium est 'res et non sacramentum.'"—DS 783 (PL 214.1121B).

[13] "In Eucharistia tria attenduntur principaliter, quorum neutrum est in homine, scilicet forma panis et vini quae est sacramentum tantum, corpus Christi sumptum de Virgine, quod est sacramentum et res sacramenti, et corpus Christi mysticum, scilicet unitas Ecclesiae res tantum et non sacramentum. Similiter in baptismo tria principaliter attenduntur scilicet character, infusio gratiae et remis-

Hugo of St. Cher, *Summa* (ca. 1233), likewise uses this triad but also introduces a variation in which the middle term is reversed to read *res et sacramentum*.[14] After the middle of the thirteenth century the standard formulation of the triad, favored also by Thomas Aquinas, becomes: *sacramentum tantum, res et sacramentum, res tantum.*

C. EVALUATION OF THE TRIADIC SCHEMA

Chapter one, part III, of this book contained an evaluation of the triadic concept of the sacrament which is an authentic contribution of scholastic theology. There it was shown how the analysis of the composition of the sacraments of the Eucharist by Peter Lombard became normative in scholastic theology. While it had the advantage of highlighting the somatic presence of Christ, it also had the disadvantage of situating the grace of the sacrament of the Eucharist outside the sacrament itself as the "thing signified but not contained in the sacrament." This conception of the relationship of the eucharistic grace to the sacrament of the body and blood, in its turn, had the effect of obscuring the vision of what is ultimately signified by the sacrament: the eschatological dimension, namely, Christ in heavenly glory, in the midst of the holy ones, as fulfillment of the eucharistic celebration. As long as the *res* ultimately signified by the sacrament was identified as the inner-power of the eucharistic body, the saving effect of reception of Holy Communion was described as a grace radiating from the eucharistic body, which enables spiritual communion with the glorified flesh of the risen Lord. But to be in communion with the glorified flesh of Christ necessarily includes being present to the risen Lord in the midst of the heavenly Church.

This early scholastic theology of the eschatological effect of participation of the sacraments of the body and blood had its counterpart in the theology of the Eucharistic Prayer and accompanying action, which was valued as a sacrificial means of the "consecration of the Body and Blood of Christ." In short, early Scholasticism understood that the proclamation of the Eucharistic Prayer attains at the level of

---

sio peccati; et constat quod infusio et remissio peccati sunt in homine; ergo eadem ratione tertium scilicet character est in homine. Ideo character potius imprimitur in baptismo quam in Eucharistia"—Stephen Langton, Cod. lat. 57, Cambridge, St. John's Coll., fol. 308va (cited from Hödl, "Sacramentum et Res," 176, n. 40).

[14] *Libellus de sacramento altaris* (ms. lat. 3627, 3640 de la Bibliothèque nationale [cf. *DTC* 7.239]).

prayer what is attained at the level of sacramental participation in the body and blood of Christ.

As previously noted, the early scholastic use of the phrase "consecration of the body and blood" was not restricted to the divine activity by which bread and wine are converted into the eucharistic flesh and blood of Christ. Rather the term had a broader field of meaning that embraced (1.) the *transitus* of the elements into the eucharistic flesh and blood, (2.) the *transitus* of the consecrated flesh and blood into the heavenly body of Christ, (3.) the purpose of the twofold *transitus*, namely, the integration of the liturgical community into this single *transitus* of Christ from suffering to glory in virtue of its self-offering made in union with Christ in the power of the Holy Spirit.

This broader meaning of the term consecration continued to be used without difficulty down through the first part of the twelfth century. It was applied to the sacrament of the body and blood. Moreover it was also applied to the Eucharistic Prayer to describe its efficacy. In the instance of the latter usage, the (1.) effect of the conversion of the eucharistic elements into the body and blood of Christ, and the (2.) effect of uniting the eucharistic and the glorified bodies of Christ, as well as the (3.) effect of ordering the earthly liturgical assembly to the heavenly Church, was attributed to the instrumentality of the Eucharistic Prayer.

However, from the middle of the twelfth century, as the focus of attention turned to the problem of working out a systematic explanation of the mystery of the somatic real presence of Christ under the forms of bread and wine, the formulation of a doctrine about the somatic presence of the whole Christ became acute. As a result, the teaching about the two bodies of Christ, the eucharistic body and the body of the crucified and glorified Lord, was pushed into the background. The major task at hand was twofold: (1.) the identification of the liturgical formula of consecration, and (2.) finding an explanation of the change of the bread and wine that could account for the presence of the whole Christ under the appearances of bread and wine. The latter problem was resolved with the development of the doctrine of transubstantiation. The former task was settled by identifying the words of Christ contained in the liturgical narrative of institution as the "essential form" of the sacrament. As a consequence, the consecratory efficacy originally attributed to the Eucharistic Prayer as a whole, as witnessed for example even in the oaths prescribed for Berengar, was devalued.

At the same time, and understandably, a narrowing of the concept of consecration began to take hold. Gradually the term consecration came to be employed exclusively to express the idea of the conversion of the bread and wine. By the latter part of the twelfth century, as reported in the first chapter of this work (above pp. 74–78), it was no longer correct to speak of the "consecration of the body and blood of Christ" in systematic theological discourse.

CONCLUSION

By way of a conclusion to this chapter, two themes call for comment. We have seen how the doctrine of the two bodies of Christ, the eucharistic body and the glorified body of the Lord, exercised considerable influence on the elaboration of the early scholastic formulations of both the composition of the eucharistic sacraments and the theology of the Eucharistic Prayer. At the same time it must be said that a satisfactory theological formulation of the identity and distinction between the two bodies, that is, the historical-glorified body and the eucharistic body, was not achieved. Rupert of Deutz (1075–1129) explains the matter in this way:

"Neither are there two bodies mentioned, nor are there two, that which is taken from the altar and that which is taken from the womb of the Virgin. Because, namely, one and the same Word . . . is above in the flesh, and here in the bread. . . . The one Word once assumed flesh from the virgin Mary and now takes the salutary victim from the altar. Therefore it is the one body which, born from Mary . . . hung on the cross and which, offered on the holy altar, daily renews the passion of the Lord for us."[15]

[15] The full text reads: "Nec duo corpora dicuntur aut sunt, hoc quod de altari et illud, quod acceptum est de utero Virginis, quia uidelicet unum idemque Verbum, unus idemque Deus, sursum est in carne, hic in pane. Alioquin et ille panis, quem heri sacrificauimus, et ille, quem hodie uel cras sacrificabimus. Plura sunt corpora, nec recte dicimus offerri ab ecclesia corpus Domini, meliusque diceremus corpora, quia cotidie pene tot offeruntur panes, quot habentur in ecclesia sacerdotes. Sed hoc prohibet causa, conuincit ratio, religio respuit. Unitas enim Verbi unitatem efficit sacrificii. Similiter enim unum Verbum et olim carnem de Maria Virgine sumpsit et nunc de altari salutarem hostiam accipit: igitur unum corpus est, et quod de Maria genitum in cruce pependit, et quod in sancto altari oblatum quotidie nobis ipsam innouat passionem Domini"—Rupert of Deutz, *De divinis officiis* 2.2 (CCCM 7.34.100–35.114 [PL 170.35A-B]).

Finally, what can be said about the Lombardian schema of the composition of the sacraments of the Eucharist which places the sacramental grace outside the sacrament? Peter Lombard himself explicitly taught that the grace of unity was available to the worthy communicant as fulfillment of what the sacrament signifies according to the divine intention. Is this explanation superior to that which views the eucharistic grace as radiating from the eucharistic body of Christ?

A solution to the question of the twofold body of Christ is at hand in the Greek tradition which employs a prototype-image theology. From this point of view, the distinction between the natural mode of presence of the crucified and risen Lord at the right hand of the Father and the sacramental mode of presence is decisive. On the subject of the relation of the grace of the Eucharist to the sacraments of the body and blood, it is theologically more accurate to speak of the grace radiating from the sacrament than it is to describe it as related to participants in the Eucharist by divine intention. However, this does not mean that some supernatural power flows from the eucharistic body and blood. The instrumental power of the sacramental body and blood is the power of the principal cause of sanctification, namely, the Holy Spirit, whom the risen Lord sent once-for-all from the Father in order to establish the Church and in order to draw humanity into communion with himself and with the members of his body the Church, and so with the Father as sons and daughters in the one Son.

Chapter Four

From Early to High Scholastic Theology of the Eucharist: The Priest Presiding at the Eucharistic Liturgy

This chapter examines the traits of the latter stage of development of the early scholastic theology of the Eucharist, which prepared the way for the thirteenth-century synthesis. We have shown elsewhere that the concentration of reflection on the mystery of the somatic eucharistic presence of Christ was typical of twelfth-century scholasticism. We identified this as an important factor behind the neglect of the broader notion of "consecration," which finally resulted in the abandonment of the usage of *consecratio corporis et sanguinis Christi* in scientific terminology, although it was retained in the Roman Canon for the rite of co-mingling of the consecrated bread and wine.

The fascination with the question of the somatic presence of Christ had the effect of redefining the term "consecration" as applied to the notion of sanctification of the eucharistic elements. Moreover, this orientation, which took the theme of the somatic presence of Christ as the starting point for a synthetic theology of the Eucharist, contributed significantly to the redefining of the role of the ordained minister, bishop, or presbyter, who presides at the eucharistic liturgy.

We have already discussed Berengar's singular contribution to the development of Latin theology of the Eucharist, namely, his analysis of the process of change whereby the elements of bread and wine become the sacrament of the body and blood of Christ (above pp. 97–102). He actually analyzed the process of change. This was new for the contemporary scene. What change takes place, and how is it to be conceived? Within the context of a way of thinking in which the real is opposed to the symbolic, questions eventually (and inevitably) arise concerning the exact time of the change, and the exact instrumental cause of the change. When and by what means does the change take place?

The basic questions have become: (1) What are bread and wine? (2) What change takes place with the bread and wine? (3) How is the change to be conceived? (4) When does the change take place? (5) By what instrumental cause does the change take place? All these are questions that have been asked explicitly since the time of Berengar.

By the close of the early scholastic period, despite various nuances concerning the nature of the change of the bread and wine, there was agreement: (1) that the change takes place at a single moment within the scope of the Eucharistic Prayer; (2) that the words of Christ contained in the liturgical narrative of institution of the Eucharist constitute the essential form of the consecration of the elements of bread and wine; and (3) that the presiding priest, reciting these words of Christ, acts as the minister of Christ insofar as Christ himself exercises a theandric act, i.e., an act accomplished by the person of the Word in and through his humanity, which serves as sacrament of the purely divine act by which the conversion of the eucharistic elements is effected.

The identification of the exact moment of consecration of the eucharistic elements, the essential form of the eucharistic liturgy, and the attribution of the consecration of the elements exclusively to the presiding priest, are the three elements which constitute the kernel of the later scholastic orientation in eucharistic theology. In contrast, the earlier scholastic explanation of the relationship of the eucharistic sacrifice to the historical sacrifice of the cross repeats an earlier tradition which focuses on the identity of the victim and the application of the efficacy of the sacrifice of the cross in the Mass. In chapter two above, Alger of Liège was cited as one who exemplifies the common opinion of the day in this regard (pp. 108–9). He bases the real identity of the Mass and the sacrifice of the cross only on the identity of the victim:

"Although the oblation of Christ once on the cross is true *(vera),* although the daily one on the altar is figurative *(figurativa),* nevertheless, indeed, here and there is the grace of our salvation . . . because here and there the true Christ is *potens ad omnia.*"[1]

This general orientation provided the background from which to rethink a number of important aspects of eucharistic theology: (1) the

[1] Text above, p. 109, n. 74.

nature and scope of the power of offering the eucharistic sacrifice conferred at ordination; (2) the representative role of the presiding priest in relation to the Church; (3) the measure of the degree of membership in the Church sufficient to authorize the exercise of leadership of the divine liturgy; (4) the representative role of the priest in relation to Christ; (5) the nature of the liturgical activity of the assisting faithful. After treating these five points, this chapter will conclude (in section VI) with an exposition of the development of the doctrine of transubstantiation.

I. THE MINISTERIAL POWER OF CONSECRATION

Toward the end of the first millennium, the German liturgical tradition introduced into the ordination rites the ritual of the handing on of the sacred instruments of the eucharistic sacrifice: the cup and paten. Together with this ritual gesture went the following formula of interpretation: "Receive the power of offering sacrifice in the Church on behalf of the living and the dead, in the name of the Father and of the Son and of the Holy Spirit." In the *Decree for the Armenians (Decretum pro Armenis)* of the Council of Florence, this formula is identified as the form of the sacrament of ordination to the priesthood.[2]

In the same decree the form of the sacrament of the eucharist is identified as

". . . the words of the Savior, by which this sacrament is confected, since the priest confects the sacrament speaking in the person of Christ. For by the power of the words themselves are converted the substance of the bread into the body of Christ, and the substance of the wine into the blood: in such a way, however, that the whole Christ is contained under the species of bread and the whole [Christ] under the species of wine. Also, the separation having been made, the whole Christ is under the consecrated host and consecrated wine."[3]

[2] "Forma sacerdotii talis est: 'Accipe potestatem offerendi sacrificium in Ecclesia pro vivis et mortuis, in nomine Patris et Filii et Spiritus Sancti'"—*Decretum pro Armenis*, A.D. 1439 (DS 1326).

[3] "Forma huius sacramenti sunt verba Salvatoris, quibus hoc confecit sacramentum; sacerdos enim in persona Christi loquens hoc conficit sacramentum. Nam ipsorum verborum virtute substantia panis in corpus Christi, et substantia vini in sanguinem convertuntur: ita tamen, quod totus Christus continetur sub specie panis et totus sub specie vini. Sub qualibet quoque parte hostiae consecratae et

In this fifteenth-century *Decree for the Armenians*, the presbyter's consecratory power over the sacrament of the Eucharist was clearly distinguished from and, in fact, also isolated from his authoritative power expressed in the *Supplices* prayer of the Roman Canon which asks that the consecrated gifts receive an added degree of sanctification through contact with the heavenly altar. The same holds true for early scholastic theology where these two powers exercised by the leader of the eucharistic liturgy are conceived as grounded in the rite of presbyteral ordination. But these two powers are, nevertheless, moved from potency to act under different conditions.

Up through the latter half of the twelfth century it was commonly assumed that the actuation of one power, that of consecration of the bread and wine, did not necessarily entail the actualization of the other power, that of offering the sacrifice in the name of the Church. The teaching of Sicard of Cremona and Lothar of Segni can serve as examples.

A. SICARD OF CREMONA (CA. 1150–1215)

Sicard of Cremona's comments on the ordination rite of presbyter is instructive. In his *Mitrale*,[4] he identifies the Holy Spirit as the divine source of the priest's ministry. This is witnessed by the ordination rite of imposition of hands: "The imposition of hands signifies the exercise of the works of the Holy Spirit."[5] Regarding the celebration of the Eucharist, Sicard's commentary on the *Te igitur* of the Roman Canon quotes the text of Honorius cited above about the light signifying the Holy Spirit.[6] At the same time he places the capability of the priest to consecrate the bread and wine on a Christological basis. He says that the priest consecrates bread and wine by "a power of consecrating conferred by the consecrated Lord."[7]

---

vini consecrati, separatione facta, totus est Christus"—*Decretum pro Armenis*, A.D. 1439 (DS 1321).

[4] Sicard of Cremona, *Mitrale, seu de officiis ecclesiasticis summa* (PL 213.13–434).

[5] "Manus impositio sancti Spiritus operum exercitationem significat"—Sicard of Cremona, *Mitrale* 2.2 (PL 213.65B).

[6] See above p. 107, n. 66; here: "Inde est quod hoc sacramentum sine lumine celebrari non debet; lumen enim significat Spiritum sanctum, qui hoc sacramentum consecrat, qui hoc digne percipientes illustrat; lumen et laetitiam designat, et hoc sacramentum nobis aeternam laetitiam donat"—*Mitrale* 3.6 (PL 213.125C).

[7] "Manus inguuntur, ut mundae sint ad offerendas hostias pro peccatis, et ut Christi crucifixi vestigia sacerdotes in misericordiae operibus imitentur, qui potestatem consecrandi a consecrato Domino sortiuntur"—*Mitrale* 2.2 (PL 213.65D).

In commenting on the *Qui pridie* of the Roman Canon, Sicard identifies the Last Supper as the historical situation in which Christ himself established the essential form by which the sacrament of the body and blood is made. He distinguishes between the spiritual power exercised by Christ at the Last Supper and its relation to the words of Christ spoken by priests in the Mass. At the Last Supper Christ "blessed":

"He poured out the grace of transubstantiation, in order that the bread might be transubstantiated into flesh; and he filled it by the Holy Spirit. . . . And see that at the uttering of these words: *Hoc est corpus meum,* the bread is divinely transubstantiated into flesh. The divine material substance of this sacrifice is the word which, coming to the element, perfects the sacrament; (just as) the Word united to the flesh effected the man Christ."[8]

His further remarks on the authoritative activity of the priest who presides at the Eucharist have to do with his role as leader of the eucharistic worship of the Church. Commenting on the whole process of sanctification that underlies the Roman Canon in the context of the *Offerimus* prayer, Sicard says that the priest

"prayed beforehand for the victim to be transubstantiated, and transubstantiated it, and offered the transubstantiated [victim] to the Father. (But) now he prays for its acceptance . . . and that he (Christ) may carry it into the sight of the divine majesty; that through its intercession before the Father, and through our reception of it, we may be filled with the blessings of celestial grace."[9]

We conclude from this exposition that the priest is given the power to act as minister of the Eucharist by ordination, in which he receives this power from Christ. This ministerial power is exercised in the

[8] "*Benedixit,* id est gratiam transsubstantiandi infudit, ut panis transsubstantiaretur in carnem; et Spiritu sancto replevit. . . . Et vide quod ad prolationem istorum verborum: *Hoc est corpus meum,* panis divinitus transsubstantiatur in carnem, divina etenim materialis substantia hujus sacrificii est verbum quod ad elementum accedens perficit sacramentum; sic verbum carni unitum efficit hominem Christum"—*Mitrale* 3.6 (PL 213.128D–129C, at 129A-B).

[9] "Super quae cum oravit pro hostia transsubstantianda, eamque transsubstantiavit, et transsubstantiatam Patri obtulit, nunc orat pro ipsius acceptione, ut . . . et in conspectum divinae proferat majestatis; ut per ejus interpellationem ad Patrem, et per ejus nostram perceptionem, repleamur caelestis gratiae benedictione" —*Mitrale* 3.6 (PL 213.131B).

Mass: a power of transubstantiation. The ministerial power is realized by the recitation of the words of Christ which are the divine form of the sacrament. Finally "consecration" is narrowly interpreted to refer only to the conversion of the bread and wine. This consecratory power of the priest is distinguished from the sanctifying efficacy of the petition by which the priest asks that the sacrament of the body and blood be accepted by the Father and, becoming the spiritual and divine flesh, become a source of blessings for the communicants.

B. LOTHAR OF SEGNI (1160/61–1216)

Lothar of Segni, afterwards Pope Innocent III, wrote *De sacro altaris mysterio* between 1195 and 1197.[10] He employs a general notion of consecration in his commentary on ordination. Here he explains that in the ordination rite the hands of the candidate for the presbyterate are anointed by the bishop in order that the candidate may know that he receives the "grace of consecrating through the Holy Spirit."[11] This grace holds for all kinds of consecrations or blessings.

Regarding the consecration of the Eucharist, Lothar records a possible difference between what Christ did at the Last Supper and what the priest does in the Mass. The Roman Canon states that Christ "blessed," and then spoke the words of institution of the Eucharist. But did he confect the sacrament by the blessing or by the words of institution? Lothar lists two possible solutions. It may be that Christ spoke the words in order to attribute to them the power of confecting the sacrament, and added a sign of blessing or some word of blessing. Then he repeated the words to instruct the apostles about the form of the sacrament. It is also possible that Christ's blessing confected the sacrament, and then he gave the form by which it should be confected in the future:

"Certainly it may be said that Christ confected by divine power, and afterward expressed the form, under which posterity should bless. For he blessed per se, by his own power. We, however, bless by that power which he infused into the words."[12]

[10] Lothar of Segni, *De sacro altaris mysterio libi sex* (PL 217.773–916).

[11] "Unguntur autem manus presbyteris ab episcopo, ut cognoscant hoc sacramento se per Spiritum sanctum suscipere gratiam consecrandi"—Lothar of Segni, *De sacro altaris mysterio* 1.9 (PL 217.779C-D).

[12] "Sane dici potest, quod Christus virtute divina confecit, et postea formam expressit, sub qua posteri benedicerent. Ipse namque per se virtute propria benedixit.

In the following chapter, Lothar says that when the priest pronounces the words of Christ,

". . . bread and wine are changed into flesh and blood, by that power of the word, by which 'the Word was made flesh and dwelt among us,' by which 'he spoke and they were made, he commanded and they were created.'"[13]

Nevertheless, Lothar does not equate the eucharistic change with creation. Rather, he uses an argument from Ambrose, that it is greater to create from nothing than to change something that already exists. Hence, "was not the word of Christ (which could create from nothing) able to change bread into flesh?"[14]

After his election as pope, in a letter of December 18, 1208, Lothar formulated a confession of faith to be taken by convert Waldensians, which contains a summary of his eucharistic theology. The converts are to confess that they do not disapprove "the sacraments . . . which are celebrated in her (Roman Catholic Church), with the inestimable and invisible power of the Holy Spirit cooperating *(virtute Spiritus sancti cooperante)* . . ."[15] In regard to the Mass, the following is made the object of confession:

"The sacrifice, that is the bread and wine, after the consecration is the (true) body and the (true) blood of (our Lord) Jesus Christ . . . in which nothing more is accomplished by a good priest or nothing less by a bad one; because it is effected not in the merit of the one consecrating, but in the word of the Creator and in the power of the Holy Spirit."[16]

Nos autem ex illa virtute quam indidit verbis"—*De sacro altaris mysterio* 4.6 (PL 217.859B).

[13] Panis et vinum in carnem et sanguinem convertuntur, illa verbi virtute, qua *verbum caro factum est, et habitavit in nobis* (Joan. I) qua *dixit, et facta sunt, ipse mandavit, et creata sunt* [Ps. 148:5]"—*De sacro altaris mysterio* 4.7 (PL 217.859C).

[14] ". . . verbum Christi non potuit panem in carnem mutare? Quis hoc audeat opinari de illo cui nullum verbum est impossibile (*Luc.* I), per quem *omnia facta sunt, et sine quo factum est nihil?* (Joan. I). Certe majus est creare quod non est, quam mutare quod est—ibid., 4.7 (PL 217.859C-D). For Ambrose, see above p. 15, n. 29.

[15] "Sacramenta a quoque, quae in ea celebrantur, inaestimabili atque invisibili virtute Spiritus Sancti cooperante . . ."—DS 793.

[16] "Sacrificium, id est panem et vinum, post consecrationem esse *verum* [—!] corpus et *verum* [—!] sanguinem Domini nostri [—!] Iesu Christi . . . in quo nihil

The consecration is attributed to the "word of the Creator" and the "power of the Holy Spirit." This is a synonym for the divine power of the Godhead as such. The term "consecration" is taken in the narrow sense of conversion of the bread and wine. There is no reference to the aspect of sanctification applicable to the priest's activity in the offering of the gifts of the Church to be sanctified through contact with the heavenly altar. But this omission is not surprising since Pope Innocent III is describing what is done by the priest as minister of Christ, not as possible representative of the Church.

Later on it would be possible to identify the sacrificial aspect of the Eucharist with the consecratory aspect by which the conversion of the bread and wine takes place, as the other side of the coin. However the inclusion of the ecclesiological within the Christological aspect of the eucharistic mystery was not available at this time. It has been argued that St. Thomas Aquinas understood the twofold representative function of the leader of the Eucharist in such a way that the ecclesiological aspect is contained in the Christological. In other words, the presiding priest is understood to act *in persona Christi capitis ecclesiae,* and therefore as representative of the Church of which Christ is the head. However, there is no proof for this thesis in the writings of Aquinas. On the contrary, in his commentary on the Sentences of Peter Lombard, Aquinas does not allow the ecclesiological relation to be absorbed by the Christological.[17]

II. PRIEST AS REPRESENTATIVE OF THE CHURCH

In the period of the early Middle Ages, as witnessed from Isidore of Seville to Remigius of Auxerre (d. 908), according to the common teaching of the Latin theologians, only the universal Catholic Church

---

a bono maius nec a malo minus *perfici credimus* [perficitur] sacerdote; *quia non in merito consecrantis,* sed *in verbo efficitur creatoris et in virtute Spiritus Sancti"*—DS 794.

[17] According to Aquinas, the authority to preside at the Eucharist as representative of the Church derives from ordination in which the priest obtains the power to consecrate the gifts of the Church *in persona Christi.* But this act is accomplished for the whole Church because the Eucharist is "sacrament of the universal Church" (*In IV Sent.,* d. 24, q. 2, 2 ad 2). Therefore, by reason of the ecclesial nature of the Eucharist, the priest acts for the whole Church, not because he consecrates the gifts of the Church in the person of Christ, head of the Church. The formal reason why he represents the whole Church is the fact that the Eucharist is a corporative act of the universal Church which takes place in favor of the Church itself.

was thought to be able to celebrate the true Eucharist of Jesus Christ. This teaching is in continuity with the eucharistic theology of the ancient North African Church. With this understanding, the local churches in communion with the *una sancta catholica ecclesia* were conceived as representing the whole Church in the eucharistic liturgy. Whence the priest who presides at the Eucharist was viewed as one who represents the whole Church by acting as liturgical leader of the local church. Generally, the axiom held that a true eucharistic liturgy cannot be celebrated except in the context of the Catholic Church. More often than not this teaching is expressed in a general way without specifying exactly what is meant by it.

However, at the turn of the first millennium, the axiom began to be defined more precisely. There existed a rather common opinion that an ecclesiological dimension of the eucharistic celebration is absolutely necessary for the realization of the Christian eucharistic celebration. But precisely what that ecclesiological content might be was a matter of debate.

Peter Damian (d. 1073) seems to have thought that the whole Church is somehow present in the eucharistic liturgy. Still, it is probable that he construed the presiding priest's activity as activity of the whole Church.[18] Odo of Cambrai seems to think in this direction where he interprets the *Orate fratres* prayer in private Masses as directed to the universal Church: "By virtue of the whole communion, the priest confects the sacramental mysteries of the Church through the grace of God."[19] Rupert of Deutz (1075–1129) teaches that the cor-

[18] Peter Damian, *Dominus vobiscum* (Opusculum 11) cap. 7–8 (PL 145.236C–238B). Typical texts: "Providerunt enim, quia quidquid in divinis obsequiis a quolibet Ecclesiae membro reverentur offertur, id etiam fide et devotione cunctorum universaliter exhibeatur"—cap. 7 (PL 145.237B); "In quibus verbis patenter ostenditur, quod a cunctis fidelibus, non solum viris, sed et mulieribus sacrificium illud laudis offertur, licet ab uno specialiter offerri sacerdote videatur; quia quod ille Deo offerendo manibus tractat, hoc multitudo fidelium intenta mentium devotione commendat"—cap. 8 (PL 145.237D).

[19] The full sentence: "Et cum non habeant quam pluraliter collectam salutent, nec plurales mutare possunt salutationes, convertunt se ad Ecclesiam, dicentes se Ecclesiam in Ecclesia salutare, et in corpore totum corpus alloqui, et virtute totius communionis in Ecclesia confici sancta mysteria per gratiam Dei, nec esse quemquam alicubi infidelium, qui vivificorum non fiat particeps et cooperatorius sacrosanctorum, dum in corpore Ecclesiae adhaereat capiti, velut utile membrum"—Odo of Cambrai, *Expositio in canonem missae* (PL 160.1057B). See Mary M. Schaefer, "Twelfth Century Latin Commentaries on the Mass: Christological and

respondence between the body of Christ, the Church, and the body of Christ, the Holy Victim, requires that the whole Church be the subject of the eucharistic sacrifice. But by this he means that the faith of the Church shared by local churches enables them to celebrate the sacrifice of the communion of churches.[20]

III. ECCLESIOLOGICAL RELATION AS CONDITION FOR LITURGICAL LEADERSHIP

In line with North African and Augustinian theology, the early medieval Latin theologians exercised considerable caution concerning the conditions under which ordained priests could be said to celebrate truly the eucharistic liturgy of the Catholic Church. In the first place, the ability of the priest to celebrate the Eucharist was measured by the degree of his membership in the Catholic Church. But there was no absolute consensus concerning the grades of membership which excluded the priest from representing the Church. Also, in the course of time, a distinction was formulated concerning what the priest can do as representative of Christ or as representative of the Church. For it was possible, at least theoretically, to conceive of the priest sanctifying the eucharistic elements as minister of Christ and, at the same time, as unable to represent the faith of the Church when he proclaims the Eucharistic Prayer of the Church.

Finally there are a variety of theological reasons advanced to explain why priests outside the Church are unable to celebrate the true Eucharist. These reasons are based both on the expected absence of elements essential to the constitution of the comprehensive Body of Christ, or the inability of the priest to represent the Church because of his deficiency of membership in the Church.

Ecclesiological Dimensions," Dissertation, Notre Dame, 1983 (Ann Arbor, Mich.: University Microfilms International, 1983) 60. In the following pages, we rely heavily on Schaefer's study of this pivotal period of formulation and crystallization of Western scholastic thought on the Eucharist.

[20] "Nam quomodo deifer panis ille non de uno sed de multis conficitur granis, et uinum illud sacrosanctum non de uno sed de multis confluxit acinis, sic nimirum non tantum habet Verbi Dei, quanta est gratia unius hominis, sed quanta est plenitudo totius corporis Christi, quod est ecclesia, quae de multis hominibus consistit, quaeque per unumquemlibet catholicae fidei hominem uniuersa ad sanctum altare in loco uel tempore quolibet assistit"—Rupert of Deutz, *De divinis officiis* 2.2 (CCCM 7.35.124–32).

The Venerable Bede (d. 735), for example, is said to have denied that heretical and schismatic priests can celebrate the Eucharist. He is reported to have given as the reason the fact that the angels would not be present. For the true Eucharist encloses also the heavenly Church. From the turn of the first millennium through the first half of the twelfth century others maintained that without the leadership of a priest who qualifies as member of the Church, the eucharistic sacrifice of the Church cannot be celebrated. This position makes the eucharistic liturgy dependent on the ecclesial status of the liturgical president and not simply on the power received through ordination.[21]

In the twelfth century the problem still remained concerning the degree of the irregular relation to the Church which disqualified priests from celebrating the Eucharist of the Church. Here opinions differed as to whether the priest could confect the sacrament as representative of Christ without being able to offer the acceptable eucharistic sacrifice. Honorius Augustodunensis held that the sacrament is not confected and the offering of sacrifice is not accepted outside the Church.[22]

Gerhoh of Reichersberg specifies that the sacraments of heretical and schismatical priests are invalid.[23] The *Summa sententiarum*, probably authored by Otto of Lucca (d. 1146), cites two opinions on the

[21] The ninth-century Florus of Lyons maintains that there is no sacrifice outside the Church: "Veri sacrificii extra catholicam Ecclesiam locus non est"—*De expositione missae* 53 (PL 119.49B [Schaefer, 71, n. 205]). Odo of Cambrai (ca. 1050–1113): "Non est enim locus veri sacrificii, extra catholicam Ecclesiam"—*Expositio in canonem missae* (PL 160.1061D [Schaefer, 71]), Rupert of Deutz (1075–1129 [Schaefer, 114–15]), and Honorius Augustodunensis (fl. ca. 1198–1130s): "Extra ecclesiam nec hoc sacramentum perficitur, nec munus oblatum accipitur"—*Eucharisticon*, chaps. 5–6 (PL 172.1252D–1254A) at chap. 6 (PL 172.1253C [Schaefer, 164]) deny that a priest can offer sacrifice outside the Church. Stephen of Autun (bishop: 1112–1135; d. 1139/40) takes the whole Church as the starting point for discussing the valid Eucharist. There is no place for sacrifice outside the Church: "Extra communionem fidelium et venerationem sanctorum non est locus offerendi verum sacrificium"—*Tractatus de sacramento altaris* (PL 172.1273–1308), here at chap. 13 (PL 172.1290B [Schaefer, 361]).

[22] Schaefer, 164.

[23] Gerhoh of Reichersberg, *Epistola ad Innocentium Papam* (A.D. 1131) in Emil Sackur, ed., MGH, *Libelli de Lite Imperatorum et Pontificum Saeculis XI. et XII. Conscripti.* Tomus III (Hannover: Impensis Bibliopolii Hahniani, 1897) 203–39, esp. at 221–22: "Non proposui ea [ereticorum sacramenta] vacuare, sed vacua ostendere, illa nimirum sacramenta, quae ab ereticis quibuslibet anathematizatis extra unitatem [a]ecclesiae data fuerint et accepta . . . *Aliter,* ait Leo Magnus, *vana est habenda consecratio,* quae nec loco fundata est nec auctoritate munita" (222).

Masses of excommunicated and manifestly heretical priests: Some hold that they are valid; others that they are invalid. The reason given for the author's preference for the latter opinion is based on the liturgical prayer. The priest says: "we offer"; one offers *ex persona totius ecclesiae.*[24] The anonymous eleventh- or twelfth-century *Epistola de sacramentis hereticorum* teaches that the heretical priest has the sacrament of the priesthood *intus,* but loses the *potestas et virtus* of the priesthood *foris.*[25] However, the tide was beginning to run in the other direction, namely, toward a downplaying of the ecclesiological status of the priest who presides at the eucharistic liturgy. In 1133 Gerhoh was opposed by Bernard of Clairvaux, and called to Rome, since the question was disputed. On that occasion Gerhoh defended his position in the monograph *Liber de simoniacis.*[26]

Around the middle of the twelfth century, Peter Lombard held that outside the Church the priest cannot celebrate a true sacrifice since the angels are not present. Hugo of St. Victor and Alger of Liège maintained the subtle distinction that echoes the teaching of St. Augustine: The priest outside the Church can celebrate a valid but not a fruitful eucharistic sacrifice.

In the second half of the twelfth century, Lothar of Segni follows Peter Lombard in formulating the common teaching that the priest sacrifices *in totius ecclesiae persona.*[27] He explains that the priest so acts "as long as the priest remains with the others in the Ark," and uses the form handed on by the tradition.[28] However, Lothar does not elaborate on the subject of the significance of the Eucharist of the priest who is separated from the Church.

IV. THE PRESIDING PRIEST AS REPRESENTATIVE OF CHRIST

The different opinions concerning the ecclesiological status which qualifies or does not qualify the priest to preside at the eucharistic liturgy, and the development of the distinction between what the priest can do in virtue of the power received at ordination, that is, confect the sacrament and offer the sacrifice, reflects an evolving the-

[24] PL 176.146B-C (Schaefer, 332).

[25] Emil Sackur, ed., MGH, *Libelli de Lite,* Tomus III. 12–20.

[26] Emil Sackur, ed. (see above n. 23) 239–72.

[27] Lothar of Segni, *De missarum mysteriis* III.5 (PL 217.844C-D (Schaefer, 456–57).

[28] Ibid., 456.

ology of the hierarchical priesthood. This also holds true for changes in the terminology employed to describe the relationship between Christ and the liturgical leader of the eucharistic liturgy.

The medieval commentaries on the Mass take up the earlier theme which depicts the priest of the New Covenant as the fulfillment of the Old Covenant priesthood; one who offers the sacrifice for the people. This description is applied to Christ and, in turn, to the ordained bishops and presbyters. In the eleventh and twelfth centuries the term *similitudo* is used to describe this participation of ordained clergy in the priesthood of Christ.[29]

In order to shed light on the ministerial action of the priest in the eucharistic liturgy, the language of drama is sometimes introduced. The priest is said to imitate the person of Christ when he recites the words of institution of the Eucharist.[30] More commonly the relation of the priest's activity to Christ is expressed by terms such as *vices Christi*.[31]

The idea that the priest represents both Christ and Church is sometimes expressed by the imagery of ambassador and embassy. The priest is called ambassador of Christ and embassy of the people to the Lord;[32] or ambassador of the Church to Christ; ambassador of Christ to us (embassy of Christ to us).[33]

V. PRIEST AND ASSISTING FAITHFUL

The relationship of the activity of the presiding minister of the Eucharist to Christ and to the Church implied for early scholasticism an

[29] In this sense, the early medieval Peter Pictor describes the priest as *similitudo* of Christ (Schaefer, 10, 24). Rupert of Deutz uses the term bearer of the person or *similitudo* of Christ (Schaefer, 98–100). In the latter case, the idea of "bearer of the person," as synonym for *similitudo*, carries with it the notion of personal presence of the one through the presence of the other.

[30] Ivo of Chartres (1040–1115 [Schaefer, 234–35]).

[31] Hildebert of Le Mans [Hildebert of Lavardin] (1057–1133) depicts the priest as *vices Christi* (PL 171.1185D–1186A [Schaefer, 276]), or "acts in place of Christ by reciting the words of institution" (ibid. [Schaefer, 269]). In this connection, Stephen of Autun states that Christ gave to the disciples the power to consecrate—*Historia scholastica*, chap. 152 (PL 198.1618A-B [Schaefer, 357]). Robert Paululus says that the priest "bears the person of Christ"—*Gemma animae* I.45 (PL 172.403B [Schaefer, 384]); *vices*—ibid. (1050–1100 [Schaefer, 134]) II.4 (411B [Schaefer, 385]).

[32] Thus Bernold of Constance.

[33] Honorius Augustodunensis describes the priest as ambassador of the Church to Christ; ambassador of Christ to us (embassy of Christ to us) (texts in Schaefer, 158).

active relation of the liturgical assembly to both Christ and the presiding minister.

Odo of Cambrai describes the faithful as "assisting by their prayers," as *cooperatores* of the holy mysteries. They cooperate as "offerers" along with the presiding priest and clergy by their desires and prayers and communicate as it were by the kiss of peace, confessing what is done.[34] Honorius Augustodunensis refers to a distinction between the "sacrifice" of the faithful and the consecration by the priest. The faithful share in the prayer of the Roman Canon: "the prayer of the people," by offering themselves.[35]

The offertory procession is seen as the place where the people offer different gifts, prefigured in the Old Testament legal sacrifices.[36] Jean Beleth (1160s) refers to the people "offering themselves," as related to the offering of "apt sacrifices."[37] While, on the one hand, Bernold of Constance (ca. 1150–1160) underscores the high degree of participation of the people,[38] Ivo of Chartes (1040–1115) understands that the people participate only by their devotion.[39]

Jean Beleth explains the offering of gifts by the faithful from the Old Covenant model.[40] This is the usual explanation given in the eleventh and twelfth centuries. In other words, the offertory procession is understood to be a continuation of the sacrificial offerings of the faithful of the Old Covenant liturgy. It symbolizes the self-offering of the individual Christian by faith and devotion which is linked to the eucharistic sacrifice of the Church. Hildebert of Le Mans (ca. 1056–1133) also describes the offertory procession in terms of the Old Covenant model. The offerings symbolize the life of faith, the sacrifice of self.[41] Likewise Pseudo-Hugo of St. Victor (ca. 1160–1165) teaches that the offertory procession signifies the offering to God and is based on the Old Covenant model.[42] Stephen of Autun (bishop:

[34] Schaefer, 70–71.

[35] Ibid., 174–75.

[36] Ibid., 171–72.

[37] ". . . tria debemus offerre: Primo nosmetipsos, postea que sunt necessaria sacrificio, scilicet panem et vinum et aquam et cetera sacrificio apta"—Jean Beleth, *Summa de ecclesiasticis officiis*, chap. 41.4–6 (CCCM 41.75–76 [Schaefer, 203]).

[38] Schaefer, 138.

[39] Ibid., 246.

[40] Ibid., 199–201.

[41] Ibid., 263.

[42] Ibid., 334–35.

1112–1135, d. 1139–1140) teaches that the priest offers the sacrifice of peace; the people offer themselves by faith and devotion:

"We offer by the thing: they offer by faith and devotion. We offer the sacraments by confecting, they offer by fulfilling vows. . . . We offer wine, and they offer as oblation a holy and devout disposition."[43]

The latter offering is symbolized by the offertory procession which draws on the Old Covenant cultic model.[44] Generally speaking the participation in the offertory procession is viewed as an activity predicated of the individual as such and not precisely interpreted as a communal act. However the idea that the whole Church participates in this offertory procession through the faithful who are present and active is not entirely absent.[45]

In the second part of the twelfth century, Robert Paululus (d. 1184) describes the faithful as offering themselves and their own.[46] The priest is said to carry out the sacrifice,[47] while the people share vicariously.[48] Sicard of Cremona also describes the offertory procession on the basis of the Old Covenant model.[49] This ritual signifies that, while the priest offers on behalf of the people,[50] the people offer by their devotion.[51] Lothar of Segni, following Peter Lombard, more generally explains that the priest alone offers in the person of the whole Church:

"However granted that only one offers the sacrifice nevertheless *offerimus* is said in the plural, because the priest sacrifices not only in his own [person] but in the person of the whole Church. Wherefore in the sacrament of the body of Christ no more is accomplished by a good, no less by a bad priest, as long as the priest remains in the ark with the others, and observes the form handed down by the dove. Because it is confected not in the merit of the priest but in the word

[43] "Offerimus re: ipsi offerunt fide et devotione. Offerimus sacramenta conficiendo, ipsi offerunt vota solvendo. . . . Offerimus vinum, et oblatam ipsi offerunt mentem sanctam et devotam"—Stephen of Autun, *Tractatus de sacramento altaris* (PL 172.1288D–1289A [Schaefer, 352]).

[44] See Schaefer, 358–59.

[45] Schaefer, 361.

[46] Ibid., 394.

[47] Ibid., 396, 380.

[48] Ibid., 396–97.

[49] Ibid., 413.

[50] Ibid., 440.

[51] Ibid., 420.

of the creator. Therefore the evilness of the priest does not impede the effect of the sacrament, just as the infirmity of the doctor does not destroy the power of the medicine. The work of the one working sometimes is impure, nevertheless the work worked is always pure."[52]

On the other hand the ordinary faithful are thought to offer through the priest in the sense that the priest transmits the prayer of the people to heaven. In sum, "only the priest is the active subject of the ritual offering. Priests are advocates and mediators for the people before God."[53]

SUMMARY (I–V)

In the eleventh century the activity of the priest presiding at the Eucharist was attributed to the whole Church which was viewed as somehow present. However, in the commentaries on the Mass of the eleventh and early twelfth centuries, a precise explanation of the relationship of the whole Church to the individual Eucharist is lacking. It is possible, however, that the notion of the whole Church as supportive of the eucharistic celebration by its prayer of faith is implied in certain texts.

In any case, the question is raised concerning the required degree of membership in the Church in order that priests be qualified to preside at a Eucharist. The Mass commentaries of the eleventh century, and up to the middle of the twelfth century, which treat this subject maintain that there is no place for the eucharistic sacrifice outside the Church. This opinion seems to have been the most common down to the end of the twelfth century.

The participation of the assisting faithful in the eucharistic liturgy is symbolized by the offertory procession. This activity is understood to signify the individual self-offering energized by faith and devo-

[52] "Licet autem unus tantum offerat sacrificium pluraliter tamen dicit 'offerimus,' quia sacerdos non tantum in sua, sed in totius Ecclesiae persona sacrificat. Quapropter in sacramento corporis Christi nihil a bono majus, nihil malo minus perficitur sacerdote, dummodo sacerdos cum caeteris in arca consistat, et formam observet traditam a columba. Quia non in merito sacerdotis, sed in verbo conficitur Creatoris. Non ergo sacerdotis iniquitas effectum impedit sacramenti, sicut nec infirmitas medici virtutem medicinae corrumpit. Quamvis igitur opus operans aliquando sit immundum, semper tamen opus operatum est mundum"—Lothar of Segni, *De missarum mysteriis* III.5 (PL 217.844C-D [Schaefer, 456]).

[53] Schaefer, 473; see also 469.

tion. In this connection the authors of early Mass commentaries refer to the *offerimus* of the liturgical prayer. Thus, for example, the *Summa sententiarum* (1140/1146) notes that the priest does not say *offero*, but *offerimus ex persona totius ecclesiae*.[54]

The phrase *ex persona* has the meaning of an exercise of the power of the one whom the acting subject represents. It is noteworthy that Peter Lombard employs the argument for the necessity of the ecclesiological aspect based on the liturgical *offerimus* without introducing the question of the priestly power of consecration bestowed through presbyteral ordination. Rather, he appeals to the implication of the liturgical prayer concerning the role of the angel of the liturgy bearing the gifts of the Church to the "altar on high." It seems, however, that angels do not assist at the Masses of priests unless they authentically represent the Church.[55]

CONCLUSION (I–V)

The thirteenth-century development of the sharp distinction between the two representative roles of the priest occasioned the promotion of the words of institution of the Eucharist to the form of the sacrament. The fixing of the moment of consecration at the recitation of the words of Christ had the effect of introducing a conceptual separation of the sacrament from the aspect of sacrifice, which fostered a theology of eucharistic sacrifice that dominated the scene up to the Council of Trent. This fixing of the moment of consecration (often resulting in a fixation on this moment) has continued to this day to constitute a serious obstacle to the task of structuring a coherent synthesis of this theme.

VI. THE DEVELOPMENT OF THE DOCTRINE OF TRANSUBSTANTIATION

In the eleventh-century (and subsequent) debate over eucharistic realism, the resolution was eventually achieved by theologians who employed philosophy. The problem was this: How can one express the symbolism and realism of the Eucharist, when contemporary thought no longer understands the implications of the ancient image

[54] PL 176.146C (Schaefer, 332).

[55] Odo of Cambrai, among others (see Schaefer, 55–57).

theology? A solution to this problem was discovered by Lanfranc, afterwards Archbishop of Canterbury, and Guitmund of Aversa (d. 1095). Both recognized that Berengar's concept of *substantia* was inadequate to a philosophical penetration of the doctrine of the Eucharist for the contemporary period. The concept of change of essence was developed first by Lanfranc in the debate with Berengar. Another contemporary of Berengar, Guitmund, speaks, as Lanfranc does, of a substantial change of the elements.[56]

Lanfranc conceives substance in such a way that it does not destroy the tension between visible and invisible. He distinguishes between substance (essence) and species (appearances). Applying this to the eucharistic bread, Lanfranc distinguishes between the substance *(substantia)* and visible form *(species visibilis);* in relation to the body of Christ, he distinguishes between the essence *(essentia)* and properties *(proprietates).* In his argument against Berengar he confesses as follows: "We believe . . . the earthly substances . . . are converted into the essence of the Lord's body."[57] Thus he retains the symbolic character of the Eucharist without abandoning realism. Visible bread is sign of the essential reality of the body of Christ hidden in it. According to Lanfranc, all things have a visible and invisible aspect. Together they constitute the unity of being. The realism of the Eucharist is secured by saying that the earthly (invisible) substance is changed into the essence of the Lord's body. In this way, he is able to affirm realism; he is able to oppose the simple identification of the historical body of Christ with the sacramental body since only the essence is present in the eucharistic bread; he is able to affirm that all which is visible in the bread remains unchanged.

Lanfranc recognizes the distinction between sacrament (symbolic reality) and the reality signified by it *(res sacramenti).* Berengar defines the substance of the elements as the perceptible properties; Lanfranc defines the substance of the elements as the essence opposed to the perceptible properties. According to Berengar, the substance of bread

[56] Guitmund of Aversa, *De corporis et sanguinis Christi veritate in eucharistia libri tres* (PL 149.1427–1494).

[57] "Credimus igitur terrenas substantias, quae in mensa Dominica, per sacerdotale mysterium, divinitus sanctificantur, ineffabiliter, incomprehensibiliter, mirabiliter, operante superna potentia, converti in essentiam Dominici corporis, reservatis ipsarum rerum speciebus, et quibusdam aliis qualitatibus . . ."—Lanfranc of Canterbury, *De corpore et sanguine Domini adversus Berengarium turonensem* (PL 150.407–42) here chap. 18 (PL 150.430B-C).

does not change into the sacrament of the body of the Lord.[58] Lanfranc, on the contrary, affirms: "We believe . . . the earthly substances are changed into the essence of the body of the Lord."[59] The teaching of Lanfranc was developed further in the twelfth and thirteenth centuries, reaching its high point with the use of Aristotelian categories to distinguish substance and accident: the visible and invisible realities of a thing.

A. THE TWELFTH-CENTURY CONTRIBUTION TO THE DEVELOPMENT OF THE DOCTRINE OF TRANSUBSTANTIATION

The debate with Berengar, as we have seen, resulted in a shifting of the discussion from the content of the sacrament to the process of change. Since the theology of metabolism was secured and also the fact of conversion in accord with the Ambrosian tradition, the interest shifted to a credible explanation of the nature of the change which would also secure the sacramental presence of the whole Christ. In the twelfth century, the process of change was formulated in terms of a change of substance. The application of the verb *transsubstantiare* to this process of change is first found in the middle of the twelfth century in the *Sententiae* of Rolando Bandinelli (b. ca. 1105), the later Pope Alexander III (1159–1181). In time the term came into common usage and eventually it received official approval at the Fourth Lateran Council (1215).[60]

In the second half of the twelfth century, the concept of change was discussed with an eye toward supporting the theology of the somatic real presence of the crucified and risen body of the Lord. Concerning the mode of the conversion of elements, three major opinions were advanced. (1.) There was the theory of consubstantiation in which the change consists in the addition of the body and blood to the bread and wine. This doctrine was considered to be consistent with eucharistic faith by Peter of Capua, while it was rejected by Peter Lombard.[61] (2.) Another theory was based on the idea of annihilation through consecration. In other words the bread and wine are understood to be simply destroyed at the same time that the body and blood begin

[58] See *Epistola Berengarii ad Ascelinum* (PL 150.66B).

[59] PL 150.430B-C (text above n. 57).

[60] ". . . transsubstantiatis pane in corpus, et vino in sanguinem potestate divina"—DS 802.

[61] Peter Lombard, *Sent.* IV, dist. 11, c. 1.

to exist under the appearances that remain. This was allowed as possible by Peter of Capua, Abelard (d. 1141), and Rolando Bandinelli (d. 1181). (3.) Finally there was the theory of conversion in which the substances of bread and wine are converted into the body and blood of Christ. Peter of Capua, Hugo of St. Victor, Peter Lombard, Peter Cantor, and Stephen Langton favored this theory. Hugo of St. Victor (d. 1141), who produced one of the most important treatises on the sacraments in twelfth century,[62] and who distinguishes first between the *sacramentum* and the *res* of the sacrament,[63] and later on also between the *species* and the *veritas* of the eucharistic body,[64] rejects consubstantiation and annihilation.

The *Glossa ordinaria* to the *Decretum Gratiani* prefers the annihilation theory,[65] as does Huguccio the canonist (d. 1210). Peter Cantor in his *Summa de sacramentis* (1191–1197) rejects annihilation. Innocent III (Lothar of Segni), favors change of being, but does not condemn the other two theories.[66] Stephen Langton (d. 1228) argues against annihilation and consubstantiation. This also holds for William of Auxerre (d. 1231), Hugo of St. Cher (d. 1263), and the theologians of his school.

Writing at the close of the twelfth century, Peter of Capua states: "Nor is it an article of faith to believe that the conversion is done this way or that way, but only to believe that the body of Christ at the

[62] Hugh of St.-Victor, *De sacramentis christianae fidei* (PL 176.173–618), esp. lib. 2, pars 8, *De sacramento corporis et sanguinis Christi* (PL 176.461–72).

[63] "Idcirco voluit Christus a nobis manducari, ut nos sibi incorporaret. Hoc est sacramentum corporis Christi, et res sacramenti corporis Christi. Qui manducat et incorporatur, sacramentum habet, et rem sacramenti habet. Qui manducat et non incorporatur, sacramentum habet, sed rem sacramenti non habet. Sicut qui incorporatur etiam si manducare non contingat, rem sacramenti habet quamvis sacramentum non habeat. Qui sumit sacramentum habet, qui credit et diligit, rem sacramenti habet. Melius ergo est illi qui credit et diligit, etiamsi sumere et manducare non possit, quam illi qui sumit et manducat et non credit, nec diligit; vel si credit [et] non diligit"—Hugh of St.-Victor, *De sacramento* 2.5 (PL 176.465B-C).

[64] Hugh of St.-Victor, *De sacramento* 2.6–8 (PL 176.465C–468A): cap. 6: "Quod sacramentum altaris et figura est quantum ad panis et vini speciem, et res quantum ad corporis Christi veritatem"; cap. 7: "Tria esse in sacramento altaris: panis et vini speciem, corporis Christi veritatem, gratiam spiritualem"; cap. 8: "Quare in specie panis et vini Christus sacramentum corporis sui et sanguinis instituit."

[65] See Aemilius Ludovicus Richter and Aemilius Friedberg, eds., *Corpus Iuris Canonici*, Pars Prior, *Decretum Magistri Gratiani* (Leipzig: Bernhard Tauchnitz, 1922) 1.1314–1352 (= Decreti tertia pars de consecratione, dist. 2, cc. 1–97).

[66] Innocent III (Lothar of Segni), *De sacro altaris mysterio libri sex* (PL 217.773–916) esp. at 4.19–20 (PL 217.869C–871D).

proclamation of those words is on the altar."[67] As a matter of fact, the theology of conversion of being developed in the fourth-century Antiochene school is difficult to understand outside the framework of the prototype-image theology of the Greek Fathers. Precisely the notion of annihilation of the substance of bread and wine is excluded by the characteristic of elevation of the reality of the eucharistic elements to the status of image through the working of the Holy Spirit (see above chapter one, esp. pp. 8–10, 18, 34–35, 40–41, 50–51, 55–56).

B. EXPLANATION OF THE CHANGE BY METAPHYSICAL ANALYSIS

The twelfth- and thirteenth-century work of Gilbert of Poitiers (d. 1154) and his followers developed the Aristotelian principles of being, as these had been mediated through Boethius (d. 524). Boethius's philosophy is characterized by its grounding on Aristotelian concepts, but in a further determination, non-Aristotelian concepts are introduced. Thus, in the conception of matter, biblical ideas from the account of creation, Platonic notions from the Timaios, and Neoplatonist concepts, above all from Augustine, are introduced. The form (of an existing being or substance), according to this philosophy, is the sum of substantial partial forms, including substantial properties. Thus humanitas, as the specific substance of the human being, is composed of corporeality, rationality, and sensibility. (In contrast to this, Aristotle conceives of form as a simple, undivided principle.) Following this type of philosophy as received through Boethius, theologians held that there is a change of material substratum; but substantial form and essential properties remain. In this context only part of the material being is changed. The majority of twelfth-century theologians held this theory, including Pope Innocent III and Peter Cantor.

The decisive development, however, came when the Aristotelian principles of being, matter and form (which had been mediated—but not fully—by Boethius), were finally accepted in their pure Aristotelian philosophical explanation. This occurred at the beginning of

[67] "Nec est articulum fidei credere quod sic vel sic fiat illa conversio, sed tantummodo credere quod corpus Christi ad prolationem illorum verborum sit in altari"—as cited by Hans Jorissen, *Die Entfaltung der Transsubstantiationslehre bis zum Beginn der Hochscholastik,* Münsterische Beiträge zur Theologie 21,1 (Münster: Aschendorff, 1965) 24.

the thirteenth century when Aristotle's definition of form as a simple, undivided principle of being was received in the work of William of Auxerre (d. 1231) and became fixed in that understanding. But in the meantime, during the twelfth century, the theological endeavors to clarify the eucharistic change on the basis of Aristotelian terminology—but as mediated by Boethius—had resulted in two opposing theories.

According to the first explanation, espoused by Alanus of Lille, transubstantiation consists in the change of the whole being constituted of matter and substantial form, that is, the material subject together with its essential properties, with the accidents remaining. According to the second theory, there remains at the change, apart from the accidents, also the substantial form and, therefore, the essential properties. A shift in thinking takes place at the beginning of the thirteenth century as the theory of Alanus of Lille gains in popularity. This became the preferred approach in the work of Stephen Langton, who criticizes Peter Cantor.

The conceptual explanation of transubstantiation as change of being, under demarcation of the metaphysical being of the essential properties, was inaugurated by Alexander of Hales (d. 1245). Transubstantiation is conceived as a change of the substance of bread and wine, constituted from matter and form, with only the accidents of bread and wine remaining.[68] Matter and form, principles of being, are distinguished from accidents. The whole matter and form of bread and wine changes; only the appearances remain, namely, the species, which are real beings.

During the thirteenth century, the majority of theologians held for transubstantiation. But consubstantiation and annihilation were not necessarily considered to be heretical, as one can see in the early writing of Albert the Great (d. 1280). But in his later work, consubstantiation and annihilation are judged to be against Catholic faith. He thought that the words of Christ, *Hoc est corpus meum*, provide an important proof against the theory of consubstantiation. According to Albert, the Lord "did not say: *'Accipite in hoc, vel cum hoc corpus meum'!*"[69] Thomas Aquinas (d. 1274) and Bonaventure (d. 1274) also

[68] Alexander of Hales, *Glossa in quatuor libros sententiarum Petri Lombardi*, IV, In librum quartum, lib. 4, dist. 11 and 12 (Bibliotheca Franciscana scholastica medii aevi cura PP. collegii S. Bonaventurae 15 [Florence: Quaracchi, 1957] 168–98).

[69] Albertus Magnus, *De corpore Domini (Liber de sacramento Eucharistiae)* d. 6, tr. 2, c. 1, no. 6 (B. Alberti Magni, Opera Omnia, vol. 38 [Paris: Vivès, 1899] 369–70).

hold that the wording of the institutional account of institution of the Eucharist is a decisive argument for transubstantiation.

C. THE VALUE OF THE THEORY OF TRANSUBSTANTIATION

The theory of transubstantiation was developed not in order to secure the fact of the essential change of the bread and wine into the body and blood of Christ. This fact was already taken for granted. Rather, it was developed to affirm the presence of the whole Christ under the forms of bread and wine, beyond the presence of his historical and glorified body and blood. In this way the doctrine overcame the alternatives: crass realism—subjective symbolism. But this doctrine has its weaknesses.

The concepts prototype–image are able to include not only the somatic real presence, but also, on the ground of its dynamism, the actual presence of the whole Christ, above all the commemorative active presence of Christ and his saving work. The doctrine of transubstantiation, however, grounded by the static concepts of substance and accidents only secures the somatic real presence conceived in a static-objective way.

The doctrine of transubstantiation supposes an ontological separation of substance and accidents in the eucharistic bread. Hence the question was posed for the High Scholastics: Do the accidents exist after the consecration without a subject of inherence? In other words, according to the doctrine of transubstantiation, the sacrament, the outward sign, is distinguished from the *res et sacramentum,* the body and blood of Christ. But how is the sign and reality held together? Unable to answer this satisfactorily, most of the theologians appealed to the divine power. This idea only favored the concept of a static, objective presence.

Decisive for the judgment about the value of the doctrine of transubstantiation is the consideration of the function it exercised in systematic eucharistic theology. This teaching holds together the visible—invisible, and maintains the levels of reality, and the openness of the world for the freedom of divine action. Concretely, the intimate relation of the eucharistic signs to the reality of Christ remains secured; but, unfortunately, a statically conceived real presence results.

The later doctrinal affirmation of the Council of Trent must be interpreted from this standpoint. The council's teaching on the subject of the somatic real presence favored a presence conceived statically. Nevertheless the council defined that in the eucharistic event, and so in the eucharistic gifts, Christ bestows himself on us. Hence there remains open the possibility, within the context of the doctrine of Trent, to express the twofold dimension of the eucharistic reality in terms of a relational-personal ontology. But this possibility was not available to theologians at that time.

As a result, the teaching of Trent contributed to the suppression of a series of important aspects of the authentic whole tradition of the theology of the Eucharist. There, in tridentine and post-tridentine theology, the cosmic salvation-history perspective of the Greek Fathers was not available. As a consequence, the idea that the bread and wine are elevated to their highest meaning is pushed aside. Instead, the work of the divinity is pictured, willy-nilly, as that of effecting the destruction of the substance, or metaphysical being of the eucharistic elements, rather than a divine working that effects the ontological elevation of the being of the elements to their ultimate meaning. In other words it ignores the old notion that the sanctifying action of the Holy Spirit does not in any sense destroy but rather perfects by transforming the object of sanctification. Also a great deal is lost by setting aside the analogy between the historical Incarnation and the eucharistic Incarnation, and introducing the analogy with the change drawn from a theory of the composition of material being.

Another effect of the exaggerated attention given to the question of securing the eucharistic presence of the whole Christ under the species of bread and wine was the shifting of theological reflection away from the eschatological aspect of the eucharistic sacraments. Lost to view was the fact that this sacramental presence, because of its relational nature, includes in itself the presence of the heavenly Church of the saints. Also the ecclesiological dimension of the Eucharist became marginalized vis-à-vis the Christological. For the outstanding problem becomes that of offering a reasonable approach to the question of the real presence of Christ in the sacrament. Since this problem was treated for itself in isolation from the rest of the mystery of the Eucharist, the way was opened to completely disengage the role of the consecrating priest as representative of Christ from his role as representative of the Church.

This step was not actually taken in early scholasticism. Nevertheless, the movement in this direction was already underway in virtue of the opinion, fostered by some, that the priest consecrates the elements as representative of Christ and offers the eucharistic sacrifice as representative of the Church. As we have seen, this distinction was used by some theologians to provide a response to what an excommunicated priest could accomplish through the eucharistic celebration even though he could not represent the Church.

Mention must be made of the lasting effect of the distinction between what the priest presiding at the Eucharist does exclusively as representative of Christ, and what he does as representative of the Church. Eventually this distinction led to the teaching that the presiding priest represents Christ through the ministerial act of consecration of the eucharistic elements and at the same time represents Christ as head of the Church offering the eucharistic sacrifice in the name of his body the Church. However this step was taken only after a gradual process of thinking through the Christological implications of the splinter tradition of eucharistic theology that came of age in the thirteenth century.

As might be expected, the question of the subject of the offering of the Eucharist was treated from different standpoints in the period from the thirteenth to the sixteenth century. The earlier tradition, which emphasized the priest's role as representative of the Church in the offering of the Eucharist, was modified gradually in order to integrate it with the increasingly dominant Christological aspect of the eucharistic sacrifice. Despite this shift, however, the dominant synthetic theology of the eucharistic sacrifice from the end of the thirteenth century to the time of the Council of Trent still affirmed that the priest represents the Church, which is the principal subject of the offering of the eucharistic sacrifice.

Only as a result of the teaching of the Council of Trent was this theological explanation of John Duns Scotus (renewed by Gabriel Biel at the end of the fifteenth century) commonly set aside in favor of a theory which identifies Christ as the principal active subject not only of the consecration of the elements but also of the offering of the eucharistic sacrifice. As a consequence of this, the moment of the consecration of the eucharistic elements through the proclamation of the words of Christ contained in the liturgical formula of the narrative of institution of the Eucharist was also identified as the moment of the reactualization of the liturgical self-offering of Christ.

Thus the (formerly dominant, overarching) ecclesiological aspect of the eucharistic sacrifice is inserted into the Christological aspect, or rather is absorbed by it.

Correspondingly, the twofold representative function of the priest in relation to Christ was understood to be realized at this liturgical moment. The priest's role as representative of the Church could only be explained systematically in the following way: (1.) The priest represents Christ by his ministerial act of consecration of the eucharistic elements, and (2.) he also represents Christ the head of the Church offering his once-for-all sacrifice in the name of all the people.

This synthetic theology of the Eucharist requires that the once-for-all sacrifice of the cross be liturgically represented, or rendered objectively present on the altar through an activity in which the priest acts exclusively as representative of Christ. As we shall see, this approach needs to be reassessed.

Finally, the separation of the grace of the sacrament of the Eucharist from the sacrament itself is a weakness fostered by the overexaggerated concentration on the reality of the somatic presence of Christ. On the grounds of the medieval debate concerning the relationship of (a.) the historical and glorified body of Christ and (b.) the sacrament of his body and blood, and stimulated by the gradual decay of biblical and patristic symbolical thinking, the use of the concept "mystical body" for the eucharistic sacrament was replaced by "true body" *(corpus verum),* while the term "mystical body" *(corpus mysticum)* was applied to the Church. Previously, the term true body referred to the Church. In early scholasticism the Church became the "mystical body," the body built up by the *sacramentum.* This teaching was passed on to the thirteenth-century theologians. Thomas Aquinas, employing the distinction of Peter Lombard, speaks of the *res non-contenta* of the sacrament as the *"corpus Christi mysticum."*[70]

St. Augustine's teaching concerning the relation of the Eucharist to the Church was received in early scholastic theology, but also changed. He taught that the whole Christ, head and body, is signified by the eucharistic species. But the medieval emphasis on the somatic real presence of Christ led to the neglect of the reciprocal relation of dependence between Church and Eucharist. The Church is now seen as made by the Eucharist. But the idea that the Church makes the Eucharist in virtue of the commemorative actual presence of Christ as host and high priest was not exploited. Rather, the Church was considered the sphere within which the Eucharist is possible.

This does correspond in part to the old theology. But in the new theology of the thirteenth century, the Church is considered to be the *res sacramenti:* the fruit of the reception of the sacrament. The Church,

[70] *Summa theologiae* 3, q. 80, a. 4.

therefore, was understood in this sense as the mystical body. This spiritualizing of the concept of Church—the separation of Church into a juridical institution and an invisible community of the holy—was a consequence of the narrow view of a spiritual Church as an effect of the Eucharist.

VII. CONCLUSION

Twelfth-century theological reflection on the sacraments of the body and blood of Christ prepared the way for the final stage of development of which the new orientation was capable. (The high point of this development was reached in the thirteenth century.) This theology of the sacraments of the body and blood of Christ gave birth to the late twelfth-century liturgical "rite" of the elevation of the host at the moment of consecration. The growing popularity of worship of the consecrated host was especially encouraged by the popular teaching that, in their gazing at the sacrament, believers could find a salutary substitute for the reception of the sacraments of the body and blood.

In the middle of the thirteenth century the feast of Corpus Christi was instituted. In 1264, Urban IV prescribed it for the whole Church. The office for the feast was assembled by Thomas Aquinas.[71] In this office, three hymns are introduced: *Pange lingua, Sacris solemniis,* and *Verbum supernum,* as well as the Mass sequence, *Lauda Sion.* In this poetry of superior rank, one can find a handy summary of the "new theology" of the altar sacrament linked with the traditional biblical and patristic concepts.

[71] Thomas Aquinas, *Officium de festo Corporis Christi ad mandatum Urbani Papae IV dictum festum instituantis* (Edit Rom. Opusculum LVII) = Opusculum XXXVII in S. Thomae Aquinatis, *Opuscula omnia,* vol. 4 (Paris: Lethielleux, 1927) 461–76. Also = Opusculum V. *Officium de festo Corporis Christi* in *Sancti Thomae Aquinatis opera omnia,* vol. 15 (Parma: Typis Petri Fiaccadori, 1864) 233–38.

Chapter Five

Eucharistic Theology: High Scholasticism to the Council of Trent

In the period of High Scholasticism up through that of the sixteenth-century schism in the Western Latin Church, theologians concentrated their attention, above all, on the mystery of the sacraments of the body and blood and the efficacy of the eucharistic sacrifice for the living and dead. Systematic reflection on the nature of the eucharistic sacrifice itself, in relation to the historical sacrifice of the cross and to the sacraments of the body and blood, was carried on only at a very low level of theological discourse.

This chapter offers a bird's eye view of the history of the theological developments of these themes from the thirteenth century to the eve of the European reformation movement which occasioned the Council of Trent. We begin by recounting the way in which the thirteenth-century doctrine of transubstantiation was received in the late medieval period. We follow this with a description of how the nature and efficacy of the eucharistic sacrifice was explained in a systematic fashion.

I. THE DOCTRINE OF TRANSUBSTANTIATION

We have already noted the widespread thirteenth-century preference for the theory of transubstantiation as the most satisfactory approach to the dogma of the somatic real presence of the whole Christ under the forms of food and drink. Moreover, since the Fourth Lateran Council (1215), which employed the verb *transsubstantiare* to express the idea of substantial conversion,[1] the theory of consubstantiation was more generally considered to be erroneous. The fourteenth-

[1] DS 802: "transsubstantiatis pane in corpus et vino in sanguinem."

century William of Ockham, a leader of so-called nominalist scholasticism, typically preferred the doctrine of consubstantiation as more in accord with Scripture. Nevertheless, he held for transubstantiation because of Church authority.

In the late medieval period, the theory of consubstantiation was clearly rejected by Church authority. Nevertheless, there was very little mention of the main objection against this explanation, namely: If bread and wine are unchanged, it stands to reason that they are not bearers of Christ's presence. They constitute only an occasion of a meeting with Christ in faith. However, in the light of the developments in the Western theology of the Eucharist since the eleventh century, it was not possible to speak of the bread and wine remaining untouched by the somatic presence of Christ.

At the outset of the sixteenth century, there remained the unsolved problem of how the constitution of the sacraments of the body and blood should be conceived. The problem could not be reduced to this question: Why can the vocal word function as medium of encounter with Christ, and not the visible or gestural word? Obviously, the answer would be that both can serve the same function. Rather, the problem that needed to be addressed is this: Why is the mode of encounter with Christ in the sacrament essentially different from that of the encounter with Christ through the medium of the vocal word that expresses the life of faith of the Church?

A. MARTIN LUTHER

Martin Luther attempted to rethink traditional Catholic theology and practice of the Eucharist. At various stages of his polemic against Rome, he singled out specific aspects of this tradition for critical analysis. In particular he found three doctrinal positions to be incompatible with the authentic whole tradition of which Scripture serves as norm: (1.) the theological justification of the practice of reception of Holy Communion under just one species, (2.) the preference for the theory of transubstantiation, (3.) the identification of the celebration of the Mass as a true sacrifice.

In what can be called the first period of Luther's criticism of Catholic eucharistic theology, after 1517, he stressed the goal of the Eucharist: communion of believers with Christ and among themselves. At the same time he rejected the scholastic defense of the practice of Communion under just one species. This practice seemed to him to contradict the witness of Scripture. Luther saw the weakness of the concomitance doctrine that was used to justify the reception of the sacrament of the Eucharist "under one species." According to this reasoning, the fact of the presence of the body and blood of Christ presumes also the presence of the whole Christ under each species (i.e., concomitantly). Consequently, the same effect results whether one receives one or both species. To Luther, this argument seemed to be founded merely on human logic, not on the will of Christ.

Luther was correct in sensing a weakness in this medieval reasoning. But he did not identify the basic weakness of the scholastic synthesis which served as background for justification of communion *sub una.* The scholastic emphasis on the content of the sacrament and the efficacy of the sacrament tended to marginalize the significative function of the sacramental signs of bread and wine. This marginalization is especially manifested in the doctrinal exposition of the theory of transubstantiation. According to this teaching, as presented in the classical thirteenth-century treatises, the appearance of bread and wine remain after the conversion, but are treated as isolated, purely accidental entities. However, from the standpoint of the law of prayer, the liturgy of the eucharist, they belong to the shape and actuality of the *corpus Domini.* They manifest the redemptive meaning of the *corpus Domini,* and are an essential element of the act of presence of the *corpus Domini.*[2]

[2] The commentary of Pope Gelasius on the necessity of reception of Holy Communion under both species is well known. In a letter to the bishops of the region of Calabria he reports having heard that "some, having taken a portion of the holy body, abstain from the blood of the holy cup—*quidam . . . sumpta tantum corporis sacri portione a calicis sacri cruore abstineant.*" He attributes this to a "superstition." He gives a theological reason why this practice is not allowed: ". . . because the division of one and the same mystery cannot come about without a great sacrilege—*quia divisio unius ejusdem mysterii sine grandi sacrilegio non potest provenire.*" Gelasius does not ground the sacrilege simply on the reception *sub una:* a practice which was allowed in certain circumstances. It was based on the preference for the superstition about the drinking of blood, or the symbol of blood, rather than the teaching of the Fourth Gospel about drinking the blood of Christ. Moreover, Gelasius identifies the two sacraments as one symbolic reality: a unified whole intended by divine institution to be received as the normal way of full participation in the eucharistic meal. This symbolic reality is to be liturgically manifested and experienced by the communicants (*Epistola 37. Gelasii papae ad Majoricum et Johannem,* in Andreas Thiel, *Epistolae Romanorum Pontificum genuinae et quae ad eos scriptae sunt a S. Hilaro usque ad Pelagium II* [Brunsberg: Eduard Peter, 1868] Ep. 37.2, pp. 450–52, at 451–52). Cf. our extensive treatment of Gelasius above in chapter one, pp. 31–58.

Luther held for the sacramental somatic presence of Christ: Christ is present *in usu*, i.e., in the accomplishment (or celebration) of the sacrament. However, this does not mean simply at the moment of the administration of the sacrament. He wanted to recover the "event" character of the eucharistic action. *In usu* means within the scope of the command of Christ. The command of Christ concerns an action: "Do this . . ." But to do this involves the distribution and the eating and drinking along with thanksgiving. Moreover, Luther does not seem to have seriously challenged the eschatological meaning of the sacrament; for if Christ makes the sign, it remains as long as the bread and wine remain. For although he is not favorable to the specific Catholic practice of ritual veneration of the Eucharist, he does not oppose bringing the Eucharist to the sick outside the liturgical celebration.

The theory of consubstantiation seems to have been preferred by Luther. He does not recognize that the ontological relation between sign and signified speaks in favor of transubstantiation. Also, after the break with Rome, he no longer sees the value of the support of church authority for transubstantiation.

II. THE DOCTRINE OF EUCHARISTIC SACRIFICE

The twelfth-century commentaries on the Mass, as we have already observed, more generally pay close attention to the ecclesiological aspect of the eucharistic sacrifice. At the same time, the influence of the eleventh-century controversy over the nature of the eucharistic sacrament of the body and blood of Christ had already turned theological speculation on the Eucharist toward an almost exclusive preoccupation with securing a credible explication of the sacrament that would secure the realism of Christ's somatic presence while avoiding the idea of a materialistic eating and drinking of Christ's flesh and blood.

More commonly, up through the middle of the twelfth century, the commentaries on the Mass held that the priest presiding at the Eucharist, if not in communion with the Church—especially by reason of excommunication as a heretic—could not represent the Church. Hence the attempt of such a priest to celebrate the Eucharist was futile.[3]

[3] See Mary Schaefer, "Twelfth Century Commentaries on the Mass: Christological and Ecclesiological Dimensions," Dissertation, Notre Dame, 1983 (Ann Arbor, Mich.: University Microfilms International, 1983)

This aspect of the problem of the ecclesial relation of the priest continued to be discussed from the thirteenth to the sixteenth centuries. But by the end of the fifteenth century, solutions had been found which rendered the question more or less academic.

The previous long-standing opinion that the exercise of the power to consecrate the eucharistic gifts received in the ordination rite of priesthood depends on the current ecclesiological status of the presiding priest was set aside in the thirteenth century. In this period of High Scholasticism, the exercise of this power of consecration of the eucharistic gifts was not considered to be hindered per se by an irregular ecclesiological status of a priest. However, there still remained that part of the tradition which questioned the authority of such priests to offer the eucharistic sacrifice in the name of the Church.

This fact shows clearly enough that High Scholastic eucharistic theology was not inclined to presuppose the organic unity between the consecration of the gifts and the sacrificial dimension of the Eucharist. According to many scholars, Thomas Aquinas, whose eucharistic theology is discussed below in chapter nine, represents an exception to the rule. However, the germ of the tendency to distinguish the consecration of the gifts by the priest acting *in persona Christi* from the offering of the eucharistic sacrifice in the name of the Church was latent in the commonly accepted opinion that the consecration of the gifts is an image of the past historical sacrifice of Christ. In other words, the consecration (recitation of the words of institution) serves only to evoke the recall of that sacrifice which could no longer be repeated: it thus serves (only or primarily) to promote devotion.

This tendency eventually led to the explicit conceptual separation of the sacrament from its sacrificial aspect. This is evident in the fourteenth and fifteenth centuries where the formal treatise on the Eucharist is reduced to the problem of transubstantiation. The subject of the sacrifice of the Mass is treated elsewhere in systematic theology, especially in the treatise on the "Last Things," in connection with the efficacy of the Mass for the souls in purgatory, the distinction between the fruits of the Mass and their modes of application, and in connection with more or less peripheral questions such as how the Mass of a heretical priest can be considered as valid.

In this connection it is noteworthy that the Dominican Robert Holkot, professor at Cambridge who died in 1349, treats the question of the consecration of bread outside the liturgy, that is, in the window of a bake shop. He presumes the possibility of this as a common opinion of the day.[4]

A. JOHN DUNS SCOTUS

John Duns Scotus (d. 1308) is the first to present a systematic theology of the eucharistic sacrifice which separates the action of the consecration of the eucharistic elements from a temporally succeeding sacrificial act. He holds that the consecration takes place through the power of the words of Christ which the priest speaks in the person of Christ. The eucharistic sacrifice is explained as the offering of the consecrated gifts by the priest in the service of the Church.[5]

Scotus is the first of the scholastic theologians to discuss explicitly the question whether Christ himself elicits a new act of oblation in the Mass. He responds that Christ offered himself once for all time on the cross. He does not make an offering immediately in each Mass, otherwise the Mass would have the same value as that of the historical sacrifice of the cross. But this latter position, according to Scotus, is shown to be manifestly untenable from the fact that the Mass can be offered frequently for the same intention. However, Scotus maintains that Christ is offered as contained in the sacrament.[6] In other words the eucharistic sacrifice is not offered immediately by Christ, but what is offered is the consecrated gifts of the body and blood of Christ. Liturgically this is expressed in the linking of the consecration of the bread and wine to the anamnesis-offering prayer of the Roman Canon: "Recalling, therefore . . . we offer . . ." Scotus grounds the limitation of the efficacious value of the Mass on the fact that the active subject of the offering is (not Christ but) the Church. The Church that offers is conceived in the congregationalist sense of the sum total of the members of the Church Militant. As offered by this universal Church, the sacrifice of the Mass is always efficacious because there are always some members who are holy and whose devotion, related to each Mass, accounts for its value.

According to Scotus, the merit contained in the oblation of the Mass is the merit of the Church. However, this merit is intimately re-

[4] Erwin Iserloh, "Die Wert der Messe in der Diskussion der Theologen vom Mittelalter bis zum 16. Jahrhundert," *Zeitschrift für katholische Theologie* 83 (1961) 44–79, at 59.

[5] John Duns Scotus, *In 4 Sent.*, d. 8, q. 1 (Paris: Vivès, 1894) 6–10.

[6] John Duns Scotus, *Quaestiones quodlibetales*, q. 20, no. 22 (*Opera Omnia*, vol. 26 [Paris: Vivès, 1895] 321).

lated to that of Christ. It is not that Christ now merits, but that he merited in his passion, and that his merit is now applied to the merit of the Church.[7] The Church recalls the sacrifice of the cross; the intensity of the remembrance determines the devotion that measures the value of each individual Mass, that is, the measure of the merit won by Christ on the cross which is applied to the merit of the Church.

In this theological explanation of the eucharistic sacrifice the priest is identified as one who acts as representative of the Church in the sacrificial offering. He presents Christ, victim of the cross, before the Father in order to plead in the name of the Church the application of the merits of Christ. Therefore the Church Militant is the principal offerer, while the priest acts as representative of the Church of which he is a member and qualified to act in this way because of this authority to represent Christ in the act of consecrating the bread and wine.

This eucharistic theology constituted the last systematic approach in medieval scholastic theology which accentuates the ecclesiological dimension of the eucharistic sacrifice. It exercised considerable influence over the next two centuries, at least as regards its essential orientation. In general, however, only a few theologians explicitly dealt with Scotus's systematic elaboration. More commonly it is simply assumed that the Mass is a sacrifice in its own right, somehow linked to the sacrifice of the cross and grounded on the institution of Christ. Moreover, the ecclesiological dimension was frequently short-circuited. More often than not, the accent was placed on the ministerial activity accomplished by the priest for the benefit of the Church, while neglecting to take account of the representative function of the priest within the relation Christ and the Church.

B. GABRIEL BIEL

At the end of the fifteenth century, Gabriel Biel, professor at Tübingen from 1484, returned to and, in a minor way, reworked the eucharistic theology of Scotus. He made Scotus's opinion his own where he teaches that the priest consecrates the gifts *in persona Christi* and offers the sacrifice *in persona ecclesiae.*[8]

[7] Ibid., q. 20, nos. 23–24 (Vivès 26.321).

[8] See Gabriel Biel, *Collectorium circa quattuor libros Sententiarum.* Libri quarti pars prima (dist. 1–14) d. 13, q. 1, dubium 2 (Tübingen: J.C.B. Mohr [Paul Siebeck], 1975) 392.42–47: "Respondet *Scotus* quod 'oblatio non pertinet ad rationem consecrationis,' quia potest eucharistia consecrari et non offerri, sicut potest consecrata conservari et non offerri 'nisi aptitudinaliter.' Et ideo, licet offerens offerat in persona

In his *Expositio canonis missae,* Biel teaches that the priest "offers the holy victim not only in his own person, but at the same time in the person of those assembled and of the whole Church." This assertion is supported by 1 Peter 2:9, which attests that the *Christifideles* are priests.[9] Elsewhere Biel states that "in the person itself of the Church, the priest says: *offerimus tibi.*"[10] More precisely he qualifies the priest as one who offers immediately and personally, and the Church Militant as offering mediately and principally *(offerens mediate et principaliter).* And because the Church is always holy, the offering is acceptable: "in her always there are holy people, whose work pleases God."[11]

---

ecclesiae, non tamen consecrat nisi in persona Christi, cuius vicem gerit etiam praecisus per ordinem et characteris potestatem, quae per praecisionem non aufertur ab eo."

[9] "Non enim in sua tantum persona sacerdos, sed simul in persona circumstantium et totius ecclesiae sacram offert hostiam. Concelebrant sacerdoti circumstantes et spiritualiter communicantes, non conficiendo cum sacerdote quod tantum sacerdotis est, sed cum eo hostiam patri a sacerdote consecratam, seque ipsos sacrificium placabile deo patri offerendo. Unde est illud in canone (*Hanc igitur oblationem servitutis nostre, sed et cuncte familie tue* et cetera); propter hoc scriptura omnes christifideles regale nominat sacerdotium. Vos estis, inquit, gens electum . . ." [etc. as per 1 Peter 2:9]—Gabriel Biel, *Canonis misse expositio,* pars prima, lectio 12 (Heiko A. Oberman and William J. Courtenay, eds. [Wiesbaden: Franz Steiner, 1963] 92).

[10] "Dicit autem 'offerimus' in plurali, licet unus solus sacerdos celebrans offerat, quia sacerdos non in sua duntaxat persona sacrificat, sed in persona totius ecclesiae"—ibid., lectio 22A (p. 196).

[11] "Est autem duplex offerens, scilicet offerens immediate et personaliter, alius offerens mediate et principaliter. Primus est sacerdos consecrans et summens sacramentum, qui ita in persona sua auctoritate tamen divina hec perficit, quod nemo alius in sic offerendo secum concurrit. Offerens vero mediate et principaliter est ecclesia militans in cuius persona sacerdos offert, et cuius est in offerendo minister. Est enim hoc sacrificium, sacrificium totius ecclesiae, in cuius signum sacerdos non ex sua persona dicit 'Oro,' sed ex persona ecclesie 'oremus.' Nec dicit in primis, 'que tibi offero,' sed *que tibi offerimus.* Et post communionem: *Proficiant nobis quaesumus, domine, hec sacramenta que sumpsimus,* quamvis ipse solus offerat et sumat personaliter, unde ecclesia offert per ipsum tanquam per ministrum quem ad hoc instituit et ordinavit. Primus offerens non semper gratus est deo, nec semper sibi placet, quia sepe peccator est. Secundum offerens deo est semper acceptum, quia ecclesia semper sancta est et unica sponsa christi pudica, casta, nesciens maculam, neque rugam, cum ergo missa semper valorem suum habet et accepta est deo. . . . Non ergo erit hoc regulariter propter offerens primum, quod nonnunquam displicet, ergo erit propter offerens secundum scilicet ecclesiam, que semper grata est deo, quia semper in ea sunt homines sancti et virtuosi, quorum actiones et merita deo placent"—ibid., lectio 26H (pp. 245–46).

The Scotistic idea that the value of the Mass corresponds to the merit of the Church Militant is consistently taught by Biel. In *Expositio,* lectio 85 (in a context in which, by contrast, he is apparently not writing under the influence of Scotus) he does state that Christ (rather than the Church) is the primary offerer of the Mass; but the reference is to the acting of Christ in the consecration of the gifts (as opposed to the offering of the sacrifice).[12] Beyond this Biel also asks about the value of the Mass from the institution by Christ and the fact that Christ is the sacrificial gift. He explains that Christ is contained in the sacrament, the fullness of grace and merit. Still, the allotment of the fruit with respect to satisfaction is limited. The merit of the offering of Christ in the Mass is less than that of the cross because Christ does not offer himself immediately. Rather: "In the office of the Mass the sacrifice and the oblation are the same, not through repeated death, but through the rememorative representation *(rememorativam repraesentationem)* of the death suffered once." He adds that Christ does not offer himself (Hebrews 9:11-12), but "we offer him and do that now, but what we do is a *recordatio sacrificii.*"[13]

C. CARDINAL CAJETAN

On the eve of the reformation movement, the Dominican Thomas de Vio, known as Cardinal Cajetan (1468–1534), one of the most renowned theologians of his day, took a different path than that of Scotus.[14] He attempted to follow the teaching of Aquinas. In his theology of the Mass, he highlights the offering of Jesus Christ, who is the sacrificial gift. As such, the Mass is of unlimited value *ex opere operato.* Hence the value of the Mass as worship of God is infinite. But as applied to individuals by intention, it is limited according to the devotion of the offerers and those for whom it is offered. Also, as offered by the priest *in persona ecclesiae* the Mass has its value in the measure of the devotion of those offering.[15]

[12] *Canonis misse espositio,* lectio 85H (Oberman and Courtenay, eds., pars quarta [Wiesbaden: Franz Steiner, 1967] 103). See Iserloh, "Der Wert der Messe," 65.

[13] "In officio autem misse idem sacrificium est et oblatio, non per iteratam mortem, sed per mortis semel passe rememorativam representationem . . . *ipsam offerimus* et nunc, sed quod nos agimus recordatio est sacrificii"—*Canonis misse expositio,* lectio 27K (Oberman and Courtenay, pars prima, p. 265).

[14] For this summary of Cajetan's eucharistic theology, we rely primarily on Iserloh, "Der Wert der Messe," 70–77.

[15] "Quum . . . sacerdos oret, et offerat in persona Ecclesiae, et quilibet fidelis sit membrum Ecclesiae, consequens est, ut quilibet per sacerdotis actus oret, et offerat:

Cajetan placed great emphasis on the unity of the cross and sacrifice of the Mass. This unity consists in the unity of the victim, i.e., the inner relation of the one victim of the cross and Mass. The difference between the two sacrifices lies in the manner of offering: a bloody manner on the cross, and unbloody in the Mass. The one sacrifice of Christ is preserved in the mode of sacrifice *(immolatitio modo)*[16] through the daily renewal of the Eucharist according to the institution of Christ. That Christ is the proper offerer in the Mass is occasionally stated by Cajetan.

Cajetan's view of the unity of the sacrifice of the cross and Mass, with Christ as proper offerer, conforms to that of Aquinas. For Cajetan, the Eucharist is a "memorial" in the sense that it initiates the recall of the passion among the participants of the liturgy. He grounds the sacrificial character of the Mass on the identity of the victim of the once-for-all sacrifice of the cross. But the sacrifice itself is not the content of the sacrament. The proof that the Eucharist is a sacrifice is the fact that the priest offers the body and blood. Cajetan is influenced by the static concept of the somatic real presence fostered by the doctrine of transubstantiation, which tended to obscure the more dynamic patristic teaching about the presence of the salvation reality of Christ and his redemptive sacrifice.[17]

D. CATHOLIC APOLOGISTS

Cajetan's point of view was not followed generally by the pre-Tridentine Catholic apologists in their debates with the Reformers. Johannes Eck and the majority of these theologians accepted the Scotus–Biel synthesis. Kasper Schatzgeyer, Franciscan Provincial at Strasbourg (d. 1527), favored a position close to that of Cajetan's theology of the Mass. This is also true of some others such as Melchior Cano,

---

et sic causaliter concurrat ad sacrificium ac per hoc quaelibet Missa singulis fidelibus prodest etiam satisfactori iuxta eorum deuotionem"—Thomas de Vio (Cajetan), *De missae celebratione,* cap. 2 "Utrum sacerdos celebrans pro pluribus, satisfaciat pro singulis," (*Opuscula Omnia Thomae de Vio Caietani* [Venice: Apud Iuntas, 1588] 147–49, at 148).

[16] See Iserloh, "Der Wert der Messe," 75–76.

[17] Cajetan does not introduce Aquinas's teaching about the presence of the historical saving acts of Christ in the sacramental celebration, that is, as instrumental causes of the salutary effects of the divine action. See Iserloh, "Der Wert der Messe," 71–77, and Edward J. Kilmartin, "The One Fruit and the Many Fruits of the Mass," in *Proceedings of the Catholic Theological Society of America* 21 (New York: Catholic Theological Society of America, 1967) 53–55.

O.P. (d. 1560), and Cardinal Hosius, the papal legate at the twenty-second session of the Council of Trent (1562), who presided over the Council's deliberations on the Mass and was responsible for the drafting of the decree on the sacrifice of the Mass.

However all the Catholic theologians, whether favorable to Cajetan or to the Scotus–Biel synthesis, ground the sacrifice of the Mass on the identity of the victim of cross and Mass, and the proof of the sacrifice of the Mass on the fact that the priest offers the divine victim in the Mass.[18]

III. EFFICACY OF THE EUCHARISTIC SACRIFICE

The early sources of the origin of the practice of the Mass stipend was treated above in chapter two (pp. 109–15). It was shown how, despite initial opposition to the system that developed in the Frankish milieu, the practice eventually became common throughout the Western Latin Church. Under precise conditions for such transactions, as well as juridical consequences established by Roman law, and with the full approval of ecclesiastical authorities, the practice of celebrating distinct Masses for distinct intentions of individual donors of offerings became the general rule in the thirteenth century. Moreover, the pastoral practice now served as the source of the theology of the efficacy of the Mass. The question to be addressed now was: What does the practice of the Church, based on the insight of faith, imply for the efficacy of the Mass?

From the thirteenth to the sixteenth centuries, the value of the fruits of the eucharistic sacrifice is the only theological question given much attention in the discussion of the theology of the sacrifice of the Mass. This subject was developed from reflection on the possible implications of the practice of limiting the application of the Mass to the intention of one donor of a stipend to the exclusion of other potential donors, and the practice of having Masses repeatedly offered for the same intention. These practices suggested that the blessings applied through the Mass for this intention are already limited in themselves before application, and not simply limited by the measure of receptivity in the beneficiaries.

But this conclusion seemed to run contrary to the fact that the Mass applies the graces derived from the redemptive sacrifice of Christ,

[18] See Iserloh, " Der Wert der Messe," 77–79.

which is of infinite value. In the light of this latter conviction of faith, how is the finite value of the Mass to be explained? Various solutions given to this question were based on one of two options. Either (1) the limitation is fixed prior to application, or (2) the limitation occurs in the application itself. More generally, in the thirteenth century theologians maintained that the limitation is fixed a priori. To explain this limitation some simply appealed to the divine will. Others employed the distinction between the value of the cross (infinite) and the value of its representation in the Mass (finite). In this latter case it was argued that the value of the representation of the sacrifice of the cross cannot be equated with that of the original offering.

Among theologians of the first rank, St. Bonaventure taught that the value of the Mass is limited a priori. This also holds for Thomas Aquinas in his *Commentary on the Sentences* where he explains that the satisfactory value of the Mass, with respect to the punishment due to sinners, is limited in *actu primo.* However, in his *Summa theologiae,* Aquinas does not agree that the Mass is limited a priori. Rather, the limitation is due to the subjective devotion of the beneficiaries.[19]

A. JOHN DUNS SCOTUS ON THE EFFICACY OF THE EUCHARISTIC SACRIFICE

Although a great deal of energy was spent on the subject of the efficacy of the sacrifice of the Mass during the period of High Scholasticism, only at the end of the thirteenth century did a truly systematic theological explanation of the measure of the limited fruits of the Mass emerge. It was developed by John Duns Scotus who based the limitation on the quality of the subjective devotion of the those engaged actively by faith in the celebration of the Mass.

In his systematic approach to the question of the efficacy of the sacrifice of the Mass, Scotus introduced an important question which had not as yet been considered. He explicitly asked whether a new

[19] "Sicut passio Christi prodest quidem omnibus quantum ad sufficientiam ad remissionem culpae et adeptionem gratiae et gloriae, sed effectum non habet nisi in illis qui passioni Christi conjunguntur per fidem et charitatem, ita et hoc sacrificium, quod est memoriale dominicae passionis, non habet effectum nisi in illis qui conjunguntur huic sacramento per fidem et charitatem"—*Summa theologiae* 3, q. 79, a. 7 ad 2. According to Aquinas, the Mass is applied by the priest to the intention of the donor of a stipend. The priest does not apply the fruits derived from the Mass. St. Francis of Assisi taught that one Mass daily in a monastery, celebrated with devotion, is better than many Masses touched by individualism.

oblation can be predicated of Christ, and concluded that this could not be harmonized with the once-for-all sacrifice of the cross. Consequently he explained that since the sacrifice of the Mass is offered indirectly by Christ and directly by the Church, the measure of the efficacy of the Mass is linked to the devotion of the Church. Here the Church, taken to be the offerer of the victim of the cross, is identified as the Church (= social body) of those living on earth at a given time. The devotion of this body is always limited.

One of the basic reasons why Scotus appealed to the self-offering of the universal Church was his conviction that every valid Mass infallibly produces fruits which are a participation in the graces derived from the sacrifice of the cross. This was the common doctrine of contemporary theology. To explain this efficacy of the Mass, theologians often appealed to the concept of efficacy of the sacraments *ex opere operato* and applied it to the Mass in an analogous fashion. However, Scotus was able to explain this presumed infallible effect by appealing to the concept of the application of the devotion of the saints of the universal militant Church who associate themselves with the Masses of the world. Since there are always some saints in the Church on earth, their participation in the Masses of the world by their intention secures the infallible efficacy of each Mass for the living and dead.

At this same time Scotus produced a systematic exposition of the distinctive fruits of the Mass which was worked out in great detail. There is the fruit applied to the Church, world, etc., for whom intercession is made in the liturgical Eucharistic Prayer; the special fruit that comes to the priest in virtue of the fact that he presides at the Eucharist as representative of the militant Church and Christ, the head of the Church; the fruit applied to the special intention for which the Mass is celebrated. This latter fruit was thought to be applied by an authoritative act of the will of the priest who is the official representative of the Church. Scotus systematized this teaching, underscoring the idea that these fruits of the Mass are applied according to different laws.

The understanding of the meaning of offerings made to the priest with the request that Mass be celebrated for a special intention is reflected in the names assigned to them. These offerings were often given the name *stipendium:* the wages of a soldier. They were considered to be a compensation for the service of the priest, and often equated with almsgiving. These offerings were not considered to be a symbolic manner of active participation of the donor in the offering of the Mass.

In short, the characteristic traits of the theology of Mass stipends as formulated by Scotus are the following: (1.) The offering for the celebration of a Mass for a particular intention was viewed as a contribution to the livelihood of the priest; (2.) the fruit infallibly derived from the Mass and applied to the intention of the donor of the offering was considered to be limited in itself by the limited devotion of the offering Church, and limited by the receptivity of the beneficiary; (3.) the fruits of the Mass were distinguished from one another on account of differences of origin and laws of application. While other opinions concerning the origin of the limitations of the fruits of the Mass were not limited to Scotus's explanation, it is his theological orientation that determined the teaching about Mass stipends and its practice up to the twentieth century.

Chapter Six

The Eucharistic Doctrine of the Council of Trent

The sixteenth-century Western Church witnessed the rejection, by theologians of the Reformation movement, of essential elements of the Catholic eucharistic faith concerning the sacraments of the body and blood of Christ and the sacrificial character of the eucharistic liturgy. This challenge to the venerable doctrinal tradition was the occasion for the dogmatic formulations of these themes in the deliberations of the Council of Trent, a council which was intended to serve as the instrument of reconciliation within the communion of churches of the Western patriarchate. This chapter summarizes the kernel of Trent's teaching on the subjects of the eucharistic sacraments and the nature of the sacrifice of the Mass. The order followed is that observed by the council itself. Thus the discussion of the sacraments of the body and blood precedes that of the Sacrifice of the Mass.

I. THE SACRAMENTS OF THE BODY AND BLOOD

On the subject of the somatic real presence of Christ in the eucharistic sacraments, the Council of Trent adopted the doctrinal position of High Scholasticism. It affirmed the doctrine of the presence of the whole Christ as a consequence of the doctrine of concomitance. In other words, it affirmed the presence not just of the flesh and blood of the crucified and risen Lord, but also of the person of the Word of God. For, the flesh and blood of the crucified and risen Lord (1) in virtue of the hypostatic union are always united to the person of the Word of God, and (2) in virtue of the resurrection and ascension are animated by the human spirit of Christ. Moreover, to a certain extent, the council approved the scholastic philosophical theory intended to support belief in the presence of the whole Christ, namely, the doctrine of transubstantiation. However, the teaching of the council on this subject was presented in such a way that it merely affirmed this real presence without situating it in the context of the whole eucharistic event. Nowadays it is clearly recognized that the proper starting point for a systematic theology of the Eucharist is the teaching about the sacrificial character of the Eucharist, not that about the sacrificial sacrament that results from the actualization of the sacrificial dimension. At Trent the preference for initiating the treatment of eucharistic theology with the sacraments of the body and blood was not motivated by systematic considerations, but rather was dictated by the agenda of the Reformers. In this regard, Martin Luther must be mentioned. For early on he mounted strong opposition to the Catholic doctrine of transubstantiation, a subject we have just discussed in chapter five.

A. COUNCIL OF TRENT: THIRTEENTH SESSION (1551)

The subject of the content of the eucharistic sacraments was treated in the thirteenth session of the Council of Trent in the year 1551. The council teaches that Christ is present not only *in signo,* but *in veritate.*[1] The council denied the theory of consubstantiation by insisting on the real conversion, and supported this denial by the use of the term transubstantiation.[2] On the other hand, the council insisted that the making of the sacrament itself is not the primary goal of the eucharistic conversion. Rather, the primary goal is the making of the sacrament for "reception by the faithful," and not to serve as object of adoration.[3] In canon 1, the council teaches that the Eucharist not only

[1] "Can. 1. Si quis negaverit, in sanctissime Eucharistiae sacramento contineri vere, realiter et substantialiter, corpus et sanguinem una cum anima et divinitate Domini nostri Iesu Christi ac proinde totum Christum; sed dixerit, tantummodo esse in eo ut in signo vel figura, aut virtute: anathema sit"—DS 1651.

[2] "Can. 2. Si quis dixerit, in sacrosancto Eucharistiae sacramento remanere substantiam panis et vini una cum corpore et sanguine Domini nostri Iesu Christi, negaveritque mirabilem illam et singularem conversionem totius substantiae panis in corpus et totius substantiae vini in sanguinem, manentibus dumtaxat speciebus panis et vini, quam quidem conversionem catholica Ecclesia aptissime transsubstantiationem appellat: an. s."—DS 1652.

[3] "Nullus itaque dubitandi locus relinquitur, quin omnes Christi fideles pro more in catholica Ecclesia semper recepto latriae cultum, qui vero Deo debetur, huic sanctissimo sacramento in veneratione exhibeant [can. 6]. Neque enim ideo minus est adorandum, quod fuerit a Christo Domino, ut sumatur *[cf. Mt 26, 26 ss],* institutum"—DS 1643.

signifies but contains the *totum Christum.*[4] Canon 2 stresses the patristic concept of conversion of being to avoid the notion of the union of the substance of bread and wine with the substance of the humanity of Christ. This concept was already found in the list of propositions attributed to Reformers formulated in 1547: "There is in the Eucharist indeed the body and blood of Our Lord Jesus Christ, but with the substance of bread and wine, so that there is no transubstantiation, but a hypostatic union of the humanity and the substance of bread and wine."[5] Canon 2 was formulated precisely to avoid the idea that a strict parallel exists between the unique hypostatic union of Logos and humanity and the eucharistic incarnation.[6]

In short the council rejects the theory of consubstantiation because it does not sufficiently secure the unity of being between the species of bread and wine and the humanity of Christ. At the same time the council approved the use of the term transubstantiation as "apt" to signify the concept of the conversion of the being of the eucharistic elements. Finally the council rejects the theory that a strict parallel exists between the historical Incarnation and the eucharistic incarnation. For while this theory underscores the notion of a profound unity between the eucharistic elements and the crucified and risen Lord, it does not affirm the substantial conversion of the elements.

[4] DS 1651; CT 7.4.1 (1961) 203.26–29 (text above in n. 1).

[5] "In Eucharistia esse quidem corpus et sanguinem D. N. Iesu Christi, sed simul cum substantia panis et vini, ita ut non sit transsubstantiatio, sed unio hypostatica humanitatis et substantiae panis et vini"—CT 5 (Freiburg i. Br.: Herder, 1911) 869.20–22. The acts of the council then continue: *"Lutherus in testamento de sacramento altaris ait: Profiteor, quod in eo veraciter corpus et sanguis Christi in pane et vino corporaliter manducatur et bibitur.* Idem in assertionibus: *Postquam vidi, quae esset ecclesia, quae aliter determinasset, nempe Thomistica, id est Aristotelica, audacior factus sum, et qui inter sacrum et saxum haerebam, tandem stabilivi conscientiam meam sententia priori, esse videl. verum panem verumque vinum, in quibus Christi vera caro, verusque sanguis non aliter nec minus sit, quam ipsi sub accidentibus suis ponunt.* Idem ad regem Angliae: *Impius et blasphemus est, si quis dicit, panem transsubstantiari"*—ibid., 22–29.

[6] J. Wohlmuth, "Noch einmal: Transubstantiation oder Transignifikation?" *Zeitschrift für katholische Theologie* 97 (1975) 430–40, esp. at 439–40. This article, which offers a valuable summary of theological debate on this question since 1949, is itself an "abstract" of the author's *Realpräsenz und Transsubstantiation im Konzil von Trient. Eine historisch-kritische Analyse der Canones 1–4 der Sessio XIII*, 2 vols., Europäische Hochschulschriften, Reihe 23, vol. 37 (Bern—Frankfurt, 1975).

II. SACRIFICE OF THE MASS[7]

Martin Luther was certainly the great opponent to the Catholic theology of eucharistic sacrifice. His critical objections to this theology influenced to a great extent the formulation of the Catholic doctrine undertaken by the Council of Trent in its decree on the sacrifice of the Mass. Let us pause for a moment to recall why Luther considered this doctrine to be erroneous.

According to Hebrews 10:1-18, Christ offered himself once-for-all. This dogmatic statement excludes the notion of another sacrifice that is pleasing to God. Therefore, if the Mass is a true sacrifice, it is a new sacrifice working against the one sacrifice. But a new sacrifice would be a human work. Therefore it would not be acceptable to God.

Luther was convinced that the Catholic doctrine of the sacrifice of the Mass describes only a human work, and that it makes of this work a means of grace. The Catholic apologists could not produce arguments that in Luther's estimation reconciled the sacrificial character of the Mass with the once-for-all sacrifice of the cross. Luther, on the other hand, was unable to discover for himself another way of resolving the apparent contradiction. One must sympathize with Luther to a degree when one considers what was presented as an acceptable theology of eucharistic sacrifice by many of the chief Catholic apologists such as Johannes Eck and H. Esner, namely, Gabriel Biel's theology of the sacrifice of the Mass. Moreover, Luther himself was well acquainted with this teaching, having studied Biel's *Expositio canonis missae* previous to his ordination to the priesthood. This explanation of Biel's provided strong support for Luther's conviction that Catholic theology erroneously attributes to the Mass a sacrificial activity that competes with the sacrifice of the cross. For, in this theory, the victim of the cross and the Mass is identical, but *not the sacrifice.* The eucharistic sacrifice is offered by the Church acting as *principalis offerens.*

The proper response to Luther's objection which offers a satisfactory approach to the inner connection between the Mass and the event of the Cross would have been the Greek patristic concept of the commemorative actual presence of the one sacrifice of the cross. At least this approach has found widespread acceptance in modern ecumenical dialogues between the Catholic Church and churches deriving from the Reformation. However, as we have seen in chapter one,

[7] [See David Power, *The Sacrifice We Offer: The Tridentine Dogma and Its Reinterpretation* (New York: Crossroad, 1987)—RJD.]

this Greek notion of commemorative actual presence never found its place in the Latin patristic tradition which provided the foundations for medieval scholasticism.

Nevertheless, it is an exaggeration to say that medieval theology entirely neglected this event-character of the Eucharist. At least one can show that Thomas Aquinas held for the real presence of the sacrifice of the cross in the Mass not as a local presence objectively realized on the altar, but rather as a presence that is metaphysically affirmed together with the salutary effects derived from the redemptive sacrifice. We take this up below in chapter nine. Beyond that, there is no really convincing evidence that medieval theology, in general, taught that the Passover event of Christ is really present in the eucharistic celebration.

A. COUNCIL OF TRENT: TWENTY-SECOND SESSION (1562)

In session twenty-two of the Council of Trent, a full decade after the decree on the Eucharist, the question of the sacrifice of the Mass was treated.

1. The Canons on the Sacrifice of the Mass

The teaching of the Council of Trent on the subject of the eucharistic sacrifice did not include a choice between the explanation of Scotus–Biel and that of Cajetan. According to the canons *de ss. Missae sacrificio,* the Mass is a true and proper sacrifice offered to God (canon 1: DS 1751). This sacrifice was instituted by Christ, who also instituted a priesthood ordered to the offering of his body and blood (canon 2: DS 1752). This sacrifice is propitiatory and can be offered for the living and dead, for pardon of sins, for satisfaction for sins, and as remedy for punishment due to sins, as well as for other necessities (canon 3: DS 1753). This sacrifice in no way detracts from the sacrifice of the cross (canon 4: DS 1754).

This defined doctrine leaves many question unanswered. There is the matter of the relation of the Mass to the sacrifice of the cross. Is the sacrifice of the Mass an offering of the body and blood of Christ made by the Church as an additional offering subordinate to the sacrifice of the cross? Is the sacrifice of the Mass a sacramental mode of being of the one sacrifice of the cross? The efficacy attributed to the sacrifice of the Mass leaves the question open as to how this efficacy is realized. Is it a matter of efficacy *ex opere operato,* or by way of intercession *ex opere operantis,* or both? Again, the Mass has the characteristic of thanksgiving and propitiation. But how are the two related? Is the Mass a propitiatory sacrifice for which thanksgiving is offered, or is it propitiatory because it is a thank-offering? Also, if the Mass is a true sacrifice does this mean that it is related only to the sacrifice of the cross, or also to the resurrection of Christ? Does a true sacrifice not include offer and acceptance?

The role of the priest in the Mass is described by Trent as that of offering the body and blood of Christ (canon 2: DS 1752). How is this role to be understood? Does the priest offer as representative of the Church to whom Christ left the eucharistic sacrifice? Does he offer as representative of Christ? Does one have to make a choice between the possible representative functions? If not, how is the twofold relationship to be conceived?

In the context of this last question the problem of the "sacramental sacrifice" can be raised. If the consecration of the bread and wine is understood both to recall and also to represent Christ's sacrifice of propitiation because the consecrated species contain the victim of the cross, the presiding priest can be identified as minister of Christ, acting in the person of Christ who offers himself through the ministry of the priest. If the consecration is seen as effecting the presence of the victim of the cross who must then be offered in a visible rite, then the presiding priest can be conceived as one who offers Christ the victim in the anamnesis-offering prayer as representative of the Church.

According to the first option the priest acts *in persona Christi* who, as head of the Church, represents His sacrifice in order that the Church might share in it by devotion. Hence the priest acts as representative of the Church of which Christ is the head by acting *in persona Christi capitis ecclesiae.* According to the second option, the priest acts *in persona ecclesiae* in the offering of the body and blood, and he acts as representative of Christ insofar as minister of the Church of which Christ is the head.

These are the options open in the context of a theology of consecration in which the event takes place through the recitation of the words of institution of Christ spoken by the priest, and in which the priest acts exclusively on the side of Christ in the midst of the eucharistic prayer. It must be emphasized that, as far as the defined doctrine of the canons is concerned, either option could be maintained since the council had no intention of making a choice between a Thomistic or a Scotistic theology of the representative role of the presiding priest.

2. *The* Doctrina de ss. missae sacrificio[8]

In the doctrine attached to the canons on the sacrifice of the Mass,[9] it is said that Christ left to the Church a visible sacrifice by which the historical sacrifice of the cross would be represented, and by which its salutary power would be applied (chapter one: DS 1740). But what is meant by saying that this visible sacrifice is a representation of the sacrifice of the cross? A liturgical rite can be said to represent the sacrifice of the cross in the sense that it contains, in a manner to be defined, the presence of that sacrifice. Also, such a liturgical rite can be said to represent the sacrifice of the cross in the sense that it depicts the sacrifice of the cross at the level of external expression.

The notion of representation in the doctrine of Trent offers problems for the interpreter. In addition to the above possible interpretations, the following profoundly important question may also be asked: Does the idea of representation leave open the question whether, by means of the visible sacrifice, [1] the assembled Church is represented to the sacrifice of the cross, or [2] the sacrifice of the cross is represented to the Church?

It is clear that the orientation of the teaching of Trent favors the understanding of the visible sacrifice as the representation of the sacrifice of the cross to the liturgical assembly. For the fathers of the council held these things in common: [1] the essential form of the eucharistic consecration is the words of Christ expressing his sacrificial disposition; [2] the Christus Passus is rendered present under the separated species; [3] the anamnesis–offering prayer expresses the Church's intention to offer itself in union with the sacramentally present Christus Passus. Also, the doctrine on the sacrifice of the Mass states that Christ is offered in an unbloody manner (DS 1743), that is, ritually. This idea can be embraced by either the Thomistic or the Scotistic points of view (the only options open to the council members in view of the theology of the moment of consecration). In the Thomistic view, the victim of the cross is represented to the Church in the consecration of the gifts, and as offered to the Father. For the sacrament is both sacrament and sacrifice in the mode of immolation.

[8] DS 1738–1750.

[9] The "doctrine" is placed before the canons in the acts of the council: CT, tom. 8, pars 8 (Freiburg i. Br.: Herder, 1919) 959.36–962.22; DS 1738–1759. Note, however, that while the doctrine reflects the general thinking of the council, the council presents only the canons as its "defined" doctrine.

In the Scotistic view, the victim is presented to the Church in the consecration as victim of the cross, but the sacrifice consists in the victim being presented to the Father by the action of the Church, principal offerer, through the ministry of the presiding priest. In both points of view there is a representation of the sacrifice of the cross to the Church at least in the sense of a liturgical representation of the victim of the sacrifice of the cross, which is the condition for the eucharistic sacrificial act of the Church. However the matter can be conceived in another way.

At present, there are some Catholic theologians who are inclined to offer a correction to the point of view which was commonly held by the Tridentine Council fathers. For example, the Italian theologian Cesare Giraudo holds that it is more accurate to say that the Church is represented liturgically to the sacrifice of Christ through the medium of the eucharistic prayer.[10] However, this opinion of Giraudo is not a conclusion that follows from the traditional Latin Church understanding of the function of the liturgical narrative of the institution of the Eucharist. Rather, it originates in an interpretation of the narrative of institution contained in the Eucharistic Prayer that is foreign (i.e., not present) to the thinking of the fathers of the Council of Trent.

The doctrinal explanation of the canons on this subject affirms the identity of the victim and offerer of the eucharistic sacrifice: Christ offers himself through the service of the priest (DS 1743). But this approach is open to one of two alternatives: The statement could be based on the idea that the eucharistic sacrifice is a sacramental representation of the once-for-all sacrifice, or it could imply that in some sense Christ offers himself anew.

The Council of Trent does not refer explicitly to the Eastern theology of the commemorative actual presence of the cross in the Mass. Trent uses the term representation (*repraesentatio*: DS 1740). But it teaches that through the offering of the body and blood of Christ under the forms of bread and wine, the Eucharist is a visible sacrifice which, in itself, has a sacrificial character. Hence in virtue of the relation established by Christ between the sacrifice of the cross and the sacrifice of the Mass, the Mass has the function of representing the sacrifice of the cross. In other words, the commemorative actual pres-

[10] Cesare Giraudo, *Eucaristia per la chiesa: Prospettive teologiche sull'eucaristia a partire dalla "lex orandi,"* Aloisiana 22 (Rome: Gregorian University—Brescia: Morcelliana, 1989) 560–72, esp. at 563–64.

ence of the sacrifice of the cross is not identified as the ground of the sacrificial character of the Mass. Rather, it is the sacrificial character of the Mass that grounds why it can represent the sacrifice of the cross.

At Trent the chief debate among the fathers and theologians did not concern the sacrificial character of the Eucharist, but the sacrificial character of the Last Supper. Therefore it was not taken for granted that the basis of the sacrificial character of the Mass is the representation of the sacrifice of the cross. For in this case the same consideration for the Last Supper and Mass would have held true. In this frame of thinking, it matters little that the Last Supper or Mass came before or afterwards.

The sacrificial trait of the Last Supper was disputed. The sacrifices of the Old Testament, of the cross, and of the Mass were generally interpreted from the standpoint of what we would now call a history-of-religions concept of sacrifice. But the question of identifying the conditions for such a concept of sacrifice in the case of the Last Supper remained problematic for some time. After long discussions, the Last Supper was finally viewed by the Tridentine fathers as a sacrifice. But not in such a way that the thought of the representation of the sacrifice of the cross played a role. In other words, the council grounded the sacrificial character in the offering of the body and blood of Christ under the forms of bread and wine. Hence this approach was open to the understanding of the mystery of the sacrifice of the Mass as a kind of new offering of Christ through which the sacrifice of the cross is represented because it already bears the trait of a sacrifice. In short, the sacrificial character of the Mass is not seen as derived from its relation to the historical sacrifice of the cross, but is, in the last analysis, simply presupposed.

Trent speaks about the sacrificial character of the Mass in the dimension of the visible cultic action. Possibly this was the only way it could explain the sacrificial character of the Mass. For the concept of commemoration, a term used by the Reformers, was suspect.[11] Also, in session twelve, canon 1, the council reflects a kind of thinking in which "thingly reality" is opposed to "sign or image." Thus it is clear that the old Greek concept of real symbol was not in the foreground of the eucharistic theology of Trent.

[11] "Si quis dixit, Missae sacrificium tantum esse laudis et gratiarum actionis, aut nudam commemorationem sacrificii in cruce peracti, not autem propitiatorium . . . an. s."—DS 1753.

In the context of the theological climate at Trent, the possibility of formulating the Christological dimension of the eucharistic sacrifice in terms of the commemorative actual presence of the sacrifice of the cross was not available. This means two things. In the first place, it is a historical fact that the council did not have the means to resolve the difficulty of Luther, and neither did Luther have the means of correcting the weak orientation of the conciliar doctrine. Secondly, it cannot be presumed that the council did not favor a particular possible theological explanation of the sacrificial character of the Mass because it did not introduce it into the discussion. Rather, the theory was not employed (or discussed) because it was not known, or not accessible, in that situation.

Karl Rahner observes that at Trent the sacrificial character of the Mass was thought to precede logically its relation to the sacrificial character of the event of the cross. This was the orientation of the systematic view of the eucharistic sacrifice at Trent.[12] The fathers of the council were not able to view the sacramentality and sacrificial character of the Mass as one reality, and to ground the sacramental character of the Mass in the sacrificial. In fact they had already excluded this willy-nilly, by deciding to treat the question of eucharistic somatic real presence and that of the eucharist as sacrament before the question of the sacrifice of the Mass.

The separation of the question of real presence and sacrifice is a clear sign that the council did not see the inner connection between the sacramentality and the sacrificial character of the Mass. Rather, an accidental connection between the two was to a great extent simply taken for granted. Both Christ and the forms of bread and wine had to be present in order that he might be offered to the Father. Hence each Mass is seen as a kind of new sacrifice related to the cross in which the priest and the victim are identical with the priest and the victim of the cross.

[12] Karl Rahner, *The Celebration of the Eucharist,* Angelus Häussling, ed. (New York: Herder and Herder, 1968) 18 = Karl Rahner, Angelus Häussling, *Die vielen Messen und das eine Opfer,* Quaestiones Disputatae 31 (Freiburg—Basel—Vienna: Herder, 1966) 28–40.

Chapter Seven

From the Council of Trent to Modern Times

After the Council of Trent, in certain Reformation circles, the traditional doctrine of the somatic real presence of Christ was denied. The spiritualized interpretation of the sacraments of the body and blood gained the upper hand. As support from tradition for this spiritualized theology of the sacraments of the body and blood, appeal was made, and not without reason, to St. Augustine of Hippo. On the other hand, the sacrificial character of eucharistic worship was not simply denied. The special opportunity for the spiritual self-offering of the individual believer in the liturgy of the Lord's Supper was not denied, or even questioned, but rather decidedly affirmed. What then was denied? More commonly, Reformation theologians reacted against the Catholic affirmation of the objective sacrificial character of the Mass as well as against the theological explanations employed to support the relation of the sacrifice of the Mass to the historical sacrifice of the cross.

At the same time, in Catholic circles, the theological endeavor to hand on Trent's teaching regarding the mystery of the Eucharistic somatic real presence of Christ was not always successful. Especially in the matter of the doctrine of transubstantiation, theologians, whether Catholic or Protestant, almost invariably misinterpreted the intention of the council. Only now, in the twentieth century, is it commonly recognized that Trent did not canonize the philosophical explanation underlying the scholastic theology of transubstantiation. Moreover, only now it is commonly recognized that the scholastic explanation of the notion of substantial change is not the only valid approach to the question, and that it is not, in fact, superior to that of fourth-century Greek theology. The same pattern of a more nuanced understanding of what Trent really intended has also developed in the matter of reflection on the doctrine of the sacrifice of the Mass.

I. THE DOCTRINE OF TRANSUBSTANTIATION

The history of Western systematic theology shows that models have been employed to shed light on various aspects of the Christian economy of salvation. Sometimes the model employed is endogenous, deriving from the data being studied. At other times it is exogenous, imported from the outside. In the matter of theological reflection on the eucharistic conversion, an example of an endogenous model is the notion of "eucharistic Incarnation," where the historical Incarnation of the Word provides a salvation-history perspective. An exogenous model of eucharistic conversion is based on the model of a change that takes place wholly within the world, thus making possible the continued existence of the appearance of bread and wine while their substances are changed into that of the body and blood of Christ.

The limitation of the model of eucharistic Incarnation, employed in Greek and Latin theology, was recognized by Western scholastic theologians. This model tends to support the idea of a kind of hypostatic union of the humanity of Jesus with the substance of bread and wine. The Council of Trent clearly opposed the strict application of the notion of eucharistic Incarnation by denying the idea of a union of Christ with the bread and wine. The council affirmed not unification but rather conversion.[1] On the other hand, Trent did not canonize the philosophical theory of transubstantiation, a theory which leads to a static concept of Christ's real presence.

More recently, in order to shed some light on this conversion, for which there is no natural analogy, various theories have been proposed. All of these new theories are also specifically concerned with affirming the active real presence of Christ in the sacrament of his substantial real presence.

A. THEOLOGICAL EXPLANATION OF THE ROLE OF THE SPIRIT IN THE SANCTIFICATION OF THE EUCHARISTIC ELEMENTS

In the Eastern tradition, the bread and wine are said to be changed by the power of the Holy Spirit. By the same power the sacramental body and blood sanctify the communicants. This activity of the Holy Spirit, derived from the Spirit's personal and proper mission, is intimately linked to the theandric activity of the crucified and risen Lord

[1] Council of Trent, Session 13, canons 2 and 3 (DS 1651–1652).

Jesus Christ in the event of the consecration of the eucharistic elements. Christ's action in Holy Communion likewise includes the action of the same Holy Spirit.

From this viewpoint it can be said that Christ himself, by a divine-human act, consecrates the bread and wine, i.e., gives the meaning that constitutes an ontological change, or change of being. In this way, Christ himself turns to the communicant of the sacraments of his body and blood, is met by the communicant who participates in the sacrament, and sacramentally draws the communicant into union with himself. On the other hand the Spirit, sent by Christ, sanctifies the bread and wine that has been given a new meaning, i.e., assimilates the bread and wine to the risen Lord, so that there is unity of being between Christ and the bread and wine. The reception of the sacrament of the presence of the whole Christ is an efficacious symbolic activity. It serves as transparency for the spiritual union of the believer with Christ based on the participation of the Holy Spirit who is the mediation[2] of the personal immediacy of Christ to the communicant and of the communicant to Christ.

In the sacramental event of the consecration of the bread and wine, the crucified and risen Lord, fully relational to the world through his glorification, relates himself to the bread and wine. But the perfect correspondence between being and meaning, the correspondence that overcomes the distance between sign and signified, is the work of the Holy Spirit. But note that the Spirit does not fill the bread and wine in such a way that the Eucharist is, in the first instance, sacrament of the Spirit. This would mean that, because the Spirit in the bread and wine is the same Spirit whom Christ possesses in fullness, one communicates with Christ by receiving the sacrament. While this concept emerges here and there in the Eastern and Western traditions, it remains marginal.

In the West it is generally explained that the power of God changes the bread and wine. The transformation is seen as an exercise of divine efficient causality accomplished by the three divine persons in common, even when the transformation is attributed to the Holy Spirit. In the theory of transubstantiation, bread and wine are changed into the body and blood, a change that seems to take place in this world. But, in fact, the change is not wholly in this world. The change

[2] "Mediation" is not to be confused with "mediator"; for the Holy Spirit is not the mediator, only Jesus is.

is from the sphere of the world to the sphere of God; for the change is into the Christ sacrificed and glorified. The theory of transubstantiation, which calls for a change of one material element into another, locks (as theory) the change within this world. The principle that one substance can change into another needs to be amplified by the consideration of the uniqueness of the eucharistic change. It is our conviction that the whole matter can be dealt with best within the theological outlook of traditional Eastern theology.

To explain the eucharistic change, the Eastern Fathers refer to the analogy with the historical Incarnation. Here a change took place from the sphere of this world to the sphere of God. There was the actualization of the potential of a created being for union with the Son in person. This union of the humanity of Jesus with the Son, from the standpoint of ascending Christology, was the consequence of the sanctifying action of the Spirit in the act of the creation of that humanity.

Corresponding to this, material things are said to be capable of being sanctified because they are used by God as means by which God and the human being, in synergism, realize man's transcendence.[3] The Incarnation of the Word of God involved a change in the assumed humanity, a higher determination that leaves intact the previous human perfections. The change that was brought about in the human reality was a change effected by the divinely endowed potency granted in a built-in potency. The actualization of this potency terminated in another being, the divine person. In other words, in the process of the sanctification of human beings, the obediential potency is actualized so that the sanctified one is constituted a new being. In the case of the eucharistic gifts, the sanctifying action of the Holy Spirit enables the elevation of the elements to terminate in Christ sacrificed and glorified. As a result, through the participation of the sacraments of his body and blood, Christ himself unites the believer to himself sacramentally. And this is a sign of the deepening of the spiritual union of the believer with Christ that is ultimately based on the participation of the Holy Spirit who is the mediation of the personal immediacy of Christ to the communicant and of the communicant to Christ.

How are bread and wine changed? By being made sacraments, by being invested with new meaning in the sphere of God, and thus by

[3] [In this manuscript, EJK often took pains to use inclusive language. I have at times made editorial changes in that direction, but not, as here, where I was afraid of losing or misrepresenting significant nuance—RJD.]

being brought into unity of being with Christ. The limitations of the unity of sign and signified pertain to the limitations of sign. In the Eucharist, the process begins with signification and ends up with the elements becoming one in unity of being with Christ. The sacraments of the body and blood are the only example of ontological sanctification which ends in unity of being between sign and signified (real symbol). But the sanctification of the bread and wine is not an instance of ontic sanctification: The sanctification is not a determination of the being-in-itself, but the determination of a being-for-human beings.

II. THE SACRIFICE OF THE MASS

During the centuries separating the Council of Trent from the contemporary Catholic Church, numerous theories have been proposed to explain the essence of the eucharistic sacrifice. All Catholic theologians have maintained that the Mass has a sacrificial character and that the sacrificial trait is expressed in the visible ritual activity of the liturgy. Beginning with this presupposition, the question that remains to be answered is this: Precisely in what does the visible sacrifice of the Mass consist?

Trent seemed to many post-Tridentine theologians to provide the key in the "doctrine" it attached to the canons concerning the eucharistic sacrifice. Here it is stated that the prophecy of Malachi about the pure oblation offered by the Gentiles is fulfilled in the Mass.[4] This teaching influenced some theologians to identify the sacrificial element of the Mass in terms of a food offering. But Trent's doctrine, in fact, supplied no clarification concerning what elements constitute the general notion of sacrifice, and wherein the Mass corresponds to this definition of sacrifice.

Among the more popular theories proposed by Catholic theologians concerning the constitution of the visible sacrifice of the Mass was the following: In the twofold consecration, the separation of the species is a sign of the separation of the body and blood on the cross. However, this theory was finally rejected as unsatisfactory, for the symbolic reference could not be identified as that which constitutes the sacrificial character of the Mass. For the twofold consecration signifies the separation of body and blood of a victim of a sacrifice; this is a comparative-religions concept of the effect of a sacrificial death.

[4] DS 1742.

The eucharistic action, on the other hand, was understood as a "true and proper sacrifice," that stands in a real relation of dependence on the once-for-all sacrifice of the cross.

Moreover, in biblical and patristic thinking, the grounding of the sacrificial character of the Eucharist in the separation of flesh from blood is inconceivable. For the terms flesh and blood, or body and blood, express the total representation of the life and the offering of it to God in sacrifice. In brief, this theory which identifies the sacrificial trait of the Eucharist with the separate consecration of the species is not biblical, because both actions represent together the total giving of Jesus.

The problem with all theologies of the Mass of the post-Reformation period originates in the search for the grounds of sacrifice in the rite itself, and not in the representation of the sacrifice of the cross. Catholic theology did not take seriously enough the fact that "sacrifice" in the history-of-religions sense was abolished with the Christ-event. In the Christ-event, sacrificial activity on the part of the creature is reduced to the obedience of Jesus before the Father, even unto death.

But how should Catholic theology employ the teaching of Trent on the sacrifice of the Mass? First of all, one has to take into account the relation between Scripture and the official teaching of the Church. The office of teaching, in its dogmatic statements, "receives" the interpretation of Scripture furnished by theologians. But Scripture also serves as a norm for the critique of the interpretation of official teaching. Hence a valid interpretation of Trent is possible that disengages the content of its statements concerning the sacrificial character of the Eucharist (derived from the particular historically conditioned narrowness of the sixteenth century), and leads it closer to the authentic whole tradition ultimately based on the primary witness of Scripture. What the council meant remains, in this way, true, but only in this way.

In the course of time from the seventeenth to the twentieth centuries, a series of theories about the sacrifice of the Mass developed which can be grouped under the titles *theory of oblation* or *theory of destruction.* The theory of oblation holds that the offering of a gift is the essence of sacrifice. In the case of the eucharistic sacrifice, influenced by the Tridentine order of treatment of the sacraments of the somatic real presence of the whole Christ and the eucharistic sacrifice, the offering of the gift of Christ was depicted as conditioned by the prior conversion of the bread and wine. Here, generally speaking, the conversion was conceived as occurring simultaneously with the sacrificial offering, but according to priority of nature and not as priority of time.

The theory of destruction was based on the principle that a change of the gift is the essence of sacrifice. Therefore, some theologians attempted to identify what it was in which this destruction of the victim of the eucharistic sacrifice might consist. The idea of "virtual death" through the separate consecration of the eucharistic gifts was often proposed. Robert Bellarmine taught that the destruction of the victim through the priest's eating and drinking of the eucharistic body and blood constituted an essential aspect of the eucharistic sacrifice. Incidentally, his insight that brings the rite of Holy Communion into the sacrificial dimension of the Eucharist is in harmony with the scriptural understanding of Eucharist. For according to the New Testament witness, sacrifice and meal cannot be separated. There will be further discussion of this theme below in our concluding chapter eleven.

Today, one recognizes that the Eucharist has a sacrificial character because of its relation to the sacrifice of the cross. From this point of view, the sacrificial character of the Mass is often explained as consisting in "sacramental representation of the offering of Jesus on the cross." This opinion offers no objective difficulty. But what does this mean? In the first place, it means that there is a visible manifestation of Christ's sacrifice. Secondly, it means that there is present under the visible manifestation the presence of the once-for-all sacrifice of Christ. However, this does not mean that the visible manifestation of Christ's sacrifice, not itself a sacrifice, becomes a visible sacrifice by the fact that there is present under it the invisible sacrifice of Christ. Otherwise all sacraments would be the sacrifice of Christ.[5] It means that when Christ's self-offering is expressed in the eucharistic celebration in the sacramental signs, this suffices for the special sacrificial character of the Eucharist. The sharing of bread and wine together with the words of institution suffices, for the eucharistic action is the visible offering of Christ himself. Other sacraments are not sacrifice because they do not represent so directly the offering of Christ himself to the Father.

The Christ-event is represented in the Eucharist under the viewpoint of its sacrificial character. This is known from the action itself: the narrative of institution and the sharing of the sacramental body

[5] Karl Rahner, *The Celebration of the Eucharist*, Angelus Häussling, ed. (New York: Herder and Herder, 1968) 19.

and blood. If we see the sacraments as realizing signs, their difference is grounded in the different relations to the Christ-event which are represented symbolically. Hence unity and difference in the sacraments are grounded in the relationality of the symbolic in which and through which Christ represents himself.

The foregoing perspective corresponds to the general way in which, at the present time, Catholic theologians ordinarily seek to explain the sacrificial character of the Eucharist as the sacramental representation of the historical self-offering of Jesus on the cross. Official Catholic theology also emphasizes the role of the recitation of the account of institution of the Eucharist as the symbolic act in which Christ, through his minister, both represents his self-offering to the Father and consecrates the elements of bread and wine to become his body and blood in the power of the Holy Spirit. However, this way of thinking, by identifying the sacrificial aspect of the Mass as sacrifice of Christ with the formula of consecration, remains somewhat insensitive to the intimate link between the Eucharistic Prayer and the rite of Holy Communion. This way of thinking clashes with biblical and patristic witness by making the sharing of the body and blood of Christ only an "integral rite" and not an essential aspect of the sacrificial dimension of the Mass.

A. AVERAGE MODERN CATHOLIC THEOLOGY OF EUCHARISTIC SACRIFICE

The Council of Trent made no choice between the theology of the Mass of the schools of the Scotists and Thomists. However, the continuing debate with the Reformers forced Catholic theologians to concentrate on proving that the sacrifice of the Mass does not derogate from that of the cross. This resulted in a strong placing of the accent on the Christological dimension of the eucharistic sacrifice. Whereas in the two centuries before the Council of Trent the ecclesiological dimension had received serious attention, this latter dimension now faded into the background.

We have already touched on the various approaches to the subject of the relation of the sacrifice of the Mass to the sacrifice of the cross from the sixteenth to the twentieth centuries. In general these approaches failed to offer a satisfactory account of the nature of the identity of the historical and the liturgical sacrifice, and of the distinction between the two. Ultimately, from the standpoint of the Christological dimension of the Eucharist, these post-Tridentine attempts failed to offer a solution to the problem of the intimate relation of the sacrament of Christ's somatic presence to the liturgical presence of his once-for-all historical sacrificial act of the cross. Increasingly, the question or problem centered around the characteristically Western idea of the "moment of consecration." The question became: How is the relationship between the "somatic presence" and the "liturgical presence" to be explained in the perspective of the Western theology of the moment of consecration in which the words of Christ contained in the narrative of institution of the Eucharist at the Last Supper constitute the essential form of the sacramental sacrifice?

In the latter part of the twentieth century, the essence of the sacrifice of the Mass is no longer sought in a ritual immolation. For some, such as Robert Bellarmine, "ritual immolation" had included the idea that the consumption of the body and blood is an essential part, and not merely a ritual activity required for the integrity of the celebration. Moreover, the teaching that the essence of the eucharistic sacrifice consists in the oblation whereby the Church offers Christ to God is recognized as expressing only an aspect of the whole mystery. In the average modern Catholic theological understanding, the idea of a sacramental representation is popular. Here the historical sacrifice of the cross is described as obtaining a new *ubi et nunc* ("place" and "time") in the sacramental world which transcends the laws of space and time.

In this connection, the term "sacramental sacrifice" is employed to convey the idea that the sacrament of Christ's somatic real presence derives from the liturgical representation of his once-for-all self-offering of the cross. In other words, it conveys the notion that the sacrifice of Christ on the cross is represented to the liturgical assembly in the action by which the sacrament of Christ's somatic real presence is constituted. In a word, the eucharistic celebration is a visible sacrifice.[6] The once-for-all historical sacrifice of Christ is the reality, source, and presupposition of the eucharistic meal, and the grounds of the cultic sacrifice of the Church.

III. THE MODERN ROMAN CATHOLIC OFFICIAL POSITION

The more recent official teaching of the Roman Catholic magisterium in this twentieth century favors this idea of sacramental sacrifice.

[6] *Sacrificium visibile* (DS 1740–1743).

However, a development appears to have taken place since the time of Pius XII's encyclical letter *Mediator Dei*, November 20, 1947.[7]

A. PIUS XII, ENCYCLICAL LETTER *MEDIATOR DEI*

This document, devoted to the subject of the liturgy, will be discussed at length below in chapter ten. For now we note only that in this letter the question of the relation of the mysteries of Christ's historical life to the liturgical year is discussed. There is an unmistakable reference to the theology of mysteries espoused by Dom Odo Casel, O.S.B., in which the Pope reacts negatively to the theological explanation of the school of Maria Laach.[8] But the insight, central to the approach of that school, concerning the fact of a presence of the historical mysteries is not explicitly rejected by the Pope. On the other hand, a preference for the traditional scholastic explanation is clearly expressed, namely, a presence of the historical saving acts in the sense of the application of graces merited by Jesus' historical living. One also detects the influence of the negative reaction of Roman theologians of that time to Casel's thought.

However, subsequent research in the area of Greek patristic literature produced evidence of a fairly widespread conviction concerning the active presence of the mysteries of Christ's life in the sacramental celebrations of the Church, especially in baptism and Eucharist. This conclusion seems to have had the effect of rendering the Roman magisterium more sympathetic to the basic insight of Casel.

The presentation of the theology of eucharistic sacrifice in *Mediator Dei* is, above all, significant for the influence it has had on subsequent official Roman teaching. It has become the normative presentation, and is based on the reception of one of the post-Tridentine scholastic theologies of eucharistic sacrifice. Pius XII employs the eucharistic theology of Thomas Aquinas as mediated through post-Tridentine Thomistic theologians. And he adopts the formulation of the sixteenth-century Jesuit theologian Robert Bellarmine, but without ascribing to Bellarmine's peculiar explanation of the essence of the eucharistic sacrifice which embraces the aspect of destruction of the sacraments of the body and blood through eating.

[7] *Acta Apostolicae Sedis* 39 (1947) 521–600.

[8] Maria Laach, Casel's home monastery, is generally recognized as the most important center of the Catholic liturgical reform movement through most of the twentieth century.

On the subject of the consecration of the eucharistic species, which he understands to pertain to the essence of the eucharistic sacrifice, Bellarmine states:

"Because the sacrifice of the Mass is offered in the person of Christ, the priest does nothing so clearly in the person of Christ than the consecration in which he says: 'This is my body' etc."[9]

Earlier in the same chapter Bellarmine had stated:

"The sacrifice is offered principally in the person of Christ. Thus the oblation following the consecration is a certain attestation that the whole Church consents in the oblation made by Christ, and at the same time offers with him."[10]

This latter text is cited by Pius XII in *Mediator Dei.*[11]

Finally, Bellarmine links the offering of Christ, Church, and minister in this way:

"The sacrifice of the Mass is offered by three; by Christ, by the Church, by the minister; but not in the same way. For Christ offers as primary priest, and offers through the priest a man, as through his proper minister. The Church does not offer as priest through the minister, but as people through the priest. Thus Christ offers through the inferior, the Church through the superior."[12]

In *Mediator Dei* we read this paraphrase:

"The priest acts for the people only because he represents Jesus Christ, who is head of all his members and offers himself for them.

[9] "Quia sacrificium Missae offertur in persona Christi: nihil autem facit Sacerdos tam perspicue in persona Christi, quam consecrationem, in qua dicit: *Hoc est corpus meum etc."*—Robert Bellarmine, *Controversiarum de sacramento eucharistiae,* book 5, chap. 27: "Solvitur ultima objectio, et explicatur in qua parte Missae proprie consistat essentia sacrificii," in *Roberti Bellarmini Opera Omnia,* vol. 4 (Paris: Vivès, 1873) 364–68, at 368.

[10] "Sacrificium autem in persona Christi, principaliter offertur. Itaque ista oblatio consecrationem subsequens, est quaedam testificatio, quod tota Ecclesia consentiat in oblationem a Christo factam, et simul cum illo offerat"—Bellarmine, *Controversiarum de sacramento eucharistiae* 5.27, p. 366.

[11] *AAS* 39 (1947) 554 (DS 3851).

[12] "Primum est, Sacrificium Missae a tribus offerri, a Christo, ab Ecclesia, a Ministro; sed non eodem modo. Christus enim offert, ut primarius Sacerdos, et offert per Sacerdotem hominem, ut per suum proprium Ministrum. Ecclesia non offert, ut Sacerdos per Ministrum, sed ut populus per Sacerdotem. Itaque Christus per

Thus he goes to the altar as the minister of Christ, inferior to Christ, but superior to the people."[13]

This theological approach excludes the teaching of Scotus–Biel, for it subsumes the ecclesiological aspect of the eucharistic sacrifice under its Christological aspect. In other words, the priest represents the Church because he represents Christ the head of the Church who offers the sacrifice in the name of all the members of his body the Church. This teaching is developed in *Mediator Dei:*

"For that unbloody immolation, by which at the words of consecration Christ is made present upon the altar in the state of victim, is performed by the priest and by him alone, as representative of Christ and not as representative of the faithful. But it is because the priest places the divine victim upon the altar that he offers it to God the Father as an oblation for the glory of the Blessed Trinity and for the good of the whole Church. Now the faithful participate in the oblation, understood in this limited sense, after their own fashion and in a twofold manner, namely, because they not only offer the sacrifice by the hands of the priest, but also, to a certain extent, in union with him. . . . Now it is clear that the faithful offer by the hands of the priest from the fact that the minister at the altar, in offering a sacrifice in the name of all his members, represents Christ, the head of the mystical body. Hence the whole Church can rightly be said to offer up the victim through Christ. But the conclusion that the people offer the sacrifice with the priest himself is not based on the fact that, being members of the Church no less than the priest himself, they perform a visible liturgical rite; for this is the privilege only of the minister who has been divinely appointed for this office; rather it is based on the fact that the people unite their hearts in praise, impetration, expiation, and thanksgiving with the prayers or intentions of the priest, even of the High Priest himself, so that in the one and same offering of the victim and according to a visible sacerdotal rite, they may be presented to God the Father."[14]

---

inferiorem offert, Ecclesia per superiorem"—Bellarmine, *Controversiarum de sacramento eucharistiae* 6.4, p. 373.

[13] ". . . sacerdotem nempe idcirco tantum populi vices agere, quia personam gerit Domini nostri Iesu Christi, quatenus membrorum omnium Caput est, pro iisdemque semet ipsum offert; ideoque ad altare accedere ut ministrum Christi, Christo inferiorem, superiorem autem populo"—*AAS* 39 (1947) 553 (DS 3850).

[14] "Incruenta enim illa immolatio, qua consecrationis verbis prolatis Christus in statu victimae super altare praesens redditur, ab ipso solo sacerdote perficitur,

On the subject of the nature of the eucharistic sacrifice, Pius XII goes beyond the teaching of the Council of Trent. "The august sacrifice of the altar . . . is . . . a true and proper act of sacrifice *(sacrificatio)*, whereby the High Priest by an unbloody immolation offers himself a most acceptable victim to the eternal Father, as he did on the cross."[15] This statement is intended to be an interpretation of the statement of chapter two of the Council of Trent's doctrine concerning the sacrifice of the Mass: "It is one and the same victim; the same now offering by the ministry of priests, who offered himself then on the cross, the manner of offering alone being different."[16]

After recalling that the priest of the eucharistic sacrifice is Jesus Christ, represented by the minister who "possesses the power of performing actions in virtue of Christ's very person," there follows this observation on the identity of victim:

"Likewise the victim is the same. . . . The manner, however, in which Christ is offered is different. On the cross he completely offered himself . . . and the immolation of the victim was brought about by the bloody death. . . . But on the altar . . . the sacrifice is shown forth in an admirable manner by external signs which are symbols of his death . . . the eucharistic species under which he is present symbolize

---

prout Christi personam sustinet, non vero prout Christifidelium personam gerit. At idcirco quod sacerdos divinam victimam altari superponit, eamdem Deo Patri qua oblationem defert ad gloriam Sanctissimae Trinitatis et in bonum totius Ecclesiae. Hanc autem restricti nominis oblationem christifideles suo modo duplicique ratione participant: quia nempe non tantum per sacerdotis manus, sed etiam cum ipso quodammodo Sacrificium offerunt . . . . Christifideles autem per sacerdotis manus Sacrificium offerre ex eo patet, quod altaris administer personam Christi utpote Capitis gerit, membrorum omnium nomine offerentis; quo quidem fit, ut universa Ecclesia iure dicatur per Christum victimae oblationem deferre. Populum vero una cum ipso sacerdote offerre non idcirco statuitur, quod Ecclesiae membra, haud aliter ac ipse sacerdos, ritum liturgicum adspectabilem perficiant, quod solius ministri est ad hoc divinitus deputati: sed idcirco quod sua vota laudis, impetrationis, expiationis gratiarumque actionis una cum votis seu mentis intentione sacerdotis, immo Summi ipsius Sacerdotis, eo fine coniungit, ut eadem in ipsa victimae oblatione, externo quoque sacerdotis ritu, Deo Patri exhibeantur"—*AAS* 39 (1947) 555–56 (partially given in DS 3852).

[15] "Augustum igitur altaris Sacrificium non mera est ac simplex Iesu Christi cruciatuum ac mortis commemoratio, sed vera ac propria sacrificatio, qua quidem per incruentam immolationem Summus Sacerdos id agit, quod iam in cruce fecit"—*AAS* 39 (1947) 548.

[16] "Una enim eademque est hostia, idem nunc offerens sacerdotum ministerio, qui se ipsum tunc in cruce obtulit, sola offerendi ratione diversa"—DS 1743.

the actual separation of his body and blood. Thus the commemorative representation of his death, which actually took place on Calvary, is repeated in every sacrifice of the altar, seeing that Jesus Christ is symbolically shown forth by separate symbols to be in the state of death."[17]

Pius XII distinguishes between two essential moments of the sacrifice of the Mass: the internal oblation of Christ *(oblatio)* and the external manifestation of the internal act *(immolatio incruenta).* Thus he differs from Trent where oblation and immolation are used as synonyms. Also the pope seems to favor a theory of an actual oblation (internal offering) of Christ in every Mass, where he says that Christ "does what he did then on the cross." It was a common opinion of the time when Pius XII was writing that an actual oblation of Christ is related to the eucharistic sacrifice; not formally a new act, but the same act which Christ elicited on the cross and which somehow remains in the glorified Christ.

In fact the Pope explicitly distinguishes between internal oblation and immolation in the following passage: "the sacrifice . . . is shown forth by external signs which are symbols of his death *(signa externa).*"[18] Nevertheless, the Pope does not explicitly identify in what the essential *immolatio incruenta* consists. Some authors held that it consists in the separate consecrations; others that it consists in the sacramental mode of the presence in that Christ's body is present under the species of bread and his blood under the species of wine in virtue of the words of consecration.

[17] "Eadem pari modo victima est, divinus nempe Redemptor, secundum humanam naturam suam et in corporis sanguinisque sui veritate. Dissimilis tamen ratio est, qua Christus offertur. In Cruce enim totum semet ipsum suosque Deo obtulit dolores; victimae vero immolatio per cruentam mortem, libera voluntate obitam, effecta est. In ara autem, ob gloriosum humanae naturae suae statum, 'mors illi ultra non dominabitur,' [Rom 6:9] ideoque sanguinis effusio haud possibilis est; verumtamen ex divinae sapientiae consilio Redemptoris nostri sacrificatio per externa signa, quae sunt mortis indices, mirando quodam modo ostenditur. Siquidem per panis 'transubstantiationem' in corpus vinique in sanguinem Christi, ut eius corpus reapse praesens habetur, ita eius cruor: eucharisticae autem species, sub quibus adest, cruentam corporis et sanguinis separationem figurant. Itaque memorialis demonstratio eius mortis, quae reapse in Calvariae loco accidit, in singulis altaris sacrificiis iteratur, quandoquidem per distinctos indices Christus Iesus in statu victimae significatur et ostenditur"—*AAS* 39 (1947) 548–49.

[18] "Redemptoris nostri sacrificatio per externa signa, quae sunt mortis indices, mirando quodam modo ostenditur"—*AAS* 39 (1947) 548.

Of course, the whole Christ is present under each species in virtue of the hypostatic union and mystery of the resurrection and glorification as defined by Trent.[19] Pius XII's encyclical letter ascribes the value of sign or symbol only to the separation of the species. The unbloody immolation is said to be "signified" or "indicated,"[20] "made manifest in a mystical manner by the separation of the species."[21]

In brief, Pius XII avoids theories, such as that of Bellarmine, de Lugo, and Franzelin, which require a real or virtual destruction of Christ, and which, especially in the case of Lugo-Franzelin, dominated the entire Catholic theological field during the pontificates of Pius IX and Leo XIII. He retains formulas dating from the end of the reign of Leo XIII, revived and propagated by Cardinal Billot, while making no reference to Billot's system. Rather, he appears to tend in the direction of those theologians who had been making the idea of sacramental sacrifice the object of their studies.

Prescinding from the various nuances of particular authors, the essentials of the theory of sacramental sacrifice may be summarized thus: The immolation of the Mass differs from the oblation. Christ offers himself in the Mass and is sacramentally immolated at the consecration of the bread and wine. The qualification "sacramental" means that it is a matter of a symbolic ritual that contains what it signifies. In virtue of the divine institution, the Eucharist renders the sacrifice of the cross sacramentally present.

This explanation of "sacramental" is based on an understanding of the special mode of sacramental being, whereby the reality signified has its proper mode of existence elsewhere but is truly contained in its symbolic representation. It is with this concept of "sacramental presence" that the explication of the eucharistic sacrifice begins, that is, the explanation of how the sacramental sacrifice is a true sacrifice

[19] DS 1651: "Can 1. Si quis negaverit, in sanctissimae Eucharistiae sacramento contineri vere, realiter et subtantialiter, corpus et sanguinem una cum anima et divinitate Domini nostri Iesu Christi ac proinde totum Christum; sed dixerit, tantummodo esse in eo ut in signo vel figura, aut virtute: anathema sit *[cf. *1636 1640].*" DS 1653: "Can. 3. Si quis negaverit, in venerabili sacramento Eucharistiae sub unaquaque specie et sub singulis cuiusque speciei partibus separatione facta totum Christum contineri: an. s. *[cf. *1641].*

[20] *AAS* 39 (1947) 548—see n. 17 above.

[21] "Animadvertendum est Eucharisticum Sacrificium suapte natura incruentem esse divinae victimae immolationem, quae quidem mystico modo ex sacrarum specierum separatione patet"—*AAS* 39 (1947) 563.

differing only in the manner of offering from that of the historical sacrifice of the cross. However, authors who hold for this sacramental theory are not in agreement concerning the nature of the presence of the sacrifice of the cross in the Mass. Is it to be attributed to a perpetual state of victimhood of the glorified Christ? Here an appeal is made to an interior offering of Christ accomplished on the cross which has become "eternal" and is externalized through the words of consecration. Others demand more, in virtue of the fact that we are redeemed by the historical redemptive work. In one way or another, they postulate the presence of the historical saving act of the cross: a metahistorical presence.

B. LETTER OF THE CONGREGATION FOR THE DOCTRINE OF THE FAITH

Since the publication of *Mediator Dei,* the official teaching of the Roman magisterium has often repeated the perspective of that encyclical on the subject of the relation of the presiding priest to Christ and the Church in the Eucharist. The Constitution on the Church of Vatican II, *Lumen gentium* no. 10, states that "The priest . . . confects the eucharistic sacrifice in the person of Christ and offers it in the name of the people of God." Here we meet the characteristic post-Tridentine scholastic theology of eucharistic sacrifice, wherein the ecclesiological aspect is subsumed under and introduced through the Christological.

There is no need to review all the modern documents of the Roman magisterium which treat this theme. It suffices to recall the content of "The Letter of the Congregation for the Doctrine of the Faith on the Subject of the Role of the Ordained Ministry of the Episcopate and Presbyterate in the Celebration of the Eucharist," dated August 6, 1983.[22]

In this letter, the CDF cites the previous official documents since Pius XII on the topic. The letter is occasioned by the prevalence of erroneous opinions concerning the question of the requirement of ordained office-bearers, bishops, and presbyters, as those alone qualified to preside at the Eucharist. On this subject the traditional teaching is restated:

"For although the whole faithful participate in one and the same priesthood of Christ and concur in the oblation of the Eucharist,

[22] *AAS* 75 (1983) 1001–9. Here one will find footnote references to all the major statements of recent official teaching of the Roman magisterium on this point.

nevertheless only the ministerial priesthood, in virtue of the sacrament of orders, enjoys the power of confecting the eucharistic sacrifice in the person of Christ and of offering it in the name of the whole Christian people."[23]

The subject of the representative function of the presiding minister is taken up in detail later on:

"However those whom Christ calls to the episcopate and presbyterate, in order that they can fulfill the office . . . of confecting the eucharistic mystery, he signs them spiritually with the special seal through the sacrament of orders . . . and so configures them to himself that they proclaim the words of consecration not by mandate of the community, but they act *'in persona Christi,'* which certainly means more than 'in the name of Christ' or even 'in place of Christ' . . . since the one celebrating by a peculiar and sacramental way is completely the same as the 'high and eternal Priest,' who is author and principal actor of this his own sacrifice, in which no one indeed can take his place."[24]

In this letter, as in other earlier documents, the formula *in persona Christi* is employed to exclude clearly the idea that the priest represents the Church by delegation from below, from the members of the Church. The error which these documents are resisting comes to this: "The advocates . . . affirm that any Christian community, by the fact that it gathers in the name of Christ . . . enjoys all powers, which the

[23] "Quamvis, enim, fideles universi unum idemque Christi sacerdotium participent et in oblationem Eucharistiae concurrant, solum tamen sacerdos ministerialis, vi sacramenti Ordinis, potestate gaudet sacrificium Eucharisticum conficiendi in persona Christi illudque totius christiani populi nomine offerendi"—CDF Letter of 6 August 1983, I 1 (*AAS* 75 [1983] 1001).

[24] "Quos autem ad Episcopatum et Presbyteratum vocat, Christus Dominus, ut iidem munera sibi credita peculiarique modo munus tam grave conficiendi mysterium Eucharisticum adimplere valeant, eos speciali sigillo per sacramentum Ordinis spiritualiter signat, 'charactere' appellato etiam in solemnibus Magisterii documentis, eosque sibi ita configurat ut ipsi dum proferunt consecrationis verba non communitatis mandato, sed agant 'in persona Christi,' quod plus sane significat quam 'nomine Christi' vel etiam 'Christi vicem' . . . , cum celebrans ratione peculiari et sacramentali idem prorsus sit ac "summus aeternusque Sacerdos" qui Auctor est principesque Actor huius proprii sui Sacrificii, in quo nemo revera in eius locum substitui potest"—CDF Letter of 6 August 1983, III 4 (*AAS* 75 [1983] 1006). The quotation which occupies the second half of this citation is from Pope John Paul II's Lenten letter *Dominicae cenae* II 8 (*AAS* 72 [1980] 128–29).

Lord intended to grant to his Church."[25] Also in the "Declaration of the Congregation for the Doctrine of the Faith on the Question of Admission of Women to the Ministerial Priesthood," the Christological argument is used to show that only men can represent Christ in the act of eucharistic consecration: "It is true that the priest represents the Church which is the body of Christ. But if he does so it is primarily because, first, he represents Christ himself who is head and pastor of the Church."[26] Hence the conclusion is drawn that, since the priest represents Christ in strict sacramental identity at the moment of consecration, the role must be taken by a man.

The teaching on the representative functions of the priest in the celebration of the Eucharist, and their ordering, does not touch the essential doctrine of the eucharistic sacrifice. On the question of the relationship between the sacrifice of the Mass and that of the cross, prescinding from *Mediator Dei,* little that is noteworthy has been taught by the magisterium in this century apart from the 1980 Holy Thursday letter of Pope John Paul II, *Dominicae cenae,* and the "Vatican Response to ARCIC I Final Report."[27]

C. LETTER OF POPE JOHN PAUL II: *DOMINICAE CENAE*

The 1980 Holy Thursday letter of Pope John Paul II, *Dominicae cenae,* treats the sacred and sacrificial character of the Eucharist.[28]

1. *The Sacred Character*

The sacredness of the Eucharist is ascribed to fact that Christ is the author and principal priest. This ritual memorial of the death of the Lord is performed by priests who repeat the words and actions of Christ, who thus offer the holy sacrifice *"in persona Christi* . . . in specific sacramental identification with the High and Eternal Priest, who

[25] "Novarum opinionum fautores affirmant quamlibet Christianam communitatem, eo ipso quod adunatur in nomine Christi ac proinde indivisa Eius praesentia fruitur (cf. *Mt* 18, 20), omnibus gaudere potestatibus, quas Dominus Ecclesiae suae concedere voluit"—CDF Letter of 6 August 1983, II 1 (*AAS* 75 [1983] 1002).

[26] "Fatendum sane est sacerdotem reapse Ecclesiam repraesentare, quae est Corpus Christi; at hoc ideo, quia in primis Christum ipsum repraesentat, qui est caput et pastor Ecclesiae"—*Inter insigniores,* 15 October 1976, *AAS* 69 (1977) 98–116, at 112–13.

[27] *Origins* 21, no. 29 (Dec. 19, 1991) 441–47.

[28] *De SS Eucharistiae Mysterio et Cultu (Dominicae Cenae),* 24 February 1980, *AAS* 72 (1980) 113–48, at II 8–9: "Eucharistiae indoles sacra et sacrificium," 127–34.

is the author and principal actor of this sacrifice of his . . ."[29] Here as elsewhere in this letter, John Paul II limits himself to the typical scholastic approach to the theology of the Eucharist, passing over the trinitarian grounding of the holiness of the Eucharist. In modern Catholic theology, the sacred character of the Eucharist is grounded on more than just this Christological basis. Its sacredness is not merely based on the fact of originating in a historical act of institution by Christ. Rather, what grounds the holiness of the Eucharist is the initiative of the Father: the self-offering by the Father of his only Son for the salvation of the world.

Here we touch on the unique New Testament understanding of the "true sacrifice" as that which is grounded on the movement of God to us. The death of Jesus is ultimately the expression of the turning of God to us. The love of the Father is the origin of the self-offering of Jesus.[30] The classical Eucharistic Prayers were constructed with this background in mind, and represent the response of the sacrifice of praise to the Father to what the Father has done in Jesus Christ for the salvation of the world. Also, in this perspective, there is the matter of the sanctifying work of the Holy Spirit who is the divine agent of the self-offering of Jesus on the cross and of the presence of this unique sacrifice in the eucharistic celebration. The sending of the Spirit at Pentecost enables the celebration of the Eucharist in which the triumph of the death of Christ is represented and the Father is given thanks for the great gift. According to the Constitution on the Sacred Liturgy of Vatican II, "All this . . . happens . . . in the power of the Holy Spirit."[31] However, there is a notable absence of the pneumatological aspect of the Eucharist in *Dominicae cenae.*

This pneumatological aspect of the Eucharist has been made especially prominent in the new Eucharistic Prayers of the Missal of Paul VI where the Holy Spirit is identified as the divine source of the "change of the bread and wine" (Eucharistic Prayer III). However, John Paul II's description of the role of the ministerial priesthood omits completely the pneumatological dimension. Rather, basing himself on Trent's decree on priesthood, canon 2, concerning the

[29] "Offertur nempe 'in persona': cum celebrans ratione peculiari et sacramentali idem prorsus sit ac 'summus aeternusque Sacerdos,' qui Auctor est principesque Actor huius proprii sui Sacrificii . . ."—*Dominicae cenae* II 8, *AAS* 72 (1980) 128.

[30] Romans 8:32, John 3:16, and numerous other places in the New Testament.

[31] Vatican II, Constitution on the Sacred Liturgy *(Sacrosanctum concilium)* no. 6.

potestas consecrandi,[32] the ministerial activity of priests is mentioned under the presupposition of its Christological grounding. Priests are said to be the acting subjects of the consecration: "they consecrate it (elements of bread and wine)";[33] "by means of consecration by the priest they become sacred species."[34]

2. *The Sacrificial Aspect*

The Eucharist is said to be "above all a sacrifice."[35] As support for this, the doctrine of Trent's Decree on the Sacrifice of the Mass, chapters one and two, is cited.[36] Also the *Respice* prayer of Eucharistic Prayer III is quoted, where the self-offering of the community is linked to the historical self-offering of Christ.[37] But on the subject of the response character of the Eucharistic Prayer, the following is said: "Since the Eucharist is a true sacrifice it brings about the restoration to God. Consequently, the celebrant . . . is an authentic priest, performing . . . a true sacrificial act, that brings men back to God."[38] Also, in the same number of the letter, we read: "To this sacrifice, which is renewed *(renovatur)* in a sacramental form."[39]

Here the same kind of confusion is discernible as that caused by Trent's use of *offerre* when referring both to the historical sacrifice of the cross and to the liturgical–ritual sacrificial act of the eucharistic celebration. Trent, as we have seen, used *offerre* not only with reference to the self-offering of Christ, but also to describe the liturgical–ritual rite of the Eucharist. The theological and terminological problem derived from Trent's mixing up of the historical self-offering of

[32] DS 1771.

[33] ". . . panem namque et vinum offerunt et consecrant . . ."—*Dominicae cenae* II 11, *AAS* 72 (1980) 141.

[34] ". . . per consecrationem sacerdotis sacrae species efficiuntur"—ibid., II 9, p. 133.

[35] "In primis autem est Eucharistia sacrificium"—ibid., II 9, p. 130.

[36] Note 46 of *Dominicae cenae,* pp. 130–31, quotes the following statement from chap. two of the doctrina from Trent's Session 22: "Una eademque est hostia, idem nunc offerens sacerdotum ministerio, qui te ipsum tunc in cruce obtulit, sola offerendi ratione diversa" (DS 1743).

[37] *Dominicae cenae* II 9, p. 132.

[38] "Quam ob rem verum cum Eucharistia sit sacrificium, hanc restitutionem ad Deum operatur. Inde vero sequitur ut celebrans, germanus sit *sacerdos* qui—peculiaris potestatis virtute in sacra ordinatione collatae—sacrificalem perficit actum homines ad Deum referentem"—ibid., II 9, p. 131.

[39] "Ad hoc igitur sacrificium, quod modo sacramentali in altari renovatur . . ."—ibid., II 9, p. 133.

Christ and its ritual expression can be resolved only by a rethinking of the inner relation of [1] the personal sacrifice of Jesus and his body the Church and [2] the outward form of the meal as its efficacious sign.

Moreover, the traditional fixing of the sacrificial act in the consecration of the eucharistic gifts by the priest needs to be critically examined. The sacrificial action of the Mass cannot be narrowed down to oblation and immolation, liturgically accomplished at the conversion, with the meal treated almost as an irrelevant sequel. From the biblical point of view, the sacrifice and meal cannot be separated. According to the narrative of institution, it is the intention of Christ to give himself in such a way that he is simultaneously received. This biblical view can be described as follows: The Passover of Christ to glory, once-for-all, makes his self-offering an abiding "being-for-us." In the action of the Eucharist, the sacrifice of Christ is proclaimed by word and represented and applied to the community in the giving over of the eucharistic gifts as food. The outward form of the representation of the sacrificial offering of Jesus is not a sacrificial rite in the commonly understood sense, but the distribution of his body and blood as food of life. The basic structure is the sacrifice of self-offering in the signs of food.

The Eucharist renders present the reality of the mystery of the cross in the form of a sacramental memorial meal of the Church. As sacrifice of the Church, it is disclosed as a sharing in the one sacrifice of Jesus. The goal of the Eucharist is the self-offering of the whole Church, head and body. Or, if you will: the goal of the Eucharist is the self-offering of the Church with Christ, or the Church's participation in the sacrifice of Christ. The visible sign of the sacrifice is the meal. There is the offering and sharing of the body and blood of Christ as food. This is accompanied by the acceptance and the receiving of him as a sharing of himself with us. The remembrance in faith of the self-offering of Christ includes the sharing in the movement of the Father to us in the sending of his Son, and the movement of the incarnate Son to the Father. We enter into both movements: the movement of the Father to us in the sharing of our love with the brethren, and the movement of the Son to the Father, for our hope and trust in him is the highest expression of worship of the Father.

Only from this biblical perspective can a basic theological statement be made concerning the sacrifice of the Church. The sharing in the body and blood of Christ makes us one body and draws us into the fate of this body. The eucharistic body of Christ does not stand by itself and is not offered as an isolated gift vis-à-vis us. Rather, Christ is there in order that believers be changed into the true body of Christ, and become themselves a holy sacrifice.

Pope John Paul refers to the awakening of the consciousness of the faithful to their participation in the eucharistic sacrifice through the ritual act of bearing the bread and wine to the altar with prayers and spiritual offerings to the end that the elements be changed so as to become the body of Christ given and the blood of Christ shed.[40] But more than this needs to be said. The special question of the particular sacrificial act of the priest must remain embedded in a broader ecclesiological context of the Augustinian body-of-Christ theology. The sacrificial action should not be narrowly conceived as coinciding liturgically with the moment of consecration of the elements, and thereby relegating the meal to the status of a nonessential, merely "integrating rite."

The further aspect of the relation of the death of the cross to the Eucharist also needs to be expressed more fully than is done in *Dominicae cenae* no. 9. Here we read: "The forms of bread and wine represent, in virtue of the conversion, in a sacramental and unbloody way the bloody propitiatory sacrifice which he offered on the cross to the Father for the salvation of the world."[41] However, in fact, in the eucharistic action, Jesus Christ encounters us in the fullness of his mission. The abiding ground of this is his death on the cross wherein his eternal priesthood is based. Here he celebrated his liturgy. From now on there is no sacrifice in the proper sense which does not include the radical self-offering of a person. The eucharistic action stands in a constitutive connection with the salutary sacrificial death of Jesus. It is only possible in the presupposition of his death. But the eucharistic celebration brings to living presence in the body and blood of the Lord his death and resurrection as center of the reality of salvation.

Regarding the relation of the Eucharist to the Last Supper, John Paul II follows Trent's teaching expressed in canon 2 of its decree on the sacrament of the Eucharist. He views the Last Supper as the moment when Christ instituted the Eucharist and, at the same time, the sacrament of the priesthood.[42] But going beyond Trent he also

[40] Ibid., II 9, p. 132.

[41] "Ita quidem propter consecrationem species panis et vini repraesentant modo sane sacramentali et incruento ipsum cruentum Sacrificium propitiatorium quod is Patri in cruce obtulit pro saeculi salute"—ibid., II 9, p. 133.

[42] Trent, Session 22, canon 2: "Si quis dixerit, illis verbis: 'Hoc facite in meam commemorationem' *[Lc 22, 19; 1 Cor 11, 24]*, Christum non instituisse Apostolos

teaches that the Last Supper was the first Mass.[43] Thus he espouses an opinion once favored by Catholic theologians but now generally denied. Rather, it is now more generally argued that the Church was constituted in the Easter-event, and that the sacraments are also Easter realities grounded on the sending of the Holy Spirit.

This living presence of the Passover of Jesus is described at Trent with three concepts: The Eucharist represents, recalls, and applies the event of the cross to the community here and now.[44] In modern, contemporary eucharistic theology it is expressed this way: The Eucharistic Prayer is the sacramental symbolic form under which the once-for-all sacrifice of Christ to God and for humanity obtains power over the assembly. Thus the relation of the sacrifice of the cross to the movement of memorial becomes clear. The Church adds nothing to the sacrifice of Christ, nor does she renew or repeat it; the Church does not of herself undertake the offering of the body and blood of the Lord. Rather, the Church is taken up into Christ's self-offering. She is enabled by grace to participate in it. Modern Catholic theologians are especially sensitive toward the use of terminology that might give the impression that the eucharistic sacrifice repeats in some sense the sacrifice of the cross.

In *Dominicae cenae* 9, John Paul II slips back into older terminology where he speaks of the sacrifice of Christ "that in a sacramental way is renewed on the altar . . ."[45] The Council of Trent never speaks of a renewal in this context, nor does Vatican II. It must be presumed that, in expressing himself in this way, John Paul II did not intend to state anything more than that the newness of the eucharistic sacrifice can only be ascribed to the repetition of the ecclesial dimension.

3. Vatican Response to ARCIC

The final document to be considered is: "Vatican Responds to ARCIC I Final Report."[46] The Anglican-Roman Catholic International Commission published the results of meetings held from 1970–1981

---

sacerdotes, aut non ordinasse, ut ipsi aliique sacerdotes offerrent corpus et sanguinem suum: an. s."—DS 1752.

[43] *Dominicae cenae* I 4, pp. 119–21.

[44] Trent, Session 22, "Doctrina de ss. Missae sacrificio," cap. 1, "De institutione sacrosancti Missae sacrificii" (DS 1739–1742).

[45] "Ad hoc igitur sacrificium, quod modo sacramentali in altari renovatur . . ."—*Dominicae cenae* II 9, p. 133.

[46] *Origins* 21, no. 28 (Dec. 19, 1991) 441–47.

in 1982.[47] The report contains documents on the subject of Eucharist, Ordained Ministry, and Authority in the Church.

The theme of eucharistic sacrifice is contained in "Eucharistic Doctrine" (Windsor 1971) II 5: "The Eucharist and the Sacrifice of Christ,"[48] and in the 1979 "Elucidation on Eucharistic Doctrine: Elucidation" (Salisbury 1979) 5: "Anamnesis and Sacrifice."[49] In the Windsor document, "Eucharistic Doctrine," the notion of memorial is employed to shed light on the relation of the Eucharist to the cross. It is alleged that, in the biblical sense, memorial was employed at the time of Christ for the Passover celebration to convey the idea of a ritual activity that makes "effective in the present . . . an event in the past." Applied to the Eucharist, it is stated that the Eucharist is

"the Church's effectual proclamation of God's mighty acts. Christ instituted the Eucharist as a memorial *(anamnesis)* of the totality of God's reconciling action in him. In the Eucharistic Prayer, the Church continues to make a perpetual memorial of Christ's death, and his members, united with God and with one another, give thanks for his mercies, entreat the benefits of his passion on behalf of the whole Church, participate in these benefits and enter into the movement of his self-offering."

Elucidation 5 of the Salisbury document thus defends the use of anamnesis to express the "traditional understanding of sacramental reality, in which the once-for-all event of salvation becomes effective in the present through the action of the Holy Spirit." It goes on to argue for the use of sacrifice as a synonym for *anamnesis* in the case of the Eucharist. This means that "the Eucharist is a sacrifice in the sacramental sense, provided it is clear that this is not a repetition of the historical sacrifice." The Elucidation concludes on this subject that, "In the celebration of the memorial, Christ in the Holy Spirit unites his people with himself in a sacramental way so that the Church enters into the movement of his self-offering."

The Vatican's response recognizes that the "most notable progress toward a consensus" on the subjects dealt with in this international ecumenical dialogue is found in the documents on the Eucharist. It notes with approval that the members of the commission "affirm 'that

[47] *ARCIC I Final Report* (London: SPCK, 1982).
[48] Ibid., 13–14.
[49] Ibid., 18–20.

the eucharist is a sacrifice in the sacramental sense, provided it is made clear that there is no repetition of the historical sacrifice' (Agreed Statement on Eucharistic Doctrine: Elucidation [hereinafter EE] 5." However, later on, a fuller exposition of Catholic doctrine regarding the Eucharist and ordained ministry is recommended to the commission:

"With regard to the Eucharist, the faith of the Catholic Church would be even more clearly reflected in the Final Report if the following points were to be explicitly affirmed: —That in the Eucharist the Church, doing what Christ commanded his apostles to do at the Last Supper, makes present the sacrifice of Calvary. This would complete, without contradicting it, the statement made in the Final Report affirming that the Eucharist does not repeat the sacrifice of Christ nor add to it. . . . —That the sacrifice of Christ is made present with its effects, thus affirming the propitiatory nature of the eucharistic sacrifice, which can be applied also to the deceased . . . including a particular dead person, is part of the Catholic faith."[50]

The relevant material in the statement Ministry and Ordination (Canterbury 1973) and Ministry and Ordination: Elucidation (Salisbury 1979) can be briefly summarized. In Ministry and Ordination (MOE) 2 it is stated that "it is only the ordained minister who presides at the Eucharist, in which, in the name of Christ and on behalf of his Church, he recites the narrative of the institution of the Last Supper and invokes the Holy Spirit upon the gifts."[51] The Vatican response notes that from the Catholic side this needs to be expanded in the following way:

"That only a validly ordained priest can be the minister who, in the person of Christ, brings into being the sacrament of the Eucharist. He not only recites the narrative of the institution of the Last Supper, pronouncing the words of consecration and imploring the Father to send the Holy Spirit to effect through them the transformation of the gifts, but in so doing offers sacramentally the redemptive sacrifice of Christ."[52]

Again the Vatican response refers to MOE 13, where it is said that in the Eucharist the ordained minister "is seen to stand in a sacramental

[50] "Vatican Response," *Origins* 21 (1991) 445

[51] *ARCIC I Final Report*, 41.

[52] "Vatican Response," *Origins* 21 (1991) 445.

relation to what Christ himself did in offering his own sacrifice."[53] The response suggests that the statement of MOE 13 be completed by adding

"that it was Christ himself who instituted the sacrament of orders as the rite which confers the priesthood of the new covenant. . . . This clarification would seem all the more important in view of the fact that the ARCIC document does not refer to the character of priestly ordination which implies a configuration to the priesthood of Christ . . . central to the Catholic understanding of the distinction between the ministerial priesthood and the common priesthood of the baptized."[54]

IV. CONCLUSION

From the sixteenth century to modern times in Catholic theological circles, the old (i.e., fourth-century) Antiochene theology of the sacramental somatic real presence of Christ under the forms of bread and wine, as received by the Council of Trent, remains normative. However, the limitations of the scholastic philosophical explanation of the conversion of the eucharistic gifts have been clearly recognized. At present more attention is being paid to other points of view, especially to that of early Greek theology. However, there does not exist at present a commonly accepted approach to a theology of conversion among Catholic theologians.

The situation regarding eucharistic sacrifice is much more complicated. In this chapter, our bird's-eye view of developments in the post-Tridentine period up to modern times singled out developments which have led to what can be described as the average modern Catholic theology of eucharistic sacrifice. It amounts to a modification of a post-Tridentine, Thomistic synthesis which consists in the addition of a modified version of the theology of mysteries developed by Dom Odo Casel, O.S.B.

[53] Ibid.
[54] Ibid.

Chapter Eight

The Practice and Theology of the Mass Stipend

On Saturday, March 23, 1991, the *Osservatore Romano* published a decree of the Congregation for the Clergy regarding Mass stipends.[1] Pope John Paul II had approved it on February 22, 1991, and ordered its promulgation with the force of law.[2] The document is divided into two sections: first a preface, and then the body of the decree in seven articles. The preface explains the motivation for the decree. The first six articles are integrated into existing legislation; the seventh requires that the faithful be instructed concerning the contents of the decree.

I. THE PREFACE

At the outset, the teaching of Paul VI's apostolic letter *Firma in traditione* is recalled:

"It is the constant custom in the Church that the faithful, motivated by a religious and ecclesial consciousness, add a kind of sacrifice of their own by which they participate in the eucharistic sacrifice more actively; in this way contributing to the needs of the Church and particularly to the support of their ministers."[3]

[1] *Osservatore Romano* 131, no. 68 (23 March 1991) 1, 5. The decree *(Mos iugitur)* is accompanied by an Italian translation and a commentary, also in Italian, by Archbishop Gilberto Agustoni, secretary of the Congregation for the Clergy.

[2] The publication of the decree in the *OR* was preceded by a note reporting that it had been approved by the Holy Father *in forma specifica,* and that it would come into force with its publication in the *Acta Apostolicae Sedis* according to the norms of canon 8, no. 1 of the Code of Canon Law. As of 4 December 1997 (*AAS* 89, no. 12), publication in the *AAS* had not yet taken place.

[3] "Firma in traditione Ecclesiae positum est, ut fideles, religioso et ecclesiali sensu ducti, Sacrificio Eucharistico, quo actuosius hoc participent, quoddam quasi sacrificium sui ipsorum adiungant, hoc modo consulentes, pro sua parte, necessitatibus

The preface of the decree then goes on to explain that

"in antiquity this contribution consisted especially in fruits of nature; but in our days it consists almost solely of money. However, the motivation is the same and the finality of the offerings of the faithful of this kind remain the same, and have been approved also by the new Code of Canon Law (canons 945, no. 1; 946)."

Nevertheless the decree recognizes that this practice, involving money, brings with it the danger of "financial exploitation or simony." For this reason the Apostolic See has always exercised vigilance regarding developments in this "pious tradition" in order to "prevent or correct . . . abuses."

The particular abuse that has occasioned this decree is described as a "relatively recent practice" in which Masses are celebrated to satisfy "collective" intentions. By this is meant the practice by which a priest accepts an offering for the celebration of a particular Mass for the particular intention of an offerer, but instead celebrates one Mass for the particular intentions of many offerers. This practice is distinguished from two others which have only a superficial resemblance to it. The first of these is the old custom whereby the faithful contribute modest gifts to the priest on the occasion of the celebration of Mass, but without "explicitly requesting that a particular Mass be applied to their particular intention." In this case the priest is allowed to unite as many offerings as correspond to the amount of money established by the diocese for a stipend Mass and apply them to one Mass. In the other custom, a number of the faithful unite their intentions and offerings, requiring only "one Mass to be celebrated for their intentions." The faithful are "always free" to do this.

The distinctive character of the recent practice—the apparent occasion of the decree—consists in disregarding the wishes of donors to have their offerings applied to a particular Mass for their particular intentions. The decree labels the arguments of those who defend this way of acting as "specious . . . and even pretexts; indeed rather they reflect a false ecclesiology."[4]

Ecclesiae, maxime vero eiusdem ministrorum sustentationi"—Paul VI, apostolic letter *Firma in traditione, Acta Apostolicae Sedis* 66 (1974) 308–11, at 308 ET: Austin Flannery, ed., *Vatican Council II: The Conciliar and Post Conciliar Documents,* rev. ed. (Northport, N.Y.: Costello; Grand Rapids: Eerdmans, 1992) 277–80.

[4] ". . . argumenta speciosa sunt, immo et praetexta, quin etiam falsam redolent ecclesiologiam" *OR* 131, no. 68 (23 March 1991) 1.

The preface ends with a reflection on the dangers of the use of the Mass celebrated with a collective intention, even when the faithful request it. It can be the occasion for the "grave risk of not satisfying an obligation in justice" with respect to the donor of a stipend. Also, if allowed to grow, it could diminish and even "extinguish in the Christian people that pious sensibility and impulse of conscience by which the motivation and finality for which stipends are offered for the celebration of Masses for particular intentions are understood and accepted." Moreover there would be the added bad effect of depriving ministers, who depend on these offerings for their livelihood, and "many particular churches" of the support they need for "apostolic activity."[5]

II. THE ARTICLES

In Article 1, no. 1 of the decree, the normative legislation of canon 948 is recalled whereby "distinct Masses are to be applied to the intentions of those from whom individual offerings *(stips)*, although small, have been offered and accepted." This means that the priest who accepts the stipend for celebrating Mass according to a particular intention is held by the "obligation from justice" either to personally satisfy the "obligation" (canon 949), or to commit it to another priest under the conditions of canons 954–955. According to Article 1, no. 2. the relatively recent practice "violates the norm," to which priests are duty-bound "in conscience."

Article 2, no. 1 grants that a single Mass can be applied according to a collective intention provided that the offerers are "previously and explicitly" advised of the procedure, and "freely consent." However, Article 2, no. 2 establishes the following conditions under which this practice is allowable: The day, place, and hour of such Masses must be publicly announced, and they may take place at most only twice a week. Article 2, no. 3 warns that the excessive extension of this practice, which is "an exception to the norm of the law," and which may be occasioned "by erroneous opinions concerning the meaning of oblations for the celebration of Masses," should be considered by bishops as an "abuse." Moreover, account should be taken of the fact that the practice could influence the faithful progressively to become

[5] Ibid., 1, 5. [In those cases where Kilmartin's translation clearly gives the precise meaning of a straightforward and unambiguous Latin (or Italian, in the case of the commentary) text, I have not thought it necessary to reproduce in every instance that original Latin or Italian text—RJD.]

unaccustomed to "offering oblations for the celebration of distinct Masses for distinct intentions, and thus to the extinguishing of the venerable custom salutary for individual souls and the whole church."

The subject of Article 3 is the use of the offerings made for the pluri-intentional Mass. Article 4 calls for vigilance on the part of officials regarding the observance of the law concerning Mass stipends. Article 5 recalls the legislation about the fulfillment of the Mass stipend obligations within a year. Article 6 refers to the responsibility of bishops to make known the contents of the decree to diocesan and religious priests and to oversee their observance. Finally, Article 7 requires that the faithful be instructed on the subject of the decree by a special catechetical instruction which highlights the following: (1) the theological meaning of "offerings given to the priest for the celebration of the eucharistic sacrifice"; (2) the "ascetical importance of almsgiving . . . of which the offerings made for the celebration of holy Masses is a most excellent example"; (3) "The sharing of goods by which the faithful, through offerings for the celebration of Masses," cooperate in the support of their ministers and in the realization of apostolic works of the Church.

III. THE OFFICIAL COMMENTARY

The content of the official commentary on the decree by Archbishop Gilberto Agustoni, secretary of the Congregation for the Clergy,[6] can be quickly summarized:

(a) The commentary identifies what is described in *Firma in traditione* as "the constant practice of the Church," and which the decree itself insists has always been motivated by the same *(iidem)* "reasons and goal." There is a

"substantial identity of the reasons and goal for which the faithful, following an uninterrupted tradition . . . ask the priests to celebrate the holy sacrifice according to particular intentions, offering them a compensation . . . called by a juridical term (indeed hardly happily, 'stipend,' and more commonly 'alms')."

Neither the decree nor the commentary provide an exact explanation of what is meant by "the constant custom of the Church" or "an

[6] Gilberto Agustoni, "A tutela di una pia e preziosa tradizione," *OR* 131 (23 March 1991) 5.

uninterrupted tradition." However both the decree and commentary obviously refer to the practice of the Mass stipend, noting that despite the fact of a change in the type of material gift offered, i.e., money instead of fruits of nature, the motivation and goal of the practice has remained the same. In this regard the commentary alludes to traditional terminology applied to the offerings which does not adequately express the religious signification of the practice. Thereby the commentary appears to call attention to the notion that the offerings are first and foremost a way of participation in the eucharistic sacrifice and only indirectly a way of contributing to the support of the Church and the ordained ministry.

(b) The commentary identifies one example of what the decree describes as a "pretext" used to justify the new form of pluri-intentional Mass, namely, that the obligation to apply the offerings of donors to the eucharistic sacrifice is fulfilled by mentioning the intentions of the offerers during the celebration of the Mass. This does not satisfy the obligation assigned by canon 948, namely, "of applying as many Masses as there are intentions."

(c) The decree describes an argument used by certain people to support the practice of the pluri-intentional Mass as reflecting a "false ecclesiology." On this subject the commentary observes: "Not infrequently one hears repeated by them that the celebration of the Eucharist is an action of the Church, and so eminently communitarian." Hence "the idea of 'privatizing' it by fixing particular intentions or wishing to destine the fruits of it according to our intention" contradicts the very nature of the Mass. Without further elaboration, this argument is judged to manifest the

"doctrinal confusion of a certain ecclesiology, concerning the infinite merits of the sacrifice of the cross, concerning the celebration of the sacrament of the unique sacrifice which Christ entrusted to the Church, and concerning the treasury of the Church of which the Church disposes."[7]

(d) The commentary musters additional support for the normative practice of having Masses celebrated for particular intentions by

[7] "Queste argomentazioni manifestano la confusione dottrinale di certa ecclesiologia circa i meriti infiniti dell'unico sacrificio della croce, circa la celebrazione del sacramento di quell'unico sacrificio che Cristo ha affidato alla Chiesa, e circa il 'thesaurus Ecclesiae' di cui la Chiesa dispone"—ibid.

appealing to the traditional doctrine of Catholic theology concerning the fruits of the Mass:

"Nor can it be forgotten that Catholic doctrine has constantly taught that the fruits of the eucharistic sacrifice are variously attributed: above all to those whom the Church herself names in the 'intercessions' of the Eucharistic Prayer, then to the celebrating minister (the so-called ministerial fruit), then to the offerers, and so forth."[8]

(e) The commentary observes that the decree deals harshly with the pluri-intentional Mass in order to attract attention to the "incalculable damage" it could cause. It could lead to the abandonment of the old tradition which relates one special intention to one Mass, and the consequent loss of monetary support for priests and apostolic works. This potential danger is cited as the basic reason for limiting the exception to the norm of law, allowed by Article 2, to two days a week in the same place of worship (Art. 2, no. 3). The limitation, along with the conditions imposed to avoid abuses, is said to be motivated by the desire to prevent the diffusion of the pluri-intentional Mass.

(f) The commentary faults priests who refuse to accept offerings for the celebration of Masses for particular intentions. They deprive the faithful of one of the most excellent ways by which the laity can participate more actively in the celebration of the Mass. Their refusal contributes to the "spiritual damage" referred to in Article 2, no. 3.

(g) Among those who theorize about new ways of support for clerics, some argue that modern priests do not need stipends, or that the practice offends the dignity of the ministry of the altar. The commentary responds to these "specious" objections by pointing out that the majority of priests worldwide are supported by stipends, and that many activities of the Church are dependent in part or totally on Mass stipends. Hence the conclusion is drawn that only those who want to be scandalized or who are affected by a "strange puritanism" could maintain that the ancient tradition is anachronistic or unworthy of providing sustenance for priests and for the works of the Church.[9]

[8] "Nè si può dimenticare che la dottrina cattolica ha costantemente insegnato che i frutti del Sacrificio eucaristico sono variamente attribuiti: innanzitutto a coloro che la Chiesa stessa nomina nelle 'intercessioni' della Prece eucaristica, poi al ministro celebrante (il cosidetto frutto ministeriale), quindi agli offerenti, e così via"—ibid.

[9] The commentary prefaces its remarks on this point with the severe: "Questa e una delle tante illusioni o utopie che mancono di riferimento alla realtà"—ibid.

IV. HISTORICO-LITURGICAL AND THEOLOGICAL PERSPECTIVES OF THE DECREE AND COMMENTARY

The most serious deficiency of the decree and commentary, from the standpoint of the history of the practice of linking material offerings of the faithful to the liturgy of the Eucharist, is the tendency to conflate several types of the general practice and, at the same time, to attribute to them the same motivation and finality. The only significant change in the practice that is mentioned in the degree and commentary concerns the variation in types of material offerings: the development from offerings of the fruits of nature to offerings of money.

In other words, the illusory impression is given of a linear development in the direction of a more perfect expression of the practice and its interpretation. However, history teaches us that there has been a somewhat complex "evolution" in the practice under consideration: a development from an original practice to later forms due to variations in the intervening period induced by significant changes in the theology of the Eucharist. In fact, when placed in its full context, the whole history of the whole Church, the subject of the decree turns out to be a particular medieval tributary of the most ancient form of the offertory ritual of the Latin Church.

The decree favors as normative practice the version of that particular tributary which was well established throughout the Latin Church in the thirteenth century (A. "Long-standing Custom of the Church"). When one examines this practice in its medieval context, one finds that the meaning of the offerings of this tributary was more generally understood at that time to be limited to the notion of almsgiving in exchange for a special application of a Mass to the intention of the donor. However the decree and commentary assign as the primary meaning the function of serving as the expression of active participation in eucharistic worship. Therefore, on the latter account, the decree presumes that only members of the Catholic Church are capable of acting as donors of such offerings (B. "Donor of Stipend").

A distinction is made between a legitimate and illegitimate form of the pluri-intentional Mass. Reasons for curtailing the legitimate form are listed (C. "Conditions of Pluri-Intentional Mass"). Among the erroneous opinions regarding the stipend Mass are enumerated the tendency to marginalize the meaning of celebrating Masses for particular intentions, or to equate them with almsgiving (D. "Erroneous

Opinions"). As a failure to respect the will of the donor of the offering, the illegitimate pluri-intentional Mass is said to constitute a violation of the obligation from justice (E. "Obligation from Justice").

These five themes (A to E) are treated in this section of this chapter. In the subsequent section, the principal systematic theological themes of the decree and commentary will be discussed. They are (A) the arguments drawn from the nature of the eucharistic sacrifice, and (B) the theology of the "treasury of the Church," as well as (C) the traditional doctrine concerning the fruits of the Mass. These theological themes are used to refute support for the illegitimate form of the pluri-intentional Mass which reflects a "false ecclesiology."

A. LONG-STANDING CUSTOM OF THE CHURCH

The description of the practice, identified as a "long-standing custom of the Church," places it in the category of an ancient observance somehow linked to a more ancient Western Church custom of the offertory procession. The latter ritual act was practiced in third-century North Africa, and possibly at Rome, and in the fourth century at Milan, Aquileia, as well as in Spain. However, when one examines the matter more closely, the ancient practice to which the decree refers is related to a completely new form of gift-giving which has roots in the seventh century, began to emerge in the eighth century in Gaul, Spain, the British Isles, and France, and was fairly widespread also elsewhere in the West by the middle of the ninth century. It is this new form, and not the much more ancient offertory procession, which is the forerunner of the Mass stipend practice, which is, in turn, the subject of the 1974 apostolic letter *Firma in traditione* of Paul VI and this 1991 decree of the Congregation for the Clergy.

There is no need to rehearse here the details of the origin of the thirteenth-century Mass stipend practice and the main lines of the theology of this practice. These themes have already been discussed above in chapters two and five.

B. DONORS OF STIPENDS

The decree identifies the practice of making offerings in connection with the eucharistic celebration as a particular mode of active participation in the eucharistic sacrifice which is open to the "faithful": the baptized who are in communion with the Catholic Church. Since such offerings are the symbolic expression not only of one's spiritual union with the sacrificial worship of Christ, but also of one's membership in the celebration of the faith of the hierarchically organized Catholic Church, it is clear that only the baptized person who qualifies on both counts is a legitimate subject of such offerings. This is the position found in the New Code of Canon Law, canon 946: "The Christian faithful" are identified as those who make such offerings in order that the Mass be applied to their intention. The old Code of Canon Law of 1917 does not stipulate whether or not the subject of the offering must be in full communion with the Catholic Church (canons 824–826).

There are two nineteenth-century Roman decisions which allow the priest to accept an "alms" *(eleemosynam)* from a non-Christian for the celebration of Mass under certain conditions which relate to the purity of the intention.[10] Also the Sacred Congregation of the Council, in a decree approved by Pope Gregory XVI, allows schismatic Greeks to offer alms for the celebration of Mass for their intention, namely, "for their conversion to the true faith."[11]

The reason for these decisions seems obvious. The stipend was not considered to be related to the Mass as a sign of the co-offering of the faithful, but only indirectly related by obliging the priest to celebrate Mass for a special intention. At that time it was the common opinion that the stipend serves the ecclesiological function of providing support for the priest. In fact, Adalbert Mayer, in his detailed survey of the history of the practice and theology of the Mass stipend, is able to cite only one publication of the nineteenth century in which the anonymous author identifies the stipend primarily as sacrificial gift "by means of which one unites oneself in the Spirit with the holy sacrifice of the Mass, just as formerly through the offering of the bread and wine."[12]

C. CONDITIONS FOR PLURI-INTENTIONAL MASSES

The occasion for the decree under consideration is the practice of applying a single Mass to the offerings of several donors without taking

[10] Responses of the Congregation of the Holy Office (12 June 1865), and of the Congregation for the Propagation of the Faith (11 March 1848). Confer Maurice de la Taille, *Mysterium Fidei* (Paris: Beauchesne, 1921) 366, n. 1.

[11] Response of the Sacred Congregation of the Council (19 April 1837). Confer de la Taille, 367.

[12] This quote is from the anonymous "Ueber den Gebrauch der Meßstipendien," *Theologisch-praktische Monatsschrift* 2/1, 4th ed. (Prague, 1828) 382–402, esp. 392, 395—as reported in Adalbert Mayer, *Triebkräfte und Grundlinien der Entstehung des Mess-Stipendiums,* Münchener theologische Studien, III. Kanonistische Abteilung, vol. 34 (St. Ottilien: EOS Verlag, 1976) 2.

into account the will of donors who expect the normative practice. This illegitimate practice of the pluri-intentional Mass is rejected because it is contrary to the normative practice, does not satisfy the obligation "in justice," and ultimately because of the danger of "financial exploitation or simony." There is indeed a legitimate practice of the pluri-intentional Mass which does not run contrary to canon law; it is, however, hemmed in by a number of conditions laid down in Article 2.

It is significant for the understanding of the theology of Mass stipends reflected in the decree to list the reasons for the limitations and conditions established in Article 2 for the practice of the legitimate pluri-intentional Mass. These reasons are related only to the possible danger of not satisfying the obligation "from justice" with respect to the donor of a stipend, the possibility of the loss of the normative practice if the exception becomes widespread, and the fact that the normative practice is an ancient custom.

The decree clearly favors the normative practice, but it does not elaborate on the reasons why it might be considered more efficacious. One supporting reason, which may be implied in the preference for the normative practice, could be the intensity of the devotion that is aroused when the focus of attention is on the single intention for which the Mass is celebrated on behalf of one donor's intention. However, nothing in the decree gives the impression that necessarily more fruit can be expected a priori from a single Mass celebrated for the particular intention of one donor, than could be expected from a Mass celebrated for the intentions of several donors of stipends. The silence of the decree on this point seems to be significant; for if this were verifiable, it would constitute the best argument against the "relatively new practice."

Concerning the illegitimate practice of the pluri-intentional Mass, it is noteworthy that what the decree of the Congregation labels as a "relatively recent practice," as well as the reasons given for excluding it, are not without precedent. This practice seems to have gained headway in recent years in Europe beginning from the period during World War II (according to reports of which this author has heard, especially from priests acquainted with the usage in Slavic lands and Italy). It is also verifiable from sixteenth-century sources, and it probably has earlier roots. Moreover, the earlier opposition of church authorities to the kind of pluri-intentional Mass rejected by the decree seems to have been based not only on the norm of the law concerning the application of one Mass in view of one stipend, but also on the motive of avoiding the scandal of financial exploitation. But this earlier opposition by church authorities does not seem to have been based precisely on the principle that the normative practice is necessarily more efficacious.

At the Council of Trent, a list of probable abuses associated with the practice of the celebration of Mass was placed before the council fathers for their consideration on August 8, 1562. Among others, the question was asked whether it should be considered an abuse "that a priest accepts alms from many people for the celebration of a Mass, then wishes to satisfy [the obligation] with only one Mass. Wherefore it seems that this abuse, above all, which is called 'mass for profit,' should be removed."[13] In the subsequent compendium of abuses, this practice is rejected.[14] This list of abuses and compendium are not found in the *Acta* of the council. Rather they served as preparation for the canons proposed on September 10, 1562. There is an allusion to the problem of financial exploitation in the Decree of September 17, 1562.[15]

Another related practice, also found in the list of abuses and compendium, reads as follows:

"Again, since it happens that annual legacies are often left for saying Masses, which legacies do not suffice to support the priest, does it seem permitted to the ordinary, that many alms of this kind could be gathered into one body, as it were, and could be retained for the support of one such person, who afterwards would be held to make commemoration in his prayers of those who would have left the legacies?"[16]

[13] "Item considerandum, an abusus sit, quod unus sacerdos a pluribus eleemosynas accipiat pro missae celebratione, deinde unica tantum missa satisfacere velit. Quare imprimis abusus ille tollendus videtur, quod quaestus nomine missae dicantur"—Stephanus Ehses, ed., *Concilii Tridentini Actorum,* Pars Quinta (Freiburg i. Br.: B. Herder, 1919) 917.39–41.

[14] "Atque imprimis, ut omnium malorum fons et radix avaritia tollatur, omnibus locorum ordinariis districte mandat, ne missas quaestus et pretii nomine a quibuscumque sacerdotibus quamvis exemptis dici permittant, illis ob hoc non prohibens eleemosynas accipere, quae a sponte dantibus offerentur"—"Compendium eorundem abusuum" (ibid., 922.11–14).

[15] ". . . above all, what pertains to avarice, conditions of any kind of commerce . . . which are not far from a simoniacal tinge . . . are completely prohibited"—*Decretum de observandis et evitandis in celebratione missarum, publicatum in eadem sessione sexta* [22nd overall session of Trent] *Tridentina sub Pio Papa quarto* (ibid., 963.1–5).

[16] "Abusus circa missae sacrificium," ibid., 918.24–28; see also "Compendium eorundem abusuum," ibid., 922.26–30.

D. ERRONEOUS OPINIONS

Article 3, no. 3 of the 1991 decree refers to "erroneous opinions concerning the meaning of oblations for the celebration of Masses." The quotation from Paul VI's apostolic letter *Firma in traditione* makes clear that offerings are a form of ritual participation in the Mass which are the expression of an interior devotional participation. Here the material oblation is calculated to contribute to a "more active participation." The active participation is identified by Paul VI as a more intimate union with Christ's self-offering. This is the fundamental "theological meaning" to which Article 7 of the decree refers.[17]

The linking of the offerings of the faithful with a mode of active participation in the eucharistic sacrifice makes sense when the donors are present at the Mass that the offering makes possible, precisely as the Mass applied to the offering of the donor. In this case, it may be expected that there will be an increase of devotion in virtue of the contribution to the ritual celebration through the offering as a way of participating in the eucharistic sacrifice.

But how does this make sense when the stipend donor is absent? The absent donor can be said to have a ritual participation since the donor makes possible the celebration itself. The devotion expressed at the time of the offering made to the priest for the celebration of the Mass for one's intention is relevant to the intention, insofar as it is the expression of the prayer of intercession of the donor for his or her intention. Moreover, the donor participates in the blessings derived from the Mass to which the offering and intention of the donor is related in virtue of the actual devotion of those physically present and participating in the ritual celebration itself.

Neither Paul VI, nor this decree of the Congregation for the Clergy discuss the question of the mode of participation of the absent donor. However, the identification of one "erroneous opinion" concerning active participation in the eucharistic sacrifice can be uncovered from the text of the decree. It is the one based on a "false ecclesiology" (preface) which downplays the value of the oblations given for the celebration of particular Masses for special intentions, which the decree judges to be "salutary for individual souls and the whole Church" (Art. 2, no. 3). The defenders of the pluri-intentional Mass who, perhaps in an unreflective way, find difficulty with this so-called

[17] ". . . eximiam significationem theologicam oblationis sacerdoti datae ut Eucharisticum celebretur Sacrificium"—*OR* 131, no. 68 (23 March 1991) 5.

"privatizing" of the Mass, could be said, according to the fairly obvious implication of the decree, to incline toward an erroneous opinion.

The thesis which focuses exclusively on the communitarian aspect of the Eucharist obviously contradicts what the classical Eucharistic Prayers of the Eastern and Western traditions affirm. Moreover, this thesis corresponds to what Pope Pius VI condemns in his critique of the teaching of the Synod of Pistoia, expressed in its decree of September 18–28, 1786, concerning the application of the fruits of the Mass.[18]

In this decree of the Synod of Pistoia, a special remembrance and intercession for particular individuals living and dead is recommended. However (and this is the precise point at which the synod begins to incur the condemnation of the magisterium) it is denied that the priest, by an act of his will, can dispense the fruit of the sacrifice to whom he wishes. Consequently, the synod draws the conclusion that it is a false opinion to hold that those who give alms to a priest, on condition that he celebrate a Mass, receive a special fruit from that Mass.

In the apostolic constitution *Auctorem fidei* of 1794, Pius VI condemned this teaching as "false" when understood as follows: "the special oblation or application of the sacrifice, which is made by the priest does not profit more those for whom it is applied, all things being equal, than anyone else; as though no special fruit comes from the special application."[19] Here the Pope rejects the thesis that the special application is meaningless. But, while affirming that the special intention is a fruitful way of participating in the Mass, Pius VI does not go on to indicate precisely why one receives this special benefit. Hence the way is left open to the scholastic thesis that the Mass in itself intrinsically involves a special fruit which must be expressly bestowed by the very nature of the case, and/or that the Mass intention is one of the ways of sharing in the sacrifice.

[18] Pius VI, apostolic constitution *Auctorem fidei*, 28 August 1794, no. 30 (DS 2630: ". . . no special fruit derives from the special application . . . for certain persons or groups of persons . . .—nullus specialis fructus proveniret ex speciali applicatione, quam pro determinatis personis aut personarum ordinibus faciendam . . ."). This document (we have quoted here from the 30th of 84 numbered paragraphs detailing the *Errores Synodi Pistoriensis*), as will be seen below, does not explicitly confirm the precise scholastic systematic position on the "fruits of the Mass" that was the common teaching of the day.

[19] ". . . specialis ipsa oblatio seu applicatio sacrificii, quae fit a sacerdote, non magis prosit ceteris paribus illis, pro quibus applicatur, quam aliis quibusque; quasi nullus specialis fructus proveniret ex speciali applicatione . . ." (DS 2630).

The Synod of Pistoia based its (condemned) conclusion on the principle that God alone distributes the fruits of the Mass to whom he wishes, and in the measure that pleases him. Pius VI affirms what the Synod of Pistoia does not deny, namely, that the application of the Mass is profitable for those for whose sake it is applied. However, the argument cited by the 1991 commentary is based on a depreciation of the relation of the Eucharist as sacrifice of the Church to the Eucharist as sacrifice of Christ. Hence the commentary traces the source of the argument to

"the doctrinal confusion of a certain ecclesiology concerning the infinite merits of the unique sacrifice of the cross, concerning the celebration of the sacrament of that unique sacrifice which Christ confided to the Church, and concerning the 'treasury of the Church,' of which the Church disposes."[20]

While those who argue from the communitarian aspect of the Church in order to reject fixed intentions, and to reject the desire to destine the fruits according to one's intention, the commentary itself argues from the mystery dimension of the celebration. The argument seems to come to this: The Eucharist is the celebration of the sacrament of the sacrifice of the cross, which has infinite value before God. Moreover, the infinite merits of the unique sacrifice of Christ constitute the essence of the "treasury of the Church." As minister of the redemptive work of Christ, the Church disposes of this treasury for the salvation of all humanity, and of particular individuals, especially in and through the eucharistic liturgy.

Another erroneous opinion is identified in the commentary where the meaning of the offering for the celebration of a Mass is understood only as almsgiving for the support of the priest. It cites the example of priests who refuse to accept offerings for Masses; or who wish to do away with the practice on the basis that priests no longer need this support; or who think it is beneath the dignity of the servants of the altar to be involved in this practice. According to the commentary this way of acting prevents the realization of one of the most excellent ways of active participation in the sacrifice of the Mass.[21]

[20] ". . . la confusione dottrinale di certa ecclesiologia circa i meriti infiniti dell'unico sacrificio della Croce, circa la celebrazione del sacramento di quel'unico sacrificio che Cristo ha affidato alla Chiesa, e circa il 'thesaurus Ecclesiae' di cui la Chiesa dispone"—G. Agustoni, "A tutela . . . ," *OR* 131, no. 68 (23 March 1991) 5.

[21] "I sacerdoti che non accettano l'impegno di celebrare la Messa secondo parti-

Certainly the terms "stipend" or "alms" do not adequately describe the function of the offerings as a liturgical way by which the faithful "more actively participate in the eucharistic sacrifice." Rather, this terminology has place where the offerings are understood to serve as an indirect way of participating in the sacrifice, namely, by supporting the priest who exercises a ministry on behalf of the donor of a gift.

This second erroneous opinion, which equates the offerings with "alms," is manifested by the tendency to consider the custom to be anachronistic or a kind of compensation that does not harmonize well with the ministry of the Eucharist. In any case, the opposition is motivated in this instance by the desire to avoid the linking of financial considerations to the celebration of Mass. This motive inspired the rejection of the usage of the practice of the Mass stipend by some medieval religious orders such as the Franciscans, Cistercians, and Premonstratensians. On the grounds that the stipend was conceived as "alms," they originally rejected this practice as unacceptable to them, although not rejecting it outright for others.

The attitude of the Society of Jesus toward this practice corresponds to that of the above-mentioned religious orders. It was derived from the founder, St. Ignatius of Loyola. He recognized as legitimate the practice of taking money as compensation for the celebration of Masses for particular intentions. Still, he refused to engage in it himself. In fact, one of the original band of Ignatius's ten companions, Simon Rodriguez, reports that they all vowed in Paris that they "would never accept anything for doing (sic!) the holy Mass." This decision was also made one of the substantials of the Constitutions of the Society of Jesus.[22] It was confirmed by the following General Congregations: VI (1608), decree 39; XVI (1730–1731), decree 25; XXII (1853), decree 42; XXIV (1892), decree 18; XXVII (1923), decrees 198–201.

The Epitome of the Institute, proposed to the Twenty-Seventh General Congregation, and sent to the provinces of the Jesuits, July 27,

---

colari intenzioni non si rendono conto di precludere uno dei modi excellenti per partecipare attivamente alla celebrazione del memoriale del Signore" (ibid.).

[22] *Monumenta Ignatiana* II: Monumenta historica societatis Jesu 64 (Rome: Gregorian University Press, 1936), "Examen generale cum declarationibus," c. 1, no. 3, p. 7: ". . . que ni quiere ni puede tener rentas algunas para su sustentación . . . . Ni tampoco (aunque a otros seria lícito) por missas o predicaciones . . ."; "Constitutiones et Declarationes," P. VI, c. 2, no. 7, p. 537: ". . . se acuerden que deuen dar gratis lo que gratis recibieron, no demandando ni acceptando stipendio ni limosna alguna en recompensa de missas o confessiones o predicar . . ."

1924, treats the subject in the section on the gratuity of ministries.[23] The principle of gratuity of ministries is affirmed and, in particular, the prohibition against accepting a stipend or alms in compensation for ministries.[24] Moreover it is forbidden to accept stipends in compensation for Masses even when the alms are used for pious purposes outside the Society of Jesus.[25] Also, the Mass(es) prescribed to be celebrated each week by the priest members of the Society for Fr. General's intention cannot be "applied by him" in such a way as to free others, not members of the Society, from the responsibility they had "contracted by accepting stipends."[26]

Also it is noted in the Jesuit Epitome that a dispensation from the law of the gratuity of ministries is not an abrogation of the law, but a relaxation of the law in individual cases.[27] This is said in the context of the report on the dispensations received from the Holy See regarding Mass stipends. Following the restoration of the Society of Jesus[28] it was found necessary to request a dispensation from the law concerning stipends for certain purposes. Such a dispensation was granted by Leo XII, September 16, 1824, and by Gregory XVI, May 13, 1838. Finally, a general dispensation was granted to the General of the Society to use freely for those in need to enable them to accept "alms" for Masses and other ministries according to the norms applicable to other priests. This dispensation was granted by Pius IX, May 10, 1859. In the communication of P. Anderledy, *Ordinatio "De stipendiis missarum"* of July 31, 1887, Pius IX is quoted as saying the dispensation is given to him and his successors. P. Werntz explained that the faculty was given not only for the support of Jesuits but also for ad-

[23] Antonius M Arregui, S.I., *Annotationes ad Epitomen Instituti Societatis Iesu* (Rome: apud oeconomum generalem, 1934) Titulus III "De Paupertate," caput III, "De gratuitate ministeriorum," nos. 524–530, pp. 514–21.

[24] Ibid., no. 525, 1, pp. 515–16.

[25] Ibid., no. 526, 1, p. 517.

[26] Ibid., no. 526, 2, pp. 517–18. Arregui here reports that the reason given for this by Father Noyelle at the 12th General Congregation (1682) is to enable the Jesuit General to refuse requests of this type more graciously *(humaniter)*. The 12th General Congregation did decree this, and the 27th General Congregation (1924) confirmed it. Whether or not, at present, a Jesuit might profit from this (i.e., by having his own Mass-intention obligations covered by the general applying some of these weekly Mass intentions to that end) is an open question, but the faculty is available to Fr. General to use.

[27] Ibid., no. 530, 2, p. 520.

[28] The Society of Jesus had been suppressed in 1773, and restored again in 1814.

vancing their work.[29] P. Ledóchowski points out that the dispensation was given for support of indigent residences, and that stipends can be taken by the provincial from colleges and residences if they do not need them for support. This purpose is said to constitute the primary reason for the dispensation.[30]

On the subject of the theological background for the typical Jesuit understanding of the theology of the Mass up through the middle of the twentieth century which explains this understanding of the Mass stipend, A. Coemans's commentary on the rules of the Society of Jesus is instructive. This work was published in 1938, and was used by tertian instructors[31] of the Society for many years, and probably is still in use in many places. In the section on the theology of the Mass as sacrifice, it is presumed (although not explicitly mentioned) that the stipend is a form of almsgiving.[32] The priest alone is identified as the celebrant of the Mass, while others are qualified as assisting. The presiding priest is described as one who offers in the name of the whole Church. The individuals present are said to participate through their individual devotion. The proper way of "hearing" the Mass is to pay attention to what the priest says and does, and to do, as far as one can, what the priest does because each has a share in the transaction which is done and celebrated.[33]

Coemans quotes Session 22, chapter 2 of the Council of Trent which was commonly understood as teaching that the Mass "renews" the

[29] Letter of Franciscus Xav. Wernz, 7 May 1910, *Acta Romana Societatis Jesu,* anno 1910 (Rome: Typis Polyglottis Vaticanis, 1911) 46.

[30] Response no. 44, "Paupertas residentiarum," 26 November 1920, *Acta Romana Societatis Iesu,* anni 1921 (Rome: apud curiam praepositi generalis, 1922) 385–86.

[31] "Tertianship," under the direction of a "tertian instructor," is the final year of the formal education/formation of a Jesuit priest. Considered as a kind of recovery of the intensive spiritual life of the novitiate (the fervor of which may have faded in the intervening years of study), it focuses on spiritual and pastoral training and activity and on a study of the *Spiritual Exercises* of Ignatius, the founder, and of the constitutions and rules of the order.

[32] Augusto Coemans, S.J., "Punctum Tertium. De Sacrificio Missae," in *Commentarium in Regulas Societatis Iesu omnibus nostris communes* (Rome: apud oeconomum generalem, 1938) nos. 176–179, pp. 99–101 (commenting on Common Rule no. 2 [Constitutions, P. IV, c. 4, n. 3]).

[33] Coemans here quotes Alfonso Rodríguez, S.J., whose *The Practice of Perfection and of Christian Virtues* (Seville, 1609) was fully or partially translated into twenty-three languages and widely used, not just by Jesuits, well into this century as spiritual reading for novices (ibid., 101).

sacrifice of the cross, through Christ's presence as priest and victim.[34] From this point of view the author predicates of the Mass an effect that is independent of the devotion of the priest or of those who are somehow present. This means that the Mass produces fruits *ex opere operato* in virtue of the oblation of Christ, and *ex opere operantis* on the grounds of the devotion of the believing participants.[35]

E. OBLIGATION FROM JUSTICE

The 1991 decree of the Congregation for Clerics refers to the fact that the priest is bound in conscience to follow the norm of the law regarding Mass stipends. The positive law of the Church entails a legal obligation. But it is also said that the priest is obliged after acceptance of the stipend "from justice" to do what the donor of the stipend requests. The meaning is not explained. According to one part of traditional scholastic theology, this would be an obligation analogous to one of commutative justice because a determinate amount of fruit is applied in relation to the special intention. Hence, if a priest accepts two offerings for particular Masses and celebrates only one, the offerer is deprived of this full share.

However, the mere fact that positive law determines that the priest is able to accept only one stipend for the celebration of a particular Mass means that it involves only a legal obligation. It does not imply *of itself* that a determinate amount of fruit is associated with the special intention, and hence that the obligation is analogous to that of

[34] "In Sacrificio Missae, teste Concilio Tridentino, 'idem ille Christus continetur et incruente immolatur, qui in ara crucis semel se Ipsum cruente obtulit . . . Una enim eademque est hostia, idem nunc offerens Sacerdotum ministerio, qui se Ipsum tunc in cruce obtulit, sola offerendi ratione diversa'"—Coemans, no. 177, p. 100 (DS 1743). [This text has often been thought to be the basis for the imprecise idea that the Mass renews the sacrifice of the cross. But one should note that the specific word "renews/*renovatur*" is not used by Trent—RJD.]

[35] "Haec omnia respiciunt effectum illum qui producitur vi ipsius oblationis Christi, quasi ex opere operato, independenter a dispositionibus Sacerdotis et assistentium. Habetur enim praeterea alius fructus qui a Sacerdote et assistentibus obtinetur ex opere operantis, sicut ex quovis bono opere, plus minus pro perfectione dispositionum"—Coemans, no. 178, p. 101. Also illustrative of the devotional theology that used to be inculcated into priests of the Roman Rite, and still widely practiced, is the list of Mass intentions which every priest of the Society of Jesus is prescribed to offer: "Catalogus Missarum et orationum quae Nostris praescribuntur (Ex *Epitome Instituti*)"—ibid., nos. 766–773, pp. 379–81.

commutative justice.[36] Nevertheless, there is the matter of the meaning of the stipend. According to the decree, it is a particular way of participating in the Mass. When the stipend is given to found a Mass, other such gifts do not have the same function. Hence it is not morally permissible arbitrarily to combine in one Mass several intentions for which one is under obligation to celebrate individual Masses. For the others cannot participate in the Mass precisely in this way. To accept another stipend in this way would be unjust. It may also be noted here that the priest, who accepts an offering with the promise to make intercession at Mass, is of course bound by that promise. But by the acceptance of a stipend he is not, on that account alone, bound precisely from justice to make intercession for the donor.[37]

V. SYSTEMATIC THEOLOGICAL THEMES OF THE DECREE AND COMMENTARY

This section of the chapter analyzes the principal systematic theological themes found in the decree and commentary and the uses to which they are put. These themes are, corresponding to the three subdivisions of this section of this chapter: the theology of the Eucharist conceived as sacrament of the sacrifice of the cross; the theology of the treasury of the Church; and the theology of fruits of the Mass.

The commentary refers to what the decree says about the "specious arguments . . . and indeed pretexts" of those who support the recent practice of the pluri-intentional Mass, and which reflect "a false ecclesiology." The decree does not spell out what this false ecclesiology might be. But the commentary identifies it with the argument which contrasts the essentially communitarian aspect of the eucharistic sacrifice with the undesirable privatizing of the Mass which results from introducing "fixed intentions" and "wishing to assign fruits of (the Mass) according to our intentions." The commentary seems to respond to this argument (branding it "the doctrinal confusion of a certain ecclesiology") in two steps.

[36] Confer Karl Rahner's references to the works of G. Rohner and K. Mörsdorf on this topic in: Karl Rahner and Angelus Häussling, *The Celebration of the Eucharist,* trans. W. J. O'Hara (New York: Herder and Herder, 1968 [German: *Die vielen Messen und das eine Opfer,* Freiburg i. Br., 1966]) 58, n. 17; 123, n. 40.

[37] Ibid., 121.

A. SACRAMENT OF THE SACRIFICE OF THE CROSS

First of all, the commentary affirms that this so-called "privatizing" of the Mass is grounded both on the fact that the sacrament of the sacrifice of the cross, with its infinite merits, is entrusted to the Church, and then, in a second step, that it is also grounded on the theology of "the treasury of the Church of which the Church disposes." It may be gathered from this point of view that the infinite merits of the sacrifice of the cross are the source of the "fruits" that derive from the celebration of the sacrament of the sacrifice of the cross. But since the sacrifice of the Mass is also the sacrifice of the Church, the theology of the "treasury of the Church" is applicable to the question at hand.

The Mass is the sacrifice of the Church in the sense that only the Church, which exists in local hierarchically organized communities, is commissioned by Christ to celebrate this sacrament of the sacrifice of the cross. Through this celebration the merits of Christ's sacrifice of the cross are applied to those actually participating in some way in the celebration of the Mass. In addition, the merits of Christ are applied to the whole Church, and to individuals for whom intercession is made in the eucharistic liturgy. But can more be said than that fruit derives from the Mass as a function of the devotion of those actually and personally involved in some way in the celebration?

The devotion of which we speak is the disposition of the participants of the Mass which is conformed to the meaning of the eucharistic sacrifice. It is prompted by the supernatural virtues of faith, hope, and love, which inspire the dedicated sacrificial attitude that issues in sacrificial service conformed to that of Christ. This devotion is incarnated in the prayer of intercession of the Mass, impelled by love, the gift of the Holy Spirit, for all the Father's children for whom Christ died. This love necessarily includes the desire for the full redemption of all humanity, and therefore of particular individuals. Through the devout intercession of the worshiping community for the whole Church and world, as well as for individuals, a contribution is made to the salvation of others; for this intercession is made in view of the work of redemption accomplished through Christ, and in view of the works accomplished in Christ by the saints.

We pray to Christ and to the saints, asking them to join in our prayer of intercession for ourselves and others; and we identify the source of the favorable response we expect as the cooperation of Christ and the saints—or rather, more precisely, we attribute the source of the favorable response we expect first to Christ alone, and then also to the value of our appeal to Christ made in union with the prayer of the saints, which is always there when we pray in communion with the prayer of the Church Militant.

It is evident that the liturgical traditions of the churches of East and West have never found any difficulty with the idea of "privatizing" the Mass in this way. Moreover, although the commentary indicates that the idea of "privatizing" is repeatedly criticized in certain circles, this writer is unable to identify any writings of Catholic theologians which fall into this category. It is not unthinkable that the commentary created this adversary out of whole cloth in order to allude to the teaching of Pope Pius VI occasioned by the decree of the Synod of Pistoia mentioned above (pp. 217–18).

When we discuss the question of the application of the fruits of the sacrifice of the cross through the eucharistic sacrifice from the sources of the eucharistic liturgy, we discover a valuable witness for the orthodoxy of the conviction of the Catholic faith that benefits accrue to those on whose behalf the eucharistic sacrifice is especially dedicated. This conviction of faith is ultimately grounded on the notion that in this economy of salvation, God the Father has determined himself to be moved by the response of the love of human beings for him and for all his children, a love which is instilled in them by the Holy Spirit.

The commentary identifies the eucharistic celebration as the "sacrament of the sacrifice of the cross." This raises the question concerning the understanding of the presence of Christ in the eucharistic celebration. The fact that the eucharistic community's sacrificial prayer is made in union with Christ who is the crucified and risen Savior, presupposes that there is a presence of Christ and his redemptive sacrifice, or rather, of Christ under the modality of offering himself to the Father for the salvation of the world. But what is meant precisely by the statement that the Eucharist is "the sacrament of that unique sacrifice which Christ has entrusted to the Church"?

The way in which this statement is phrased leads one to suspect that it is a paraphrase of a commonly heard statement, namely, that the once-for-all sacrifice of Christ is sacramentally re-presented in the Mass. But in the same breath, those who speak this way add that this does not mean that the sacrifice of Christ is repeated. Rather it means that the sacrifice of the cross is "renewed sacramentally" or "sacramentally re-presented."

Now the somatic real presence of Christ under forms of bread and wine can indeed be described, with reference to the numerous Masses celebrated daily throughout the world, as a sacramental re-presentation of the crucified and risen Lord. In other words, it is correct to say that the sacramental real presence of Christ under forms of bread and wine is repeatedly presented, occurs, or is re-presented in each eucharistic celebration. But the once-for-all sacrifice of Christ is not re-presented in this sense. This sacrifice is always present to the Church, since Christ himself is always actively present to the Church in all her essential activities, as well as to the faithful in their daily lives.

In the Eucharist, the only new activity is that of the Church. Consequently, we are correct in saying that the eucharistic community, through its eucharistic worship, is newly presented to the once-for-all sacrifice of Christ. Indeed the community does not continually present itself to the sacrifice of Christ from its own resources, but rather is re-presented. In the power of the Holy Spirit, the Church is re-presented to the unique sacrifice of Christ, and is enabled to make an appeal in the most intensive ritual way to the salvific will of the Father in, with, and through Christ. And by reason of the measure of devotion of the Church, which naturally is increased through active participation in the eucharistic sacrifice, the efficacy of this celebration as petition for the needs of the living and dead is realized.

The devotion that accounts for the efficacy of the eucharistic sacrifice cannot be simply described as the mental attitude of love that prompts one to do something without any real consequences for one's subsequent activity. The devotion that conforms to the eucharistic sacrifice must be understood as the actual disposition directed towards the meaning of the eucharistic sacrifice. It is the readiness to follow God's demands in actual service. It is prompted by that love which is the proximate cause of devotion; by that love which grounds the dedicated attitude of the mind that issues in obedient activity. In the eucharistic celebration, it is made evident that the proper attitude, grounded in faith and love, is the sacrificial attitude conformed to that of Christ.

B. TREASURY OF THE CHURCH

The commentary indicates that the doctrine of the treasury of the Church is applicable here. But how is this doctrine related to the intercessory prayer made in the Eucharist for various intentions? What new idea is included in the notion that the Church "disposes" of the treasury of the Church? Are we to think that there are two different acts of "disposing" and "interceding" which follow different laws? Are we to imagine that the Church exercises a kind of juridical act through its official ministers in the eucharistic celebration by which the infinite merits of Christ's redemptive sacrifice are applied to the various intentions for which the Mass is celebrated? And are we to distinguish this activity from the intercessory prayer made in the Eucharist for special intentions? We may suppose that in the commentary "treasury of the Church" means what Paul VI states in the apostolic constitution "The Doctrine of Indulgences." Here he observes that this treasury should be conceived "not (as) an amount of goods on the model of material riches, which are accumulated through centuries, but (as) the infinite and inexhaustible value which the expiations and merits of Christ have before God . . . also the prayers and good works of . . . Mary and of all the saints."[38] Paul VI also says:

"The Church, using her power of/as minister of the redemption of Christ the Lord, not only prays, but dispenses authoritatively to the aptly disposed Christian faithful the treasury of atonement of Christ and the saints for the remission of the temporal punishment";[39]

or that "the Church, as the minister of redemption, authoritatively dispenses and applies the treasury of the atonement of Christ and of the saints."[40] This is said about indulgences. But how is this to be explained theologically, and how is this doctrine related to the eucharistic sacrifice?

Until now, no common theological explanation has been achieved on this point among Catholic theologians; although the more common opinion in the scholastic tradition seems inclined to describe the application of indulgence as an act of jurisdiction. But can this activity be explained under the formality of prayer itself? At this juncture, it is sufficient to observe that the theological basis on which the doctrine

[38] "Qui quidem non est quasi summa bonorum ad instar materialium divitiarum, quae per saecula cumulantur, sed est infinitum et inexhaustum pretium, quod apud Deum habent expiationes et merita Christi Domini . . . Praeterea . . . et . . . orationes ac bona opera Beatae Mariae Virginis et omnium Sanctorum . . ." —Paul VI, apostolic constitution, *Indulgentiarum doctrina* II 5, *AAS* 59 (1967) 11–12.

[39] "In indulgentia enim Ecclesia, sua potestate utens ministrae redemptionis Christi Domini, non tantum orat, sed christifideli apte disposito auctoritative dispensat thesaurum satisfactionum Christi et Sanctorum ad poenae temporalis remissionem"—ibid., IV 8, p. 16.

[40] ". . . ope Ecclesiae quae, ut ministra redemptionis, thesaurum satisfactionum Christi et Sanctorum auctoritative dispensat et applicat"—ibid., norm 1, p. 21.

of the treasury of the Church is ultimately grounded is the reason why the eucharistic sacrifice includes fixed intentions for individual persons. This theological basis is also the reason why the Church "blesses" the desire that special benefits accrue to these fixed intentions for the particular needs of the persons for whom they are applied. But what, precisely, is the theological basis on which the doctrine of the treasury of the Church is ultimately based?

The commentary on this decree, as we have seen, refers to the infinite merits of Christ's sacrifice, the sacrament of which Christ has entrusted to the Church. As a consequence, the theology of the treasury of the Church "of which the Church disposes," is relevant to the subject of the efficacy of the Mass for individual intentions. For this treasury is essentially the "infinite merits" of Christ before God, but also includes the merits of the saints accomplished in and through Christ. From this standpoint it is understandable that, especially in the celebration of the Eucharist, the Church can "dispose" of the treasury of the Church in favor of the whole Church, the world, and individual persons. But what does "dispose" in the context of the eucharistic celebration mean?

The value which the sacrifice of the cross has before God cannot be disposed of by a juridical act of the Church. Rather, the holy Church's tendency toward perfect love entails the desire that all sinfulness, and its consequences, be eliminated from humanity. This tendency is grounded in the salvific will of God which is focused on the redemptive work of Christ, and as a consequence in the holiness of the Church which depends on the redemptive work of Christ, and which has the ministry of contributing to the salvation of the world.

The salvific will of God is made historically accessible in and through the activity of the holy Church. This activity includes not only the preaching of the gospel and witness to this preaching by concrete works of loving service to others, but also the prayer of the Church. In the latter case we are faced with the mystery of the efficacious prayer of the Church before God, which is an appeal in and through Christ for the offering by God of the graces needed by human beings for their salvation. The conviction of the Church that her prayer is heard finds its theological basis only in the divine decision to enter into a covenant relation of love with humanity through Christ's response of love as representative of all humanity.

God's offer of love necessarily implies the possibility of a response of love through the gift of faith by which God is moved to bestow his grace. This is verified in the one acceptable response of Christ, and in the response of love made by the holy Church in, with, and through Christ. On this ground the Church is confident that her prayer made for others is heard by God and answered by God's offer of his blessings, which are bestowed on condition that the ones for whom the Church prays are open in faith to receive these graces.

Above all, in the Eucharistic Prayer the Church intercedes in union with Christ for the whole Church, for the world, and for individuals. The Church appeals to the salvific will of God in virtue of the value of the redemptive work of Christ. This prayer makes manifest that, in the economy of salvation, the Father offers himself to be loved through the twofold self-communication of the incarnate Word and Spirit, and that the answering response of love is possible in union with Christ's once-for-all response of love. Moreover, according to the ontology of love, the divine offer of love necessarily includes the capacity of receiving the love of creatures; for by its very nature love is fulfilled in mutually exercised self-communication. When this love of the Father is expressed with reference to love for the Father's children by praying for their salvation, the Father is "moved" to hear this prayer of intercession.

Ultimately the treasury of the Church is the salvific will of God the Father, source of the mission of the incarnate Word. What the Church appeals to is this salvific will, but it appeals to it in union with Christ's intercession grounded on his historical and human response in his self-offering on the cross, which is the uniquely acceptable response to the Father's salvific will.

C. THEOLOGY OF THE FRUITS OF THE MASS

While the objection against including fixed intentions is easily met on the grounds of traditional liturgical practice that is supported by dogmatic teaching concerning the eucharistic sacrifice and the treasury of the Church, the opposition against "wishing to destine fruits of (the Mass) according to our intentions" is another matter. This latter expression, as formulated by the commentary, does not seem to be intended as a simple synonym for the idea of fixed intentions. Rather, it appears to express opposition to a specific theological understanding of the laws governing the distribution of the divine blessings which are associated with the celebration of a Mass.

The commentary answers this objection by an appeal to Catholic doctrine:

"Nor can it be forgotten that Catholic doctrine has constantly taught that the fruits of the eucharistic sacrifice are variously attributed: above all to those that the Church herself names in the 'intercessions' of the Eucharistic Prayer, then to the celebrating minister (the so-called ministerial fruit), then to those offering, and so forth."[41]

This statement could mean one of two things. It could mean, first of all, that Catholic doctrine has always taught that the fruits, or blessings, derived from the eucharistic sacrifice benefit those for whom the Church prays in the intercessions of the Eucharistic Prayer, as well as the presiding minister, and those who are engaged in a special way by reason of their offerings, etc. For indeed Catholic doctrine has always taught that the eucharistic sacrifice is beneficial in this way.

However, the commentary also employs the technical language of the thesis of traditional scholastic theology which maintains that special "fruits" derive from the Mass as such, independent of any consideration of the devotion of those participating in the Mass, i.e., those actually present, or participating by way of a stipend, whether physically present or absent. These fruits are distinguished among themselves and are applied to various subjects according to special laws. Moreover the commentary also qualifies this as "Catholic doctrine." Since it is well known that the magisterium of the Catholic Church has accepted this scholastic teaching in varying degrees since the High Middle Ages, it is arguable that the commentary is referring explicitly to this scholastic position.

However, the scholastic theology of the fruits of the Mass, although accepted in some measure by the magisterium, and also expressed in official documents, has not yet been fully stated and guaranteed by the magisterium itself. Certainly the scholastic teaching contains a grain of truth, but it is not necessarily materially identifiable with what is actually binding in faith. Moreover, if one can judge by publications over the last four decades, the majority of Catholic theologians are opposed to the kernel of this scholastic thesis. They hold that there is "one fruit" of the Mass, which fruit is derived from Christ's redemptive work, and which is measured by the devotion of those participating in the Mass, and by the devotion of those in whose favor intercession is made through the eucharistic sacrifice.

[41] See above, n. 8, for the Italian text.

It may be suggested that the commentary inserts the scholastic thesis merely to point out the grain of truth it contains. What must be held, as doctrine guaranteed by the instinct of the faithful, and by the teaching of the magisterium, is the conviction that fruit derives from the Mass for the whole Church, and the world, and individuals for whom the Church prays in the eucharistic sacrifice; and especially for those who actively participate in the celebration as well as for those in favor of whom the eucharistic sacrifice is celebrated. This is especially witnessed by the liturgy of the Eucharist itself.

If the scholastic theology of the fruits of the Mass is only tentatively introduced in the commentary with the words, "Nor can it be forgotten," this doubtless indicates that it is considered to have only a marginal value; for if this scholastic theological position could be theologically verified, it would be the best argument to propose against the argument based on a "false ecclesiology."

The decree refers to the priest "applying" the Mass "for" the intention of the donor of a stipend, or the more favored expression: the faithful make offerings for, or the priest accepts offerings for, "the celebration of a Mass according to a particular intention." But nowhere in the decree itself is the value of the particular Mass for the particular intention based on the classical scholastic thesis that a special fruit, intrinsic to the Mass itself, independently of any consideration of those actually participating in the Mass, accrues to the intention of the person in whose favor the priest applies this special fruit.

VI. CATECHETICAL INSTRUCTION CONCERNING THE THEOLOGY OF THE MASS STIPEND

In the latter half of this century papal documents have reflected a certain caution regarding key aspects of the traditional scholastic theology of Mass stipends and, at the same time, have turned to more recent orientations of Catholic theology on the subject. For example, a part of the traditional scholastic theological position teaches that distinct fruits derive from the celebration of the Mass as such, independently of the devotion of those who in some way actually participate in the Mass, and are applied according to distinct laws. This thesis was formerly used to explain why it is more advantageous for priests to "celebrate" Mass rather than attend as "hearers." However, since the middle of this century, papal documents have passed over this argument when urging priests to prefer to celebrate private Masses or to concelebrate rather than attend after the manner of laity.

The opportunity presented itself to Pius XII when, in an allocution delivered on 2 November 1954, he spoke of the importance of a priest's devotion in connection with Mass. He states that it is possible for a priest to receive more fruit from hearing a Mass with devotion than from celebrating it negligently.[42] This seems to imply that in both cases the measure of fruits is determined by the measure of devotion. In other words, there is no ministerial fruit automatically bestowed in virtue of the fact that the priest acts as chief celebrant of the liturgy. Also Paul VI, in the encyclical letter *Mysterium fidei,* speaks of the abundance of particular graces that come to the priest from the celebration of private Masses,[43] but he does not mention the so-called ministerial fruit that would be the best argument for the practice of celebrating private Mass rather than simply assisting.

In the matter of the so-called special fruit that comes from the application of the Mass to the intention of the donor of an offering, Paul VI, in *Firma in traditione,* relates the offering of the faithful to the desire to participate more actively in the eucharistic sacrifice in order than they might "unite themselves more closely with Christ offering himself as victim, thus deriving more abundant fruit from the sacrifice."[44] Here the Pope refers only to the devotion of the faithful as the measure by which the fruit of the sacrifice of Christ is applied. He simply passes over the traditional thesis concerning the application of a special fruit *ex opere operato* to the intention for which the Mass is celebrated.

The 1991 decree of the Congregation for the Clergy, which makes its own this teaching of Paul VI, also passes over the traditional scholastic theology of offerings made for the celebration of Masses. In this case the preference for the normative practice over that of the pluri-intentional Mass would have been best supported by that traditional scholastic explanation of the meaning of Mass stipends. The of-

[42] ". . . sane fieri potest, ut quis maiorem fructum capiat ex Missa pie religioseque audita quam ex Missa leviter et neglegenter celebrata . . ."—Pius XII, Allocution on the occasion of the establishment of the liturgical feast of Mary, Mother of God and Queen of Heaven and Earth, 2 November 1954, *AAS* 46 (1954) 666–77, at 669.

[43] Paul VI, encyclical letter *Mysterium fidei, AAS* 57 (1965) 753–74, at 762.

[44] ". . . Christo . . . arctius sociantur et abundantiorem fructuum copiam inde percipiunt . . ."—Paul VI, apostolic letter *Firma in traditione, AAS* 66 (1974) 308–11, at 308.

ficial commentary on the decree does introduce the key element of the traditional scholastic theology of Mass stipends, namely, the concept of the differentiation of fruits of the Mass applied according to different laws. However, it remains unclear how this reference is to be interpreted. All of this indicates that the magisterium is open to a new way of understanding the theology of Mass stipends, while at the same time it is reluctant simply to relegate the traditional explanation to the historical past.

This last observation brings us to the pastoral problem raised by Article 7 of this decree. How is the directive requiring that the faithful be instructed about the theological meaning of "offerings given to the priest for the celebration of the eucharistic sacrifice" to be carried out? Perhaps the best approach is to begin with an explanation of the various aspects of what modern Catholic theology teaches about the theology of the Mass stipend. In a second step, this teaching should be compared to corresponding aspects of the classical scholastic synthesis; and, in a third step, reasons should be given, where applicable, for disregarding the position of the classical synthesis. With regard to this third step, this task is completed when the official teaching of the Roman magisterium on this subject is identified along with the areas where there exist legitimate differences of theological opinion among Catholic theologians.

The characteristic aspects of this new theology of Mass stipends which are "received" by the magisterium, as well as the contrasting aspects of the traditional theology of Mass stipends which are placed alongside them and still "retained," along with the reasons for the preferences for the modern options where applicable, can be summarized as follows:

(A) The Mass entails the sacramental representation of the sacrifice of the cross. But in what sense? Is the sacrifice of the cross represented to the liturgical community in order that the community be enabled to come into contact with it; or, is the liturgical community represented to the sacrifice of the cross? In either case, does the mystery of the eucharistic sacrifice consist in the sacramental presence of the historical sacrifice of the cross? The Roman magisterium seems to favor the idea that the sacrifice of the cross is represented to the liturgical community. However the concept of representation of the liturgical community to the sacrifice of the cross is also a viable option.

(B) This sacramental presence takes place in order that the community might share in a sacramental way in the graces derived from the redemptive work of Christ. Hence the eucharistic celebration is a means of application of the fruits of the sacrifice of the cross. This is the authentic teaching of the Catholic Church confirmed by the Council of Trent.

(C) This sacramental presence of the once-for-all sacrificial self-offering of Christ does not imply, in any sense, the presence of a new oblation on the part of Christ. Moreover, in the glorified state, discrete acts are not possible on the part of the humanity of Christ. The newness of each eucharistic sacrifice is attributed to the renewed self-offering of the liturgical assembly. The idea that the eucharistic sacrifice is above all an action of Christ is frequently met in the teaching of the magisterium. What is meant by this, however, remains obscure. The statement that the eucharistic sacrifice is efficacious *ex opere operantis Christi* is open to several interpretations and is not sufficiently clarified in modern official teaching.

(D) The thesis concerning the *ex opere operato* effect of the Mass which is based on a supposed new action of Christ lacks a solid theological basis. Moreover, there is no convincing argument for predicating that fruits derive from the Mass *ex opere operato* in virtue of the divine will. Rather this thesis is based on the unproven assumption that every celebration of Mass involves an efficacy analogous to the so-called efficacy of the sacraments which consists in the infallible offer of grace *ex opere operato*. Still, the Roman magisterium to this day has not explicitly rejected the notion of fruits derived from the Mass independently of the devotion of those who somehow actively participate in the celebration of the eucharistic sacrifice.

(E) Fruits derived from the Mass are a function of the devotion of members of the Church who actively participate in the eucharistic worship and are received according to the measure of the devotion of those who offer or those for whom the offering is made. For no other source of blessings derived from the Mass can be identified. The classical doctrine of distinct fruits of the Mass applied according to different laws still forms a part of the tradition which has not been completely discarded by the magisterium.

(F) As subjects of the offering of the Mass are included all the Christian faithful who are actively related to the particular Mass through physical presence and, therefore, those whose devotion determines the measure of fruits derived from the celebration. The notion that the members of the universal Church participate in the Masses of the world by their intention is valid insofar as this means that their prayer affords support for those engaged in the celebration of particular Masses. It should also be said that those who make offerings for the celebration of Masses participate in the celebration as persons who make possible the eucharistic celebration. But their devotion in making the offering does not account for the measure of the fruits of the Mass when it is celebrated. As in the case of the members of the Church universal, the divine response to the expression of their devotion does not have to wait until a Mass is applied to their offering.

The notion that the holy members of the Church who unite themselves in the offering of the "Masses of the world" are a source of blessings which derive from these Masses is a part of the traditional teaching of Catholic theology which was explicitly formulated in the thirteenth century. The teaching about the Eucharist as involving the offering of the universal Church continues to find place in the teaching of the magisterium, but the exact meaning of this teaching is not sufficiently determined.

(G) The application of a Mass to the offering of a donor is made by the priest. Thereby a relationship between a gift and a particular Mass is established by the liturgical leader. However, the priest does not, precisely speaking, apply the fruit of a particular Mass to the intention of the donor of the offering. For the fruits of the Mass are not applied according to different laws. Rather, there is one fruit which is applied according to the divine dispensation to all in accord with their devotion.

From this point of view it is imprecise, theologically speaking, for a priest to promise to offer Mass "first intention" for this or that person. This language implies what has now become theologically questionable, namely that the priest has control over blessings derived from the Mass. However, the Roman magisterium has not yet explicitly rejected the idea that the priest has a role in the assignment of the special fruit of the Mass which is related to the special intention for which the Mass is celebrated.

(H) The application of a number of offerings of donors to a particular Mass does not, in itself, necessarily result in a diminishing of the efficacy of the Mass for the intention of the individual donor. For, always, the efficacy of the Mass is measured by the quality of the devotion of the participants. Nevertheless, the Roman magisterium still speaks of the relatively greater efficacy of the normative practice of the Mass stipend, but without sufficiently clarifying the basis for this position.

VII. CONCLUSION

The 1991 decree of the Congregation for the Clergy *(Mos iugiter)* is suggestive regarding the special role of the magisterium as mediator in the process of promoting a better theological understanding of the practice of the Mass stipend. It is of utmost importance that this role be explained in the catechesis on this subject. For there exists the danger that what the magisterium has to say about a theological issue, such as this one, which is still in the process of maturation, is taken to be a final authoritative solution rather than viewed as presenting a theological problem still remaining to be resolved.

It should be evident that the modern approach to the theology of the Mass stipend has much in common with the theology of the tributary of the old offertory procession as it was practiced in the Roman sphere of influence from the end of the first millennium until the end of the twelfth century. At the same time, the practice of the Mass stipend which was approved in that milieu also corresponded to that theology.

By contrast, the modern practice of the Mass stipend (the subject we have been discussing) corresponds to the medieval German version of a secondary tributary of the old offertory procession which, when implemented by precise determinations from Roman law, became the normative practice in the Western Catholic Church and has remained so down to the twentieth century.

However, the modern approach to the theology of the Mass stipend does not harmonize well with the theology of the Mass stipend which is appealed to in order to ground that practice. Correspondingly, the 1991 decree of the Congregation for the Clergy has much in common with the theological stance that lies behind the decision of the Roman Synod of 826. But, at the same time, its practical decision stands in sharp contrast with that of the ninth-century synod. That synod clearly favored what corresponds to the pluri-intentional Mass and renders a negative judgment regarding the contemporary ninth-century German version. On the other hand, our 1991 decree champions the German version of the practice which became normative and has been in vogue in the West since the thirteenth century.

In short, the official teaching of the Roman magisterium on the subject of the theology and practice of Mass stipends can serve as one example of what is true of practically every aspect of official teaching concerning the theology of the Eucharist in this period of renewal of doctrine and practice. By placing what is new alongside what is old, the magisterium poses a challenge to theologians to strive to attain a new and higher synthesis of theory and practice. In this way the magisterium contributes significantly to the task of the reformulation and deepening of eucharistic theology. This contribution, however, is realizable only to the extent that the Roman magisterium enters into the theological dialogue as mediator both of the valid insights of traditional doctrine and of the valid insights of contemporary theology.

Part Two

Theology

Introduction

Overview of the History of the Western Latin Theology of Eucharistic Sacrifice

Part two of this book treats only the subject of a systematic theology of the eucharistic sacrifice based on the authentic whole tradition of Catholic eucharistic faith. Part one, as we have seen, contains an outline of salient features of the various stages of the history of eucharistic theology of the Western Catholic tradition. This included the history of the theology of eucharistic sacrifice. This historical information provides the indispensable background for a proper evaluation of a systematic theology of the sacrifice of the Mass that can claim to be faithful to the Catholic tradition.

Here, at the outset of Part two, as an aid to situating a systematic theology of the Mass within the proper historical context of the whole Catholic tradition and, in particular, as a help to identifying the synthesis of the peculiar splinter tradition of the eucharistic theology of the Latin Church, this introduction supplies a brief summary of salient features of the evolving understanding of the sacrificial dimension of the eucharistic liturgy at key stages from the first to the twentieth century.

(1) The New Testament sources present a theology of spiritual sacrifice, the offering of one's whole being (body and spirit) in the service of God, that is, in the life of faith which is expressed in the preaching of the Gospel of Jesus Christ, the loving practical service of one's neighbor, and in communal activity of worship.

(2) In the second century the emphasis fell on the eucharistic cultic expression of this spiritual sacrifice of the priestly community. This theology was supported by references to the prophecy of Malachi 1:10-12.

(3) During the third century, a shift took place from emphasis on the self-offering of the Christian assembly to the more explicit awareness

that in the Eucharist the Church offers sacrificial worship in union with Christ. With the orientation being placed on the Christological aspect of the eucharistic sacrifice, the reference to the prophecy of Malachi was displaced by that of the sacrifice of Melchizedek which was viewed as type of the eucharistic sacrifice of Christ the high priest.

(4) From the fourth to the sixth centuries, in both East and West, theological reflection centered on the problem of the active presence of Christ as priest and victim in the liturgical self-offering of the Church. The Eastern tradition drew on the notion of the commemorative actual presence of the sacrifice of the cross, while the Western tradition generally viewed the presence of a sacrificial action of Christ in the offering of the Church as situated in a looser relation to that of the historical sacrifice of the cross.

(5) Especially from the seventh century onward in the Western Church, under the influence of Eastern theology, the mediatorial action of the ordained minister in the eucharistic liturgy was modeled on Old Testament priesthood. At the same time, the liturgical president was understood to represent the Church in the eucharistic sacrifice, and only so was qualified to represent Christ the high priest of the Mass.

(6) At the end of the first millennium, in the Western Church of the ninth to the tenth century, the distinction between the sacrificial activity of Christ in the Mass and that of the historical self-offering on the cross is underscored. The distinction between the efficacy of the historical sacrifice of the cross related to original sin and the offering of the daily sacrifice for daily sins, a viewpoint in vogue since the sixth century, is commonplace. The need for the priest to be a member of the Church in order to function as president of the eucharistic sacrifice of the Church continues to be underscored.

(7) From the eleventh century through the thirteenth century, there is in the Western Church no further theological development of the relation of the eucharistic sacrifice to that of the cross. However, the understanding of the relation of the presiding priest to Christ and the Church does undergo change. The priest is now thought to be qualified to celebrate the Eucharist, at least as regards the confection of the sacrament of the body and blood, in virtue of the "power of consecration" conferred at ordination. The previous necessity of certain grades of membership in the Church as condition for the presiding priest to represent the Church is played down while, at the same time, the ec-

clesiological dimension begins to be subsumed under the Christological dimension. Also at the same time, the notion of the participation of the laity in the offering of the eucharistic sacrifice is understood to be effected precisely through the mediation of the presiding minister on the model of the Old Testament high priest.

(8) In the fourteenth century and onward up through the beginning of the sixteenth century, the eucharistic sacrifice is conceived as the offering of Christ, the victim of the cross through the ordained minister. The Church receives the fruits of the offering which are the application of the fruits of the historical sacrifice of Christ. According to the Scotus–Biel theory, the consecration of the bread and wine is accomplished by the priest acting as representative of Christ. On the other hand the presiding priest also acts as representative of the Church which is the principal offerer of the eucharistic sacrifice.

(9) At the outset of the sixteenth century, Martin Luther rejected the teaching that the Mass is a sacrifice in the proper sense. Rather, in the Mass the sacraments of the body and blood enable the realization of participation in a holy communion with the victim of the sacrifice of the cross. The Council of Trent taught that the sacrifice of the cross happened once-for-all. Therefore Christ's priesthood is eternal. The ordained member of the hierarchy who presides at the Eucharist is the minister of Christ. The eucharistic celebration is a memorial celebration of the once-for-all historical sacrifice of the cross. The event of the cross is represented and its saving power bestowed.

At Trent the concepts of "memorial," "representation," and "application," are used but not clearly defined in the doctrinal exposition on the subject of the sacrifice of the Mass. The memorial is conceived as happening objectively in the ritual event of the Eucharist, and not simply in the subjective memory of individuals. The representation is more than the outward image; it includes the reality. Memorial and representation involves the "new pasch," the *transitus* to the kingdom.

The application of the historical sacrifice of the cross in the Mass is explained in this way: The Mass is propitiatory because the same priest and victim of the cross is present, because there is a bestowal of the fruits of the cross. Nothing is added to the cross. What is received is the fruit of the bloody immolation. But to receive it, one must have proper dispositions.

There are several difficulties with the teaching of Trent. The New Testament references to the historical self-offering of Jesus Christ are meshed with concepts of sacrifice derived from Old Testament animal sacrifices. There is the tendency to confuse statements about the liturgical activity with dogmatic statements. In Trent's doctrinal exposition, chapter one, it is said that Christ gave his body under the appearances of bread and wine to be offered by priests. Here there is reference to the outward sign; *offerre* is used in the sense of a common cultic term. But in chapter two we read that Christ offers himself as he did on the cross. Here *offerre* is a New Testament sacrificial concept.

This mixing of terms drawn from both (non-Christian) cultic activity and the event of the cross led to permanent difficulties. When they are not distinguished, one seeks the act of offering to God at the level of signs in the liturgical action. In this way one is led back to a pre-Christian concept of sacrifice; for example, the theory of the mystical immolation of Christ, a "virtual death." Moreover the offering of the sacrifice of Christ is seen as objectivized in the Mass independently of the offering of the Church. One could, therefore, say that Christ's sacrifice becomes present at the moment of consecration, that is, at the moment of the recitation of the words of Christ contained in the liturgical account of the institution of the Eucharist. This moment becomes the holy moment when the liturgical community should join itself to the sacrificial action of Christ. The anamnesis-offering prayer which follows enables the participants of the liturgy to articulate liturgically their intention of offering themselves in union with the self-offering of Christ to God the Father, and to plead for the acceptance of their self-offering.

Thus, one of the most basic difficulties with Trent's teaching about the eucharistic sacrifice is the use of *offerre* for both the historical self-offering of Jesus Christ and the liturgical offering of bread and wine. The use of this verb for the historical self-offering of Christ on the cross and the use of the same term for the liturgical-ceremonial ritual act became an obstacle to the recovery of the ancient doctrine of the mystery of the eucharistic sacrifice.

(10) From the seventeenth to the twentieth centuries, Catholic theologians described the eucharistic sacrifice almost exclusively from the standpoint of the role of Christ. But the sacrifice of Christ is conceived as somehow located in the external rite; for example, the mystical separation of body and blood. However, the French Oblationist School brought some balance to this approach by highlighting the offering of the Church linked to the offering of Christ.

(11) From the early part of the twentieth century, beginning with the research of the German monk Dom Odo Casel, O.S.B., a new ap-

proach to the subject of the relationship of the eucharistic sacrifice to the historical sacrifice of the cross was undertaken in the Western Church. Here the interest turned to the Greek patristic idea of the commemorative actual presence of the cross in the Mass. Speculative aspects of Casel's theology, however, are only partially accepted. The further development of explanations of the mystery presence of the act of the cross in the Mass includes systematic considerations of the role of the Spirit in relating the sacrifice of the assembly to the sacrifice of the cross. Also, the attempt is being made at present to redefine the role of the priest, as leader of the eucharistic sacrifice, in relation to the Eucharist as the act of the whole assembly.

Chapter Nine

Eucharistic Sacrifice According to St. Thomas Aquinas

The average modern Catholic theology of eucharistic sacrifice corresponds in great part to the thirteenth-century systematic approach of St. Thomas Aquinas which was rescued from partial oblivion in the wake of the sixteenth-century controversies over the Mass. From the latter part of that century to the twentieth century this theological synthesis became increasingly influential. In our own time it has been adopted by the Roman magisterium in its ordinary teaching and slightly adapted to the exigencies of modern scientific studies.

In effect, the only alternative to Aquinas's approach within the tradition of scholastic theology was in fact the common teaching from the fourteenth to the sixteenth centuries. But, in the judgment of prominent and influential theologians, this late medieval approach proved to be untenable, or at least "inopportune." This was particularly true when Catholic theology was forced to defend the teaching of the Council of Trent on the subject of the sacrifice of the Mass against the objections of the Reformers. However, as we shall see, this late medieval approach, mostly forgotten in the post-Tridentine period, does contain an important insight that is now finally being given the attention it deserves. For in the most recent past, theologians have been attempting to integrate into a higher synthesis both the fundamental insights of Aquinas and the theology of the sacrifice of the Mass of the late medieval period.

Without doubt, the theology of eucharistic sacrifice of St. Thomas Aquinas constitutes an outstanding example among the thirteenth-century contributions to this subject. On the following pages the essential elements of his synthesis are treated in summary fashion.

I. THE THOMIST SYNTHESIS

The sacrifice of the Mass is located liturgically within the context of the Eucharistic Prayer and symbolic action which is a formulation of the eucharistic faith of the Church. The Eucharistic Prayer itself is the liturgical expression of that differentiated activity of the life of faith which falls in the category of worship of God: a communal activity of the Church which takes place in union with Christ who is the High Priest of the worshiping community. Beginning from this point of view, Aquinas takes account of the liturgical expression of the ecclesiological and Christological dimensions of the eucharistic sacrifice found in the canon of the Mass.

A. THE ROLE OF THE LITURGICAL ASSEMBLY

What the worshiping community does in the eucharistic celebration is accomplished in virtue of the baptismal character by which the members are configured to the priesthood of Christ. Through this "certain participation in the priesthood of Christ,"[1] the whole Church participates in the eucharistic worship of which Christ himself is the author and principal actor. Hence there is a sacramental basis for the possibility of the worship of the community in union with Christ which is described as a kind of participation in the priesthood of Christ but not simply as a participation in the personal, unique priesthood of Christ which, by definition, is incommunicable.

B. THE ROLE OF THE PRESIDING PRIEST

The intimate organic unity between the worship of Christ, the High Priest of the Church's worship, and the worship of the Church is conditioned by the special role of the presiding priest who proclaims the Eucharistic Prayer in the name of the Church. The authority of the priest to preside at the eucharistic liturgy as representative of the Church is accepted by Aquinas as a given. He bases this authority on the sacrament of holy orders by which the candidate is elevated to the rank of presbyter. Through this sacrament, according to the teaching of the day, the candidate obtains the power to accomplish the act by which the gifts of bread and wine, which signify the self-offering of

[1] Cf. *Summa theologiae* 3, q. 63, a. 3 c: "Manifestum est quod character sacramentalis specialiter est character Christi, cujus sacerdotio configurantur fideles secundum sacramentales characteres, qui nihil aliud sunt quam quaedam participationes sacerdotii Christi ab ipso Christo derivatae."

the Church, are made a consecrated offering. But this activity, in which the presiding priest consecrates the gifts, acting in the person of Christ *(in persona Christi),* is not proposed as the formal reason why the priest is able to act as representative of the whole Church.

In other words, it is not precisely because the priest consecrates the gifts in the person of Christ the head of the Church that he represents the Church of which Christ is the head. Rather, he represents the whole Church because of the nature of the eucharistic sacrament. It is because the Eucharist is accomplished for the whole Church; it is because the Eucharist is "sacrament of the universal Church."[2] Therefore, by reason of the ecclesiological nature of the Eucharist, the priest acts for the whole Church, not immediately because he consecrates the gifts *in persona Christi, capitis ecclesiae.*

Later on in the Thomistic school—not to be identified simply with the teaching of Aquinas himself—not only is the consecration understood to be a commemorative representation of the once-for-all self-offering on the cross, the accent is also placed on a sacramental renewal of the self-offering of Christ through the ministry of the priest. The idea that through the priest, acting in the person of Christ, Christ offers himself to the Father as head of the Church leads to the conclusion that the priest, in his sacramental role, also represents the Church of which Christ is the head. In this way the ecclesiological dimension of the sacrifice could be conceived as included in the Christological dimension. One could conclude that the Church offers the sacrifice "through the hands of the priest," insofar as he acts in the person of Christ, head of the Church.

Aquinas himself recognizes that the consecration of the gifts signifies in a sacramental way Christ's once-for-all sacrifice of the cross. But scholars debate over the question whether he also went beyond this and held for a sacramental representation of the historical sacrificial act of the cross, or whether, as we think, he simply followed the common opinion of the day. We will return to this question below.

C. THE MOMENT OF CONSECRATION

Following the common teaching of the day, Aquinas locates the consecration of the bread and wine within the Eucharistic Prayer at

[2] "Ipse solus [i.e., the priest] potest gerere actus totius Ecclesiae qui consecrat eucharistiam, quae est sacramentum universalis Ecclesiae"—*In IV Sent.,* d. 24, q. 2, a. 2 ad 2.

the moment of the recitation of the words of Christ which are contained in the liturgical narrative of the institution of the Eucharist, and which identify the bread and wine as Christ's body and blood "given and shed." These words, the essential form of the sacrament of the Eucharist, are understood to be spoken by the priest *quasi ex persona Christi.*[3] What they signify is realized by the divine power which changes them into the body and blood of Christ offered once for all for the salvation of the world. Hence this sacrament is both "sacrifice" and "sacrament": sacrifice as offered and sacrament as food of life. However the ecclesiological representative function is also included, since the priest must have the intention of doing what the Church does in obedience to the will of Christ, that is, of accomplishing the sacrament through reciting the words of Christ as representative of Christ.

From the standpoint of sacrificed body, the twofold elements, described as the body given and blood shed, represent sacramentally what happened on Calvary when the sacrificed body was marked with the blood of the cross once-for-all. Thus Aquinas can speak of the twofold consecration as the image of the passion of Christ, and the result of the consecration as the real presence of the Christus Passus under the form of bread and wine. There is, therefore, an organic link between the historical sacrifice of the cross and the eucharistic sacrifice. This link has multiple elements consisting in (1.) the identity of the victim of the cross; (2.) the presence of Christ under the signs of the passion; (3.) the identity of the principal priest, namely, Christ the high priest who acts through the ministerial priest; (4.) the application of the fruits of the cross, *ex opere operato,* in and through the eucharistic sacrifice.[4]

[3] "Si sacerdos sola verba praedicta proferret cum intentione conficiendi hoc sacramentum, perficeretur hoc sacramentum, qui intentio faceret ut haec verba intelligerentur quasi ex persona Christi prolata, etiamsi verbis praecedentibus hoc non recitaretur"—*ST* 3, q. 78, a. 1 ad 4.

[4] According to the younger Aquinas, limited fruits are offered through the Mass *ex opere operato.* The older Aquinas, however, seems to have attributed the limitations of the fruits of the Mass applied *ex opere operato* to the measure of the devotion of those for whom the Mass is offered or of those who offer it. Or, more precisely, as regards intercession for others, the fruits are limited for the dead only by reason of the devotion of the offerers, and applied according to divine justice. The same is also true of the fruits for the living, namely, by reason of their devotion, etc. On this matter, cf. Karl Rahner and Angelus Häussling, *The Celebration of the Eucharist* (New York: Herder and Herder, 1968) 47, 79, 81–82.

D. THE SACRAMENTAL PRESENCE OF THE MYSTERY OF THE HISTORICAL REDEMPTIVE ACT

Aquinas held that the redemptive power of the sacrifice of the cross is applied *ex opere operato* in and through the Mass. This was the common theory among contemporary scholastics. Also, according to some modern scholars, Aquinas does not seem to have moved beyond the common teaching of the day concerning the question of the presence of the past historical sacrifice of the cross in the Mass which was confined to the application of its salutary effects.[5]

In his study of the Western tradition, on the question of the relation of the sacrifice of the Mass to the historical sacrifice of the cross, Dom Odo Casel, O.S.B., argued that Aquinas held for a mystery presence of the historical sacrifice of the cross objectively realized in a sacramental mode of existence on the altar.[6] More recently, on the other hand, in his monograph on the subject of the sacramental crisis of the concept of sacrament in Luther and in the scholasticism of the Middle Ages, Ferdinand Pratzner argues that Aquinas did not go beyond the common opinion of the day, namely, that the separate consecration of bread and wine has the value of a commemorative sign which elicits the subjective recall of the historical passion.[7] Alexander Gerken follows Pratzner, identifying the cause of Aquinas's conclusion as the lack of a relational ontology of person in the Thomist perspective. According to Gerken, such a relational ontology implies the presence of the historical passion wherever the risen Lord is present. Christ, who became the man for others through the actualization of his relational nature, is present sacramentally as the one who offered himself to the Father for us. Person and act are inseparable.[8]

[5] ". . . quae profecto mysteria, non incerto ac subobscuro eo modo, quo recentiores quidam scriptores effutiunt, sed quo modo catholica doctrina nos docet, praesentia continenter adsunt atque operantur . . . eximia sunt christianae perfectionis exempla, et divinae gratiae sunt fontes ob merita deprecationesque Christi"—Pius XII, encyclical letter *Mediator Dei, AAS* 39 (1947) 580.

[6] On this subject, cf. Bernhard Poschmann, "'Mysteriengegenwart' im Licht des hl. Thomas," *Theologische Quartalschrift* 116 (1935) 55–116; Johannes Betz, *Die Eucharistie in der Zeit der griechischen Väter* I/1 (Freiburg: Herder, 1955) 248.

[7] Ferdinand Pratzner, *Messe und Kreuzesopfer: Die Krise der sakramentalen Idee bei Luther und in der mittelalterlichen Scholastik,* Wiener Beiträge zur Theologie 29 (Vienna: Herder, 1970) 70–76.

[8] Alexander Gerken, "Kann sich die Eucharistielehre ändern?" *Zeitschrift für katholische Theologie* 97 (1975) 415–29, at 427–28, n. 17.

1. Anscar Vonier

Dom Anscar Vonier's interpretation of Aquinas's teaching on this issue can serve to illustrate a popular view of Aquinas's position that is held in many circles today.[9] He explains how Aquinas conceives the Eucharist as *"sacramentum"* not only in the sense of other sacraments but as sacrifice. Aquinas certainly teaches in an explicit way that this sacrament is both sacrifice and sacrament, or rather the one thing is both a sacramental sacrifice and sacrificial sacrament. He states that this sacrament differs from others in that it is a *sacrificium* "and so there is a difference of condition."[10]

The sacrament, according to Aquinas, is most fully expressed in the consecration: a sacramental representation of Christ's passion, and as such is a sacrifice. The perfection of this sacrament is not in the rite of Holy Communion, but in the consecration of the elements: "The perfection of this sacrament is not in the use, but in the consecration of the *materia.*"[11] "The representation of the Lord's passion is performed in the very consecration of this sacrament, in which the body ought not to be consecrated without the blood."[12] Hence the sacrament is essentially realized in the consecration, which is the representation of Christ's passion, since the body and blood are consecrated separately.

As far as the Mass is concerned, "the sacrament itself is the principal thing" distinguished from the prayers for the living and dead, and from Holy Communion which is required for the integrity of the celebration. Thus the Mass, said by a sinner or holy man, is the same in value because the same sacrament is performed.[13] In short, to offer Mass is simply *conficere sacramentum.* The use that is made of the sacrament follows upon the existence of the sacrament.[14] The use belongs to the perfection of the sacrament, just as the operation is the

[9] Anscar Vonier, *A Key to the Doctrine of the Eucharist* (Westminster, Md.: Newman, 1948) passim.

[10] ". . . et ideo non est similis ratio"—*ST* 3, q. 79, a. 7 ad 1.

[11] ". . . cum alia sacramenta perficiantur in usu materiae, percipere sacramentum est ipsa perfectio sacramenti; hoc autem sacramentum perficitur in consecratione materiae"—*ST* 3, q. 80, a. 1 ad 1.

[12] "Repraesentatio dominicae passionis agitur in ipsa consecratione hujus sacramenti, in qua non debet corpus sine sanguine consecrari"—*ST* 3, q. 80, a. 12 ad 3.

[13] "Quantum ergo ad sacramentum, non minus valet missa sacerdotis mali quam boni, quia utrobique idem conficitur sacramentum"—*ST* 3, q. 82, a. 6.

[14] "Hoc sacramentum perficitur in consecratione materiae; usus autem fidelium non est de necessitate sacramenti, sed est aliquid consequens ad sacramentum"—*ST* 3, q. 74, a. 7.

second perfection of a thing.[15] The distinction of effects follows the composition of this sacrament. Having the nature of a sacrifice insofar as offered up, it functions as sacrifice. Conversely, having the nature of a sacrament insofar as partaken, it affords spiritual food for the soul.[16]

According to Aquinas, Christ was offered *in proprie specie* on Calvary and is offered *in specie sacramenti* on the altar. But how is the sacrament understood to be a sacrifice? Vonier interprets Aquinas's thought in the following way. What is contained in the sacrament is known through the signs that constitute the sacrament. The sign signifies sacrifice; the words work sacramentally according to the power of signification.[17] The eucharistic representative sacrifice contains a representation of the broken Christ on Calvary. The phase of Christ dead on the cross is represented realistically. Hence we have a memorial in the sense of the representation of the real death of Christ which took place in historical time. Christ is not immolated anew but the immolation on Calvary is rendered present through the eucharistic body and blood. There is one sacrifice of Christ of which the sacrament is the representation of the natural sacrifice. The act is new, not the sacrifice. There is the repetition of the thing in the sacramental sphere; i.e., of the thing that is [in the natural sphere] immutable in itself.

This interpretation of Vonier seems to go beyond the evidence. In *ST* 3, q. 83, a. 1 the question is asked: Whether Christ is immolated in the sacrament? Two reasons are given. First, the Augustinian saying is introduced: the image of a thing bears the name of the thing. On this point Aquinas has already stated that the separation of the species is a "certain image representative of the passion of Christ, which is his true immolation."[18] Second *(alio modo)*, Aquinas refers to the fact that

[15] "In his verbis: *Accipite et comedite,* intelligitur usus materiae consecratae, qui non est de necessitate hujus sacramenti . . . . Et ideo nec haec verba sunt de substantia formae. Quia tamen ad quamdam perfectionem sacramenti pertinet materiae consecratae usus, sicut operatio non est prima, sed secunda perfectio rei, ideo per omnia ista verba exprimitur tota perfectio hujus sacramenti"—*ST* 3, q. 78, a. 1 ad 2.

[16] "Hoc sacramentum simul est sacrificium et sacramentum; sed rationem sacrificii habet, inquantum offertur; rationem autem sacramenti, inquantum sumitur. Et ideo effectum sacramenti habet in eo qui sumit, effectum autem sacrificii in eo qui offert, vel in his pro quibus offertur"—*ST* 3, q. 79, a. 5.

[17] *ST* 3, q. 78, a. 4 ad 3, and ibid., ad 2.

[18] ". . . imago quaedam est repraesentativa passionis Christi, quae est vera ejus immolatio"—*ST* 3, q. 83, a. 1; cf. 3. q. 79, a. 1.

through the sacrament we are made participants of the fruits of the passion.

As for the first mode, Aquinas recalls that Christ is also immolated in the figures of the Old Covenant; as for the second mode, however: "it is proper to this sacrament that in its celebration Christ is immolated."[19] Here Aquinas makes immolation coterminous with representation and application. But he does distinguish between representation and application because application belongs to the New Covenant while only representation belongs to the Old Covenant. Aquinas also says that the celebration of this sacrament is the "representative image of the passion . . . just as the altar represents the cross on which Christ was immolated in his own nature."[20] And in the same article, the priest is said to be the image of Christ, in whose place and by whose power he pronounces the words that make the consecration; and so in a certain way the priest and victim are the same.[21]

Now none of these texts, and similar texts in Aquinas, prove Vonier's thesis which corresponds to that of Casel, and which exercised a decisive influence on Casel's systematic thinking. There can hardly be any doubt that Aquinas held the common opinion of his day that the separate consecration of the bread and wine has the value of a commemorative sign which elicits the subjective recall of the historical passion, as Pratzner has concluded. However, Pratzner has not reckoned with what is axiomatic for Aquinas, namely, that the historical living of Christ is really present in all sacramental celebrations of the Church: a presence in which one or other event of Christ's life is highlighted, and to which corresponds the offer of the proper dispositions to respond to the represented saving event.

2. *Presence Metaphysically Affirmed*

However, this mystery presence of the historical redemptive work of Christ is not conceived as grounded on a timeless trait ascribed in virtue of the nature of the saving acts of the historical Jesus. The idea

[19] "Quantum ad secundum modum, proprium est huic sacramento quod in ejus celebratione Christus immoletur"—*ST* 3, q. 83, a. 1.

[20] "Sicut celebratio hujus sacramenti est imago repraesentativa passionis Christi, ita altare est repraesentativum crucis ipsius, in qua Christus in propria specie immolatus est"—ibid., ad 2.

[21] "Sacerdos gerit imaginem Christi, in cujus persona et virtute verba pronuntiat ad consecrandum. . . . Et ita quodammodo idem est sacerdos et hostia"—ibid., ad 3.

that the saving acts of Christ become "eternal," and therefore can become sacramentally present in an objective way in and through the sacraments, is not found in Aquinas's writings. Nor does he hold that the saving acts enjoy a timeless character in virtue of which the liturgical community is rendered present to these acts through the medium of the sacramental rite. It is from this latter perspective that the Italian theologian Caesare Giraudo understands the function of the Eucharistic Prayer, namely, to render the liturgical community present to the foundational act of Christ's Passover from suffering to glory.[22]

Aquinas teaches that all the actions and passions of Christ are causes of our salvation. Accordingly, they are really present to humanity being sanctified. This is possible because, from the divine perspective, removes of space and time are not relevant to the ultimate intelligibility of the human living of Jesus. The Angelic Doctor agrees that the passion of Christ *as corporeal* cannot effectively cause the salvation of all humanity at all times. But he does not agree that the passion of Jesus cannot act as instrumental cause of salvation in virtue of the spiritual power of the divinity united to it. Hence the passion of Christ is efficacious according to the divine disposition through spiritual contact, namely, through faith and the sacraments of faith. What this means is that the principal cause, God, employs the instrumental cause, the historical living of Jesus, to produce the effect in the beneficiary, and this effect is realized in and through the necessary response of faith.

According to Aquinas, the presence of the event of the historical living of Jesus signified by the particular sacrament is a presence in the "recipient" of the sacramental celebration in the sense of instrumental cause modifying the effect of the action of the principal divine cause of sanctification. The effect is the transmission of the attitudes of Christ conformed to the particular historical event of Christ's life signified by the sacramental rite. It is, therefore, a presence metaphysically affirmed.

Aquinas based this teaching on the grounds of the revelation that there is a single *transitus* of the world to the Father inaugurated by Jesus, and into which *transitus* humanity is to be incorporated through its response of faith. In his understanding, the removes of space and time are, from the divine perspective, not relevant to the

[22] Cesare Giraudo, *Eucaristia per la Chiesa: Prospettive teologiche sull'eucaristia a partire dalla "lex orandi,"* Aloisiana 22 (Rome: Gregorian University/Brescia: Morcelliana, 1989) 606–16.

ultimate intelligibility of the historical mysteries of Christ's life. As has been stressed over the last few decades by Catholic systematic theologians, it is axiomatic for Aquinas that the human living of the incarnate Son is the divine instrument of salvation, and therefore the historical mysteries of Christ are present to all human beings, working their salvation.

This teaching is recalled by Brian McNamara with reference to the eucharistic sacrifice.[23] From the standpoint of the realist metaphysics of Aquinas "all the actions and passions of Christ instrumentally work for our salvation in the power of the divinity"[24] Thus the principal cause, the instrument, and the effect, are coexistent. This means that God, acting through the humanity of Christ, effects the *transitus* from fleshly existence to that of the spiritualized body. The world is saved by the upward human growth of Christ to the ultimate glorification of his humanity. There are not two different types of *transitus.* Rather, there is the single *transitus* of Jesus in which human persons are incorporated through spiritual contact with the *Christus patiens, moriens, et resurgens.*

For St. Thomas, the effect of the presence of the historical acts in the sacramental celebration of the Church is a certain modification of the configuration to Christ, which by its very nature orders the faithful to Christian worship, of which Christ is the author. The primary configuration comes through the baptismal character by which Christians are configured to the "priesthood of Christ," which is a "certain participation in the priesthood of Christ."[25] The modification of this configuration includes a real participation in the attitudes of Christ that were expressed in his historical actions and passions. These attitudes are transmitted through the medium of the sacramental celebrations. They are ultimately present in us because of the presence of the historical saving acts themselves.

In the case of the eucharistic sacrifice, there is the presence of the *Christus patiens* to us with the effect that we participate in his sacrificial attitude, in his *transitus* to the Father from suffering to glory. This reality of the presence of the *Christus patiens* to us in the eucharistic

[23] Brian McNamara, "Christus Patiens in Mass and Sacraments: Higher Perspectives," *Irish Theological Quarterly* 42 (1975) 17–35.

[24] "Omnes actiones et passiones Christi instrumentaliter operantur in virtute divinitatis ad salutem humanam"—*ST* 3, q. 48, a. 6.

[25] *ST* 3, q. 63, a. 3 c (see above, n. 1).

sacrifice is of the same order as in the other sacraments. However, there is also the presence of the Lord himself under the species of bread and wine. Here the Lord is present sacramentally as the *Christus Passus.*

Aquinas argues in *ST* 3, q. 48, a. 6 for this presence of the historical living of Christ in the sacraments in the following way: He poses the objection: Corporeal agents act efficiently by contact. But the passion of Christ is corporeal. Therefore the passion of Christ cannot efficiently work the salvation of humanity of all times.[26] To this he responds as follows:

"With reference to the second objection, it must be said that the passion of Christ, although corporeal, has however spiritual power from the divinity united to it; and thus efficacy occurs through spiritual contact, namely through faith and the sacrament of faith, according to the saying of the apostle in Romans 5:25: 'whom God presented as one who propitiates through faith in his blood.'"[27]

The passion of Christ is corporeal, but it has "a spiritual power from the divinity united to it." Hence the *virtus salutaris* is the power of the principal cause. The passion is effective as instrument, that is, the power of the principal cause is the instrumental power of the passion. On the one hand, the spiritual power of the passion is identical with the action of the principal cause working through the passion, and the action is located in the effect.

Elsewhere, in *ST* 3, q. 62, a. 5, the question is asked: Do sacraments have power from the passion? Three objections are given which tend to a negative response. The passion of Christ pertains to the Word insofar as made flesh. But the sacraments have a power which causes grace in the soul. Such a power must be attributed to the Word insofar as divine, not insofar as made flesh. However, the Word vivifies bodies insofar as made flesh. In this first objection, following Augustine, the passion of Christ is viewed as instrument of the Word with respect to the vivification of our bodies. The second objection introduces the

[26] *ST* 3, q. 48, a. 6 obj. 2.

[27] "Ad secundum dicendum, quod, passio Christi licet sit corporalis, habet tamen spiritualem virtutem ex divinitate unita: et ideo per spiritualem contactum efficaciam sortitur, scilicet per fidem et fidei sacramentum, secundum illud Apostoli, Rom. 3, 25: *Quem proposuit Deus propitiatorem per fidem in sanguine ipsius*"—*ST* 3, q. 48, a. 6 ad 2.

relation between the act of faith and the sacraments. Here a saying of Augustine is introduced: What is proclaimed in the sacraments, namely, the faith of the Church, becomes effective because it is believed, not because it is said. However, the faith on which the efficacy of the sacraments depends embraces all the mysteries of the humanity of Christ and especially his divinity. So at least the special power of the sacraments cannot be confined to the passion. The third objection begins with the idea that the sacraments are ordered to the justification of the human being. Since justification is attributed to the resurrection, sacraments have more power from the resurrection than from the passion of Christ.

Reacting to these objections *(sed contra),* Aquinas recalls that the sacraments flow from the side of Christ, through which the Church is saved. From this it follows that sacraments have all their efficacy from the passion of Christ since God effected our liberation from sin and sanctification through the humanity of Christ not only by way of merit but also by way of satisfaction.

The matter is explained in the *corpus* of the article. A distinction is made between the sacraments as separated instrumental causes and the humanity of Christ which is an instrument conjoined to the divinity. The divinity is the principal cause of grace, the humanity of Christ is the conjoined instrument, and the sacraments are the separated instrumental causes of grace. Hence the salutary power in the sacraments derives from the divinity of Christ acting through his humanity. This sacramental grace is ordered to remedying the defects resulting from sin and to perfecting the soul in those things that pertain to the worship of God in the religion of Christian life. However, Christ liberates us from sin through his passion, especially by way of merit and satisfaction. In addition, he initiated through his passion the rite of the worship of God according to the Christian religion by offering himself to God. Consequently, the sacraments of Christ have power from the passion of Christ, the power which is united to us through the reception of the sacraments. The sign of this is the water and blood signifying baptism and Eucharist.[28]

[28] "Respondeo dicendum, quod sicut dictum est art. 1 huj. quaest., sacramentum operatur ad gratiam causandam per modum instrumenti. Est autem duplex instrumentum: unum quidem separatum, ut baculus; aliud autem conjunctum, ut manus. Per instrumentum autem conjunctum movetur instrumentum separatum, sicut baculus per manum. Principalis autem causa efficiens gratiae est ipse Deus, ad quem comparatur humanitas Christi sicut instrumentum conjunctum; sacramentum

In the light of the foregoing, Aquinas responds to the objections. The Word vivifies the soul as principal agent; the flesh and the mysteries accomplished in it work instrumentally for the life of the soul as well as for the life of the body *(ad primum).* The fact that Christ lives in us by faith means that the power of Christ is united to us by faith. Since the power especially pertains to the passion of Christ, we are liberated from sin through faith in the passion *(ad secundum).* Regarding justification, it is attributed to the resurrection by reason of the *terminus ad quem* which is the newness of life through grace and attributed to the passion by reason of the *terminus a quo,* namely, the remission of fault *(ad tertium).*

E. FAITH AND SACRAMENT

The connection between faith and sacraments concerns the working of the sacrament in the "recipient." The power of the sacrament derives from faith and the passion of Christ. The faith which receives the effect of the sacrament is effected by God through the sacrament, i.e., through the accomplishment of the sacramental sign. But how, in fact, is faith effected through the sacrament? In *ST* 3, q. 60, a. 7, Aquinas speaks of "word" as the form of the sacrament. He proceeds from the meaning of the word fixed by faith. This word, as form of the sacrament, works in the sacrament because it is believed: "To the first objection it must be said, as Augustine says *(Tract.* 80, *in Joan):* 'The word works in the sacrament, not because it is said,' that is, according to the exterior sound of the voice, 'but because it is believed,' that is, according to the meaning of the words, which is held by faith."[29] Hence

autem sicut instrumentum separatum. Et ideo oportet quod virtus salutifera a divinitate Christi per ejus humanitatem in ipsa sacramenta derivetur. Gratia autem sacramentalis ad duo praecipue ordinari videtur: videlicet ad tollendos defectus praeteritorum peccatorum, inquantum transeunt actu, et remanent reatu; et iterum ad perficiendam animam in his quae pertinent ad cultum Dei secundum religionem vitae christianae. Manifestum est autem ex his quae supra dicta sunt, quaest. 48 et 49, quod Christus liberavit nos a peccatis nostris praecipue per suam passionem, non solum sufficienter et meritorie, sed etiam satisfactorie. Similiter etiam per suam passionem initiavit ritum christianae religionis, *offerens seipsum oblationem et hostiam Deo,* ut dicitur Ephes. 5. Unde manifestum est quod sacramenta Ecclesiae specialiter habent virtutem ex passione Christi, cujus virtus quodammodo nobis copulatur per susceptionem sacramentorum; in cujus signum de latere Christi pendentis in cruce fluxerunt aqua et sanguis, quorum unum pertinet ad baptismum, aliud ad Eucharistiam, quae sunt potissima sacramenta"—*ST* 3, q. 62, a. 5 c.

[29] Ad primum ergo dicendum, quod, sicut Augustinus dicit super Joan. (tract. 80, a med.), *verbum operatur in sacramentis, non qui dicitur,* idest, non secundum

Aquinas concludes that different languages do not affect the power of the sacraments to signify.[30] Rather, the supra-individual faith of the Church enters into the constitution of the sacrament, and this happens once-for-all.

F. THE EFFICACY OF THE EUCHARISTIC SACRIFICE

Regarding the efficacy of the eucharistic sacrifice, a distinction must be made between the earlier opinion of Aquinas and that expressed in the *Summa theologiae.* In his earlier *Commentary on the Sentences,* the efficacy of the eucharistic sacrifice regarding satisfaction for punishment due to sin is considered to result *ex opere operato* and to be limited a priori. Suffrages, in general, are efficacious by way of satisfaction for sin only for the one for whom they are applied. Moreover, the value is limited in itself and allotted according to divine justice.[31] The satisfaction value of the cross is also considered to be applied through the Mass *ex opere operato,* i.e., independently of the faith and devotion of the Church. In itself, this value is of unlimited efficacy. However, as ordered through the Mass, it is limited before application according to the divine disposition.[32] It is also limited *in actu secundo* by the limited devotion of the offerers and of those for whom it is offered.

Regarding the effect *ex opere operantis,* Aquinas teaches in the *Supplementum* that the Mass offered by a sinful priest does not profit insofar as the Mass is his action. But insofar as he *gerit personam totius ecclesiae,* or acts in the name and as commissioned by whose who have the Mass said, the prayer of such a priest, although a sinner, is beneficial for the dead *(suffragia talis sacerdotis, quamvis peccator, defunctis prosunt).* Thus the Mass as *opus operatum* produces of itself effects unlimited *in actu primo,* but the actual effect of the *opus operatum* is also measured by the disposition of those offering the Mass.[33] Also the dispositions of those who offer the Mass limits the effect received

---

exteriorem sonum vocis, *sed quia creditur,* idest, secundum sensum verborum, qui fide tenetur"—*ST* 3, q. 60, a. 7 ad 1. [The passage from Augustine is the much-quoted one where he says (about baptism): "Detrahe verbum, et quid est aqua nisi aqua? Accedit verbum ad elementum, et fit Sacramentum. . . . Unde ista tanta virtus aquae, ut corpus tangat et cor abluat, nisi faciente verbo: non quia dicitur, sed quia creditur?"—Augustine, *In Joannis evangelium tractatus CXXIV,* tract. 80.3 (PL 35.1840)—RJD.]

[30] *ST* 3, q. 60, a. 7 ad 2.

[31] *In IV Sent.,* d. 45, q. 2, a. 4, qc. 3, sol. 2; cf. also *Supplementum* q. 71, a. 12.

[32] Ibid.; cf. also *Supplementum* q. 71, a. 14 ad 2.

[33] *Supplementum* q. 71, a. 3 c.

by those for whom the Mass is offered. Consequently, the Church as a whole takes part in the offering and accounts for its effects.

In his more mature thought, found in the *Summa theologiae,* Aquinas holds that while the nature of the sacrifice of the Mass is sufficient to satisfy for all punishment due to sin, it is limited according to the "quantity" of the devotion and fervor of charity of those offering.[34] Therefore, since the effects are always finite, they are multiplied with the repetition of the offering. The sacrifices of the old covenant, on the other hand, are not *ex sui* unlimited regarding satisfaction.

The efficacy of the application of the fruits of the redemptive sacrifice is applied in the Mass according to the intention of the Church ritually expressed in the Eucharistic Prayer, and according to the intention of the presiding priest in the case of the special intention.

II. SUMMARY AND CONCLUSION

The foregoing exposition of Aquinas's theology of the eucharistic sacrifice proceeds from his understanding of the representative ministry of the presiding ordained minister in relation to the Church and Christ. Then the nature of the eucharistic action of Christ and the Church is examined together with the liturgical activity in and through which the consecration of the eucharistic elements takes place. Next Aquinas's understanding of the organic relation between the historical sacrifice of the cross and the eucharistic sacrifice is examined together with his theory concerning the presence of the historical redemptive acts in the eucharistic celebration.

A. SUMMARY

An explanation, summarizing in six points Aquinas's view of the peculiar efficacy of the eucharistic sacrament, completes our presentation.

1. *The Ministry of the Eucharistic Prayer*

The Eucharistic Prayer, the liturgical expression of the worship of the Church, is proclaimed by the priest who presides in the name of the whole Church. His authority to assume this role derives from

[34] "Inquantum vero est sacrificium, habet vim satisfactivam. Sed in satisfactione magis attenditur affectus offerentis quam quantitas oblationis. Unde et Dominus dicit Luc. 21, de vidua quae obtulit duo aera, quod *plus omnibus misit.* Quamvis ergo haec oblatio ex sui quantitate sufficiat ad satisfactionem pro omni poena, tamen fit satisfactoria illis pro quibus offertur, vel etiam offerentibus secundum quantitatem suae devotionis, et non pro tota poena"—*ST* 3, q. 79, a. 5 c; cf. also 3, q. 79, a. 7 ad 3.

ordination which confers the power to consecrate the gifts of the Church in the person of Christ. This leadership role is performed by the priest for the sake of the whole Church because he alone "consecrates the Eucharist which is the sacrament of the universal Church."[35] The formal reason for assigning to the presiding priest the role of representative of the whole Church derives from the nature of the Eucharist, namely, a corporate act of the universal Church which takes place in favor of the universal Church.

2. The Two Representative Functions of the Presiding Priest

The priest who presides at the Eucharist represents both Christ and the Church. These two representative functions are really distinguished, and yet they are inseparable from one another. For the accomplishment of the eucharistic sacrifice requires that the priest, acting as minister of Christ, has the intention "of doing what the Church does" *(faciendi quod facit ecclesia)* in obedience to Christ's institution.

3. The Action of Christ and the Action of the Church

Between the action of Christ and the action of the Church in the eucharistic celebration there exists an intimate organic unity. For the priestly act of the Church is based on a participation in the priesthood of Christ. This participation is effected sacramentally through the baptismal character by which believers are configured to the "priesthood of Christ," and which is a "certain participation" in that priesthood.[36] The manner of participation of the whole Church in the eucharistic worship is by devotion and in union with the presiding ordained ministerial priest who proclaims the Eucharistic Prayer in the person of the whole Church.

4. The Consecration of the Eucharistic Gifts of the Church

[a] The consecration of the bread and wine takes place through the instrumentality of the words of Christ inserted in the liturgical narrative of institution of the Eucharist. These words are spoken by the presiding priest with the intention of acting "as it were from the person of Christ" *(quasi ex persona Christi)*.[37]

[35] "Ipse solus potest gerere actus totius Ecclesiae qui consecrat eucharistiam, quae est sacramentum universalis Ecclesiae"—*In IV Sent.*, d. 24, q. 2, a. 2 ad 2.

[36] *ST* 3, q. 63, a. 3 c (cf. above, n. 1).

[37] "Si sacerdos sola verba praedicta proferret cum intentione conficiendi hoc sacramentum, perficeretur hoc sacramentum, quia intentio faceret ut haec verba intelligerentur quasi ex persona Christi prolata"—*ST* 3, q. 78, a. 1 ad 4.

[b] The separate consecrations represent sacramentally what happened historically on Calvary, namely, the separation of the blood from the body of Christ in death. Hence the twofold consecration is an "image of the passion of Christ," and the effect of the consecration is the somatic real presence of the crucified Lord under the forms of bread and wine. For this reason the sacrament is called "immolation of Christ."

5. The Historical and the Eucharistic Sacrifice

There is an organic link between the historical sacrifice of the cross and the eucharistic sacrifice. This intimate relationship consists in the identity of the sacrificial victim of the cross and of the eucharistic sacrifice, the identity, in other words, of the principal priest, Christ the High Priest who acts through his ministerial priest. Moreover, it is the fruits of the sacrifice of the cross that are applied in and through the eucharistic sacrifice. These fruits are offered *ex opere operato* and are limited before application by the divine will (Aquinas junior); the limitation of the fruits applied depends on the measure of the devotion of those in whose favor the Mass is offered or who offer (Aquinas senior).

In his *Commentary on the Sentences,* Aquinas views the efficacy of the Mass as satisfaction for punishment due to sin as an effect that follows *ex opere operato* and that is limited a priori.[38] In the *Summa theologiae,* however, Aquinas teaches that the sacrifice of the Mass, according to its nature, is sufficient to satisfy for all punishment due to sin. The limitation derives from the limited devotion of those who can benefit from it.

6. The Eucharistic Presence of the Historical Sacrifice of Christ

The idea that the historical sacrifice of the cross is present, in the sense that its redemptive power is applied in and through the eucharistic sacrifice, is the common doctrine of all scholastic theology. Aquinas also held for the presence of the historical sacrifice of the cross in the eucharistic celebration (contra F. Pratzner). But he does not favor the notion of the mystery presence of the historical sacrifice of the cross objectively realized in a sacramental mode of being on the altar (contra Odo Casel). Rather, it is a presence in the willing participant in whose favor the sacramental celebration takes place. It is a presence in the sense of an instrumental cause which modifies

[38] *In IV Sent.*, d. 45, q. 2, a. 1, qc. 3, sol. 3.

the effect of the action of the principal cause, the Holy Spirit, on the subject of the sacrament. This modification of the effect of the divine action consists in the transmission of the historical attitudes of Christ conformed to the situation of the life of faith that is signified by the particular sacrament.

The presence of the historical living of Christ in the event of the sacramental celebrations was maintained by Aquinas on the grounds of revelation. According to Scripture, there is a single *transitus* of the world to the Father inaugurated by Jesus and into which humanity is to be incorporated through the response of faith. Hence, from the divine perspective, the removes of space and time are not relevant to the ultimate intelligibility of the historical mysteries of Christ's life.

Aquinas poses this objection to the question of the universal relevance of the passion of Christ. He concludes affirmatively because, while the passion of Christ is corporeal, it possesses a spiritual power from the divinity united to it. This *virtus salutaris* being the power of the principal cause, the passion of Christ is efficacious "according to the divine disposition." In other words, the passion of Christ is always efficacious insofar as the power of the principal cause is the instrumental power of the passion according to the "divine disposition."

However, the efficacy of the passion is conditioned by what enables "spiritual contact," namely, a contact realized "through faith and the sacraments of faith, according to the saying of the apostle: 'God, in fact, has presented Jesus who died on the cross as a means of pardon of sin for those who believe in him' (Romans 3:25)."

In this explanation Aquinas identifies the "spiritual power" with the action of the principal cause working through the passion: an action located in the effect. On the other hand, the required "spiritual contact" is conditioned by "faith and the sacraments of faith."

The foregoing consideration poses this question: Does the power of the sacrament depend on faith "according to the saying of Augustine: 'The word of God accomplishes the sacrament not because it is said, but because it is believed'"?[39] Aquinas answers a few pages later in this way: Christ lives in us through faith (Ephesians 3:17). Hence the power of Christ is linked to us "through faith" *(per fidem)*. But the power of remission of sins, namely, the power which propitiates for sin, pertains in a special way to the passion of Christ himself. Therefore, especially through faith in his passion, persons are liberated

[39] *ST* 3, q. 60, a. 7 ad 1 (see above, n. 29).

from sin according to Romans 3:25. "And thus the power of the sacraments, which is ordered to bear away sins, is chiefly from faith in the passion of Christ."[40]

B. CONCLUSION

The problem of the connection between faith and the sacraments concerns the working of the sacrament in the recipient. The power of the sacrament derives from two sources: faith and the passion of Christ. Faith, which receives the effect of the sacrament, is effected by God through the sacrament, namely, through the accomplishment of the sacramental sign.

How is this faith effected through the sacrament? In *ST* 3, q. 60, a. 7, Aquinas speaks of the word as the form of the sacrament. He proceeds from the meaning of the word that is fixed by faith. This word, as form of the sacrament, works in the sacrament because (quoting Augustine) it is believed: "The word works in the sacrament, not because it is said, but because it is believed."[41] From this observation Aquinas concludes that different languages do not affect the power of the sacraments to signify.[42] Rather, the supra-individual faith of the Church enters into the constitution of the sacrament, and this happens once-for-all.

THE PECULIAR EFFICACY OF THE SACRAMENTS

According to Aquinas, God has determined that the effect signified by the sacraments is dependent on the occurrence of the sacramental sign. Thus God has established a real relation of dependence of the grace signified on the sacramental sign. The sacramental celebration constitutes a historical expression of the divine offer of grace. It differs from other such expressions insofar as belonging to the category of the communal worship of the Church.

The life of faith is one and is expressed in different ways, all of which have the aspect of confession of faith, service of the neighbor, and worship of God. The differences between the various ways in which the life of faith is expressed, and the difference in the degree of realization of the life of faith and resulting deepening of this life,

[40] "Et ideo virtus sacramentorum, quae ordinatur ad tollenda peccata, praecipue est ex fide passionis Christi"—*ST* 3, q. 62, a. 5 ad 2.

[41] *ST* 3, q. 60, a. 7 ad 1 (see above, n. 29).

[42] Ibid., ad 2.

allow for the relative superiority of the sacramental acts by which the life of faith is consciously realized, and in the setting of the actualization of the covenant between God and his people.

Chapter Ten

Twentieth-Century Contribution to the Theology of Eucharistic Sacrifice

There is a certain correspondence between the twelfth- and twentieth-century contributions to the articulation of the Catholic tradition of eucharistic theology. The early scholastics prepared the way for the eventual formulation of a theology of the sacramental somatic presence of Christ, and also established the main lines of a theology of eucharistic sacrifice. This scholastic formulation has, basically, perdured down to this century. Twentieth-century Catholic theologians, on the other hand, have contributed a number of insights which are paving the way for a new, more adequate, and more truly systematic theology of the Eucharist.

The constructive theology of eucharistic sacrifice which was elaborated within Western scholastic theology and which held pride of place there for over eight hundred years was guided principally by the *lex credendi;* but it still did not manage to integrate all the dogmatic principles required for a truly systematic exposition. Moreover, the potential contribution of the *lex orandi* was not taken into account. In short, the contribution of the law of prayer was made solely on the basis of the requirements of the law of belief, rather than awarded its own proper role in the construction of a truly systematic, and authentically Catholic tradition of eucharistic sacrifice.

The essential traits of the Catholic scholastic theology of eucharistic sacrifice have remained in place over a surprisingly long period of time. Developments took place within its closed system, and have led, over the course of time, to what is generally recognized as the best exposition of which that synthesis is capable. However, even though this modern average Catholic theology of eucharistic sacrifice has received additional authoritative status through being sanctioned by the official magisterium of the Catholic Church, its weaknesses are now clearly recognized.

This chapter, on the subject of the modern Catholic theology of eucharistic sacrifice, looks beyond that theology to something better. For it is our purpose here to identify and describe what we judge to be significant recent contributions toward the formulation of a more adequate and more truly systematic theology of eucharistic sacrifice. To this end the stages of the historical development of these insights are traced from the outset of this century down to its last decade. In the following and final chapter of this book, a systematic theology of eucharistic sacrifice will be constructed which first identifies those contributions of the second "theological millennium" which remain valid today, and then integrates these valid contributions into the original dynamic and global dimension of the Eucharist which has been emerging from the systematic ordering of the investigation of twentieth-century insights derived above all from the law of prayer *(lex orandi)*, but also from neglected dogmatic tenets *(lex credendi)* pertaining to Christology, pneumatology and saving faith.

I. DOM ODO CASEL, O.S.B. (1886–1948)

Dom Odo Casel, a member of the monastery of Maria Laach, is best known for founding the school of Theology of Mysteries which became the focus of attention of some European theological circles at the close of World War I. The movement was born from the desire to give to the liturgical movement a theological foundation conformed to the spirit of the liturgy as well as to Scripture and to the teaching of the Fathers of the Church. The name "Theology of Mysteries" or "Mystery Theology" is owed to the fact that this theology explains the whole of the redemptive work of God, but especially the liturgical life of the Church, with the help of the concept of "mystery" drawn from early Christian tradition. The main protagonists and adversaries of this "school" have come from Germany.

Casel was concerned with deepening the understanding of the very essence of Christianity. To this end, he turned his attention to the mystery of Christian worship which is the ritual expression of the essence of Christian religion. This approach was deemed proper because of the two main characteristics of Christian religion. First, Christianity proclaims truth that is not fully grasped by reason, truth that cannot find an adequate model in the realm of ordinary human experience.

Second, Christianity is based on a historical deed of the past, the redemptive work of Christ, that is in some fashion made contemporaneous with all generations.

Because of the transcendent nature of Christianity, Casel was convinced that it is necessary to approach its essence through symbolism rather than through the methods of discursive reasoning. The contemporaneity of the history of Christ, the real contact of this history with Christians of all generations, is the fact that must be reckoned with in theological discourse. Speculative methods of course have their place, but liturgy offers new horizons far beyond the possibilities of speculative thought. Liturgy brings to our consciousness the awareness of the real, concrete relation of the person of Christ and his redemptive acts to the basic activity of the Church, especially to the chief rites of the Church, the sacraments.

Casel recognized the importance of the anthropological aspect of Christian liturgy, namely, that it answers to the common need of human beings to make invisible realities manifest by sensible signs. But his main preoccupation was with the role of the liturgy in the prolongation of the redemptive work of Christ. The fact of the Incarnation itself calls for the continuation and application of the mystery of Christ in exterior worship. According to him the "mystery of worship" *(Kultmysterium)* includes a twofold reality: the exterior rite and the invisible reality. For this concept he appeals to the ancient Christian view of mystery as a supernatural reality, revealed, made accessible, concretized, and localized in ritual actions.

Casel lamented the decline of sacramental theology after the High Middle Ages, especially in the neoscholastic synthesis. Neoscholastic theology of the sacraments paid scarcely any attention to the sacramental rite itself, concentrating uniquely on the efficacy inherent in the sacrament as the instrumental cause of supernatural grace bestowed on the individual subject. This synthesis neglected the point of view of the Fathers of the Church, who were accustomed to consider the holiness that the sacraments possess in themselves: an objective holiness. In this regard Casel underlines the primacy of the Christological dimension of the economy of salvation, which for him finds its deepest meaning in identifying "grace" with Christ himself and his whole redemptive work. In short, grace is not simply a power that flows from that salvific work. Rather, to share in the mystery of redemption through Christ is not so much to receive a "grace," as it is an elevation of the whole person through contact with Christ, and his redemptive work.

Since the various forms of Christian worship are a means of participation in the redemptive work of Christ, that which can be said about the economy of salvation in general holds also for the liturgy of the Church. In this case Casel makes use of the Greek term *eikôn* to express what the public worship of the church "images," namely, the mystery of salvation. This term is used in the patristic sense, where "image" conveys the idea of participation in the reality signified, or more precisely, is the epiphany of the quintessence of the thing represented.

According to Casel, the mystery of Christian worship, what worship images and so re-presents, or reactualizes, is the very kernel of the redemptive work of Christ, namely, the passage of the Lord *(transitus Domini)* from death to life. This mystery is made present liturgically; that is to say, the liturgical rites of the Church contain the redemptive drama in act. This redemptive drama in act constitutes the *Kultmysterium,* or mystery of worship.

The mystery of redemption is present in the variety of ways in which salvation is offered to human beings in all circumstances of life. Casel begins one of his major monographs with the observation that "the word *Mysteriengegenwart* is tautological, since presence belongs to the essence of mystery."[1] The liturgy of the Church is a special mode of this presence. When Casel says that sacraments are mysteries, he means that they are ritual actions in which the redemption *(Heilstat)* wrought by Christ is made present under the sacramental signs. The divine reality present in the sacraments is the work of redemption in its integrity and totality. That work, accomplished in the past, historically and in time, is now present in an atemporal way and without distinction of parts; that is, it is "sacramentally" present.

Following Aquinas, Casel reminds us that the passion is not present according to its natural manner of being, as it was historically, *in tempore,* and also not merely *in signo,* but sacramentally. Because it is not *in tempore,* it is, therefore, present *secundum modum substantiae,* without historical "before" or "after," precisely in its kernel as the salvific act of the God-man. Hence metaphysical hypotheses concerning the impossibility of a renewal of historical acts, and the like, simply do not apply in the case of the sacraments.[2]

[1] Odo Casel, O.S.B., "Mysteriengegenwart," *Jahrbuch für Liturgiewissenschaft* 8 (1928) 145–224, at 145.

[2] Ibid., 191.

In Casel's opinion, this is precisely the mode of sacramental presence, *"in mysterio,"* about which the Fathers, and Thomas Aquinas, speak. Casel appeals to the analogy between the presence of Christ *per modum substantiae* in the eucharistic species, and the presence of the redemptive acts in the rites of the Church. Christ can be rendered present in many places *per modum substantiae,* i.e., without temporal succession. Likewise the divine power can, and does, reactualize at different times and places the passion of Christ that took place at Calvary. The sacramental presence of the redemptive acts of Christ is a mode of presence that transcends space and time.

What is present is the quintessence of the redemptive act, the act of Christ. Hence the accessory circumstances are not present. But, one must ask, what is this substance of the redeeming act of God in Christ? Here Casel appeals to positive theology; the Scriptures, the Fathers, and the liturgy affirm this presence.

Viktor Warnach, a close associate of Casel, provided a relatively more precise explanation that Casel did not oppose. Warnach explains that the death and resurrection are present insofar as they are the transformation of the earthly Christ into the glorious Redeemer. This transformation through suffering to glory, a metaphysical act, is the substance of the Mystery. The action by which Christ passed from suffering to glory, as representative of humanity, has opened the way to God for all humanity. It transcends all finite limits, sums up the whole of the work of redemption, and constitutes the real content of *Mysteriengegenwart.* Hence there is present in the cultic rites something more than the "grace" of redemption.[3]

Since the sacraments effect the real presence, though sacramental, of the work of redemption, Casel concludes that the believing members of the Church, those who participate in the liturgy of the sacraments, are made participants in redemption.

Christian liturgy is the ritual performance of the redemptive work of Christ in the Church and through it, therefore, the presence of the divine salvific act under the veil of the symbol.[4] The *Mysterium* is a holy ritual action in which the redemptive event becomes present

[3] Viktor Warnach, O.S.B., "Zum Problem der Mysteriengegenwart," *Liturgisches Leben* 5 (1938) 9–39. Cf. Johannes Betz, *Die Eucharistie in der Zeit der griechischen Väter* I/1 (Freiburg: Herder, 1955) 250.

[4] Casel, "Mysteriengegenwart," 145

under the rite. Since the community of worship performs the rite, it takes part in the redemptive act, and by that attains salvation.[5]

Casel is opposed to the traditional Western scholastic view which assumes that the presence of the work of redemption is adequately explained by the presence of the effects of the redemptive work. The work of redemption, as he sees it, is present not only insofar as the believing participants are sanctified by its power. For beyond this presence by believing/sanctifying participation, he also sees the substantial presence of the passion of Christ, and this presence is prior in nature to the sanctifying effect on the believer. This is the thesis of Casel. However, he is not a systematician; his theology at times lacks consistency. Sometimes, for example, he seems to speak of the presence of the pneumatic Christ, the crucified and risen Lord, by which the passion is made present. For example:

"The Spirit of Christ, or more clearly expressed: the pneumatic Lord, is present in the Mysteries, and through them is continually present and active in the Church . . . . But this pneumatic presence of Christ stands in closest relation to his historical redemptive act, makes this present, and transfuses the fruit of grace into the Church."[6]

At other times Casel seems to come close to the "*effectus* theory" of scholastic theology, at least in the case of baptism:

"It is a fact that baptism is a dying and rising with Christ. Therefore Christ dies and rises in it, as we showed above from Paul. A mere bestowal of grace does not fulfill the concept of baptism. On the other hand, the redemptive act of Christ is not present in baptism in the same way as in the Eucharist; for, in relation to the presence of the body and blood of Christ through transubstantiation, there is a more objective presence of the redemptive act. But (in baptism) it is present in the power of Christ, the *virtus participata a Christo,* and in the moment of baptism, that is, the application of the sacrament. But that *virtus participata a Christo* is, nevertheless, something thoroughly objective."[7]

[5] Odo Casel, *Das christliche Kultmysterium* (Regensburg, 1932; 2nd ed., 1935; 3rd ed., 1948; 4th ed., 1960) 102; Eng. trans.: Dom Odo Casel, *The Meaning of Christian Worship and Other Writings,* ed. Burkhard Neunheuser (Westminster, Md.: Newman, 1962).

[6] Casel, "Mysteriengegenwart," 162.

[7] Ibid., 203.

From the fact that the sacrifice of Christ is reactualized in the Eucharist, Casel argues to the real presence of the passion of Christ in the other sacraments. Since the other sacraments are really sacraments, and thus represent and communicate the one mystery of salvation, it follows that they also contain, in an analogous way, the redemptive act.

"Although the Eucharist is the queen of the sacraments, the other sacraments are also truly sacraments. Their essence must, therefore, be essentially analogous to that of the Eucharist. The Eucharist contains the redemptive act of Christ: so too must the other sacraments contain it in a sacramental manner of being."[8]

Casel situates the Christian *Kultmysterium* within the whole of the divine plan of salvation that was gradually revealed through the divine action that led up to the Incarnation of the Logos. In the working out of this plan, Casel awards a special place to the Hellenistic mystery rites.[9] He sees them as a providential preparation for the advent of the Redeemer. The Divine Logos, who directs the history of humanity, oriented forms of cult that express an obscure search for the true God. Especially the Greek mystery religions manifest the striving of the *anima naturaliter christiana* to satisfy its yearning for union with the divine source of all being.

Within the variety of Greek mystery religions, Casel identifies a sacred tradition. It is the myth of the Lord of the mystery *(Kyrios),* who effects his *epiphany* among suffering humanity. He shares human suffering and dies. But death is not the end. The Kyrios revives *(apotheosis),* returns to life in a victory through which the whole of nature revives and lives on. Human beings become associates with the fate of the Kyrios, and acquire salvation *(sōtēria)* through the ritual reenactment of the myth of the dying and rising of the Kyrios. This ritual imitation is an effective memorial by which the initiates are afforded the anticipation of full communion with the Kyrios to be gained after death.

Casel insists that the Greek mysteries are spiritually superior to the more primitive rites that celebrated the rebirth of nature. He locates the basis of these mysteries in the psychological need for union with God, a need that God has instilled in the human being. This exigency

[8] Ibid., 200–1.

[9] For Casel's understanding of the Hellenistic mystery rites as background for the Christian sacraments, see esp. chap. 3, "Antike und christliche Mysterien," in *Das christliche Kultmysterium*, 75–89.

is fulfilled in Christian revelation, which satisfies humankind's aspirations for redemption. Thus Christian religion is conformed to the *eidos* of mystery religions. However, there is the difference between them that Christian religion is based on a *true* supernatural revelation of God in his Son.

What Christianity possesses is a true mystery, a revelation in act. This mystery of Christianity is the accomplishment of the eternal plan of God. It is the mystery hidden in God from eternity, realized by God in time through Christ's life, death-glorification-sending of the Spirit; it is the mystery of Christ. This mystery, which reaches its fulfillment in God himself, when God will be all in all, is summed up in Christ: the Savior and Head of his body the Church. The Church participates in this mystery through her essential activity, especially in the mystery of worship. Christian worship is *Kultmysterium:* the reactualization of the redemptive act of Christ to the end that believers may participate in it and be glorified with the Kyrios.

According to Casel, liturgical action is the "ritual celebration and representation: a rendering present of a divine work, on which the existence and life of a community is grounded."[10] Therefore liturgy understood, "in the sense of the execution and realization of the New Testament mystery of Christ in the Church . . . in view of her sanctification and glorification, . . . is the central, and essentially necessary activity of Christian religion."[11]

From this premise it follows for Casel, that "the life of the Kyrios Christus . . . is to be co-lived in the Church Year . . . to be celebrated."[12] However, this Church Year is "a unified mystery. It has its high point in the mystery in the highest sense, the paschal sacrament, the Easter mystery, that has each Sunday, in a certain measure, a revival . . . . The mystery is always the whole." Always it is a question of the "whole mystery of redemption," although under different points of view.[13] "If therefore the Mass also primarily represents and reactualizes the Lord's death on the cross, yet secondarily and *ex obliquo* the whole work of salvation . . . ."[14]

[10] Ibid., 79.

[11] Ibid., 46.

[12] Ibid., 94.

[13] Ibid., 96–97.

[14] Odo Casel, et al., review of Fr. Diekamp, *Katholische Dogmatik nach den Grundsätzen des hl. Thomas,* vol. 3, 6th ed. (Münster i.W., 1932), in *Jahrbuch für Liturgiewissenschaft* 12 (1932 [publ. 1934]) 231.

The basic motif is the celebration of the saving act of Christ in a holy action. The central form of this cultic reality is the Eucharist, above all in its celebration at Easter, and in the feasts of the year, and on Sunday. Alongside these central feasts, other feasts developed in the course of time, feasts in which always the same whole saving work of Christ is celebrated and shared under different standpoints. Each feast has its high point in the Eucharist.

"The holy year is like a whole image of the eternal plan of salvation of God, and contains the mystery of Christ. But within this cycle, the mystery unfolds for the eye, that is not yet, as in the world beyond, able to view the whole with one glance. As the whole year contains the divine presence, so the event of salvation, that primarily sanctifies it, newly guides the individual day upward with itself . . . . So we celebrate each day in the Mass the whole mystery of salvation, and nevertheless the Incarnation is present to us in the divine words at Christmas and Epiphany, the passion and the resurrection of the Lord at Easter. Always the meaning of the mystery of Christ is the divine presence, not merely human thinking."[15]

SUMMARY

Lack of space prevents further elaboration here. Rather, we must be content with the following observations commonly underscored in the various articles and monographs descriptive of Casel's theology of mysteries.[16]

(A) Casel's approach to sacramental theology is above all from the center of the sacramental action itself, not from the common religious symbolism and the comprehensive reality of faith. Also he sought to approach the mystery through the liturgy. To accomplish this task, he was convinced of the need to return to origins, to early Christian

[15] Casel, *Das christliche Kultmysterium*, 99.

[16] See, for example, Charles Davis, "Dom Odo Casel and the Theology of Mysteries," *Worship* 34 (1960) 428–38; E. Dekkers, "La liturgie, mystère chrétien," *La Maison Dieu* 14 (1948) 30–64; D. O'Callaghan, "The Theory of the 'Mysteriengegenwart' of Dom Casel, A Controversial Subject in Modern Theology," *Irish Ecclesiastical Record* 90 (1958) 246–62; Arno Schilson, *Theologie als Sakramententheologie: Die Mysterientheologie Odo Casels* (Mainz: Matthias-Grünewald, 1982) 274; also: A. Schilson, "Erneuerung der Sakramententheologie im 20. Jahrhundert: Ein Blick auf die Anfänge bei Romano Guardini und Odo Casel," *Liturgisches Jahrbuch* 37 (1987) 17–41.

times. The freshness and purity of the beginnings was thought to provide better ground for attaining the mystery of worship than the Christianity of the contemporary rationalistic world.

(B) What are the decisive contributions of Casel that provide impulses for contemporary sacramental theology? In the first place he succeeded in overcoming the narrowness of the concept of sacrament, as well as the misunderstanding of sacrament as a kind of thingly instrumental cause of grace. He succeeded in bringing to light the fact that the mystery, biblically witnessed, as the presence of the divine salvation in Christ through the Church, is not to be equated with an abstract grace that is mediated in the cultic event of the sacraments. Rather, it is a sharing in the divine life, and hence the becoming holy of men and women happening through the drawing of believers into the saving acts of Christ in an ecclesial celebration.

He succeeded in creating the awareness that the dynamic power of the historical past saving work of Christ is placed in the cultic action of the Church, indeed, in the Church as a whole, whose essence actualizes itself in the individual sacramental, as well as liturgical accomplishments in varying degrees of density. In his synthesis, the Church plays a decisive role in the accomplishment of the sacraments. The Church is the ultimate bearer of Christian worship, and hence of the sacraments. But all her actions remain determined by the presence of the Christ. For the Church is the visible Lord, that is, Christ becomes visible to us in the visible Church. Through her we touch him, and in him God. All activity of the Church is sacramental.

Casel sees the roots of Christian life in the chief sacraments: baptism and Eucharist. Faith as the comprehensive determination of Christian being is of course recognized by Casel; but he accents the sacramental celebration of the mystery in which alone the full Christian fellowship is realized.

(C) What are the specific impulses for Catholic theology which are derivable from Casel's theology? There is the awareness of the sacramentality of the whole Christian reality. Also he communicated a rich understanding of the content of the Christian sacrament. In his writings one encounters the notion that sacraments mediate to the faithful, through the saving act of Christ present in the sacrament *"in mysterio,"* and through their participation therein, access to the divine life as the true salvation of human beings. Accordingly, the central cultic actions of the sacraments are to be valued as mediating the true divine life in the midst of time.

Casel understands that sacraments are *in genere signi.* But beyond that they are real symbols of salvation, and therefore instrumental causes of sanctification. In this connection, Casel, in dependence on Anscar Vonier, cites Thomas Aquinas, *ST* 3, q. 60, a. 1 c.[17] However, he adopts the thesis—which Vonier (inaccurately) attributes to Aquinas—about the "sacramental world" having its own new laws which operate outside the limits of space and time, being thus able to concentrate things of the past, present, and future at a particular present point in time.[18]

Finally, Casel calls attention to the importance of accentuating the mediating reality of the Church in the sacraments, herself stamped by the Christus-Mysterium. For "the way of the individual to Christ goes by way of the Church." In sacraments the Church herself witnesses and realizes herself in her unique binding to Christ. The ecclesial body of Christ actualizes its only ground of life, Jesus Christ and his saving act, and brings this to expression in uniquely dense ways in the real symbolic events of the sacraments, borne by Christ and the Church.

Recovery of the idea that sacrament is a sign-reality, a symbol, an image, is a special contribution of Casel. Casel makes use of the notion of symbolic action characteristic of "primitive man," as found in ancient mystery religions. In this understanding symbol is not something divorced from the concrete symbolic event that is mediated. Rather, what is mediated is actually present in the symbol. As the symbol makes present the symbolized, so the symbolic action, on the ground of a corresponding sharing makes present the desired event. Casel stresses the symbolic action, the celebration. The elements of the action come in for secondary consideration.

Casel's analogy with pagan mysteries requires cautiously critical evaluation. But his stress on the cultic character of the sacraments, as well as their ecclesial dimension, are important contributions. His example of keeping the liturgical action before the eye in his reflection is important for all.

A. REACTIONS TO CASEL'S THEOLOGY OF MYSTERIES

Casel identifies his concept of Christian mystery with the kernel of the divine revelation in Christ. He based his argument on tradition,

[17] Anscar Vonier, *A Key to the Doctrine of the Eucharist* (London: Burns, Oates and Washburn/Westminster, Md.: Newman, 1925) 17–26.

[18] Ibid., 35–44.

namely, on Scripture, on the liturgical texts, and on the authentic interpretation of Scriptures and liturgy found both in the liturgical theology of the Fathers of the Church as well as in scholastic theology, above all the theology of Thomas Aquinas.

Moreover, he introduces a comparison between the Hellenistic mysteries and Christian worship in order to demonstrate that the mystery of Christian worship was already obscurely revealed in these cultic forms of expression of the search for the "unknown God" (Acts 17:23). These non-Christian mysteries are understood to be inspired by God to orient the participants toward the mystery of Christ, "that they should seek God, in the hope that they might feel after him and find him" (Acts 17:27).

Finally Casel supports his thesis with an argument based on the *analogia fidei:* the substantial presence of Christ in the eucharistic gifts supports the thesis that the multiple presence of Christ's redemptive act in the liturgy is possible. If God can, by his power, effect Christ's substantial presence in the eucharistic bread and wine wherever the Eucharist is celebrated, he can also effect the presence of Christ's redemptive act itself. The fact that he does so is proved by the sources of Christian revelation, which attest that the Mass is the reactualization of the sacrifice of Calvary. Since the mystery of Christ is one single reality, it is but a short step to conclude that the fact of the active presence of Christ in the other sacraments of the Church includes the presence of his redemptive act.

The reaction to Casel's thesis focused on his interpretation of the sources he employed. In addition, speculative considerations were introduced in the attempt to shed some light on the real relation between the saving acts of Christ and the liturgical celebrations that recall them.

1. *Yield of Comparative Religion*

In general, scholars agree on the theoretical possibility of analogies between Hellenistic mysteries and Christian worship. But the dependence of Christian forms of worship on mystery religions, a thesis of the old History-of-Religions School, has not been proved, and is not in favor among scholars today. However, in the Hellenistic culture in which the nascent Church found itself, it was customary to borrow symbolic forms of expression, and adapt them to Christian usage. Certain Fathers of the Church were also inclined to consciously interpret the content of Christian worship with concepts drawn from the

Greek understanding of reality. Clement of Alexandria says to the Greeks of his day: "Come I want to show you the Logos and the mysteries of the Logos, and I intend to explain them to you in images that are familiar to you."[19]

The question of the relation of Christian mysteries to Hellenistic mysteries is a matter about which contemporary scholarship tends to be more cautious than Casel. Some have criticized Casel's exclusive use of later forms of mystery religions, forms which may have been influenced by Christianity itself! Moreover, many specialists in the field of comparative religion judge that the doctrinal resemblances between the Hellenistic and Christian mysteries are quite superficial or practically nonexistent.[20]

2. *Sources of Revelation*

Casel bases the theology of mysteries on positive theology. According to him, his theology of mysteries is the traditional teaching of the Church, to the exclusion of all those elaborated by human reason. However, many of his critics are convinced that this thesis is really inspired by what he discovered in the data of comparative religion rather than what was there to be discovered in Christian tradition.

a. Scripture

Casel minimized the relation between the Hebrew and Christian understanding of communal celebrations of the mighty acts of God in salvation history. He espoused the thesis that the concept of cultic mystery, as he described it, was foreign to the Old Testament. On this subject Casel was challenged before World War II by D. Winzen, among others, who pointed out that the world of the psalms was bound to the fundamental idea of mystery.[21] Today there is a widespread consensus in scholarly circles that the usages in the messianic communities of Judaism, above all the Passover, supplied the principal sources

[19] Clement of Alexandria, *Exhortation (Protreptikos)* chap. 10, GCS 12 (Leipzig: Hinrichs, 1905) 84.6–7; PG 8.240B.

[20] Cf. the following for a summary of critical remarks on this theme: Louis Beinaert, "Symbolisme mythique d l'eau dans le baptême," *La Maison Dieu* 22 (1950) 94–120; Louis Bouyer, *Liturgical Piety* (Notre Dame: University Press, 1955) 86–157; Jean Gaillard, "Chronique de liturgie: La théologie des mystères," *Revue thomiste* 57 (1957) 510–51; Hugo Rahner, *Greek Myths and Christian Mysteries*, trans. Brian Battershaw (London: Oxford, 1963).

[21] D. Damase Winzen, "Note complémentaire et réponse à quelques critiques . . . ," *Les questions liturgiques et paroissiales* 24 (1939) 108–13, at 111.

of the original forms of liturgical expression in the Christian religion, and that the liturgical memorial rites of Judaism were considered to "reactualize," in some sense, the past saving acts of Yahweh for the benefit of his people.

Casel believed that he had discovered in Romans 6:1-11 the key New Testament source for his theology of mysteries. Scholarly opinion seems to agree that this text does point to a certain operational presence of the mysteries of Christ in the one being baptized, but that the precise mode of operational presence cannot be deduced from the text with any degree of certainty.

b. Fathers of the Church

Patristic scholarship does not oppose the thesis that the actual presence of the historical mysteries of Christ's life is central to the patristic theology of Christian liturgy. This holds especially for the Eucharist, but also for baptism. However, Casel's identification of his explanation of the way *(quomodo)* of this presence with the whole patristic tradition is challenged. It is theoretically possible that one or other Father of the Church conceived the presence of the historical saving act in a way that relates positively to Casel's point of view, but no one has as yet offered a convincing argument in support of Casel's claim that his elaboration is in continuity with the whole patristic tradition.

c. Constructive Theology

Casel emphasized the primacy of the liturgy as the privileged source of the theology of worship, and employed a descriptive or kerygmatic theology that focuses on liturgy as pertaining to the order of doing *(ourgia)*. He had little patience with the speculative theology of the scholastic schools. In his estimation, a kerygmatic theology of the liturgy best describes the event of the liturgical celebration by which the participants are inserted into the saving work of Christ that is represented by the symbolic language of liturgy, both verbal and gestural. The sacramental theology of the scholastic tradition, Casel complained, tended to abstract from the liturgical event and speculate on the dynamics of the event of sanctification with the help of exogenous philosophical principles, such as efficient causality.

While modern theologians do not dispute the limitations of much of scholastic theological reflection on the theology of the sacraments, they are not as confident as Casel was about a primacy of the liturgy as source of the theology of the liturgy, a primacy which would entail a certain downgrading of other sources of theology. In other words, Casel's point of view implicitly makes the liturgy, the law of prayer *(lex orandi),* into the law of belief *(lex credendi).* Thus he swings the pendulum to the other end, effectively reducing the other sources of theology to a minor role.

The liturgical act itself communicates knowledge in the process of its realization by the symbolic language, verbal and gestural, that has the power of arousing in the participants some resonances with divine realities. A descriptive theology of the liturgy resembles the process of knowledge by participation. Such a theology seeks to articulate what the symbolism of the rites intends to convey, and what experiential knowledge derives from full participation in the liturgy. The openness and ambiguity of liturgical symbolism provides a source of many insights. This symbolism is indeed susceptible or capable of evoking theological reflection. But a theology that remains wholly on the phenomenological level is not adequate to meet the needs of a Catholic theology of liturgy. Liturgical sources are a true *locus theologicus.* But they are not the only source of theological knowledge of the liturgy. The witness of the liturgy must be complemented by other sources, including Scripture, the teaching of the Fathers, and dogmatic definitions of the Church, along with the ordinary teaching of the official magisterium. There is also the matter of the role of speculative theology, that seeks the ultimate meaning of the liturgy.

Constructive theology, or systematic theology, attempts to lend intelligibility to the liturgy by the use of rigorously defined notions and precise analogies. Whereas descriptive theology runs the risk of elevating subjective experience to a theory, theology of the logical type is always in danger of operating with a limited and arbitrary understanding of the reality of the liturgy. Since the richness of the mystery of the liturgy can never be completely captured by any constructive theology, it is necessary that the acquisitions of descriptive theology be properly integrated with a theology of the logical type, namely, that which utilizes the formal object of metaphysics, i.e., being insofar as being transcends the opposition between the abstract and concrete. There is communication on the philosophical plane between logical and phenomenological considerations. Only by the phenomenological is the philosopher able to prove the consistency of the real insofar as formed from existents. This type of communication is of great significance for the theologian, who sees in existence the creative work of the divine Logos.

This constructive theology, if it is to be successful, must be dominated in its method by the *analogy of faith.* In the attempt to clarify each and every aspect of the revealed truth, it must do so with the aid of all of the other aspects of revealed truth. This constructive theology is successful to the extent that it shows the relationship between the various aspects of the one revealed truth to all the other aspects.

The relationship of each aspect of revealed truth to all the others is the principle of intelligibility in Christian theology. In this connection, it must be noted that a realist metaphysics has a key role in a theology of the constructive type. For the problem of understanding is involved. In a realist view of understanding, the solution to any problem is grasped within the problem itself. Any kind of "abstraction" that provides an escape from experiential reality has no place. What is provided by theology of the logical type is a level of understanding that transcends that of descriptive, kerygmatic theology. But it is a level of understanding that derives from the data of the sources of theology.

Summary

Theology of liturgy is one way of doing theology. This theology aims at a unified comprehension of the mystery of the divine and human. It does not escape the task of seeking to articulate the connection between the liturgical symbolic actions and the whole mystery of the life of faith within the scope of the comprehensive Christian perception of reality. The law of prayer implies, in a prereflective way, a comprehensive grasp of the whole life of faith. On the other hand, one must reckon with the limits of any particular liturgical tradition as lived practice of the faith. In order to deepen the knowledge of the mystery of the liturgy, other sources of theological knowledge must be introduced along with the liturgical-practical grounding of knowledge of faith.[22]

B. CONTEMPORANEOUS APPROACHES TO THE PROBLEM

Many attempts have been made to shed light on the content of the mystery of the liturgy. In the time before Casel's death the contempo-

[22] For further remarks on this subject, cf. the observations made on the subject of the "methodological approach to the theology of the Eucharist" contained in the introduction to this book. [This "methodological approach . . ." has been lost, or perhaps Kilmartin never got to it before his death. The editor's introduction contains my reconstruction of such a methodological essay, pieced together mainly from what Kilmartin has written in various places in this and other works—RJD.]

raneous contributions of Catholic theologians reflected the presupposition that in some sense there is a real, active presence of Christ in Christian liturgical celebrations, a presence which is distinguished from his "substantial" presence in the eucharistic sacraments of his body and blood. But the various attempts at shedding light on the relationship between the historical saving acts of Christ and the liturgical celebrations of the Church have covered a wide range of possibilities.[23] Some representative theories are described below. The first group pertains to the period before the death of Casel; the second to the period before the Second Vatican Council. It is noteworthy that a more sympathetic reception of Casel's basic insight took place after his death in 1948.

1. *Virtual Presence of Redemptive Acts*

In his own day, Casel generally had to contend with a Thomistic approach to the problem favored by the prevailing scholastic theology of the time. According to this understanding, the historical passion of Christ is swallowed up in the flow of time. Nevertheless the glorified Christ retains the power and marks of the passion. Christ, present in the liturgy, acts in virtue of the power of his past redemptive acts. This thesis is reducible to what is called "presence through effects" insofar as the benefits received from the liturgy are derived from the historical redemptive act. It is sometimes confused with the original theory of Gottlieb Söhngen, who opposed Casel during the latter's lifetime, but who afterwards became more receptive of Casel's basic insight.

2. *Presence of the Redemptive Acts*

Among the less promising proposals intended to support Casel's position is that attributed to D. Feuling. He suggested that the key to the problem should be sought in the fact that Christ lived on earth not with a human existence but only with a divine existence in virtue of the hypostatic union. This ecstasy of being extended to the ecstasy of acting. Hence the human acts of Christ participate in the "eternity" of the Word. This theory met with no success.[24] However, it is noteworthy

[23] The monograph of Theodor Filthaut, *Die Kontroverse über die Mysterienlehre* (Warendorf: J. Schnellsch, 1947), contains the most complete summary of the exchange between Casel and his critics up to the end of World War II.

[24] D. Feuling's theory is cited by Gottlieb Söhngen, "Le rôle agissant des mystères du Christ dans la liturgie d'après les théologiens contemporains," *Les questions liturgiques et paroissiales* 24 (1939) 79–107, at 103–4.

how the appeal to the hypostatic union, in one way or another and right from the earliest beginnings of Christian theology, has played a significant role in the attempts to relate the presence of the historical saving acts of Christ to the Christian liturgy.

During Casel's lifetime, Viktor Warnach, as noted above,[25] appealed to the metaphysical act by which Christ passed from suffering to glory. This transformation of the earthly existence of Christ is the mystery of the Kyrios present in the liturgy. The action by which Christ passed from suffering to glory, as representative of humanity, has opened the way to God for all humanity. It transcends all finite limits, sums up the whole of the work of redemption, and constitutes the real content of the mystery of worship.[26] Casel did not oppose this solution. We have already mentioned the fact that Casel adopted Vonier's thesis about the "sacramental world" having its own new laws which operate outside the limits of space and time, being able to concentrate things of the past, present, and future at one point.[27]

3. Presence of Redemptive Acts in and through Effects (G. Söhngen)

Among the most outstanding opponents of the teaching of Odo Casel on the subject of the relationship of the mysteries of Christ's life to the various forms of the liturgy of the Church must be numbered Gottlieb Söhngen. In his 1938 monograph *Der Wesensaufbau des Mysteriums,*[28] Söhngen explained that the Christ who suffered, the Christus Passus, still bears the marks of his passion and under this formality is present in the liturgical mysteries. This absolute and substantial presence implies the virtual presence of the historical redemptive acts of Christ and grounds the objective presence of the past saving acts which are realized (in their effects) in the individual subject of the liturgical celebrations. In a later work, published in 1946 on the subject of the theology of the eucharistic sacrifice, *Das sakramentale Wesen des Messopfers,* he modified his original theory, developing the idea of the active and relative presence of the sacrificial acts of Christ

[25] See above, n. 3.

[26] The theory of Viktor Warnach is repeated in his later publications on the subject, for example: *Agape: Die Liebe als Grundmotiv der neutestamentlichen Theologie* (Düsseldorf: Patmos, 1951) 371–400; "Mysterientheologie," in *Lexikon für Theologie und Kirche,* 2nd ed. (Freiburg: Herder, 1962) 7.724–27.

[27] Vonier, *A Key to the Doctrine of the Eucharist,* 35–44.

[28] Gottlieb Söhngen, *Der Wesensaufbau des Mysteriums,* Grenzfragen zwischen Theologie und Philosophie 6 (Bonn: Peter Hanstein, 1938).

grounded on the sacramental action which is a sacrifice.[29] This latter explanation was clarified further in an article written in 1953.[30]

In his original proposal Söhngen developed his theology of the presence of the historical redemptive work of Christ in the sacraments that began with a concept of sacrament that reflects the traditional orientation of neoscholastic theology which, as we have seen, was criticized by Odo Casel. In other words, the notion of *signum efficax gratiae* is applied to the Christian sacraments in such a way that the focus of attention is on the sacramental efficacy, not the symbolic act accomplished by the Church. The effect of the sacramental celebration, which comes to the foreground, is identified with the proper reality of the sacrament, and this perspective determines his solution to the problem of the presence of the saving acts of Jesus in the sacraments.

But if Söhngen appears to be inclined to favor the old scholastic theory of presence through effects, his thought was actually turned in another direction. He asks: How is the presence of the saving act linked to the effect? But he does not settle for the question: Does it come before the effect as cause? Rather, he goes on to ask: Is the presence of this historical saving act only linked to the effect in this relationship, or is the one to be conceived as in the other? Is the effect itself a share in the mystery itself in such a way that the mystery realizes itself as the effect?

The way that Söhngen understands the matter is illustrated by his interpretation of the Pauline teaching on baptism in Romans 6:2-11. In Romans 6:5, Paul says that the baptized dies with Christ the same death, that is a death which has the same content, namely, death to sin and passage to life. The difference lies in the mode of death: the historical death of Christ on the one hand, and the sacramental death of the baptized on the other. The mystery, or the divine life, by which the death of Christ leads to life, and by which the sacramental death of the baptized led to life, is the same. Hence, in baptism, the death of Christ is reproduced in the baptized in the sense that the effect of life, in the mystery of Christ's death, is reproduced in the baptized.

The effect of baptism, therefore, is the real imitation of the death of Christ in the recipient of baptism. This ontological imitation, or

[29] *Das Sakramentale Wesen des Messopfers* (Essen: Augustin Wibbelt, 1946).

[30] "Christi Gegenwart in uns durch den Glauben (Eph 3, 17): Ein vergessener Gegenstand unserer Verkündigung von der Messe," in Franz Xaver Arnold and Balthasar Fischer, eds., *Die Messe in der Glaubensverkündigung,* 2nd ed. (Freiburg: Herder, 1953) 14–28.

transformation, of the beneficiary is the real reproduction, or representation, or reactualization of the death of Christ. The process is substantially identical in both cases, and both are realized by the action of the Kyrios who bears the new principal of life of the baptized as life-giving Spirit.

One sees from this baptismal theology that "mystery" has a very precise meaning, narrower than the more general notion applied to the historical saving acts of Jesus. In short, mystery is the secret content of the saving acts of Christ and of the presently enacted sacramental celebrations. Since mystery is supratemporal it is able to penetrate through the historical activity of humanity.

"Mystery" is thus conceived as the reality of salvation: the presence of the divine life in the midst of historical and ethical reality. The starting point for the question of the mystery presence is the divine mystery that, in the saving work of Christ, is accomplished on Jesus himself. This mystery is again accomplished in an efficacious symbol or image in the Church and on the individual. Söhngen holds that the historical fact itself is not reactualized in the mystery of worship. For the historical death of Jesus is not the divine mystery that is reproduced in the mystery of worship, or rendered present "under the veil of the symbol" according to the saying of Dom Casel. The historical fact is simply passed and cannot be reactualized. But the divine mystery of the Lord, who lives as the glorified Lord who passed through death, is continually present: a reality existing in eternity.

A typical formulation of Söhngen's thesis is the following: The mystery presence is the presence of the divine saving acts in their mystery or secret content of salvation. In this way he emphasizes the divine saving acts rather than the supratemporal aspect of the historical redemptive acts of Christ. This distinction sets off his approach from that of those who argue that there is a presence of the historical saving acts of Jesus under the veil of the symbol. For Söhngen it is not the presence of the historical saving acts but the mystery of the saving acts. On the other hand, Söhngen is careful to state that it is not a presence of the supratemporal mystery unrelated to a historical reality of the redemptive acts of Jesus. Rather, the mystery has penetrated history in Jesus' redemptive work and so obtained from it a permanent trait.

The essential relation of the mystery of salvation to the historical life of Jesus holds for the sacraments. From the perspective of Söhngen the saving work of Christ becomes really present in us in and with the divine mystery which works on us. In a word, the past saving acts achieve presence again in the operation of the supratemporal mystery on us, namely, in the sacramental effect.

It is evident that Söhngen's theory is based on a concept of sacrament in which what the sacrament contains lies enclosed in its effect on us. The mystery reactualized in us is understood to be distinguished from the effect of its application to the subject of a sacrament, but at the same time inseparable from that effect. Hence the effect of the sacrament in its full reality is described by Söhngen as the spiritual real imitation of the saving acts of Christ.

The notion may be expressed as follows: The mystery is the proper sacramental reality come about through the imitation of Christ. This sacramental imitation of Christ in his saving work is not an image existing between the salvation-history prototype and the sacramental effect in the Church. The structure is not linear: prototype—image—effect. We do not, as it were, come upon the sacramental presence of the historical saving acts and *then* insert ourselves into it somehow by faith. No, the image exists in and with the sacramental reality which is the effect through imitation, or through conformity, but so that this imitation is the shaping power in the effect. The imitation has the pneumatic-dynamic being of a spiritual effective power.

Mystery, the supratemporal content of salvation, exists actually in the effect. The effect is the application of the saving work of Christ: conformity to Christ. But this effect takes place through representation of the saving work of Christ realizing itself in us. Thus the application of the saving work of Christ is the representation of the saving work of Christ in us, and so attribution of the fruits of this saving work. The effect, by imitation, creates conformity to Christ and so actualizes the saving work of Christ in us. The presence of the saving work of Christ is the reproduction of the conformity to Christ in virtue of the life-giving Spirit of Christ.

Söhngen can also say that the "sacrament" is accomplished in us (sacrament = mystery) by Christ. Hence we are conformed to Christ and his saving work. In this way Christ and the mystery of the saving acts of Christ are represented in us and by us (i.e., our being conformed to Christ which requires the response of faith).

Application to the Theology of the Eucharist

Söhngen applies this theology to the sacrificial action of the Mass which consists in the self-offering of the community. This sacrifice of the Church is conceived as the reproduction of the sacrifice of Christ accomplished in us and by us inwardly, that is, by the life-giving Spirit of Christ. The sacrificial death of the Lord is reactualized in that he works in us in the mystery of worship, i.e., the communication of divine life, while our act is conformed with his saving act, or imitates the historical sacrificial offering of Christ himself.

The sacrificial act of Christ on the cross offering himself by himself is not represented in a kind of sacramental imitation that comes between the historical act and its effect on the liturgical community. Rather, the sacrificial act of Christ on the cross is reproduced in the Spouse of Christ, the Church. This means that in the Mass the historical sacrifice of Christ on the cross becomes the personal sacramental sacrifice of the Church. The representation of the historical sacrifice of Jesus in the case of the Eucharist is an application made first to the Church and then to the individual believers, whereas in the case of the other sacraments the application is to the believers first and so to the Church. The substantial real presence of the sacrificed body and blood results from the change of the bread and wine so that they become a "consecrated offering." According to Söhngen this sacrament of the body and blood is identified as the sacrificial gift of the Church in the anamnesis-offering prayer of the Roman Canon. It is through this liturgical co-offering of the sacrificed body, marked once-for-all with the blood of the cross, that the sacrificial death of Christ, reproduced spiritually and really in the Spouse of Christ, the Church, is represented.

[Söhngen's Later Position]

This earlier thesis of Söhngen is determined in part by his rejection of the opinion that the historical sacrifice of the cross as historical act can be truly re-presented in the sacrament. In his later work Söhngen follows a position more consistent with the basic insight of Casel and Vonier. Söhngen now maintains that the consecration of the bread and wine by the priest acting *in persona Christi* signifies both the sacrificial act of Christ and the offering of his sacrificed body and blood as food of eternal life. The sacrament of the Eucharist, insofar as holy food, contains the Christus Passus under foreign forms: the Christ exalted through his sufferings. This is a substantial, or absolute presence of the spiritualized, glorified body of the risen Lord. Insofar as sacrificial action, the consecration is a commemorative representation of the sacrificial action of the cross. What Christ himself does through the priest is a sacrificial action that imitates his historical sacrificial act of the cross. It is a sacrificial action that symbolically represents the historical self-offering of the cross.

This sacrificial act of Christ is an actual presence of the sacrificial act of the cross in a sacramental mode of being. But it is not an "absolute" sacrificial act really distinguished from that of the cross. For it draws its reality from the historical sacrificial act. It is a relative sacrifice in that it is a sacrificial deed relative to the cross. It is also a relative sacrifice in that it relates to the Church for which and through which it is offered.

On the subject of the relationship between the substantial and relative presences of Christ, Söhngen offers this solution. The sacramental sacrificial action is made on the reality of the Christus Passus sacramentally present. Without the absolute presence, the sacrificial action would be made on the gifts of the Church: the elements of bread and wine. Without the actual and relative presence of the sacrifice of the cross, there would be no true and proper sacrifice.

4. Summary

a. The Original Thesis of G. Söhngen

The application of the sacrifice of the cross in the Mass is a reactualization of the mystery of salvation. What is reactualized is the suprahistorical content of the mystery of the cross. From this follows the attribution of the fruits of the historical sacrifice to the faithful. The reactualization of the divine content of the sacrifice of the cross is located in the faithful and received by faith. Thus the presence of the sacrifice of the cross in the Mass is the presence of the sacramental imitation realized in and by believers. This means that the dynamic conformity to Christ in his historical self-offering on the cross is the new element of the memorial of the sacrifice of the cross.

The mystery of the sacrifice of the cross is identical with that of the eucharistic sacrifice. But in and through the Eucharist Christ offers himself, not in himself, but in the sacramental sacrifice of the body of Christ, the Church. In other words, the Christus Passus represents his sacrifice in the sacramental mode of being which constitutes the sacrifice of the Church. This notion excludes the idea that the sacrifice of the Church is added externally to the sacrifice of Christ, or that it is a continuation of the sacrifice of Christ, or included in the historical sacrifice of Christ. Rather, the sacrifice of the Church is the sacramental mode of existence of the sacrifice of Christ.

But how is the substantial real presence of Christ under the signs of his passion related to the reactualization of the sacrifice of the cross in and by the faithful? The substantial real presence of the body and blood of Christ under the signs of the passion supports the presence of the mystery of the historical sacrifice of Christ in the believers. The sacrificed body of Christ marked once-for-all with the blood of the cross is the Father's sacrificial gift to us. Consequently, through the co-offering of the Church, through the return of this gift with thanksgiving, the sacrificial death of her Lord is represented spiritually and really in the self-offering of the Spouse of Christ.

b. Söhngen's Later Position

Söhngen's later position works with the notion of the actual and relative presence of the sacrifice of the cross. The presence of a suprahistorical content of salvation according to its salvific efficacy is related to the actual and relative presence of the historical saving act itself. The memorial of the passion of Christ is a sacrificial action in which the death of Christ is represented and made fruitful for the Church. The presence of the Christus Patiens in the sacrificial action is a presence in act of the suffering of the Lord, for it is represented in a sacrificial action which takes place here and now, and imitates the sacrifice of the cross accomplished once-for-all in a bloody manner. But it is a relative sacrifice, referring back to the cross of which it is the memorial and to the Church for whom and through whom it is offered. The sacrifice of the cross is not repeated; the new reality is the participation of the Church in the worship of Christ in order to derive benefits from the cross.

The presence of the Christus Passus is a substantial and absolute presence under foreign forms: a presence of a spiritualized body caused by the Holy Spirit. The unity of the substantial presence and relative presence of the passion of Christ is explained by Söhngen as follows: The Christus Passus, the *res et sacramentum* of the *sacramentum tantum,* is the foundation for the actual presence of the passion, and remains after the sacrificial action. The Christus Patiens, the presence of Jesus in the act of the passion, is that through which the substantial presence of Christ is fully realized. Hence, without the Christus Passus, the sacramental action would be made on the reality of the elements of bread and wine. On the other hand, without the actual and relative reactualization of the sacrifice of the cross there would be no proper sacrificial action.

The vital connection between sacraments and faith is clear: The presence of Christ by faith enters our daily life through the sacramental celebrations. The presence of Christ in the sacraments is realized as personal presence through faith which recognizes this presence and draws nourishment from it.

C. INITIAL REACTION OF THE ROMAN MAGISTERIUM: POPE PIUS XII'S ENCYCLICAL LETTER *MEDIATOR DEI*

From the period of the Reformation to the twentieth century, the yield of magisterial teaching on the subject of the sacrifice of the Mass has been very lean. In this regard Pius XII's encyclical letter, *Mediator Dei*, November 20, 1947,[31] represents an important intervention into that field of the theology of the liturgy in general and the theology of the Mass in particular. A part of what he states about the sacrifice of the Mass has become the standard position of subsequent papal documents. This teaching can be quickly summarized.

1. *Activity of the Faithful*

In the eucharistic liturgy the laity offer with the priest the prayers of thanksgiving, praise, impetration, and expiation. On the other hand, they offer the Victim through the hands of the priest and offer themselves with the priest.[32] This teaching is repeated in Vatican II's Constitution on the Sacred Liturgy where it speaks of the function of the liturgical rites and prayers: through this activity (the liturgical rites and prayers) the people learn to offer through the hands of the priest and to offer themselves with him offering himself.[33]

The General Instruction of the Roman Missal of Pope Paul VI presents the theology of the Eucharistic Prayer in the following way: "The center and highpoint of the whole celebration has a beginning *(initium)*, namely the *Prex eucharistica*, that is, a prayer of thanksgiving and sanctification *(sanctificationis)*."[34] The contents of the *Prex* are listed as follows: thanksgiving, acclamation (Sanctus); epiclesis for

[31] Pius XII, encyclical letter *Mediator Dei, AAS* 39 (1947) 521–95.

[32] Ibid., 556.

[33] Vatican II, Constitution on the Sacred Liturgy, *Sacrosanctum concilium* no. 48.

[34] "Nunc centrum et culmen totius celebrationis initium habet, ipsa nempe Prex eucharistica, prex scilicet gratiarum actionis et sanctificationis"—Paul VI, *Institutio generalis missalis romani* no. 54, in *Missale Romanum* (Rome: Typis polyglottis vaticanis, 1970) 39; also in Reiner Kaczynski, ed., *Enchiridion documentorum instaurationis liturgicae: Ordo Missae* (Turin: Marietti, 1976) no. 1449, vol. 1, p. 488.

consecration of gifts and communicants; narrative of institution and consecration; anamnesis; oblatio (offering prayer); intercessions; final doxology. Under "narrative of institution and consecration" the General Instruction states that

"the sacrifice is accomplished by the words and actions of Christ, which Christ instituted at the Last Supper, when he offered his body and blood under the species of bread and wine, and gave to his apostles to eat and drink and left the mandate to them of perpetuating the same mystery."[35]

In the oblation following the anamnesis, it is said that the Church offers the Victim to the Father and offers itself.[36]

2. The Function of the Eucharistic Prayer

In general the function of the prayer is described as the medium by which the congregation joins with Christ in confession of the wonderworks of God and in the oblation of the sacrifice. But what is the special value of the Eucharistic Prayer in the celebration of the Mass according to the *Ordo Missae/Institutio generalis*? The notion of contribution to the integrity of the rite of the sacrament, or to the integrity of the sacrament itself, comes to mind. Which is it?

Pius XII uses the notion of "integrity" of the eucharistic sacrifice to identify the function of Holy Communion: "Communion pertains to the integrity of the sacrifice *(ad . . . integritatem habendam)* . . . . It is an error to say that Mass is not lawful without the communion of the faithful."[37] Here the Pope refers to the teaching of the Council of Trent which defended the lawfulness of the practice of the celebration of Mass without the communion of the faithful.[38] Moreover, Pius XII

[35] "Verbis et actionibus Christi sacrificium peragitur, quod ipse Christus in Cena novissima instituit, cum suum Corpus et Sanguinem sub speciebus panis et vini obtulit, Apostolisque manducandum et bibendum dedit et iis mandatum reliquit idem mysterium perpetuandi"—*Institutio generalis* no. 55 d, p. 40; Kaczynski, *Ordo Missae* no. 1450 d, vol. 1, p. 488.

[36] "Oblatio: per quam in ipsa hac memoria Ecclesia, eaque praesertim hic et nunc congregata, in Spiritu Sancto hostiam immaculatam Patri offert. Intendit vero Ecclesia ut fideles non solummodo immaculatam hostiam offerant sed etiam seipsos offerre discant, et de die in diem consummentur, Christo mediatore, in unitatem cum Deo et inter se, ut sit tandem Deus omnia in omnibus"—*Institutio generalis* no. 55 f, p. 40; Kaczynski, *Ordo Missae* no. 1450 f, vol. 1, p. 489.

[37] Pius XII, encyclical letter *Mediator Dei, AAS* 39 (1947) 562–63.

[38] Trent, Session 22 (1562) *Canones de ss Missae sacrificio,* canon 8 (DS 1758).

identifies two errors: [1] that the Mass is unlawful without the communion of all in attendance, on the grounds that this goes against the divine institution; [2] that insistence on the requirement of the supper of fraternal assembly along with the eucharistic sacrifice seems to make Holy Communion communally celebrated, "as it were, the culmination of the whole celebration." But, says Pius XII, the eucharistic sacrifice is, by its nature, the unbloody immolation of the Victim, "mystically signified in the separate consecration of the elements." He concludes: "However, the holy banquet pertains to the integrity of it and participation in it by communion of the august sacrament."[39]

On the subject of the new liturgy of confirmation, Paul VI states that the prayer and laying on of hands before the essential rite of confirmation "contribute to the integral perfection of the same rite (Latin rite of confirmation) and to the fuller understanding of the sacrament."[40] The new *Ordo Confirmationis* explains that, "The imposition of hands . . . with the prayer *Deus omnipotens,* although it does not pertain to the valid conferral of the sacrament, however contributes much to achieving the integrity of the rite and fuller understanding of the sacrament."[41] The Eucharist Prayer thus seems to be best described as contributing to the integrity of the rite, certainly not to the integrity of the sacrament.

3. *The Subject of the Eucharistic Sacrifice*

In the Western tradition, it is noteworthy that the priest has been seen as the representative of the universal Church, and consequently also of those assisting at the liturgy. The question still remains theoretically open whether those who are present physically and those absent who join their intentions with the "Masses of the world," can both be said to participate in basically the same way in each Mass. Pius XII does not attempt to deal with this question formally. While the question is not now raised by official Catholic theology, it still remains part of the tradition. However, the majority of Catholic theologians who have written on this subject in recent years tend to explain that those absent can, by their intention and prayers, support the faith of actual participants, but they are not able to participate directly in

[39] *Mediator Dei,* p. 563.

[40] Paul VI, apostolic constitution *Divinae consortium naturae, AAS* 63 (1971) 657–64, at 664; Kaczynski, no. 2600, 1.812.

[41] *Ordo Confirmationis* (Rome: Typis polyglottis vaticanis, 1971; 2nd ed., 1973) no. 9, p. 18; Kaczynski, no. 2611, 1.817.

the offering of each Mass. For the divine response to prayer is not conditioned by the celebration of Masses.

4. Words of Consecration

Finally there is the matter of the theology of the "moment of consecration" which is unique to the Latin scholastic tradition. The narrative of institution as such recalls to the participants the meaning of the celebration. It is also the theological center of the prayer; it explains the petition for the sanctification of the gifts of the Church and for the sanctification of the communicants, and it explains the anamnesis-offering prayer. But in the Western tradition, the words of Christ spoken over the bread and wine are understood to be the essential form of the sacrament. These words thus constitute the moment when the sacrament is realized, namely, when the bread and wine are converted into the body and blood of Christ. Thus, while the words are spoken by the presiding minister, they are understood as being spoken by Christ through his minister. This act is one accomplished only by the minister acting *in persona Christi* in the midst of the prayer of faith of the Church.

This act of consecration does not simply render present the somatic Christ under the species of bread and wine. For what is signified is the body given and the blood shed for the salvation of the world. The representation of the death of Christ occurs with the act of conversion of the elements. The somatic presence of Christ and the representation of the sacrifice of Christ are simultaneously achieved in the act of the consecration of the elements.

5. Representation of the Sacrifice of Christ

But what is meant by the idea that the death of Christ is "represented at the moment of the consecration of the elements"? The post-Tridentine theories, which sought to find the visible sacrifice of the Mass in the separate consecration of the elements, proposed a "mystical mactation" of Christ at the level of the sacramental signs. Thus they espoused the idea of a sacrificial rite, the structure of which was the sacrifice of the self-offering of Christ in the signs of the food. This is a pre-Christian concept which is now generally discarded in current Catholic theology.

Nowadays the average Catholic theology of the Mass favors the idea of a ritual offering of the self-offering of Christ in the signs of the food. But it takes this form: There is an objective representation of the self-offering of Christ on the cross in the signs of the food at the moment of consecration. This theory presupposes that there is a real relation to the cross as a consequence of the presence of the same priest and victim (Christ), and because there is an application of the blessing of the cross in and through the celebration. But in addition, this theology affirms that the representation of the sacrifice of the cross is a sacramental reactualization of the once-for-all historical engagement of Jesus on the cross. The idea that in the act of consecration a sacramental representation of the sacrifice of the cross is realized in the sense that the historical sacrifice is re-presented or reactualized also seems to be favored by official Catholic theology today. However, Pius XII in *Mediator Dei* did not attempt to settle this basic question.

6. Influence of Odo Casel on Pius XII's Encyclical Letter Mediator Dei

Pius XII's encyclical letter *Mediator Dei* was influenced significantly by Casel's theology of mysteries, as well as by the literature which that theology occasioned. The encyclical's formulation of the definition of liturgy is close to that of Casel. In a very explicit way the whole of the liturgical action is identified with the work of Christ: "The sacred liturgy . . . constitutes the public worship of the mystical body of Jesus Christ, namely the head and his members.[42] [This is] the public worship which the society of Christian faithful pays to its founder and through him to the eternal Father."[43]

Moreover, Pius XII accentuates Casel's typical stress on the permanent presence of Christ and his saving activity in the life of the Church. This is said above all with reference to the exercise of the ministry of the High Priest of the liturgy.[44] The saving work of Christ is rendered living and present by means of the exercise of his priesthood: the "priesthood of Jesus Christ."[45]

In the encyclical letter *Mystici corporis*, Pius XII teaches that believers are joined to Christ through the mystery of the cross.[46] He explains that our sanctification is not realized independently of the historical fact of the Christ-event, by which redemption was objectively obtained,[47] and bases the relation of the historical saving acts to the liturgy on the actual presence of Christ.[48] *Mediator Dei* develops these ideas by

[42] Pius XII, encyclical letter *Mediator Dei, AAS* 39 (1947) 528–29.
[43] Ibid., 528.
[44] Ibid., 522.
[45] Ibid., 529.
[46] Pius XII, encyclical letter *Mystici Corporis Christi, AAS* 35 (1943) 193–248, at 205.
[47] Ibid., 206.
[48] Ibid., 218.

calling to mind the belief that "In every liturgical action the divine founder is present together with the Church." A list of modes of his presence is given: "He is present in the august sacrifice of the altar, the person of the priest, and especially under the species of bread and wine; he is present in the sacraments by his power . . . which makes them instruments of grace"; and he is present, finally, in the prayer of the Church (Matthew 18:20).[49]

This presence in the liturgy is always seen in relation to the historical mysteries.[50] For the goal of the liturgy is to lead Christians to "enter again his path of sorrow, and thus finally to share his glory."[51] Therefore the liturgy is a liturgy of the historical Christ, and not of the glorious, pneumatic Christ.[52]

In *Mediator Dei,* Pius XII develops the idea that the mystery of the cross is living and actual through the centuries.[53] The actual presence of Christ in liturgical action is considered to be the basis of the presence and efficacy of the historical work of salvation in the liturgy.[54] This actual presence of Christ in the liturgy is always seen in relation to the historical mysteries of salvation.[55] In other sacraments, apart from the Eucharist, Christ is present "in the sacraments *virtute sua,* which he infuses into them as effective instruments of sanctification."[56] So the mysteries are present in the sacraments, in the first place in virtue of the actual presence of Christ, and in the second place in virtue of the symbolic power of liturgical rites.

But what can be said about the presence of the historical events of redemption? In the case of the sacraments in general, Pius XII follows traditional scholastic theology. Casel's thesis opposed this, insofar as that theology was content with the instrumental cause-effect schema. For Casel, the schema symbol-historicity holds. Sacraments are in *genere signi.* But they are also real symbols of salvation, and therefore instrumental causes of sanctification.[57] In this connection we have al-

[49] *Mediator Dei,* p. 528.

[50] Ibid., 597.

[51] Ibid., 579.

[52] Ibid.

[53] Ibid., 529.

[54] Ibid., 528.

[55] Ibid., 577–79.

[56] "Praesens adest in Sacramentis virtute sua, quam in eadem transfundit utpote efficiendae sanctitatis instrumenta"—ibid., 528.

[57] See Schilson, *Theologie als Sakramententheologie,* 274.

ready seen how Casel adopted Vonier's thesis about the "sacramental world" having its own new laws which operate outside the limits of space and time, being able to concentrate things of the past, present, and future at one point.[58]

Pius XII makes use of Casel's insight concerning the active presence of Christ in all liturgical action. Nevertheless, in the matter of the relation between the historical saving acts and the Christian liturgy, he distances himself from Casel's thesis concerning the presence of the historical saving acts in the liturgy of the Church. This is best exemplified in the Pope's remarks on the subject of the presence of the mysteries of Christ's life in the liturgical year. Pius XII states:

"These mysteries *(mysteria)* are constantly present and operate, not in the way that some recent writers talk (*effutiunt* = chatter), but in the way that Catholic doctrine teaches us."[59]

The encyclical affirms the actuality of the mysteries of Christ's life. Christ continues "that journey . . . which he . . . began in his mortal life . . . with the intention of bringing men to know his mysteries, and in a way to live by them."[60] These mysteries are "examples of Christian perfection, as well as sources of divine grace, due to the merits and prayers of Christ."[61] They are present in virtue of the actual presence of Christ and his power: "Christ himself who is ever living in his Church."[62] "Hence the liturgical year" is, concludes Pius XII, "not a mere external representation of the past, nor a pure, bare remembrance of the events of a former age."[63]

[58] See Vonier, *A Key to the Doctrine of the Eucharist*, 35–44.

[59] "Quae profecto mysteria, non incerto ac subobscuro eo modo, quo recentiores quidam scriptores effutiunt, sed quo modo catholica doctrina nos docet, praesentia continentur adsunt atque operantur" (perhaps best translated: "These mysteries . . . not in that uncertain and vague way, which certain recent writers hold . . .") —*Mediator Dei*, p. 580.

[60] "Qui (Christus) . . . iter pergit, quod quidem in hac mortali vita . . . ipse pientissimo eo concilio incepit, ut hominum animi mysteria sua attingerent ac per eadem quodammodo viverent"—ibid.

[61] "Eximia sunt christianae perfectionis exempla, et divinae gratiae sunt fontes ob merita deprecationesque Christi"—ibid.

[62] "Christus ipse, qui in sua Ecclesia perseverat"—ibid.

[63] "Quapropter liturgicus annus . . . non frigida atque iners earum repraesentatio est, quae ad praeterita tempora pertinent, vel simplex ac nuda superioris aetatis rerum recordatio"—ibid.

The encyclical does not seem to envision the mode of presence of the mysteries of Christ's life in any other way than that of a presence *in us* by the effects of the mysteries which, although located in the past, exercise exemplary and efficient instrumental causality. The mysteries are present in the symbolic power of the liturgical rites, which both refer the Church to the mysteries of Christ and bestow the grace of the mysteries.[64]

The objective character of the sanctification given through the liturgy is affirmed. The efficacy of the sacraments and the eucharistic sacrifice derive "first of all and principally" from the act itself (*ex opere operato*).[65] On the other hand, the ritual activity instituted by the Church is "efficacious *ex opere operantis,* since the Church is holy and acts in union with Christ."[66]

On the subject of the sacramental sacrifice of the Mass, formulas close to that of Casel are employed. But the real death of Christ is not said to be renewed, or even rendered present, in the Mass: "The sacrifice of our Redeemer is shown forth . . . by external signs which are the symbols of his death."[67] When it is said that Christ "does, what he already did on the cross,"[68] the reference is only to the sacrificial oblation (unbloody oblation, as opposed to bloody oblation).

It is also noteworthy that the Holy Office complained to the archbishop of Salzburg that the German translation of *Mediator Dei* gave the impression that Pius XII favored Casel's theory by employing *Mysteria* in place of "mysteria."[69] The translation seemed to suggest that the Pope agrees with those "who teach that the Mysteries are present in liturgical worship, not historically but mystically and sacramentally, but nevertheless really."[70] However, Casel's theology of mysteries was not explicitly, or implicitly, declared untenable by *Mediator Dei.* Rather, the encyclical wanted a more precise statement

[64] Ibid.

[65] "Quae efficacitas, se de Eucharistico Sacrificio ac de Sacramentis agitur, *ex opere operato* potius ac primo loco oritur"—ibid., 532.

[66] ". . . tum efficacitas habetur potius *ex opere operantis Ecclesiae,* quatenus ea sancta est atque arctissime cum suo Capite coniuncta operatur"—ibid.

[67] "Redemptoris nostri sacrificatio per externa signa, quae sunt mortis indices . . . ostenditur"—ibid., 548.

[68] "Summus Sacerdos id agit, quod iam in Cruce fecit"—ibid.

[69] See *Mediator Dei,* p. 580.

[70] ". . . qui docent mysteria in cultu liturgico praesentia esse non historice, sed mystice ac sacramentaliter, sed tamen realiter" (see DS 3855, footnote).

at the level of dogmatic theology. The letter of the Holy Office does not go beyond the judgment of the encyclical. It merely states that the Pope does not favor Casel's view.[71]

Thus, while Pius XII was not content with Casel's formulation, it seems clear that he did not reject Casel's basic insight. Moreover, since the middle of the 1950s, it was becoming quite clear to theologians that while many aspects of Casel's theology of mysteries needed to be corrected, his basic insight deserved serious attention. A number of monographs began to appear, particularly in the area of biblical and patristic studies, as well as in the field of speculative theology, which tended to support the idea of the sacramental re-presentation of the historical saving work of Christ in the eucharistic liturgy. But no consensus has emerged in the matter from the standpoint of speculative theology. Differentiated judgments have appeared in the matter of the support given by Scripture and patristic tradition to the idea of the mystery presence of the historical saving acts of Christ.

CONCLUSION

The encyclical of Pius XII does not accept the possibility of an objective mode of sacramental presence of a reality that naturally has ceased to exist in the past. However, it affirms the possibility of a natural and sacramental presence of an existing entity: the Christus Passus. The encyclical takes for granted that the historical mysteries exist insofar as they have affected Christ. It is the crucified and risen Lord who is present in the liturgy. But there is also the matter of the *efficient causality* exercised by the historical mysteries in the liturgy. The "*effectus* theory" appeals to the virtuality left by the salvific acts on the glorified humanity of Christ. This virtuality acts morally inasmuch as, through it, Christ impetrates the grace that he now bestows. The encyclical certainly accepts this point of view. But does it say more?

Nowhere does the Pope suggest that some element of the historical saving acts of Christ has survived. Moreover, the line of development of the theology of the encyclical does not lead to seeking the key to the mystery presence *exclusively* in the human acts themselves! Rather, the presence of the Kyrios is presented as the ground of the relation between the historical saving acts and the liturgy of the Church.

[71] See J. Hild, "L'Encyclique 'Mediator Dei' et le mouvement liturgique de Maria-Laach," *La Maison Dieu* 14 (1948) 15–29.

The encyclical says more than that the historical mysteries exist insofar as they have affected Christ. A causal unity, at the level of efficiency, is affirmed between the historical mysteries and liturgical activity. It has been suggested, however, that this latter consideration excludes the idea of a permanency of the salvific work, based on the divine power contained in the historical mysteries. Rather, according to this suggestion, a virtual presence of the historical mysteries, insofar as they have affected Christ, is sufficient to explain the causal nexus between the historical mysteries and the liturgical communication of the grace of Christ.

Thus, according to Antonio Piolanti, the encyclical is open to what alone can explain this connection. There is the perennial will of Christ to effect the redemption of humanity (Hebrews 10:5-7). This was expressed in all the actions of Christ's earthly life. This will passed into eternity in the final act of the cross and remains unchanged in Christ's glorified life. It is this human intention of Christ, expressed in separate acts during his earthly life, and become stabilized once for all in the glorified Lord, that binds the historical saving acts to the liturgy.[72]

Whatever may be conjectured concerning the openness of Pius XII to Piolanti's solution, the proposal itself is not satisfactory, for it labors under the same weakness that is characteristic of many of the recent attempts to find an element of the saving work which enjoys a participation in the divine eternity. What all these attempts have in common is the inability to offer a satisfactory explanation that does not itself cry out for further explanation.

II. DEVELOPMENT IN THE POST-CASELIAN PERIOD

A. FROM 1948 TO THE SECOND VATICAN COUNCIL

1. *Presence of an Element of the Redemptive Acts*

Many Thomists, for example, J. Gaillard, have appealed to the immobile act of beatific love which they identify as the soul of the redemptive acts.[73] This immobile act, by which Christ ultimately willed and merited salvation, continues to cooperate instrumentally for our salvation with the divine will. This act of beatific love is the *mysterion* of the saving acts present in the liturgy. L. Monden and E. Schillebeeckx

[72] Antonio Piolanti, "Il mistero del culto e l'eucaristia," *Divinitas* 5 (1961) 115–38.

[73] Jean Gaillard, "Chronique de liturgie: La théologie des mystères," *Revue thomiste* 57 (1957) 510–51.

have proposed that the human saving acts of Christ are personalized by the Word.[74] Hence they participate in a duration proper to the hypostatic level, i.e., in the eternity of the Word. The beatific vision is organically part of the foundation of the presence of the saving acts of Christ in the liturgy.

Hans Urs von Balthasar

Hans Urs von Balthasar seems to be inspired by the concept of the Eucharistic Prayer, viewed as the performative form of the eucharistic faith. He understands that the Eucharistic Prayer and accompanying symbolic action is a palpable, visible expression of the spiritual self-offering of the Church, a response to the Father's fidelity to his people which has its definitive expression in the self-giving of the Son as the embodiment of the Father's covenant with humanity. This response is a visible expression of the participation of the Church in the response made by the Son of God in his humanity to the mystery of what the Father has done in him for the salvation of the world. The faith of Christ himself belongs to the mystery of God in Christ. His response of faith is the unique response which summarizes and grounds the response of all humanity. It is the embodiment of the covenant of humanity with the Father, the sealing of the covenant of humanity with the Father on the side of humanity.

This palpable, visible liturgical expression of the response of the Church is made in union with the response of the Word in his humanity which sealed the covenant. Hence it is the expression of participation in the mystery of God in Christ. This response of the faith of the Church is a participation in the faith of Christ. Balthasar speaks of an "ontic" participation which makes possible the conformity of believers to the meritorious response of Christ.

In short the spiritual self-offering of the Church is a participation in the response of the faith of Christ to the Father's fidelity to his covenant. It is the acceptable response to the inclusion in the new covenant made *in Christo,* that is, in the power of Christ inasmuch as the risen Lord sends his Spirit from the Father to draw humanity into union with himself so that human beings may participate in the new

[74] Louis Monden, *Het Misoffer als Mysterie: Een Studie over de heilige Mis als sacramenteel Offer in het Licht van de Mysterieleer van Dom Odo Casel,* Bijdragen-Bibliothek, Deel II (Roermond-Maasiek: J. J. Romen & Zonen, 1948); E. H. Schillebeeckx, *Christ the Sacrament of the Encounter with God* (New York: Sheed and Ward, 1963) 59–61.

covenant relationship between God and humanity of which Christ himself is the *substantial covenant.* Likewise it is a response made *cum Christo:* a participation in Christ's faith response to the Father's covenant initiative. Finally it is a response made *per Christum:* through the sharing in the one Passover of Christ to the Father which is the only way of salvation.

From this consideration one sees that the Church, which expresses its nature in the Eucharistic Prayer, is primarily the place where God and humanity encounter one another in the faith of Christ. The Church is the community of believers that shares in the mystery of God in Christ through faith. This faith is not a first step, something that stands before the mystery, but the first and indispensable way of sharing in the mystery. We can conclude, then, that the community which calls itself Church of Christ is in reality only the believing Church. However, no believing Church exists without prayer; for prayer is the communal performative form of the faith through which the basic act of faith is actualized, and which brings about participation in the mystery of God in Christ.

The actualization of this life of faith in the liturgy through the medium of prayer is *sacramental* inasmuch as it represents and actualizes the life of communion with God and among the faithful. In fact such prayer belongs essentially to all sacramental celebration because the activity of worship belongs essentially to the celebration of sacraments.

By means of the Eucharistic Prayer, the primary public expression of the faith of the Church, the faithful are enabled to express and realize their participation in the response of Christ's self-offering to the Father. This enablement results from the divine action effecting the transmission of the sacrificial attitude of Christ.[75]

2. *The Instrumental Activity of the Humanity of Christ: Formally the Same in History and Liturgy*

J.-H. Nicolas bases his approach on the fact that the humanity of Christ is the instrumental cause of his own death, resurrection, and glorification. This humanity is also the instrumental cause of the

[75] Hans Urs von Balthasar, "Fides Christi," in *Sponsa Verbi: Skizzen zur Theologie II* (Einsiedeln, Johannes Verlag, 1961) 45–79. Cf. Angelus Häussling, "Odo Casel—Noch von Aktualität: Eine Rückschau in eigener Sache aus Anlaß des hundertsten Geburtstages des ersten Herausgebers," *Archiv für Liturgiewissenschaft* 28 (1986) 357–87, at 383–84.

grace bestowed in the liturgy. The efficacy of the liturgy comes from the activity of the humanity of Christ that prolongs what rendered efficacious the historical redemptive acts themselves in order to draw believers into the mystery of his death and resurrection. In both instances, namely, of the historical redemptive acts and of the liturgical event, the same instrumental agent is at work and the same action is present. The action that took place in the redemptive acts is *formally* identical with that of the action that takes place in the liturgy. This explains why the formal effect of the liturgical action is assimilation to the redeeming Christ, not to the glorious Christ. According to Nicolas, this is the position of Thomas Aquinas.[76]

3. *Memory—Faith—Holy Spirit in Relation to the Liturgical Presence of the Redemptive Act of Christ*

In the past few decades a number of authors have touched on the relationship between memory, Spirit, and the presence of the saving work of Christ in the lives of believers and Church. While faith in the dimension of memory is a familiar theme in contemporary discussion concerning what happens in Christian liturgy, a common approach to this subject has not yet been realized. The more familiar approach tends to make a sharp distinction between a biblical concept of "cultic memorial," and the subjective remembrance of the participants of the commemorative liturgical act. In other words, the concept of *anamnesis* is used to underscore the fact that more is involved in the liturgy than the subjective recall of the community of faith that takes place through symbolic language, verbal and gestural. "Anamnesis" is, therefore, identified with an objective act, in and by which the person or event commemorated is actually made present, is brought into the realm of the here and now. Thus the Eucharist is the "recalling" before God of the one sacrifice of Christ in all its accomplished fullness so that it is here and now operative in its effects in the souls of the redeemed.[77]

In the opinion of many modern theologians, this notion of "objective memorial" may be useful for preaching, that is, in order to emphasize the fact of Christ's active saving presence in the liturgy. However, it does not adequately express the intimate relation between the activity

[76] Jean-Hervé Nicolas, "Reactualisation de mystères rédempteurs dans et par les sacrements," *Revue thomiste* (1958) 20–54.

[77] See W. Jardine Grisbrooke, "Anaphora," in J. G. Davies, ed., *The New Westminster Dictionary of Liturgy and Worship* (Philadelphia: Westminster, 1986) 13–21, at 18 (quoting Gregory Dix, *The Shape of the Liturgy*, 243).

of the believing community and the mystery presence of Christ and his saving work.

a. Anthropological–Psychological Considerations

In order to bring some further understanding to the problem of the relationship of memory—faith—Holy Spirit to the mystery presence of Christ's saving acts in the liturgy, many modern theologians begin with some observations on the nature and function of human memory. We will now summarize some of the more important of these observations.

In the past few decades a number of authors have touched on the relationship between memory, Spirit, and the presence of the saving work of Christ in the lives of believers and in the life of the Church.

(1.) M. Bellet, for example, observes that the remembrance of Christ as Savior is born of the experience of Christ realizing his mission in our lives. Hence the liturgical anamnesis is the work of the life of faith awakened by this experience. As act of the life of faith, the liturgical anamnesis recalls the past saving work of Christ as continually present in order to give meaning to our lives.

"The anamnesis is a work, an act of faith; impossible outside it. It is the faith in the 'dimension' of memory. This is why the passed is there as surmounted in the present, and in a present that is the unfolding of the 'Eternal' in our time; and by this likewise, the passed is recognized without difficulty . . . Christ as act (as Word: acting word) realizes himself in us, in the heart of real history . . . in order that we might live."[78]

(2.) M. Giuliani. In the context of a general discussion of the theological meaning of the recalling of the events of Christ's life in meditation, M. Giuliani, writing two decades earlier, had already gone a step further than Bellet by inserting a brief reference to the role of the Spirit in the process of recalling in faith. According to him, the Risen Lord enables the believer to live from the death and resurrection of Christ because he sends the Spirit from the Father. In the Spirit we are enabled to remember the actions of Jesus. This remembrance transforms the history of Jesus, according to the flesh, into a mystery actually present and living for us. The movement of faith, recalling

[78] Maurice Bellet, "Anamnèse I: la mémoire du Christ," *Christus* 76 (1972) 520–31, at 530.

the mysteries of Christ's life, actualizes them anew. They are continually reborn, and made fruitful by the Spirit who enables the believer to be personally united to them in memory:

"It is because Christ risen makes us live from the resurrection by communicating without cease his Spirit that we are able 'to remember' the gestures of Jesus (John 2:22; 12:16; 14:26; 15:26; etc.), and that this remembrance transforms the history of Jesus according to the flesh into mysteries actually present and living for us."[79]

Early on in this same article, Giuliani asks: How does faith render present the gospel story? His answer is that the " 'movement of faith' mystically actualizes the reality, old perhaps in history, but always reborn and fruitful through the Spirit." In this connection, Giuliani observes that Ignatius Loyola, in his *Spiritual Exercises*, does not think of making the past present. The gospel contemplation does not mimic the scene that it causes to be relived. It renders it present to the soul, which perceives it as a sign and receives spiritual fruit from it.[80]

(3.) G. Martelet agrees with Giuliani.[81] The attention given by Giuliani to the role of the Spirit in the economy of salvation is more typical of recent Catholic theologians who underscore the economy of the Spirit. Walter Kasper summarizes this new perspective in his essay on the "Church: Place of the Spirit."[82] From the analysis of the sources of Scripture that refer to the Spirit, he concludes that the Spirit is the power of the new life experienced by Christians. The working of the Spirit is especially evident where newness arises. In the time of the Church, the Spirit makes the newness of the new, that is realized in Jesus Christ, available to the world. Hence the activity of the Spirit consists in integrating humanity into Christ: the Spirit is the bond of unity between humanity and the Trinity.

The Spirit works in all creation, leading all reality to fulfillment in Jesus Christ. Wherever egoism is overcome, wherever one trusts in

[79] Maurice Giuliani, "Présence actuelle du Christ," *Christus* 2 (1954) 97–107, at 107.

[80] Ibid., 100.

[81] Gustave Martelet, "Présence actuelle du Christ," *Christus* 5 (1955) 39–62, at 56 (he quotes the passage just cited from Giuliani).

[82] Walter Kasper and Gerhard Sauter, *Kirche—Ort des Geistes,* Kleine ökumenische Schriften 8, ed. Hans Küng and Jürgen Moltmann (Freiburg—Vienna: Herder, 1976).

ultimate meaning, the Spirit is at work. But the Spirit is also Spirit of the Redeemer. As such the Spirit hands on the tradition of Jesus Christ and, at the same time, hands on Jesus Christ himself. In this sense the Spirit can be called the living memory of the People of God.[83]

(4.) J.-Cl. Sagne, in his description of the memory of the heart, expands further on the line of thought of Giuliani. Sagne's development begins with the notion of memory as the historical presence of our past which determines our personality. The presence is evoked consciously by the desire that awakens it. He distinguishes between memory as a faculty, and as the living ground of the faculties of intellect and will. Human beings are gifted with the aptitude to register and conserve events, words, etc., which affectively mark their personalities. But they also possess an inexhaustible living ground of acts of knowledge and love, i.e., memory as source whence our life unfolds in movements of knowledge and love. The memory is present in a subconscious way at all times. It is evoked by the *desire* which can either awaken or suppress it. The source that awakens particular acts of knowledge and love is the desire of God which the Creator engraves in the creature. This desire is the source of our innate capacity to be drawn by the Father to return to our living origin. The desire is grounded on the Spirit of God who configures us to Christ, as children of God.

It is the living Word of God at the source of one's personal being, giving itself to human beings from within themselves, that is this inexhaustible ground of acts of knowledge and love. The living Word of God, dwelling in the person, turns that person toward the Father. This profound memory is the trace and imprint of the creative gesture of God and the appeal to recover it. To have memory in this sense, in the sense of this profound memory, is to be called to return to the living origin by the God who is present.

Memory, as the aptitude to register and conserve events and words, must be distinguished from the desire of God engraven in the creature by the Creator. The profound memory pertains to the order of a movement of the whole of creation toward God. This desire, which awakens the memory of our origin, can be called memory of the heart. This memory of the heart is the source of our innate capacity to be drawn by the Father to return to our living origin. It is grounded

[83] Walter Kasper, "Elemente einer Theologie des Geistes," in *Kirche—Ort des Geistes*, 30–36.

on the presence of the Spirit who configures us to God in the likeness of Christ, as children of God. This same Spirit awakens the desire of God by his inspirations, calling us to go forward in fidelity to the original appeal of God to conform to the image in which we were made. In this sense the Spirit is the living memory of Christians, the one who continually calls them on the way of faith after the initial appeal of God already contained in baptismal grace.[84]

B. THE POST-CONCILIAR PERIOD

1. *Thomism and the Theology of Mysteries*

a. F. Pratzner (B. Neunheuser; A. Gerken)

Aquinas distinguishes between sacrifice and sacrificial gift: "This sacrament is called 'sacrifice' insofar as it represents the passion itself of Christ, however it is called 'victim' insofar as it contains Christ himself . . . who is the *hostia salutaris,* as it is said in Ephesians 5."[85] Sacrifice and victim are not the same. They appear to be different levels in the sacrament. The sacrifice seems to move in the outer sphere of the symbolic representation of the sacrament. The proper content of the sacrament lies in the real presence of Christ as sacrificial victim. From this source the efficacy of the sacrifice of the cross flows to the sacrifice of the Mass.

There is a definite relation between the sacrifice of the cross and the sacrificial victim of the Mass. But can we speak of an identity, according to Aquinas? The fulfillment of the Old Testament types touches only the victim, not the sacrifice. The New Testament sacrifice contains *ipsum Christum passum.*[86] The Eucharist is the perfect sacrament of the passion of the Lord "insofar as containing *ipsum Christum passum.*"[87]

Commenting on Aquinas's presentation of the distinction between the eucharistic sacrifice and the sacrificial gift of the Eucharist, F. Pratzner judges that, in the matter of the theology of the sacrifice of

[84] Jean-Claude Sagne, "La mémoire du coeur," *La vie spirituelle* 132 (1978) 184–99.

[85] "Ad tertium dicendum, quod hoc sacramentum dicitur *sacrificium,* inquantum repraesentat ipsam passionem Christi; dicitur autem *hostia,* inquantum continet ipsum Christum, qui est hostia salutaris, ut dicitur Ephes 5"—*Summa theologiae* 3, q. 73, a. 4 ad 3.

[86] *ST* 3, q. 75, a. 1 c.

[87] "Eucharistia est sacramentum perfectum dominicae passionis, tamquam continens ipsum Christum passum"—*ST* 3, q. 73, a. 5 ad 2.

the Mass, Aquinas simply repeats the theological explanation of the majority of the theologians of his time.[88]

Pratzner's analysis of Aquinas's understanding of memorial, representation, etc., in the context of the Eucharist also furnishes him with evidence that Aquinas repeats a theological tradition already exemplified in early scholasticism.[89] His interpretation of key texts of Aquinas's doctrine on the relation of the Eucharist to the cross can be summarized as follows:

(1.) Basic Statement: "This sacrament is a/the sign of the passion, and not the passion itself."[90]

(2.) Interpretation in the *Summa theologiae*: "this sacrament has a threefold signification, one indeed with respect to the past, namely, inasmuch as it is the commemoration of the Lord's passion, which was a true sacrifice";[91] "this sacrament is called sacrifice, in so far as it represents the passion itself of Christ."[92]

(3.) What does "commemoration" and "representation" mean? Pratzner offers these alternatives: (a.) These words refer to a real, sacramental presence of the passion of Christ (representation); an objective memorial filled with the reality of the redemptive act (commemoration); (b.) a representative image of the past redemptive act; a merely subjective recalling of the past redemptive act.

(4.) Pratzner's solution: Aquinas compares the "sacrament of the paschal lamb" with the "sacrament of the Eucharist." The former prefigures the passion; the latter is rememorative of the passion.[93] From this comparison, Pratzner concludes that both sacraments have the same essential function relative to the sacrifice of the cross, with the difference that one points to the future, and the other to the past. "But," says Pratzner, according to Aquinas "sacrifices of the old law contained that true sacrifice of the passion of Christ only in figure, ac-

[88] Ferdinand Pratzner, *Messe und Kreuzesopfer: Die Krise der sakramentalen Idee bei Luther und in der mittelalterlichen Scholastik,* Wiener Beiträge zur Theologie 29 (Vienna: Herder, 1970) 95–97.

[89] Ibid., 70–76.

[90] "Hoc sacramentum est signum passionis Christi, et non ipsa passio"—*In IV Sent.*, d. 12, a. 3, sol. 1 ad 2.

[91] "Hoc sacramentum habet triplicem significationem; unam quidem respectu praeteriti, inquantum scilicet est commemorativum dominicae passionis, quae fuit verum sacrificium"—*ST* 3, q. 73, a. 4 c.

[92] Text above in n. 85.

[93] *ST* 3, q. 73, a. 5 c.

cording to the saying of Hebrews 10:1: 'The law contained only a shadow of the future goods, not the image of the reality itself.'"[94]

Responding to the objection that one of the forms of the eucharistic species is superfluous, Aquinas says that the value of the twofold form lies in its representative function: "to represent the passion of Christ in which the blood was separated from the body."[95] Aquinas always speaks of the same representative meaning when he refers to the passion of Christ in relation to the twofold form of the eucharistic sacrament.

The idea that the Eucharist is a representative image of the past redemptive act is also repeated in a synthetic way in the first question on the rite of the Eucharist: "Whether Christ is immolated in this sacrament."[96] Here Aquinas gives, as his own opinion, two reasons why "the celebration of this sacrament is called immolation of Christ." First,

> "the celebration of this sacrament . . . is a certain representative image of the passion of Christ, which is his true immolation . . . . Another way is the effect of the passion of Christ, namely, because we are made participants of the fruit of the Lord's passion. Whence in a certain Sunday secret prayer, it is said: 'As often as the commemoration of this victim is celebrated, the work of our redemption is exercised.'"[97]

According to Pratzner, the second reason bears on the effect of the passion of Christ, and does not imply the "presence of the passion of Christ in the sacrament of the Eucharist."[98]

Pratzner concludes that Aquinas contrasts the sacrament of the Eucharist, "as a representative image, with the true sacrifice, that Christ

[94] "Sacrificia enim veteris legis illud verum sacrificium passionis Christi continebant solum in figura, secundum illud Hebr 10,1: *Umbram habens lex futurorum bonorum, non ipsam rerum imaginem*"—*ST* 3, q. 75, a. 1 c.

[95] ". . . ad repraesentandum passionem Christi, in qua seorsum fuit sanguis a corpore separatus"—*ST* 3, q. 76, a. 1 ad 1.

[96] "Utrum in hoc sacramento Christus immoletur"—*ST* 3, q. 83, a. 1.

[97] "Celebratio autem hujus sacramenti . . . imago quaedam est repraesentativa passionis Christi, quae est vera ejus immolatio . . . . Alio modo quantum ad effectum passionis Christi, quia scilicet per hoc sacramentum participes efficimur fructus dominicae passionis. Unde in quadam dominicali oratione secreta dicitur: *Quoties hujus hostiae commemoratio celebratur, opus nostrae redemptionis exercetur*"—*ST* 3, q. 83, a. 1 c.

[98] Pratzner, *Messe und Kreuzesopfer,* 72, n. 52.

offered for us once for all on the cross."[99] According to Pratzner, the concepts of *memoria* and *repraesentatio*, as used by Thomas in connection with the sacrifice of the Mass, "many times have a subjective sense. Therefore, according to Thomas, the sacrifice that we daily offer in the Mass, is not the sacrifice of Christ himself, but rather a memorial and image of that sacrifice, in which that one sacrifice of Christ is no longer perceived as present."[100]

Pratzner contests the statement of B. Neunheuser that, according to Aquinas,

"The Eucharist is a sacrifice as sacrament of the body and blood of Christ; the accomplishment of the sacrament, i.e., the conversion, the placing of the twofold form of the body and blood of Christ, is simultaneously the sacrifice, celebrated by the consecrating priest, who here, as instrument of the Lord offering himself historically on the cross, represents the one sacrifice of Christ."[101]

Especially on the basis of *ST* 3, q. 79, a. 1 and q. 83, a. 1, Neunheuser summarizes Aquinas's teaching on the Eucharist as sacrifice in this way: "The Eucharist is image *(imago repraesentativa)* of the passion of Christ, but image full of effective power."[102] He understands *effectus* to include the idea that the Eucharist is a sacrament in which the one sacrifice of Christ is present. Pratzner, however, argues that *effectus,* in this context, means for Aquinas "the fruits of the passion, which are shared with us in this sacrament principally through Christ, who is contained therein."[103] He refers to *ST* 3, q. 79, a. 1 c: "the *effectus* of this sacrament ought to be considered first and foremost from what is contained in this sacrament, that is Christ." From this Pratzner concludes: "Only . . . through him (Christ) is the effect of his passion sacramentally present."[104]

Pratzner observes that Neunheuser follows D. Winzen, who thinks that Aquinas maintained the sacramental presence of the historical sacrifice of the cross on the basis that "the sacramental reality is

[99] Ibid., 72.

[100] Ibid., 74.

[101] Burkhard Neunheuser, *Eucharistie in Mittelalter und Neuzeit,* Handbuch der Dogmengeschichte IV/4b (Freiburg—Vienna: Herder, 1963) 40.

[102] Ibid., 41.

[103] Pratzner, *Messe und Kreuzesopfer,* 74, n. 62.

[104] Ibid.

strictly determined by the sacramental form."[105] Also P. Wegenaer is cited, as agreeing with Winzen, that Aquinas grounds the sacrificial character of the Mass on the essence of the Eucharist as sacrament.[106] However, Pratzner's analysis of the texts of Aquinas leads him to the conclusion that Aquinas neither shows sympathy with the old "sacramental idea," nor offers a reasonable facsimile for it.

How Can the Past Historical Acts of Jesus Be Present Now?

Pratzner does not simply appeal to the fact that duration is a purely analogous term used of an occurrence in the spiritual and personal domain and of happenings in the material domain.[107] From this standpoint it can be said that the historical redemptive work of Christ is passed, but remains present in its spiritual and personal aspect in Christ forever.[108] This solution, however, does not answer the question posed above. Ferdinand Pratzner refers to the idea of sacramental–memorial and concludes that the self-offering of Christ is present in the sacramental sign since sacrament cannot be separated from sacrifice. Here he points out that Aquinas failed to integrate the presence of the passion of Christ with somatic presence in the Eucharist because he followed the opinion of the day which situated the historical sacrifice simply in the past.[109]

Alexander Gerken refers to Pratzner's assessment of Aquinas's theology of the relation of the sacrifice of the cross to the Mass with approval. Aquinas does not hold for the presence of the passion of Christ in the ontological, full meaning it had in Greek image theology. Gerken seeks the reason for this in the failure to see person as relational, the failure to recognize "that the presence of his act, that is his death and resurrection, is likewise the presence of his person and vice versa."[110]

[105] Damasus Winzen, ed., in the "Kommentar" to *Das Geheimnis der Eucharistie, Die deutsche Thomas-Ausgabe,* vol. 30 (Salzburg—Leipzig: Pustet, 1938) 566.

[106] Polykarpus Wegenaer, *Heilsgegenwart: Das Heilswerk Christi und die Virtus Divina in den Sakramenten unter besonderer Berücksichtigung von Eucharistie und Taufe,* Liturgiewissenschaftliche Quellen und Forschungen 33 (Münster, Aschendorff, 1958) 63.

[107] See Karl Rahner, *The Celebration of the Eucharist* (New York: Herder and Herder, 1968) 16–17, n. 8.

[108] Ibid., 23, n. 16.

[109] Pratzner, *Messe und Kreuzesopfer,* 70–71.

[110] Alexander Gerken, "Kann sich die Eucharistielehre ändern?" *Zeitschrift für katholische Theologie* 97 (1975) 415–29, at 427–28, n. 17.

b. Brian McNamara

Brian McNamara maintains that in accord with the divine dispensation, the presence of the historical realities of Christ's life is ultimately intelligible without recourse to the principle that such a historical reality has been rendered timeless by God. His contribution to the problem of *Mysteriengegenwart* is important because it introduces into the discussion considerations that frequently have been overlooked in the literature on this subject.[111]

Generally it has been assumed, (1.) that because the historical life of Christ is passed, it cannot be rendered present in the liturgy. On the other hand it has also often been assumed, however the explanation, (2.) that some element of the redemptive act can indeed be made timeless, or "eternal." As for this latter approach, which has become the favored position since the time of Odo Casel, it is not supported by any proper analysis of the relation between time and eternity. The former approach, however, which in earlier times was often the favored theological position, is inconsistent with a realist metaphysics (which constitutes a presupposition of Catholic sacramental theology). The solution to this dilemma is to be sought through a proper understanding of eternity and time.

b/1. Eternity and Time.[112] Let us consider, in the first place, the "divine plan" of salvation from the perspective of God. From this point of view, there is no priority of the divine plan before its realization. Why? Because God's immutability and simplicity exclude temporal succession in God. God is simply outside (i.e., beyond, not limited by) time. "Eternity," as predicated of God, means total simultaneity. In other words, what God knows, wills, and effects, God knows, wills, and effects *eternally.*

The fact that God knows, wills, and effects time-conditioned events, does not imply that there is a divine concurrence, in the sense that God and the world become parallel successions. The relation of eternity to time is the relation of eternal divine action to its consequent term. From this consideration it follows that no occurrence in the world can become timeless. Therefore the sacrifice of the cross cannot

[111] Brian McNamara, "Christus Patiens in Mass and Sacraments: Higher Perspectives," *Irish Theological Quarterly* 42 (1975) 17–35. For most of the remainder of this section, with its six subsections (b/1 to b/6), we will be giving a detailed summary of McNamara's position as he presents it in this article.

[112] Ibid., 20–24.

become timeless. Only a failure to grasp the difference between eternity and time can lead to the idea that the sacrifice of the cross has become "timeless."

Space and time are relations that arise in and with created existence. In a theological context, they are intelligible as the medium in which God makes his divine plan known and within which the divine plan operates. Spatial and temporal conditions are relevant to occurrences as occurrences. The death on the cross is always linked to the circumstances of the death of the cross. On the other hand, spatial and temporal conditions are not relevant to the basic meaning of occurrences. The basic meaning of the sacrifice of the cross, of what occurred, is independent of the circumstances of the death *as meaning*. Nevertheless this meaning cannot be simply abstracted from the circumstances, and be identified as a timeless reality.

Conclusion. The spatial and temporal duration involved in the realization of the divine plan is altogether relevant to the term of the plan. On the other hand, it is not relevant to God's eternal knowing and acting. God is simply outside time.

b/2. The Ways of Understanding the Divine Plan.[113] We can speak of a threefold perspective involved in the understanding of the divine plan of salvation. There is the (1) *experiential perspective.*[114] This experiential measurement of historical succession allows for the past to be present only in its effects, and in memory. From this point of view the notion of historical simultaneity is unintelligible. Thus the event of the cross, experienced as a circumstantial once-for-all, is simply past. The idea that Christ is "born at Christmas" can only mean that Christ is born again in our subjective memories. But the notion that the birth of Christ, the same that took place in Bethlehem, is really present now, makes no sense.

The (2) *biblical perspective*[115] views salvation history as a process, the progressive realization of the divine plan of God. From this point of view, as well as from that of kerygmatic theology, the understanding involved is that of the understanding of a process as a process. Consequently, biblical and kerygmatic theology conclude, with respect to the liturgy, that we correctly commemorate the historical life of Christ,

[113] Ibid., 24–28.
[114] Ibid., 25.
[115] Ibid., 25–26.

which culminated in his resurrection-glorification, in Christian worship. We commemorate it as objective redemption. However, in the liturgy Christ is present as the one who has suffered, has died, and has been glorified. He is present as the Glorified Lord, always able to make intercession for us (Epistle to the Hebrews). But the historical mysteries are not present, for they lie in the past.

Not satisfied with this outlook, which sees all in the light of the resurrection, theologians have sought ways of explaining more precisely the relationship between the historical life of Christ and the liturgy. But all attempts to "eternalize" the redemptive acts of Christ as a whole, or to discover a supra-temporal element within, or underlying, the historical actions of Christ have proven unsuccessful. They fail to take account of the distinction between time and eternity. But also there is the more serious objection that they threaten to introduce tenets of docetism into the theology of the Incarnation. It is not possible to abstract some essential element of the human life of Christ without bringing into question the belief that the Word redeemed the world by his subjection to the circumstances of particular places and times.

The whole matter, however, must also be seen from the (3) *divine perspective.*[116] It is clear that from the standpoint of God, the ultimate meaning of the world is the *transitus* of the incarnate Word to the Father. Historically completed on the experiential level, it is still to be completed at the higher level of the divine plan. Temporal succession and spatial duration are relevant to humanity's involvement in this *transitus* of the world to the Father, which reached its climactic expression in the Christ-event, and is continued in the age of the Church. However, such succession and duration are not relevant to the ultimate intelligibility involved. For the Incarnation as a whole is a single *transitus* to the Father in the divine plan. The incarnate Word is the sole response of the world to the gratuity of God. Hence the Church today sets out "in Christ" to make explicit in its life, on the level of time, the single *transitus* of the Son to the Father.

The humanity of Christ, living and dying a human life and death, is the how and why of salvation. The instrumentality of this humanity cannot be adequately expressed by the scholastic notion of power. The earthly life of Christ is central to the divine plan for each individual. The intelligibility involved is the intelligibility of historical events. Christian insight grasps in the life of Christ, and in the liturgical cele-

[116] Ibid., 26–28.

brations, the single movement of the world to the Father. But what is the relation of the mysteries of Christ's life to the liturgy?

b/3. Causality and the Liturgy.[117] The concept of "efficient causality" has been introduced into the discussion of the relation of the historical saving acts of Christ to the liturgy, especially the chief rites of the Church. It is a firm tenet of Catholic theology that the saving acts of Christ's life exercise instrumental efficient causality in the liturgical event of the sanctification of believers.

The metaphysical analysis of efficient causality yields these conclusions: Agent and effect are simultaneously present to one another. The agent is not present before the effect of the action is realized. The action is identical with the effect. The action is not in the agent, nor between the agent and effect. "Power" is not really different from the action, and so not from the effect. The instrument used by the agent is itself an agent acting, insofar as it is used by the principal agent. Therefore the intelligibility of the action is not be to sought in the instrument, but in the agent.

Conclusion. Efficient causality is the relation of effect to cause, and its reality is found in the effect as proceeding from the cause. The change is the effect; the agent is not changed by acting. When we apply the foregoing analysis to God's acting in relation to the world, the following conclusions are reached:

(1) God is present to humanity by acting on humanity. Christ as man is the instrumental agent. Hence the humanity of Christ is present to the human being on whom God is acting. Since the divine perspective knows the Incarnation as a single *transitus* to the Father, God acts through the entire *transitus* of Christ. Hence, in the liturgy, the entire *transitus* of Christ is present.

(2) In the sacramental action a divine activity occurs that is found in the participants of the liturgy. This divine action is a matter of the configuration of the participants to Christ. Since the divine activity is mediated by the *transitus* of Christ, the entire *transitus* is present to the participants of the liturgy taking the effective form of configuration to Christ.

(3) The power of the historical mysteries is the power of God, who acts on the participants of the liturgy through the instrumentality of

[117] Ibid., 28–30.

the life of Christ. This power is found in the liturgy as the effect of the divine action. This power of the mysteries is identically the power of the principal agent, God.

(4) The life of Christ, as intelligible instrument of the divinity, cannot be understood without a complementary understanding of the nature of the principal agent. It is impossible to see how the life of Christ can be effective now apart from the divine plan of God. God eternally knows, wills, and effects through the life of Christ. Temporal and spatial relations are relevant to the occurrence of the effect of God's acting through the instrumentality of the life of Christ; they are not relevant to, and cannot alter, the intelligibility of the timeless action of God.

b/4. The Teaching of Thomas Aquinas.[118] Aquinas teaches that God is the principal efficient cause, and that the mysteries of Christ's life are the instrumental cause, of our salvation. The agent, instrument, and effect are simultaneously present. The "power" of the mysteries is identified with the agent as agent (*ST* 3, q. 56, a. 1 ad 3), and with the action of the principal agent (*ST* 1–2, q. 112, a. 1 ad 1), and is found in the effect.

Thus the timeless God, before whom all events are present (*Contra gentiles* 1.66–67; *ST* 1, q. 14, a. 13) acts on a time-conditioned world. The time-conditioned occurrences are the consequent term of God's eternally willing (*Contra gentiles* 2.35). The divine instrument of salvation is the actual earthly living of the incarnate Son. Therefore the mysteries of Christ's life are present in the liturgy.

In the economy of salvation God is the principal efficient cause; the humanity of Christ is the instrument of the divinity (*ST* 3, q. 48, a. 6). The instrumental cause is applied *(applicatur)* spiritually by faith and corporeally by sacraments (*De veritate* 27.4). Because the humanity of Christ is instrument of the divinity *ex consequente,* all actions and passions of Christ instrumentally work for human salvation *in virtute divinitatis* (*ST* 3, q. 48, a. 6). The effect follows from the instrumental cause according to the condition of the principal cause. Since God is the principal cause, and the resurrection of Christ the instrumental cause, of our resurrection, our resurrection *"sequitur"* the resurrection of Christ "according to the divine disposition at a certain time" (*In 1 Corinthians* 15, lect. 2).

[118] Ibid., 30–32.

b/5. Objections and Responses.[119] Concerning Efficient Causality and the Presence of the Mysteries of Christ, the following difficulties can be listed.

Objection 1: The idea that the human living of Christ in the past is the efficient instrumental cause of our sanctification now lacks intelligibility.

Response 1: If God intends humanity to be saved through the instrumentality of the human living of Christ as a whole, then the human living must be present to the participants of the liturgy here and now.

Objection 2: How can events of the past be present here and now?

Response 2: The past cannot be reactualized. But in the perspective of the divine plan, duration lacks meaning; every occurrence is present to the timeless God.

Objection 3: The passion of Christ must occur before its "sacramental" presence.

Response 3: In the perspective of a realist metaphysics, agent, instrument, and effect are co- existent.

Objection 4: There is a power in the liturgy that is not identifiable with the actual actions and passions of Christ.

Response 4: In a realist metaphysics the only power acknowledged is that of the principal agent, acting though the instrumental agent, both present to the effect.

Objection 5: The methods of biblical and kerygmatic theology are different from those of the systematic theologian. The resulting expressions are products of different operations. It is preferable to approach religious questions from the phenomenological and kerygmatic point of view.

Response 5: Theological work aims at a unified comprehension of the mystery of the divine and the human. There are ordered levels of understanding in theology. The terms that arise as products of conceptions may be understandable from the experiential and biblical point of view. But they lack intelligibility at the level of ultimate intelligibility. Concepts, such as "prolongation of the mysteries of the life of Christ," "the deepest reality of the passion of Christ," "enduring element of the saving act," connote empirical categories that merely present problems for further understanding.

[119] Ibid., 32–33.

b/6. Solution to the Mystery–Presence Problem.[120] The principal agent in the economy of salvation is the Father who acts through the instrumentality of the life of Christ. The presence of this instrumental cause in the liturgy stems from the ultimate lack of intelligibility in temporal succession and spatial duration. Difficulties with this point of view arise only on the experiential level, where past is past. The presence of the historical mysteries is the presence of agent to effect. Whereas the distinction between objective and subjective redemption must be maintained from the lower, experiential perspective, this distinction loses meaning from the perspective of the divine plan. In the latter case, the ultimate intelligibility is the identity between subjective and objective redemption.

The effect of the presence of the principal and instrumental cause on the participant of the liturgy is some "modification of the configuration to Christ." This does not imply that the historical actions and passions of Christ are reproduced in the one being sanctified. Rather, it means that there is a real participation in the attitude of Christ expressed in the historical actions and passions of his earthly life. The divinely intended transmission of the human attitudes of Christ, present to the participants of the liturgy because of the (instrumental) presence of the historical life itself, is common to all liturgical celebrations. However, modifications are proper to different forms of liturgy.

At the experiential and biblical level of perception, it is correct to affirm the presence of the glorified Christ in the liturgy of the Church, and to affirm that he can die no more, and that in him we are objectively redeemed. But at the higher level, the metaphysical level that demands ultimate intelligibility, it is necessary to hold that the historical mysteries themselves are the efficient cause of our salvation.

The reality of the presence of Christ, suffering and dying, in the Eucharist is intelligible because of the transcendental perspective in which removes of time and space are ultimately unintelligible. The effect in us is our participation in the sacrificial attitudes of Christ.

The reality of the presence to us of the sacrifice of Calvary in the eucharistic sacrifice is of the same order as the presence of the historical mysteries of Christ's life in the other sacraments. The added dimension lies at the level of the ritual celebration. The Eucharist presents us with a sign significance that is more palpable.

[120] Ibid., 33–35.

In each sacrament, different historical realities of the life of Christ are present as the instrumental action of the Father on us, depending on the meaning of the liturgical activity.

2. *Modifications of Casel's Theory*

a. Johannes Betz

Johannes Betz views the mystery of the eucharistic liturgy as the coming of Christ to us: offering and distributing the elements of the sacred meal. This presence of Christ suggests static nearness in space and active presence: presenting himself to us, proffering his saving action.[121] The pneumatic Christ is identified as the principal minister of this celebration of the faith of the Church. He fulfills this role by his self-offering and the distribution of self as the food of the Christian feast. This actual presence of the person of Christ as sacrificial subject is visibly represented and mediated by the reality of Church. For the assembly of the faithful that merits the title Church of Jesus Christ is the earthly mode of manifestation of the heavenly high priesthood of Christ, namely, the ecclesial body of Christ, the fundamental sacrament of redemption.

The Eucharist is principally a commemorative celebration of the work of redemption *(anamnesis)*. But this entails more than a stimulus to evoke the experience of the subjective presence of the past redemptive work of Christ in the conscience of Christians. Rather, the memorial celebration is itself the medium of the objective presence of the redemptive work.

As anamnesis, the Eucharist is the actual presence of the sacrificial deed of Jesus from Incarnation to glorification. How is this presence related to the substantial presence of Christ in the sacraments of his body and blood? According to Betz, the actual presence of the sacrificial deed of Jesus is objectivized in the somatic real presence of Jesus as victim (sacrificial object) and is rooted in it. However, the somatic real presence comes about within the horizon of and as a moment of the sacrificial event. The recognition of the priority of the sacrificial dimension of the eucharistic celebration vis-à-vis the somatic presence is indispensable as the starting point for a systematic elaboration of the theology of the Eucharist. The fact that the basic structure of the

[121] Johannes Betz, "Eucharist: E. Theological Explanations," in Karl Rahner, ed., *Sacramentum Mundi* (New York: Herder and Herder, 1968) 2.263–66, and *Encyclopedia of Theology: The Concise Sacramentum Mundi* (New York: Seabury, 1975) 455–59.

Eucharist is sacrifice–sacrament is demonstrated by Betz from the following considerations:

Acceptance by God is essential to a sacrifice. God accepts the sacrifice of the Church because it is the sacramental representation of the sacrifice of Christ. Just as God accepted Jesus' sacrifice on the cross, and as a sign of his acceptance raised Jesus' body from the dead, so he accepts the sacrificial gifts of the Church which are the sacraments of the once-for-all sacrifice of Jesus, and fills them with Jesus' life, transforming them into the bodily presence of Jesus. Thus eucharistic body and blood as signs of the redemptive death of Jesus and also of his resurrection, are revealed as sacraments of purification from sin and communication of divine life.

The consecration concerns the substance of bread and wine. According to Catholic teaching the substance of bread and wine is transformed into the bodily being of the person of Christ. The form in which Jesus' presence comes (food) shows that it is to be consumed. It is ultimately intended to serve as nourishment, not primarily as object of adoration. The consecration of the eucharistic elements serves as preparation for the sacrificial meal in which the sacrificial action of Eucharist is brought to completion. For the activity by which Christ gives himself to the communicants is a sacrificial activity.

In general the sacrificial gift stands for the giver. Its acceptance by God means the acceptance of the giver. And in the concrete, the acceptance by God consists in the self-communication of God to the person. By sharing in the sacraments of the body and blood, the believer enters into the closest union with the sacrificial action of Christ offering himself to the Father and to the Father's children; and through this movement the believer is united to the Father. The somatic real presence of Christ makes possible the deepest encounter of Christ with the Christian.

In short, Holy Communion constitutes the goal of the Christian Eucharist. Betz qualifies the reception of the sacraments of the body and blood as "the indispensable act, at least of the priest." Moreover, by this he means that it completes the symbolic meal as an essential, and not merely integrating, part of the Eucharist.[122]

What Betz has to say about the basic structure of the Eucharist represents the contemporary common approach of Catholic theology,

[122] Betz explicitly rejects the teaching of Pius XII in *Mediator Dei,* where Holy Communion is described as (only) an "integrating part" of the Eucharist (DS 3854).

namely, the presence of the historical sacrificial act of Jesus in a manner through which we can assimilate and appropriate it, namely, in a sacrificial meal. However, there still remains the problem concerning the explanation of the possibility of a past historical act becoming actually present.

The most popular solution to the problem of the liturgical presence of the reality of the historical act of the cross seems to be based on the possibility of historical saving acts becoming "eternalized," and therefore present in the risen Lord as the one who subsists in the Logos, and is glorified forever. This is the path taken by Betz. He begins by calling attention to the ecclesial dimension that comes to the foreground of the eucharistic liturgy. Christ is said to relate his saving work to the eucharistic liturgy in such a way that he makes the act of the Church into the temporal mode of appearance and presence of that historical redemptive act. At the same time the connection is actualized by the working of the Holy Spirit. When he asks how the presence of the historical past saving acts is possible, his response begins with the identification of the acting subject in the case of the incarnate Lord.

From the standpoint of dogma, the acting subject is the eternal person of the Logos, acting through his humanity. Hence Betz concludes that the saving deeds of Jesus have become in a sense "eternal. They have a perennial quality and are always simultaneous with past finite time." Besides this, Betz continues, these acts are "somehow taken up into the glorified humanity of Jesus which, according to St. Thomas (*Summa theologica*, III, 62, 5; 64, 3), remains the efficacious *instrumentum conjunctum* of the exalted Lord. Those past salvific actions, being taken up into the divine person as also into the human nature of Jesus," are present forever in the risen Lord as the one who subsists in the Logos and is now glorified forever. This consideration leads to the conclusion that the past saving acts "can now assume a new spatiotemporal presence—in and through a 'symbolic reality.' This is an entity in which another being enters and reveals itself, is and acts. The real essence of the symbol as symbol is not its own physical reality, but the manifestation and presentation of the primary reality which is symbolized in it."[123]

[123] Betz, "Eucharist: E Theological Explanations" 265/458. Cf. also Johannes Betz, "Die Gegenwart der Heilstat Christi," in Leo Scheffczyk, et al., eds., *Wahrheit und Verkündigung: Festschrift M. Schmaus* (Munich—Vienna, 1967) 2.1807–26.

b. Cesare Giraudo (H. B. Meyer; A. Darlap; E. J. Kilmartin)

In his thesis, *La struttura letteraria della preghiera eucaristica,*[124] Caesare Giraudo presented the results of a retrospective inquiry into the history of the literary form of the Eucharistic Prayer. The inquiry attempted to place in relief the common structure which is identifiable in particular "formularies" (see following paragraph). It is retrospective in that it moves from the various stages which pertain to the development of the form and which are indispensable to the task of outlining a history of the form itself. The study begins with the literary form of Nehemiah 9 seen in relation to formularies revolving around the typology of covenant. The author places in relief the fundamental bipartite structure of formulas of covenant and prayer formulas (Part One). Then the literary form of the series of Jewish berakoth is analyzed (Part Two). The investigation closes with an analysis of the literary form of selected types of primitive Christian anaphoras (Part Three). This literary study evokes a number of theological problems which are noted, but not treated *ex professo.* It is thus a work that is preliminary to further inquiry that will be more specifically theological and dogmatic.

As used by the author "literary form" refers to the literary unity derived from a proper internal structure, which is expressed by the mutual ordering of elements that compose it. Between form or formula (form of expression) and formularies (set of fixed formulas) there is a movement from the abstract to the concrete. The term structure derives from *struere* which refers to the construction of an edifice. As employed in architecture, the term structure refers to the art of connecting a series of architectonic elements. A series of structural elements constitutes what is defined as an architectonic unity.

There is an analogy between architectonic structure, the structure based on principles of architecture, and literary structure. The prayer formularies, for example, are like the framework of an edifice in which is perceptible the dynamic articulation of the elements and relative play of forces. In this work, Giraudo's intention was to provide a comprehensive perception of that framework of the elements differentiated and reciprocally ordered, namely, the literary structure.

Giraudo's more recent volume, *Eucaristia per la chiesa,* contains much of what was originally written in *La struttura . . . ,* as well as

[124] Cesare Giraudo, *La struttura letteraria della preghiera eucaristica: Saggio sulla genesi letteraria di una forma: tôdâ veterotestamentaria, berakâ giudaica, anafora cristiana,* Analecta Biblica 92 (Rome: Biblical Institute, 1981).

the content of a number of the author's articles dealing with the theological implications of that thesis.[125] It is intended to draw out, *ex professo,* the theological implications of the Eucharist which takes as point of departure the *lex orandi.* Here the eucharistic theology of the first theological millennium is contrasted with that of the second theological millennium of the Western theological tradition. The former begins with the *lex orandi,* and results in a global view of the eucharistic celebration; the latter with the *lex credendi,* and results in the highlighting of important aspects of eucharistic theology which nevertheless remain unintegrated. He concludes that a return to a theology of the Eucharist, grounded on the *lex orandi,* is required in order to complete the new theology of the Eucharist. This task is the subject of Giraudo's extensive if not exhaustive study.

Eucaristia per la chiesa—Part One

To reach the goal of a more dynamic vision of the Eucharist, a more synthetic and global understanding of the central ritual act of the Church, the focus of attention is concentrated on the Eucharistic Prayer, which tells us why we celebrate the Eucharist. Thus, the first part of *Eucaristia per la chiesa* endeavors to bring to light the dynamic of the Eucharist through the analysis of the formulas of classical Eucharistic Prayers of the East and West. The second part aims at identifying those contributions of the second "theological millennium" which still remain valid today, and to integrate them into the original dynamic and global dimension of the Eucharist which emerges from an investigation of the *lex orandi.*

The idea that the law of prayer establishes the *lex credendi* is explained in the more general discussion of the concept of *locus theologicus.* Liturgy is a font of theology; it incorporates and hands on the Catholic sense of things. In short, liturgy is the norm of prayer that establishes the norm of belief. In liturgy we actually do (i.e., live, make real) theology; and we ought to believe in accord with what we do. On the other hand, dogmas are also sources of theology. But the relation between liturgy and dogma is not explained simply by subordinating the one to the other. The norm of belief cannot be reduced to fixed formulas which cannot be varied; so too with prayer. The eucharistic font of theology has its own special contribution to make.

[125] Cesare Giraudo, *Eucaristia per la chiesa: Prospettive teologiche sull'eucaristia a partire dalla "lex orandi,"* Aloisiana 22 (Rome: Gregorian University/Brescia: Morcelliana, 1989).

However, as Giraudo observes, the scholastic theology of the Eucharist of the second theological millennium proceeded, with unrelieved narrowness, only from the law of belief to the law of prayer. Doctrinal teaching on the Eucharist was organized into a synthesis and presented as the theology of the Eucharist. Accordingly, this method abstracted from the primitive and natural context of this theology, namely, the liturgy. If the law of prayer, the Eucharistic Prayer, determines and explicates the law of belief, and if this is indeed the doing of theology, then the voice of the Church should be heard when she speaks to her divine partner in that moment of maximum relative tension of which the one and other are capable. One should be attentive to the Eucharistic Prayer through which a vision of the Eucharist emerges that is dynamic, and that is not reductively thematic and partial, but global.

Liturgical texts, in relation to action, bring the faith to expression; they are not mere instruction for believers; they contain a variety of literary genres and theologically relevant ways of speaking which cannot be reduced to one category; and they are more than just the vehicle of ideas. Liturgy offers a holistic view in which the strengths and limitations of dogmatic teaching on the subject of the sacraments can be properly evaluated.

Having thus recalled (chapter one) the methodological problem relevant to the construction of a systematic theology of the Eucharist,[126] Giraudo turns (chapter two) to the path from Scripture to liturgy which leads to an interpretation of the theological content of Genesis 2–3. This is the pericope that contains the normative account of the ideal relation between humanity and God, and the historical rupture of that relationship. Knowledge of this relationship is required because the eucharistic *lex orandi* dictates that reflection on the Eucharist be based on this narrative.[127] From there, the author proceeds (chapter three) to the stories of the once-for-all reconciliation events (or foundational events)—events anticipated by a prophetic sign which provides the normative form of the repeatable ritual expression of that reconciliation. From the analysis of these stories, found in the Old and New Testament, there emerges a striking parallel between the structure of the dynamic of the Old and New economies of salvation. Special attention is paid to the corre-

[126] *Eucaristia,* chap. 1, 1–33.
[127] Ibid., chap. 2, 36–79.

spondences between the prophetic signs of the last supper of the Israelites in Egypt and the Last Supper of Jesus with his disciples. These correspondences point both to the foundation events of covenant (the passage through the Red Sea and the passage of Jesus from death to life occurring in the near future), and to the repeatable memorial rites (the Hebrew Passover and the Christian Passover of the distant future), both of which render the participants present to the salvific efficacy of the respective foundation events.[128]

The next step (chapter four) consists in and analyzes the theological and ritual framework of the Hebrew Passover that is contemporaneous with the first-century Christian era. The presentation is made on the basis of scriptural sources as read and interpreted in the light of rabbinical sources. On the ground of convergence of testimony from the Jewish tradition, the conclusion is drawn that the Passover *haggadah,* in its essential structure and form goes back to the period anterior to the destruction of the Temple, and that "its formularies were on the lips of Jesus" at the Last Supper.

The purpose of this chapter is to provide background for the understanding of the relations between (1.) the prophetic sign of the Last Supper of Jesus, (2.) the foundation event of the Lord's death and resurrection, and (3.) the ritual celebration of the Eucharist of the Church.[129]

What the reader may have already anticipated, is made explicit in chapter five, namely, the connection between the Hebrew Passover and the Last Supper of Jesus.[130] Here the author supplies an interpretation of the Last Supper of Jesus from the background of the knowledge gained by the investigation of the Jewish Passover meal as it was celebrated at the time of Jesus. Giraudo argues on the basis of the work of Joachim Jeremias, but especially from the analysis of the accounts of the institution of the Eucharist that "the Last Supper of the Lord . . ." was "a true and proper Hebrew Paschal celebration."[131] But the analysis of the institutional words of Jesus furnish the "argument of greatest weight, which convinces us to consider the last supper of the Lord as a Paschal celebration."[132]

In chapter six the author turns to the question of how the prophetic sign, given on the eve of the foundation events of the Old and New

[128] Ibid., chap. 3, 80–117.
[129] Ibid., chap. 4, 118–61.
[130] Ibid., chap. 5, 162–275.
[131] Ibid., 163.
[132] Ibid., 186.

Covenants, intervenes in the ritual moment, not only at the level of the theological dynamic but also at the level of the literary dynamic. In order to explain the dynamic of the Eucharistic Prayer, and to see how the prophetic sign works at the literary and theological levels, the author turns to the model of Old Testament prayer known as *todâh,* or confession. The discussion of the Eucharistic Prayer shows that it has the same structure. In both cases the prophetic sign is the *locus theologicus* that supports and grounds the celebration. Moreover, in both cases the embolism can be found either in the anamnetic or in the epicletic sections of types of Jewish and Christian liturgical prayer.[133]

Noteworthy from the standpoint of Western theology of the Eucharist is the discussion of the consequences of the isolation of the Words of Institution from the anaphora. This isolation is something that occurred in and became characteristic of the splinter-tradition development of Western eucharistic theology. It supported the idea of equating the Last Supper with the first Mass and the one-sided view of apostles and successors as celebrating Mass *in persona Christi* [in contrast to *in persona ecclesiae*], that is, doing what Christ did at the Last Supper.[134]

The last chapter of the first part of the book, chapter seven, presents a theology of the Eucharist derived from the *lex orandi.*[135] As with Jewish prayers of feasts, two basic types of classical Eucharistic Prayers are found. In the one the prophetic sign (institution narrative) is placed (as an embolism) in the anamnetic section; in the other, in the epicletic section. A detailed analysis of examples of "anamnetic" and "epicletic" types is given. From this investigation it becomes clear that the Words of Institution can be understood only by seeing them as embedded in the whole Eucharistic Prayer, and by recognizing the intimate link of this narrative with other elements of the Eucharistic Prayer. The central problem of the role and meaning of the Words of Institution is resolved by showing that the embolism functions in a way that is analogous to Jewish liturgical prayer. At the end of this chapter, an excursus examines the new Eucharistic Prayers of the Roman Missal of Pope Paul VI.[136]

[133] Ibid., chap. 6, 276–381.

[134] Ibid., 336–45. This subject has been discussed elsewhere in this book, so we need not take it up again here.

[135] Ibid., 382–517.

[136] Ibid., 506–17.

According to Giraudo, the classical Eucharistic Prayers have the same basic structure: anamnesis (remembrance) and epiclesis (petition). The narrative of institution can be found in either section. The difference in structure corresponds to two types of Jewish prayer modeled on the Old Testament theology of covenant: the relationship which Yahweh has established with his people as a result of their accepting covenant partnership and its consequences. The Eucharistic Prayers relate especially to those Jewish prayers which contain a reference to some specific past saving act of God that is relevant to the present situation, or include a scriptural text in which God's promise of fidelity takes the form of a direct address. Examples of the latter usage are found in prayers associated with special feasts understood as instituted by Yahweh to be the occasion of a special bestowal of blessings.

In the "anamnetic type" of Eucharistic Prayer (e.g., Chrysostom, Byz) the anamnesis contains the narrative of institution of the Eucharist. Thus it already takes up the command: Do this in remembrance of me. This remembrance is continued in the anamnesis-offering prayer where the community explicitly expresses its obedience in a prayer that recalls the whole Christ-event. The subsequent epiclesis of the coming of the Holy Spirit is a petition for the acceptance of the community's obedience which results in the change of the gifts of bread and wine, symbols of the community's self-offering, and the sanctification of the communicants of the body and blood of Christ. Intercessions for others follow as an extension of the epiclesis.

In the "epicletic type" (Alexandrian Mark; Third Eucharistic Prayer of the Sacramentary of Paul VI; the old Roman Canon [which does not explicitly mention the Holy Spirit in either epiclesis]), the anamnesis is interrupted by the epiclesis for the coming of the Spirit to sanctify the gifts. In turn this epiclesis is interrupted by the resumption of the anamnesis through the recitation of the narrative of institution of the Eucharist and its continuance in the anamnesis-offering prayer. Then the epiclesis for the coming of the Holy Spirit to sanctify the communicants is taken up. Intercessions for others follows as an extension of the epiclesis.

b/1. Eastern Antiochene Eucharistic Prayer Type. Giraudo then shows how the Eastern Antiochene type (Chrysostom, Byzantine)—with its structural elements of (1) anamnesis, (2) institution narrative, (3) anamnesis-offering prayer, (4) epiclesis, (5) intercessions—can serve as an example of the theological outlook common to Eucharistic Prayers which contain a specific reference to the role of the Holy Spirit.[137]

(1) *Anamnesis*. The introductory prayer of pure praise of the Holy Trinity, Father, Son and Holy Spirit is followed by the recall of the mighty works of God in creation and redemption through Christ in the power of the Holy Spirit. A special mention of the institution of the Eucharist as an event of salvation history is included by the insertion of a . . .

(2) . . . version of the *Narrative of Institution of the Eucharist,* based on the New Testament accounts. It is an object of thankful remembrance and so sets the tone for the complete fulfillment of the command of remembrance: Do this in my memorial. The narrative of institution is the theological center of the Eucharistic Prayer. It is the grounds for the shape of the celebration; the grounds for the shape of meaning of the celebration: It explains why the anamnesis-offering is made; why the epiclesis for the sanctification of the bread and wine and the sanctification of the communicants occurs.

The narrative of institution in this liturgical context, also takes on the function of intercessory prayer. It has the trait of appeal to the Father to respond to what he established through Jesus Christ as a ritual way of participation in the mystery of Jesus' once-for-all Passover from suffering to glory. In a word, it has a role analogous to that of the recall of the institutional act of Yahweh which founded special feasts of the people of the former covenant, and which served to remind Yahweh of his institutional act and its purpose: the bestowal of his blessings on his people.

(3) *Anamnesis-Offering Prayer.* This prayer explicitly formulates the community's intention to obey the institutional command: "Do this in my memorial." The anaphora of Chrysostom (Byzantine) reads: "Remembering this saving commandment and all the things that were done for us . . . offering you your own from your own in all and through all, we hymn you, we offer you also this reasonable and bloodless service . . ."

With the words "recalling" the saving work of Christ, "we offer," the community presents bread and wine designated (implicitly) as the symbolic expression of the assembly's self-offering made in union with the self-offering of Christ himself, which he made at the Last

[137] Ibid., 443–52.

Supper in the rite of the bread and cup, and historically fulfilled in the death of the cross.

(4) *Epiclesis for the Sending of the Spirit.* The Father is petitioned to send the Holy Spirit to sanctify the gifts of the Church and to sanctify those who participate in the sanctified gifts. The anaphora of Chrysostom reads:

"We offer you this reasonable and bloodless service, and we beseech . . . you, send down your Holy Spirit on us and on these gifts set forth; and make this bread the precious body of your Christ and that which is in the cup the precious blood of your Christ."[138]

The order of the sanctification of the communicants and sanctification of the gifts can be reversed, as in an Alexandrian type, the Der-Balizeh papyrus. In this latter type, the epiclesis for sanctification of the elements by the Spirit comes before the narrative of institution, and the petition for the sanctification of the communicants comes after the narrative. *But the gifts sanctified are always ordered to the sanctification of the communicants.* From this perspective it is understandable why the epiclesis for the sanctification of the communicants cannot be placed before the narrative of institution and the anamnesis-offering prayer; and it is also understandable why the order of the twofold epiclesis after the anamnesis frequently petitions for the sanctification of the communicants and then for the sanctification of the gifts which are ordered to the sanctification of the communicants.

The *epiclesis for the sanctification of the participants* represents a second theological center (after the narrative of institution) of the Eucharistic Prayer. The petition that the faithful be sanctified through Holy Communion attains at the level of prayer what is intended through the reception of the sacraments of Christ's body and blood by faith, namely: (1) communion with the Lord, (2) unity among the members of the Church, (3) anticipation of the fulfillment of the end-time through the food and drink of immortality.

(5) *Intercessions.* The intercessions for Church, world, and particular persons are an extension of the epiclesis. As a petition for the participation of all humanity in the salvation accomplished by Christ, they are the expression of the Church's love for the Father's children.

[138] Text (with commentary) in R.C.D. Jasper and G. J. Cuming, eds., *Prayers of the Eucharist: Early and Reformed*, 3rd ed. (Collegeville: The Liturgical Press, 1990) 133.

Conclusion. The literary structure of the Eucharistic Prayer shows that it is a unified prayer directed to the Father as the source of all, and to the Son and Holy Spirit. It mirrors the dynamic relation of the partners of the new covenant in the history of salvation realized fully through Christ in the power of the Spirit. The thankful recognition of the Father's action in Christ (anamnesis) is followed by the petition that the continuing fidelity of the Father to his people be expressed and realized through the sanctifying action of the Holy Spirit by which the communicants are brought to Christ (epiclesis for sanctification of communicants) and by which Christ is brought to the communicants (epiclesis for sanctification of the bread and wine). The extension of the epiclesis in the intercessions is the expression of the Church's desire that all humanity be brought within the sphere of the new covenant people. The commitment of the Church to the new covenant is expressed explicitly in the anamnesis-offering prayer.

The *transitus* of the liturgical community to the Father is expressed liturgically in the Eucharistic Prayer. The *transitus* of Christ himself is recalled but is not represented objectively and sacramentally to the assembly in the Eucharistic Prayer. For the Eucharistic Prayer is prayer of the Church. Thus the axiom remains intact: Sacramental celebrations are acts of the Church in which the Church manifests and realizes itself as body of Christ, of which Christ is the head and in which the Holy Spirit is the mediation of the presence of Christ to the Church and the Church to Christ.

The response to the prayer of the Church is represented sacramentally in the sacraments of the body and blood of Christ. Holy Communion enables sacramental communion with Christ as the one who gives himself to the Father for humanity. He gives himself as the "man for others" to draw the believers into personal communion with himself and so into communion with the Father. He does this through the sending of the Spirit as his Spirit to enable the communicants to share in his sentiments of self-offering. In the power of the Holy Spirit the sacramental communion with Christ becomes the medium of spiritual, personal communion with the risen Lord.

In the eucharistic celebration, the Holy Spirit is manifested both as the source of the faith in which the Eucharistic Prayer was formulated as memorial of the death of the Lord, and the source of the response of the assembly to the content of this performative form of the act of faith. The Holy Spirit "anoints" the prayer of the Church and "anoints" the participants of the liturgy so that, through the medium of the prayer, Christ comes to the assembly and the assembly to Christ. The Holy Spirit is also the source of the sanctification of the eucharistic gifts of the Church and of the sanctification of the communicants of the sacraments of Christ's body and blood. In this way also the Spirit is seen as the one who brings Christ to the communicants and the communicants to Christ in such a way that spiritual unity between Christ and the communicants, and between the communicants themselves, is deepened.

b/2. Theological Consequences. The foregoing analysis of the Antiochene Eucharistic Prayer, which despite minor differences corresponds to other classical Eucharistic Prayers, shows that the content is a formulation of the covenant response of the liturgical assembly to the Father's fidelity to his covenant with humanity fulfilled in the special missions of the Son and Holy Spirit. The response corresponds to the personal response of faith of the incarnate Son in his humanity for what the Father had done in him for the salvation of the world. It contains the memorial of the past saving acts of the Father in salvation history, culminating in the Christ-event; commitment to the covenant relationship; petition for the divine help to maintain the covenant relation; petition for the salvation of the world.

b/3. Function of Ritual Activity. As performative form of the activity of faith of the eucharistic community, the ritual act serves as medium through which the faithful are rendered present in memory to the self-offering of the Son of God in his humanity, which culminated in his Passover from suffering to glory. However, the community is rendered present under the formality, not of passive spectators, but of active participants in Jesus' uniquely acceptable response to what the Father has done in him for the salvation of the world. And this means that responding in faith to the mystery of God in Christ, the community is not only related to Christ's self-offering, but also that the actively present Christ relates his once-for-all self-offering to that of the community of faith. This reciprocal personal relation is grounded on the work of the Holy Spirit who both brings Christ to the faithful and the faithful to Christ.

b/4. Essence of Active Participation. The active participation of the assembly is realized by the individual believer's degree of agreement with the religious attitudes expressed verbally and gesturally in the ritual act, and which mirror the sacrificial attitudes of Jesus expressed at the Last Supper and in the event of his historical death of the cross.

Eucaristia per la chiesa—Part Two

In the second part of his study,[139] Giraudo takes up the subject of the characteristic eucharistic theology of the Western tradition which developed during the reflection of the second "theological millennium." His intention is to identify what elements are essential for the understanding of the Eucharist of the pre- and post-Tridentine periods, to evaluate them and, finally, to offer some insights concerning the proper approach to the construction of a renewed eucharistic theology that suits the third "theological millennium."

The first part of Giraudo's chapter eight[140] reviews the pre-Tridentine problematic and the related teaching of the Council of Trent. This entails a review of the controversy over the sacrament of the "real presence" and its pastoral consequences (eucharistic devotion). The second part of the chapter[141] treats the speculative reduction of the Mass to the consecration of the gifts. Here it is shown that theologians and liturgists of the second millennium had no grasp of the literary structure and theological dynamic of the Eucharistic Prayer. They reduced the matter to a "central space" with the result that the narrative of the institution of the Eucharist was poised in the air without access to the other elements of the structure.

Chapter nine[142] provides an analysis of the post-Tridentine problematic from the background of Trent's teaching about the sacrificial nature of the Eucharist. The analysis of Trent's Sessions 13 (1551) and 22 (1562) shows that the council fathers were concerned with affirming the immediate and substantial relation of the Mass to Calvary, with the consequence that the Mass has a sacrificial character. The council was not able to offer a theological explanation for its solemn definition that the Mass is a sacrifice. But since the sixteenth century theologians have attempted to supply this need. Chapter ten completes the study with a synthesis and pastoral conclusions.[143]

[139] Ibid., chaps. 8–10, 519–637.
[140] Ibid., 520–40.
[141] Ibid., 540–56.
[142] Ibid., 557–91.
[143] Ibid., 594–637.

Summary

The main points of Giraudo's contribution can be quickly summarized as follows:

[1] The first theological millennium held the law of prayer to be normative for the law of belief. In the second millennium the law of belief took pride of place.

[2] The reintegration of the law of belief into the law of prayer requires restoring the account of institution of the Eucharist into the literary-theological movement of the whole Eucharistic Prayer.

[3] The narrative of institution of the Eucharist together with the anamnesis-offering prayer form a unit. The anamnesis states what the Church is doing in view of the narrative of institution: making memorial of the death and resurrection through the offering of eucharistic gifts.

[4] The second unity, the epiclesis-intercessions, is linked to the first. Here the reason is given why the Church acts, namely, in view of the transformation of the elements and the consequent transformation of the communicants. The intercessions enlarge on the petition for the transformation of the gathered Church, to that of the universal Church.

[5] The Eucharistic Prayer is a liturgical reality and so bearer of theology. The typical configuration is inherited from Old Testament-Jewish liturgical prayer: discourse on the relation between two partners of a covenant. The attitude of the human partners is that of confession of the fidelity of God and confession of the human condition of sinfulness. The ultimate goal is confession of the Lord who alone is able to re-establish the sinner in covenantal relationship.

[6] The law of prayer affords a global and dynamic vision of the ecclesiastical mystery which requires seeing the key to the ultimate reading of the eucharistic celebration in the epiclesis for the transformation of the participants.

As ordered to the Father, the dynamic of the celebration turns between the ritual memorial of the body of Christ given for the remission of sins (narrative-anamnesis) and the petition that the body of the Church be built up through the remission of sins. Corresponding to the *todâh,* the Eucharistic Prayer is a revelation of the relational otherness of two partners. To confess sin in the content of the covenant discourse is to recall to God his great works and to proclaim to us his constant fidelity. Focusing on God and human beings at the same time, the Eucharistic Prayer creates a strong vertical tension, which, however, will not be authentic if it lacks verification in daily life. The vertical and horizontal dimensions so interpenetrate one another in the Eucharistic Prayers that the one is not given without the other.

[7] Recovering the unity of the eucharistic mystery requires the recovery of the concept of sacrament as understood in the law of prayer. In the perspective of the law of prayer the Mass is understood as the sacrament of the sacrifice of the cross through the ritual renewal of the sign of bread and cup which Jesus gave at the Last Supper for that purpose.

To recover the dynamic dimension inherent in the concept of sacrament, and thus move to a global vision of the Eucharist, the notion of representation is useful. There is a profound relation between the institution of the Eucharist, the sacrifice of the cross, and the Mass. Giraudo insists that the idea of representation of a saving event through ritual memorial is not specific to one or other religion. It was known to Israel and was applicable to the Hebrew Passover (contra Casel). However, Giraudo records with approval the warning of Gamaliel that the idea of representation takes the direction of representing the liturgical participants to the foundation event, not vice versa.

Giraudo employs the notion of *ripresentazione misterica,* or sacramental representation *(ripresentazione sacramentale)* in line with O. Casel, but with a new orientation. He speaks of the saving event "which at the level of space-time is passed—but which now rises to *presenzialità eterna*—and projects us eschatologically toward the fulfillment of the future kingdom." Thus, according to him, the categories of "profane history," where past is not present and the present is not the future, are literally transcended. The distinction is made between "profane historiography," a "physical science," and "salvation history" which is "meta-physical" *(meta-fiscia).*[144] Regarding this theme he quotes Casel: "On this subject Dom Vonier, in direct dependence on Saint Thomas Aquinas, has reason to say that the laws of space and time do not hold for the sacramental world."[145]

Giraudo formulates his understanding of the relationship of the eucharistic sacrifice to the historical sacrifice of Christ in this way: The

[144] Ibid., 615.

[145] Ibid., 615, n. 53.

sacrificial character of the Eucharist is grounded on the representation of the assembled community to the historical sacrifice of the cross, that is, "to the unique event of the death-resurrection of Jesus."[146]

What is presumed in the average modern Catholic view, insofar as it employs the basic insight of Casel, is the idea that the foundational event of the death-resurrection has, in some sense, taken on a supratemporal quality. Therefore it can be rendered present through the memorial of the death of the Lord, that is, obtain a sacramental objective presence in and through the visible rite: a visible presence to the liturgical assembly. Giraudo agrees with Casel that the historical saving work of Christ is the foundational event of the new covenant which, as foundation event, transcends history and so is accessible to each moment of the history of salvation.

[8] The question of what effects the *ripresentazione misterica* is answered as follows:

". . . it is the sacramental sign, or rather it is the salvific dynamic that underlies it; better still, it is God who represents us to the *salutaris virtus* of the *sacrificio ephapax* in the mediation of the sacramental sign. The subject passively considered, that is represented, is the assembled Church which celebrates by the 'ministry of priests.'"[147]

The actualization of the foundation event is attributed by him to the activity of the life of faith which grasps the possibility given in the obedient accomplishment of the prophetic sign instituted at the Last Supper. That prophetic sign pointed to the near future of the historical event of the death of the cross, and also to the distant future where it would serve as the ritual-cultic means of participation in the foundational event. Through this ritual activity the liturgical assembly is presented to the foundational event, and so enabled to bind itself by faith to the salvific efficacy of the foundational event.

Both the average Catholic view and that of Giraudo agree on a key concept, namely, that the meaning of the foundational event is so bound to the historical event itself that the meaning, which also transcends history, implies a supratemporal quality of the historical event. In virtue of this quality some element of the historical saving act of Christ, the kernel, becomes perennial in the glorified Christ and so is capable of being represented in the eucharistic celebration.

[146] Ibid., 616, n. 54.
[147] Ibid., 620, n. 68.

The average Catholic position views the representation as taking place in and through the ritual action to the Church in an objective way. Giraudo, on the other hand, argues that the saving act is made accessible in virtue of the representation of the community to it through the ritual act of the Church.

Hence it is not the event of the death-resurrection of Jesus that communicates with us. Rather, we communicate in the unique event through participation in the bread and cup, or are made to communicate. The sacrifice of the cross is once-for-all; the prophetic sign of the Last Supper is once-for-all. The sacramental repetition has its active subject: God who represents us to the saving power of the once-for-all sacrifice in the mediation of the sacramental sign. The passive subject, that which is represented, is the gathered Church, which celebrates by the ministry of the priest.

[9] The dynamic understanding of the permanent real presence. The sacramental presence is ordered to Communion. The sacramental Communion must be seen in the light of the fact that this is our sacramental representation to the death-resurrection of Jesus. The preferential reference to the dynamic dimension of the real presence is the epiclesis. With this the *law of prayer* gathers the eucharistic mystery into the trinitarian action: an action which from the sphere of the eternal is extended toward our "now," as at the petition the Father sends the Spirit to bring to fullness the transformation of the body in virtue of which we are to be eschatologically transformed.

[10] Giraudo concludes by identifying the single most significant modern contribution to the renewal of eucharistic theology of the Latin Church. It is the recovery of the pneumatological dimension of the eucharistic epiclesis of sanctification. In his opinion the insertion of a liturgical epiclesis for the transformation of the oblation which *follows the narrative of institution* of the Eucharist is recommended in order to make further progress. In this regard the suggestion is made that the Latin Church adopt anaphoras from the East, or model some new Eucharistic Prayers after the Eastern structure.[148] In any case Giraudo advises that Catholic theology should not be content with the

[148] [This suggestion is the special topic of a recent article by Giraudo: "Anafore d'Oriente per le Chiese d'Occidente," in Robert F. Taft, ed., *The Christian East, Its Institutions & Its Thought, A Critical Reflection: Papers of the International Scholarly Congress for the 75th Anniversary of the Pontifical Oriental Institute, Rome, 30 May–5 June 1993* (Rome: Pontificio Istituto Orientale, 1996) 339–51—RJD.]

narrow splinter-theology of the Eucharist that has dominated the Latin Church since the High Middle Ages. Above all, Catholics should abandon the "chronometrical concept" of the mystery of transubstantiation.

c. Hans Bernhard Meyer

H. B. Meyer has reported favorably on the work of Giraudo.[149] In his 1989 book *Eucharistie,*[150] he situates the theory of mystery presence of the Italian theologian in the context of the notion of memorial, a basic category of the biblical understanding of worship. The notion of memorial conveys the idea that since God and his people remember one another, they represent themselves to one another, and give themselves a share in one another. The *Christusanamnesis,* which happens in the word of preaching and in the petition for its spirit-worked actualization in the liturgical worship of the Christian assembly, is witnessed in an especially clear way in the celebration of the Eucharist.

Meyer underscores the fact that the memorial, as effective word of preaching and word of prayer, is constitutive for the sacramental sign *(Realsymbol),* in which Christ represents himself and his saving work through the working of the Holy Spirit to his community and in which the community is present to God and his saving activity through Christ in the Holy Spirit. Meyer recalls Johannes Betz's understanding of the liturgical-real symbolic shape of mediation of this representation. Betz labels it the commemorative actual presence of the saving acts and—insofar as Christ is principal agent in the worship of the Church—a personal actual presence.[151] Liturgically, it is constituted as an anamnetic-epicletic dialogue which represents to us the Lord and his saving act which, as action proper to the Eucharist, is bound to the elements of the meal, the bread and wine, the eating of which mediates the communion with the substantially present Lord and with his body, the Church.

Meyer concludes that from the point of view and conceptualization of Betz, developed by Lothar Lies, among others,[152] it is the anamnesis

[149] Hans Bernhard Meyer, "Odo Casels Idee der Mysteriengegenwart in neuer Sicht," *Archiv für Liturgiewissenschaft* 28 (1986) 388–95.

[150] Hans Bernhard Meyer, *Eucharistie: Geschichte, Theologie, Pastoral. Gottesdienst der Kirche,* Handbuch der Liturgiewissenschaft, Teil 4 (Regensburg: Pustet, 1989) 448–49.

[151] Ibid., 449.

[152] Lothar Lies, "Verbalpräsenz–Aktualpräsenz–Realpräsenz: Versuch einer systematischen Begriffsbestimmung," in Lothar Lies, ed., *Praesentia Christi.* Festschrift Johannes Betz zum 70. Geburtstag (Düsseldorf: Patmos, 1984) 79–100.

of the person and saving work of Christ happening in the word-sign action which spans the distance from the Passover of the Lord to the liturgical celebration. In the dynamic of the liturgy and the sacraments, this anamnesis of the person and saving work of Christ represents Christ and his saving work in the mode of commemorative and personal actual presence. In the case of the Eucharist, this anamnesis also represents Christ and his work in the mode of his substantial (somatic) real presence which is grounded in this commemorative and personal actual presence. However, Meyer raises the question whether one might be more advised to draw on another way of thinking with Cesare Giraudo. Meyer thus suggests that it would be more accurate to say that the liturgical activity does not "render present Christ and his saving work." In other words, we are the ones who "ought to enter newly into the presence of his person and saving work in the medium of the ritual cultic activity."

Chapter Eleven

A Systematic Theology of Eucharistic Sacrifice

This chapter provides a systematic outline of the theology of eucharistic sacrifice which attempts to integrate the more recent contributions of Catholic theologians into an authentic whole. In the interest of aiding the reader to make a more informed judgment about the orientation of our work and its resulting systematic presentation of the mystery of eucharistic worship, we will begin with a presentation and explanation of our method.

I. METHODOLOGICAL ACCESS TO THE THEOLOGY OF THE EUCHARIST[1]

The proper methodical access to the eucharistic theology of a particular liturgical tradition begins by identifying its shape of meaning and shape of celebration. The phrase *shape of meaning* signifies the form of accomplishment which gives to the celebration its meaning and through which its individual aspects obtain their theological significance, are linked to one another, and are integrated into the whole. Here the term *shape* of meaning refers to the formal structure of the celebration as a whole as well as the individual aspects which are constitutive of it and integrated into it. The shape of *meaning* determines the theological significance of the Eucharist as a whole as well as its individual aspects. In the concrete, the shape of meaning of the Eucharist is the ritual representation of the covenant relation between God and his people. Consequently, it is identified as an efficacious event of communication of the grace of the covenant.

[1] On this subject, cf. Hans Bernard Meyer, *Eucharistie: Geschichte, Theologie, Pastoral. Gottesdienst der Kirche,* Handbuch der Liturgiewissenschaft, Teil 4 (Regensbrug: Pustet, 1989) 441–60.

The phrase *shape of the celebration* refers to the material expression of the formal shape of meaning. To this belongs all which is constitutive for the symbolic actions of the celebration: words, gestures, elements and actions, personal and social factors, and the ordering of the whole celebration. The identification of the shape of meaning originates from the observation of the celebration itself. The data of the history of the practice and theology of the Eucharist is made use of insofar as it interprets the celebration and insofar as this interpretation finds its precipitate in eucharistic liturgies (specifically, the classical Eucharistic Prayers of East and West in their accompanying ritual).

The essential individual aspects of the shape of meaning of the Eucharist can be described as follows. In general, they are symbolic acts which cause by signifying: (1) they are instituted by God and supplied with the promise of God's saving actions; (2) they involve the mutual remembrance of God and his people by which they are present to one another and share in a holy partnership; and (3) they possess a sacrificial character and meal character which are, just as is the substantial real presence of Christ, specific eucharistic aspects.

The meal character is bound to the sacrificial character of the eucharistic celebration. Insofar as Jesus instituted the memorial of his self-offering in the symbolic actions of the Last Supper, the sacrificial and meal aspects are inseparable from one another. A sacrificial event is constituted in the form of a ritual meal process. This means that the meal character belongs to the shape of the celebration, because the meal has to do with the *modus quo,* not the *id quod* of the celebration. Insofar as the meal contains formal elements of meaning, these elements are already part of the essential traits of sacrifice and communion.

The individual aspects of the shape of meaning are ordered to one goal: communion in the Holy Spirit with Christ and through him with the Father, but also communion with the body of Christ in the unity of the Holy Spirit (that is, in and with the Church). This means that the Eucharistic Prayer, as performative form of the eucharistic faith of the Church, articulates a theology of covenant modeled on that of the old covenant established and actualized between Yahweh and his people. However, this theology is enfleshed with the content of the new covenant, namely, the mystery of the economy of the triune God in relation to the new people of God, the social body of which the crucified and risen Lord is head.

The trinitarian and ecclesiastical aspects of the Eucharist are expressed in the accounts of institution (Paul/Luke) which are liturgically integrated into the early Eucharistic Prayers. They are witnessed explicitly in the epiclesis, or petition calling on the Father to send the Spirit to effect the transformation of the eucharistic gifts of bread and wine which, in turn, is linked to the petition for the transformation of those who partake of the sacraments of the body and blood of Christ. The first petition looks to the existence of the sacraments of Christ's body and blood; the second petition gives the reason for the first petition, namely, that the eucharistic body of Christ might be the sacramental means of building up the body of Christ, the Church, through the sanctification it affords to the individual believing communicant.

The sacramental sign of the Spirit-worked communion with Christ and with the members of his body is the epicletic word of prayer and the reception of Communion. In this twofold aspect the celebration reaches its high point: the newly realized covenant with God in the Church filled with the Spirit of Christ and united through him under the sacramental signs with and in Christ.

The comprehensive shape of meaning of the Eucharist reflects the fact that the Eucharist constitutes the central self-realization of the Church of Jesus Christ that occurs at the level of liturgical action. For this celebration has a katabatic-anabatic basic structure in and through which God and people are bound together. This binding happens through the actualization of the covenant relationship in which the (katabatic) self-gift of the Father through Christ in the Holy Spirit to human beings finds the faith response of the (anabatic) self-gift of human beings through Christ in the Holy Spirit to the Father.

H. B. Meyer suggests that the formal liturgical-theological shape of meaning, namely, the symbolic form of accomplishment of the eucharistic celebration, can be described by the concept "blessing-commemoration."[2] In the New Testament *eulogia* stands for a benevolent action by which God bestows his grace on humankind or by which humankind acknowledges the goodness of God. Blessing, in other words, can refer to the holy self-mediation of God or to the praise of God. The blessing-activity is actualized verbally and/or gesturally, as well as by bestowal of a gift, or by any combination of these three. The use of this concept "blessing-commemoration" is especially fitting for the Eucharist because the element of gift contained in the concept *eulogia* is open to a specific eucharistic interpretation. The mutual giving and receiving of the gift of the bread and wine expresses the self-offering of God

[2] Ibid., esp. 456–57.

in Jesus Christ to humanity, effected through the Holy Spirit, sanctifying individuals and establishing fellowship of the believers in the Lord, and also the self-offering of individuals to God as well as that of the liturgical community united to Christ through the Holy Spirit.

The integration of the individual aspects into the blessing-memorial form of celebration can be formulated in the following way. The Eucharist is a symbolic sign action as blessing-commemoration. The reciprocal blessing-commemoration shows it is of divine institution. The blessing of God (objective genitive) includes the memorial of God's saving work. On the other hand, the liturgical assembly obtains access to God's saving work in the ritual because of enablement through divine institution. Since Christian faithful enter through this blessing-memorial into the event of the self-gift of God to the world and of the world to the Father, which Christ accomplished in his Passover, the celebration includes the sacrificial aspect (sacrifice of Christ and Church). Also it embraces the communion character. For the covenant, the communion between God and creatures, is an aspect of the katabatic-anabatic action.

The shape of the celebration consists in this: The community assembled in the name of Jesus proclaims the mystery of the Passover of the new dispensation. The prayer of praise and petition over the meal elements: (1) recalls Jesus Christ and his saving work; (2) petitions for communion with the Lord's body: head and members; and (3) obtains it in the sharing of the sacraments of the body and blood of the Lord. The individual elements of the shape of the celebration are: (1) the being assembled of the community; (2) the presidency of ordained ministry as expression of the soteriological dimension *(in persona Christi)* and the ecclesiological aspect *(in persona ecclesiae)*; (3) preaching and commemoration; (4) petition; (5) offering and receiving gifts of the meal.

A. STARTING POINT FOR A SYSTEMATIC EXPOSITION OF EUCHARISTIC SACRIFICE

Attaining the goal of a more dynamic vision of the Eucharist, of a more synthetic and global understanding of the central ritual act of the Church, requires an analysis of the classical Eucharistic Prayers of the patristic age which tell us why we celebrate the Eucharist. These Eucharistic Prayers convey the idea that the specific dynamic of the ritual reconciliation is the interaction between two bodies: the ecclesial and sacramental. This implies that the transformation of the eucharistic elements is subordinated to the eschatological transformation, that is, to the reconciliation of all those who participate in the eucharistic communion.

1. *From the Literary-Theological Analysis of the Eucharistic Prayer to the Systematic Theology of Eucharistic Sacrifice*

With the first step completed, that is, the analysis of the formulas of the classical Eucharistic Prayers of the East and West, the second step amounts to an assessment of those contributions of the second "theological millennium" which remain valid today. Then, in the third step, the dogmatic data of the Western Catholic tradition, which received its fullest official expression in the Council of Trent, is integrated into the original dynamic and global dimension of the Eucharist which has emerged from an investigation of the *lex orandi.*

The most fruitful approach to the problem allows the classical Eucharistic Prayers to serve as guides. This is to give full weight to the *lex orandi:* that which is prayed everywhere, always, and by all. To do this properly, however, requires the use of a complex methodology involving biblical, liturgical, and dogmatic exegesis. Of the three steps outlined in the paragraph above, the first is relatively easy. So also is the second step, the enumeration of the dogmatic data that must be integrated into the comprehensive understanding of the Eucharist such as it is expressed in and through the eucharistic symbolic language, both verbal and gestural. The main difficulty and real challenge, however, comes with the third step: the attempt to integrate the dogmatic data into the comprehensive perception of the Eucharist that impregnates and structures the eucharistic faith and practice of an ecclesial tradition.

a. *Relation of the Law of Prayer to the Law of Belief*[3]

The history of the theology of the Eucharist shows that the law of prayer was the starting point for theological reflection during the first theological millennium. This should come as no surprise. For only after knowledge is acquired through observation of what most directly manifests this reality of the Christian economy of salvation does the possibility present itself of gaining new knowledge through

[3] In this section we follow the more detailed treatment of the topic in Cesare Giraudo, *Eucaristia per la chiesa: Prospettive theologiche sull'eucaristia a partire dalla "lex orandi,"* Aloisiana 22 (Rome: Gregorian University/Brescia: Morcelliana, 1989) 14–26.

relating the subject under investigation to other aspects of the same economy. This historical observation implies a certain preference for the law of prayer vis-à-vis the law of belief.

On this subject, the witness of the *Indiculus de gratia* of Prosper of Aquitaine, secretary of Leo I around the year 435, is instructive. In chapter 8 of this work,[4] Prosper refutes the Semi-Pelagians by appealing to the witness of tradition regarding the necessity of grace for the first step toward sanctification. Then he calls for a consideration of the witness to the necessity of grace conveyed by the ritual orations which petition for all those in need of grace from "evil people" to catechumens: "Let us consider the rites of the priestly supplication in order that *(ut)* the law of prayer establish the law of belief."

Prosper invites the reader to proceed to the determination of the *lex credendi* from a consideration of the law of supplication. Evidently he presupposes that the Semi-Pelagians recognize the law of prayer of supplication, namely, that all pray in the same way. They should draw from this the law of belief about the necessity of grace. However, Prosper implies a universal axiom to which the particular application is subjected. The matter, can be formulated thus:

"The law of prayer determines the law of belief. *Atqui,* We pray that grace be granted to 'evil people.' Ergo, we ought to believe that 'evil people' need and are granted grace that is necessary for conversion."[5]

In his work *De vocatione omnium gentium,* Prosper refers to 1 Timothy 2:1 and concludes: It is the *lex supplicationis* that the Church observes. The divine command is a law of supplication, a *lex data* to which corresponds the *lex recepta* by the whole Church. The law of supplication as received *(lex supplicationis recepta)* issues in the concrete supplications made by the Church to God. This law of supplication is understood to embrace three levels: (1.) the divine command given to the Church; (2.) the reception by the Church in obedience and handed on in practice; (3.) the concrete supplications that the Church makes to God in ritual prayer.[6] In the *Indiculus de gratia* Prosper refers

[4] The entire chapter is reproduced in DS 246.

[5] See Giraudo, *Eucaristia per la chiesa,* 18.

[6] Prosper of Aquitaine, *De vocatione omnium gentium* 1.12 (PL 51.663D–665A) [also preserved as *De vocatione gentium* 2.4, spuriously attributed to Ambrose (PL 17. 1086B–1088A)]; Eng. trans.: P. de Letter, *St. Prosper of Aquitaine: The Call of the Nations,* Ancient Christian Writers 14 (Westminster, Md.: Newman/London: Longmans, Green and Co., 1952) 51–53. See Giraudo, *Eucaristia per la chiesa,* 18–19.

only to the third of these levels.[7] The argument of this work is founded on the major premise having universal value. The criterion of the *lex orandi* is its universality: what is prayed everywhere, always, and by all.

In short, the statement "Let us consider the rites of priestly supplication in order that the law of prayer establish the law of belief," comes to this: "Let us consider the rites of priestly supplication in order that the *lex orandi* (universal), as particularized in the prayer for grace for evil people (done universally), establish the *lex credendi* (universal), as particularized in the prayer for conversion of evil people."

As Prosper understood the matter, the term *locus theologicus* would be apt to describe liturgy. Especially today this theme is finally receiving the attention it deserves. As a font of theology, liturgy incorporates and hands on the Catholic sense of things. But it is more than a locus of support of a way of conceiving the data of faith. As in the case of dogmas, which are another *locus theologicus,* one must think about identity of content and variability, or richness of formulation of expression of the life of faith. Both liturgical texts and dogmas are expressed in fixed formulas which maintain their connection with specific historical contexts and cultures. They can change in their materiality and yet serve to express the same faith. Nevertheless, in the case of liturgy and dogmas there is continual need of verification of the criteria for guaranteeing that there be no deviation of the formulation from the content.

It is correct to affirm that liturgy is the norm of prayer that establishes the norm of belief. In liturgy we "do" theology, and we ought to believe in accord with what we do. But what liturgy qualifies as norm of prayer? Must this be discovered by the application of the law of belief? What is the connection between the law of belief and the law of prayer? In other words, one must challenge the legitimacy of the claim—made by most Western theology of the second millennium—that, ultimately, it is dogma that establishes the norm of prayer.

Dogma is a *locus theologicus,* as is liturgy. But the relation between liturgy and dogma cannot be simply described in terms of a relationship of dependency. Dogma serves to confirm what is witnessed by liturgy. But the witness of liturgy *per se* does not derive from dogmatic formulas. *Per accidens,* of course, there are many examples of the insertion of dogmatic formulas into classical Eucharistic Prayers.

[7] Giraudo, *Eucaristia per la chiesa,* 19–20.

The question of the relationship between the law of prayer and the law of belief has been raised especially in this century within Catholic theological circles. Given the fact that during the second theological millennium the constructive theology of liturgy and, in particular of the seven sacraments, took as starting point the law of belief, it is not surprising that the relationship between the law of prayer and law of belief was expressed in terms of a subordination of the law of prayer to the law of belief. Nowadays, however, it is generally recognized that the two sources of theology provide complementary material. The recognition of this fact sheds light on the weakness of a constructive theology of the Eucharist that is content with first organizing systematically the doctrinal teaching on this subject, and only then introducing the witness of the law of prayer, and indeed only insofar as it supports its already established synthesis.

This traditional dogmatic method that has dominated in the West abstracts from the primitive and natural context of the theology of the liturgy. If the *law of prayer,* the Eucharistic Prayer, determines and explicates the law of belief, if this law of prayer is, in fact, the "doing" of eucharistic theology, then the voice of the Church should be heeded when she speaks to her divine partner in the moment of maximum relative tension of which the one and other are capable. One should be attentive to the Eucharistic Prayer, through which emerges a vision of the Eucharist that is dynamic, and that is not reductively thematic and partial, but global. New knowledge of the Eucharist becomes available and grows only on condition that reflection tend toward a comprehension of the mystery that is always more synthetic and global.

It is not difficult to list a number of dogmatic teachings about the theology of sacraments in general, or the theology of particular sacraments, which are so imposed on the liturgical texts as to cancel out the witness of the liturgy itself. In such cases this results in the erection of a theological synthesis that unduly limits the potential for the development of a genuine systematic presentation of the subject under discussion.

A classical example of the subordination of the *lex orandi* to the *lex credendi* in Western scholastic theology is the formulation of the theology of the moment of consecration. There is no doubt that this development shattered the fragile equilibrium that the early scholastic theological synthesis of the Eucharist continued to maintain well into the twelfth century. Karl Lehmann's observation on this aspect of the scholastic theology of the Eucharist is not exaggerated when he says:

"The concentration on the concept of consecration has abridged liturgically and ecclesiologically the theological fullness of the Eucharistic Prayer (with anamnesis, epiclesis, intercessions, doxology) in a disastrous way. In this narrowing is grounded a part of the thematic of the sacrificial character of the Mass which, to this day, has not been sufficiently unraveled."[8]

In our day, at the end of the second millennium, this traditional scholastic theology of the Eucharist is being subjected to strong negative criticism by Catholic theologians for the first time in many centuries. The main reason for this negative criticism stems from the isolation of the instituting words of Jesus. These words are contained in the liturgical formula of institution of the Eucharist within the Eucharistic Prayer as the formula of consecration enacted by Christ the High Priest through the presiding ordained minister. The isolation of these Words of Institution is recognized as the product of a splinter tradition of the Western Latin Church that takes as point of departure the Christological dimension, to the neglect or exclusion of the ecclesiological, and is nurtured exclusively by dogmatic considerations.

The resulting synthesis, the product of one strain of medieval scholastic theology that gained the upper hand in the post-Tridentine period, tends to foster the erroneous understanding of the Eucharist as a sacramental celebration that takes place within the Church rather than as *the* sacramental celebration *of* the Church. In other words the liturgical assembly of the Christian faithful seems merely to provide the proper context for the celebration of the Eucharist, rather than being the active subject of the celebration itself. When the understanding of the mystery of the Eucharist is developed from this (exclusive) Christological perspective, it tends to favor an old tradition found especially in sources from the pre-Chalcedonian churches which speak of the Eucharist as memorial of the Last Supper with the implication that it was the first Mass. Moreover, this latter conclusion is used to support the exaggerated claim that the apostles and their successors act exclusively as representatives of Christ when they recite the words of consecration contained in the liturgical narrative of institution of the Eucharist, that is, repeat sacramentally the historically unrepeatable act which Christ accomplished at the Last Supper.

[8] Karl Lehmann, "Gottesdienst als Ausdruck des Glaubens: Plädoyer für ein neues Gespräch zwischen Liturgiewissenschaft und dogmatischer Theologie," *Liturgisches Jahrbuch* 30 (1980) 197–214, at 210.

Traditional Catholic theology of the second theological millennium with its dominant Christological orientation has promoted the idea that the eucharistic moment of consecration represents a unique case as regards the shape of celebration of a Christian sacrament. In this erroneous idea the words of consecration, while pronounced by the human minister of Christ, are in reality words spoken by the risen Lord in and through his minister. In order to account for this unique case, and to distinguish this unique case from the role of the presiding minister when reciting the Eucharistic Prayer, the medieval theologians developed the distinction between *in persona Christi* and *in persona ecclesiae.* However, an investigation of the liturgical employment of narratives of institution of biblical feasts of the Old Covenant as well as Jewish liturgical prayers shows that the narrative of institution of the Eucharist, situated in the movement of the Eucharistic Prayer as direct address to the Father, finds its counterpart in the numerous embolisms (insertions into an already existing structure) of biblical and Jewish prayers, and some collaterals in the embolisms of non-anaphoric Christian prayers. The function of the addition of biblical witness to God's promise through prophetic oracles is to recall to God his commitment to his covenant relation and to assure God's people of the salvation-history value of the liturgical activity.

When the liturgical narrative of institution is understood from this perspective, the employment of the concept *in persona Christi* to explain the function of the minister who presides at the eucharistic celebration provides an indispensable key to the understanding of the Christological aspect of the eucharistic mystery. Granted. But how does one move from this notion to that of the representative role of the presiding priest in relation to the liturgical assembly that merits the title Church of Jesus Christ? A proper response to this question requires the introduction of another, and more balanced, key, namely, *in persona ecclesiae.*[9]

The words of Christ found in the liturgical account of institution are pronounced by the priest acting *in persona Christi.* But the priest is also the authorized minister of the Church. While conducting the Church's prayerful discourse with the Father, he pronounces the words which Christ pronounced in the unrepeatable situation of the Last Supper in

[9] Cf. Giraudo, *Eucaristia per la chiesa*, 336–45, regarding the preference for the employment of the concept *in persona ecclesiae* as starting point for the explanation of the twofold representative role of the priest who presides at the Eucharist.

view of the immediate future, and above all in view of the future liturgical celebration of the Church. At the heart of the eucharistic worship, the authorized minister intervenes and in his oration pronounces the same words "in the person of the praying Church by the speech of Christ,"[10] that is, in the name of the Church which here prays with the words of Christ. The words of consecration are words of Christ not immediately in the mouth of Christ but in the mouth of the Church, authoritatively represented by its ordained minister. And, vice versa, the ordained minister is the only [also only the] authorized voice of the Church who is called to pronounce them in virtue of the order of interaction, received in an eminent way.

To be sure, the liturgical account of institution of the Eucharist exercises a function that transcends that fulfilled by the biblical accounts found in the Synoptics and 1 Corinthians 11. The liturgical accounts differ from the biblical witness in that no one of them simply repeats a biblical account. Rather, liturgical accounts borrow mainly from one or two accounts, and they often introduce elements from other accounts with the intention of so formulating a more adequate "historical" description of the institutional event. However, this intention does not account for the introduction of the liturgical account into the Eucharistic Prayer. Rather, the context itself provides the key to the role played by the institutional account.

Introduced into the context of prayerful discourse, the liturgical account of institution takes on the role of a prayer of petition. This epicletic function is, in fact, highlighted in virtue of the intimate connection that is made between the liturgical narrative and anamnetic-offering prayer, and the subsequent intimate link placed between this group and the epiclesis for the sanctification of the gifts of the Church and the participants who share in the sacraments of the body and blood.

A significant number of modern Catholic theologians, who are concerned especially with the theology of the chief sacraments of the Church, show a decided preference for an approach to the theological interpretation of the traditional sacraments of the Church in which they are identified as ecclesial events of the liturgy. Beginning with the fact that sacraments of the Church are, indeed, forms of the liturgy of the Church and not ecclesial activities which are enclosed in liturgical celebrations, the theologian is in a position to properly assess the

[10] Ibid., 344.

strengths and weaknesses of the traditional school theology of the Latin Church.[11]

This liturgical perspective fosters appreciation for the word of prayer of the liturgical celebration. It is recognized, and correctly so, as more expressive and significative than any synthesis of dogmatic statements about the various aspects of the seven sacraments. With regard to the Eucharist, this turn to the liturgical nature of this ecclesial activity renders obsolete many theories of school theology. For example the turn from the scholastic schema of objectivized cause-effect to the interpersonal, symbolic concept of sacramental accomplishments has rendered obsolete the old theory of "Mass fruits." Theological thinking that takes seriously the understanding of the activity of worship as an interpersonal event of encounter recognizes the unsuitability of the traditional cause-effect schema.

Likewise, when the Eucharistic Prayer is recognized precisely as a performative form of the act of faith of the Church, the traditional emphasis on the Words of Institution as the sacramental formula appears misdirected. School theology defends the concentration of its attention on the words of consecration on the grounds that this sacramental formula has been fixed juridically and dogmatically. However, this theology of the moment of consecration in which the words of Christ are identified as the essential form of the sacrament holds true only within the splinter theology of the Western scholastic tradition. Angelus Häussling correctly points out the danger of scandal that is inherent in the scholastic elaboration of the essential form of the Eucharist. "Soon the suspicion of magic or sacramentalism must arise when, in the theological discussion and instructional mystagogy, the 'sacramental formula' appears all too important." He also gives attention to another undesirable result of the exaggerated esteem for the so-called words of consecration vis-à-vis the whole Eucharistic Prayer:

"It leads to the elevation of the priest, because he speaks the words of Christ in the account of institution according to 1 Corinthians 11 and the Synoptic Gospels, to the role of the one acting *in persona Christi,* (and finally representing the person of Christ himself . . .) in such a way that he is no longer, as the rite clearly shows, receiver with and in the celebrating assembly (which is the Church) and so remains and

[11] See Edward J. Kilmartin, "Sacraments as Liturgy of the Church," *Theological Studies* 50 (1989) 527–47.

must remain. Otherwise, as the logical consequence, a sacramentalistic clericalism results that works destructively."[12]

b. The Integration of the Law of Belief into the Law of Prayer
As with prayers from Jewish feasts, two basic types of classical Eucharistic Prayers are found. In the one, the prophetic sign is placed in the anamnetic section; in the other, in the epicletic section. From a detailed analysis of examples of "anamnetic" and "epicletic" types, it becomes clear that the function of the narrative of institution of the Eucharist (the prophetic sign) can only be understood insofar as it is embedded in the whole Eucharistic Prayer, and intimately linked to the other elements of the prayer. The central problem of the function of the narrative of institution in the overall shape and structure of the Eucharistic prayer is resolved by showing that this embolism functions in a way that is analogous to comparable embolisms of Jewish liturgical prayer.

Having drawn out the consequences of the law of prayer, the task remains to integrate the dogmatic data, or law of belief, into the law of prayer. But what are these dogmatic data? In other words, what are the enduring contributions to the dogmatic theology of the Eucharist that originated in the pre- and post-Tridentine periods?

b/1. The Pre-Tridentine Problematic and the Related Teaching of the Council of Trent. In the period from the ninth to the thirteenth centuries, the question of the nature of the sacraments of the body and blood was worked out and the speculative reduction of the eucharistic sacrifice to the moment of consecration of the elements of bread and wine was achieved. The reception of this teaching by the Council of Trent signaled the end-point of this splinter-tradition created by scholastic theology.

Analysis of the theological treatises on the subject of the Eucharist produced during this whole period, especially on the subject of the speculative reduction of the Mass to the consecration of the gifts, shows that theologians and liturgists had no grasp of the literary structure and theological dynamic of the Eucharistic Prayer. They reduced the whole problematic to an imaginary "central space" within the Eucharistic Prayer, with the result that the Words of Institution

[12] Angelus Häussling, "Odo Casel—Noch von Aktualität? Eine Rückschau in eigener Sache aus Anlaß des hundertsten Geburtstages des ersten Herausgebers," *Archiv für Liturgiewissenschaft* 28 (1986) 357–87, at 377.

were poised in the air without access to the other elements of the structure.[13]

b/2. The Post-Tridentine Period. The post-Tridentine problematic derives from the background of Trent's teaching about the sacrificial nature of the Eucharist. An analysis of Trent's Sessions 13 (1551) and 22 (1562) shows that the fathers were concerned with affirming the immediate and substantial relation of the Mass to Calvary, with the consequence that the Mass has a sacrificial character. The Council was not able to offer a theological explanation for its solemn definition that the Mass is a sacrifice. But since the sixteenth century, theologians have attempted to supply this need. The classical explanations can be classified as claiming that the Mass is sacrifice: (1) because immolation (sixteenth–seventeenth century); (2) because oblation (seventeenth–twentieth century); (3) because representation, convivial memorial (twentieth century).

B. EUCHARISTIC THEOLOGY AT THE THRESHOLD OF THE THIRD MILLENNIUM

The first theological millennium took the *lex orandi* as guide for the formulation of eucharistic theology. In the second millennium, the *lex credendi* took pride of place. The reintegration of the *lex credendi* into the *lex orandi* after the manner of the first millennium remains the task of the future and will be the achievement of the third theological millennium.

At this juncture it is not possible to predict the way in which the presumed systematic theology of the eucharistic sacrifice that will result from this reintegration will be developed, for various possibilities exist. For example, it is possible to begin with the notion of Communion in order to integrate the eschatological aspect of the eucharistic celebration into the proposed synthesis. This would take the eucharistic celebration as a sacramental sign of the heavenly banquet, and then demonstrate that Communion, sacrifice, and the sacramental somatic presence of the whole Christ are essential aspects of the one mystery of the Eucharist that ultimately consists in a Holy Communion of the crucified and risen Lord with his heavenly and earthly Church; and that all the other effects of this celebration of the life of faith are included in this effect, namely, the *res tantum sacramenti.*

[13] Giraudo, *Eucaristia per la chiesa*, 520–56.

One can also undertake the task of constructing a systematic theological exposition of the Eucharist beginning with its sacrificial dimension. This is, in fact, the route that we recommend, as will be increasingly clear in the rounding off of this chapter. In following this route, however, it is important that the following sequence of steps be maintained.

1. Starting Point: An Analytical Model

The starting point is an analytical model, a conceptual image, constructed with a view to highlighting essential elements, their relations, and the principles of the reality being studied. Such models are useful as a means of simplification of complex and amorphous social realities. They are the starting point for the development of a theory that can shed further light on the reality being studied. But their usefulness depends on their correspondence with that objective reality.

The history of Western systematic theology shows that models have been employed to shed light on various aspects of the Christian economy of salvation. Sometimes the model employed derives from the data being studied (endogenous), at other times it is imported from the outside (exogenous). In the matter of theological reflection on the eucharistic conversion, an example of an *endogenous* model (derived from the data being studied) is the notion of "eucharistic incarnation," where the historical Incarnation of the Word provides a salvation-history perspective for understanding the eucharistic presence of Christ. An *exogenous* model (imported from the outside) of the same is the theory of transubstantiation, based on the model of a change that takes place wholly within the world and the possibility of the continued existence of the appearance of bread and wine while their substances are changed into that of the body and blood of Christ.

The classical theological example of the use of an exogenous model is that employed in Catholic ecclesiology from the seventeenth century to modern times. It is the theory of Robert Bellarmine in which the Church is described as a juridically perfect society modeled on a constitutional monarchy. At present, at least in most Catholic theological circles, this model is recognized as based on principles worked out through nontheological sciences and as not taking account of the most essential aspects of the ecclesial reality. Vatican II has given support for a new orientation by stressing the idea that the unique model of the Church is that of church-mystery. In order to clarify the relationship between the social structures of the Church and the mystery of the Church, the model of the Incarnation is introduced in *Lumen gentium* no. 8.1. The use of this model, drawn from the history of salvation, leads to new knowledge of all aspects of the life of the Church. Its value derives from its endogenous character.

The process by which the theologian gets behind a particular theological explanation of some aspect of the life of faith and identifies the model that determines the whole synthesis can lead to some very interesting and important results. This is especially verifiable in the case of the traditional Western scholastic theology of the sacraments. All too often it will be found in this instance that the model is exogenous: imported from outside the subject under investigation. The analytical model which should be employed in the case at hand derives from analysis of the classical Eucharistic Prayers. Since the shape of meaning of the various classical Eucharistic Prayers is essentially the same, it is also possible to begin with a particular one of these Eucharistic Prayers.

Obviously, the adherence to the model based on the classical Eucharistic Prayers avoids the danger of developing a concept of eucharistic sacrifice that is foreign to the Christian economy of salvation. That this danger was not always avoided in the past is demonstrated by the post-Tridentine theories of eucharistic sacrifice which were based on history-of-religions concepts that clashed with the authentic Christian biblical concept of sacrifice.

2. *The First Step*

The first step of this process requires the integration of the eucharistic account of institution into the literary-theological movement of the whole Eucharistic Prayer. This is accomplished in two basic steps: [1] by showing how the narrative of institution and the anamnesis-offering prayer form a unit, with the latter prayer stating what the Church is doing in view of the command: "Do this in my memorial," i.e., making memorial of the death and resurrection of Christ through the offering of elements; [2] by showing how the second unity, the epiclesis-intercessions, is linked to the first. Here the reason is given why the Church acts, namely, in view of the transformation of the elements and the consequent transformation of the communicants. The intercessions enlarge on the petition for the transformation of the gathered Church, to include that of the universal Church.

C. CONCLUSION

The analysis of the literary-theological movement of the Eucharistic Prayer shows that it is a unified prayer directed to the Father of Jesus Christ. The typical configuration of the prayer proves to be an inheritance from Old Testament-Jewish liturgical prayer, in the form, namely, of discourse on the relation between two partners of a covenant. The attitude of the human partners is confession of the fidelity of God and confession of the human condition of sinfulness. The ultimate goal is confession of the Lord who alone is able to re-establish the sinner in covenant relationship.

The Eucharistic Prayer provides a global and dynamic vision of this ecclesiastical mystery which requires identifying the epiclesis of transformation of the participants as the key to the ultimate meaning of the eucharistic celebration. This epiclesis, explicitly or implicitly, expresses the properly theological dimension of sin (our condition of creaturely existence) and of the reconciliation that Christians are called to live in a special way at the moment of celebration of the Eucharist.

As ordered to the Father, the dynamic of the celebration turns between the ritual memorial of the body of Christ given for the remission of sins (narrative-anamnesis) and the petition that the body of the Church be built up through the remission of sins. Corresponding to the *todâh* the Eucharistic Prayer expresses the relational otherness of two partners. To confess sin in the content of the covenant discourse is to recall to God his great works and to proclaim his constant fidelity to the liturgical assembly. Focusing on God and on human beings at the same time, the Eucharistic Prayer creates a strong vertical tension which, however, will not be authentic if it lacks verification in daily life. The vertical and horizontal dimensions so interpenetrate one another in the classical Eucharistic Prayers that the one is not given without the other.

From the analysis of the Christological dimension of the Eucharistic Prayer, the Eucharist emerges as a symbolic reality that enables the liturgical assembly to participate in the once-for-all death and resurrection of Christ through the renewal of the ritual of the bread and cup, which Jesus gave at the Last Supper for that purpose. The idea that the eucharistic celebration is the liturgical medium of participation in the single *transitus* of Jesus from suffering to glory is gleaned from the Eucharistic Prayer itself, from the *lex orandi.* This notion is expressed in Catholic theology by the phrase "sacramental representation." But how is the idea of representation of a saving event in and through the ritual memorial to be understood? An adequate response to this question is not supplied by the Eucharistic Prayer itself. However, a valuable clue to the correct interpretation is indeed supplied by the law of prayer. For it is evident that the orientation of the Eucharistic Prayer is from the ecclesial assembly to the Father of Jesus Christ. From this point of view it appears that the eucharistic assembly is presented sacramentally to the once-for-all saving event accomplished in Jesus Christ for the sake of all humanity.

II. SYSTEMATIC SALVATION HISTORY-LITURGICAL THEOLOGY OF EUCHARISTIC SACRIFICE

What is described as salvation history is the history of the divine offer of personal communion to human beings and the free response of the creatures. The effect of the divine offer of "self-communication" is attained to the extent that it provokes the response of the human being. The human response cannot be described as a "self-communication," but rather as the "offering of self" to receive the meaning of one's life from God; or, more precisely, as the freely chosen openness to the divine gift which alone gives ultimate meaning to human existence.

Through the revelation of God in Jesus Christ the divine gift is identified as the self-communication of the Father through the Son in the Holy Spirit, which consists in the so-called divinization of human persons. Moreover, according to the gospel of Jesus Christ, this trinitarian self-communication admits of degrees. The progressive deepening of this personal communion with the individual persons of the Trinity happens through the exercise of the psychological aspect of the life of faith: the life of trust and hope in, and love of, the triune God.

The high point of the salvation history process takes place in the special missions of the Word and Spirit which occur in the Christ-event, namely, the Incarnation life, death, and glorification of the Word Incarnate. The special mission of the Word has two dimensions. There is the Incarnation of the Word, the expression of the Father's fidelity to his covenant: the sending of his only Son. Also there is the response of the Son of Man in his humanity to the Father's work in him: the embodiment of the fidelity of humanity to the covenant relation with the Father. In the special mission of the Word, the Holy Spirit is the divine source of the sanctification of the humanity of Jesus of Nazareth by which that humanity was elevated to unity of person with the Word.

The response of trust, hope, and love made by the Incarnate Word in his humanity was a response of faith: of trust, hope, and love: dispositions engendered by the Holy Spirit. This response of faith by Jesus, carried on through the whole of his life, can be described as the progressive upward growth of his humanity toward the goal of the highest possible embodiment of the acceptable response to the covenant initiative of the Father in him. This goal was attained in the event of the death of Jesus on the cross.

A. PARTICIPATION IN THE MYSTERY OF GOD IN CHRIST

Ordinary human persons participate in the new covenant on the side of Christ's response of faith by accepting in trust, hope, and love what the Father has done in Christ for the salvation of the world. This acceptance in faith, of course, entails differentiated responses to the claims of the Father made in the concrete situations of life, just as in the case of Jesus' responses in the various situations of his life of faith.

The response of faith of ordinary human persons can be described as a participation in the life of faith of Jesus insofar as the response is conformed to the meritorious attitudes of Christ. The possibility of this active participation is not a matter of simple human endeavor based on the subjective memory of the New Testament accounts of the life of Jesus. Rather, it is based on the working of the Holy Spirit, who is the mediation of the personal immediacy of believers to Christ and of the divinely transmitted conformity to the spiritual attitudes of Christ.[14]

[14] Heribert Mühlen supplies this clarification of the notion of "mediated immediacy" by introducing a distinction between two modes of direct action of the Spirit in the economy of salvation. There is the direct action of the Spirit without mediation as in the case of the bestowal of special charisms. Also there is direct action of the Spirit that involves human mediation. This holds in the case of the inspiration of Scripture through the instrumentality of inspired authors.

In both these cases, the divine action is "immediate" in the sense of direct action; in one kind of divine action, however, it is also mediated.

The notion of "mediated immediacy" is applied to the role of the Spirit as "mediation of the mediator," namely, Jesus Christ. The accent is placed on the fact that the Spirit does not exercise the role of mediator, but rather is mediated in the theandric act of the risen Lord, under the formality of the spirit of Christ. Hence the mystery of the personal immediacy of the Church to Christ can be expressed with the formula: the one and the same Spirit in Christ and in the believing members of the Church. See Heribert Mühlen, *Una mystica persona. Die Kirche als das Mysterium*

The Holy Spirit, sent by the risen Lord from the Father, is the divine source of sanctification of willing subjects: source of the ontological state of "divine adoption." But also the Spirit is the source of the psychological reality of the life of faith which flows from the state of being child of the Father in the incarnate Son.[15]

B. EFFECT OF PARTICIPATION IN THE NEW COVENANT

The effect of participation in the New Covenant is the integration into the single *transitus* of Jesus to the Father, a gradual process that takes place through response to the concrete situations of life that are conformed to the attitudes of the Jesus of history in virtue of the inspiration of the Spirit working in the believing disciples of Christ. The integration of the believer into the single *transitus* of Jesus takes place through the action of the Holy Spirit transmitting the appropriate attitudes of Christ conformed to the concrete situations of the life of Christians that require a response of faith. Such a transmission is always offered by the Holy Spirit, but it is only bestowed on willing subjects who freely accept it under the movement of the Spirit. In other words, the action of the Spirit attains its goal when, under the movement of the Spirit, there occurs a free response of saving faith on the part of the believer.

In this process it is the Holy Spirit that is the principal agent: the Holy Spirit sent from the Father by the risen Lord, and therefore the cause of sanctification in the time of the Church. The eternal divine activity of the Spirit is found as a consequent term in the believer; there, in the believer, the action, the power, and the effect are identical. At the same time the Spirit, as principal cause, employs the

---

der Identität des heiligen Geistes in Christus und den Christen: Eine Person in vielen Personen, 2nd rev. ed. (Munich—Vienna: Schöningh, 1967) §§ 11.70–11.82, esp. 11.75 and 11.77.

[15] Mühlen points out that "the analogous character of the mediating functions of Jesus and of his Spirit is manifested in the fact that one cannot say that the Logos is in the strict sense one and the same in the Father, in his human nature, and in us, for that would mean the 'extension' of the hypostatic union also to us. Still less can one say . . . that the Father is in the strict sense one and the same in the Son, in the Holy Spirit, and in us. The Holy Spirit, however, is, in the strictest sense, one and the same in the Father, in the Son, in the human nature of Jesus, and in us! The Spirit is, without qualification, the universal mediation which, on the basis of [his] going out from the Father and from the Son, mediates all with all"—ibid., § 11.77.

agency of the human living of Jesus. The Spirit works through the human living of Jesus in the sense that this human living modifies the action of the principal cause in keeping with the divine plan in which the world is saved only through the single *transitus* of Jesus from the world to the Father.

This single *transitus* of Jesus is the only way to the Father, for there can be no other response acceptable to the Father. It is completed in Jesus Christ, who is now glorified. But it is not completed in the history of humanity. According to the divine plan, while the historical living of Jesus was completed in the coordinates of space and time, it remains the instrumental cause of the conformity to Christ effected by the divinely intended transmission of the spiritual attitudes of Christ that are bestowed on willing subjects.

From the divine perspective, removes of space and time are not relevant to the ultimate intelligibility of the divine plan. The divine knowing is eternal, without succession; all historical events are equally present to it. Also according to the divine plan the world is saved through the single *transitus* of Jesus. Divine causative knowledge has determined this relation between Jesus' Passover and the passage of all humanity from this world to the kingdom. Consequently, we can speak of the real presence of the historical saving actions to the effect of the action of the Spirit conforming the believer to Christ's attitudes.

The *virtus salutaris* working through the instrumentality of the historical living of Jesus is, of course, the power of the Holy Spirit which produces the effect. The action of the Spirit, the agency of the human living of Jesus, and the effect are coexistent in the person willingly being conformed to the psychological attitudes of Christ. Hence with St. Thomas Aquinas, we can say that there is a real presence of the saving acts of Jesus in the beneficiary of the action of the Spirit. However, it is not to be understood as a local presence in virtue of a process of "eternalization" of the saving acts. All such postulates fail to make the distinction between the eternity of God and the consequent terms that flow from the divine eternal knowing, willing, and acting.

The consequent terms of the divine eternal decisions do not become eternalized. This is not possible, nor is it required in order that they be agents of the sanctification of humanity. For the ultimate intelligibility of these acts is determined by the divine plan in which removes of space and time are irrelevant. However, the presence of these saving acts is a presence metaphysically affirmed.

C. PARTICIPATION THROUGH LITURGICAL CELEBRATIONS

Liturgical ritual prayer and its accompanying symbolic action can be described as performative forms of the activity of the life of faith. The ritual-cultic expressions of the life of faith of the Church are ultimately structured by the Holy Spirit who is the source of the life of faith. Through that medium of liturgical ritual activity believers are enabled to express their own psychological conformity to the worship of Christ grounded on the Spirit's transmission of the spiritual attitudes of Christ, which correspond to the content of the concrete liturgical celebration. In this way the participants are drawn into communion with the historical saving works of Christ really present as agents of the work of the Spirit. In this way they are united to Christ in his worship of the Father.

The accomplishment of the ritual act as performative form of the faith of the Church (ecclesial dimension) evokes the individual believer's response of faith (participants of the liturgy) to the offer of the trinitarian self-communication appropriate to the human and social situation of the life of faith being lived in the mode of ecclesial celebration of the life of faith.

D. PARTICIPATION THROUGH EUCHARISTIC CELEBRATION

The Eucharist can be described as the corporate act of the ecclesiastical community by which it actively participates in the mystery of God in Christ, namely, the New Covenant. This participation takes place on the side of the response of faith of the incarnate Son to what the Father has accomplished in him for the salvation of humanity. The participation in the response of Christ consists in the self-offering of the members of the community of faith conformed to that of Christ which had its most climactic expression, never to be surpassed, and never to be repeated in historical space and time, in the event of the Cross. The participation takes place by way of prayer and by way of sacramental communion of the body and blood of Christ.

This most characteristic form of expression of the life of faith of a Christian community derives its shape of celebration (religious meal) and shape of meaning (blessing-prayer) from the traditions of the Last Supper of Jesus with his disciples recounted in the New Testament. Therefore it includes the two basic dimensions which correspond to the activity of Jesus at that supper: the giving of thanks to God and the distribution of the food and drink as symbols of the participation of his disciples in his prayer and fate.

The command, "Do this in my memorial," found in the Pauline/Lucan traditions of the accounts of institution, is not to be understood simply in the sense of "imitate what I have done in order to bring to mind what happened once-for-all on the first Holy Thursday." It means: "Do this in your communal worship service of God at table, or let it serve as norm for the shape of your table worship." "Do this in my memorial" contains the idea of offering thanksgiving and praise to the Father for what he has done in Jesus Christ for the salvation of the world. Also the command implies that the doing is carried out in order to participate in the new relationship of the "many" with the Father realized through Jesus' response of total self-giving to the Father in obedience and love unto the death of the cross. In addition the command presupposes that the doing takes place in the spirit of dedicated attitude of mind oriented to the active service of the demands of the New Covenant revealed in Jesus' words and works, impelled by the love of the Father.

There is also the matter of the participation in the New Covenant relationship between the Father and humanity in Christ through the eating and drinking of the bread and cup over which the prayer of praise is pronounced. Doing this "in my memorial" is a means of communion with Jesus Christ himself: Take, eat and drink; this is my body given and blood shed. In this invitation is expressed the idea that participation in the New Covenant is "sacramentally" enacted through communion with the person of Jesus attained in the eating and drinking, and "spiritually" realized through conformity with the attitude of total self-dedication of Jesus through which the disciples meet the demands of the New Covenant.

1. Designations for the Memorial of the Death of the Lord

The names given to the memorial of the death of the Lord are instructive. They emphasize one or other aspect and so are often indicative of the comprehensive way in which the celebration of the faith is understood. In the New Testament the holy meal aspect is featured with the designations "the breaking of bread" in Acts 2:42–47, and "the Lord's supper" in 1 Corinthians 11:20. In the third- and fourth-century North African Church the "Lord's" *(dominicum)* was a common name, which points to the source and principal actor. On the other hand, from the second century onward, the terminology of sacrifice was frequently applied. Initially, the emphasis was placed on the sacrifice of the Church which was foretold by the prophet Malachi (1:10–12). But in the third century, the favorite Old Testament text, understood to be a foreshadowing of the Eucharist, became the sacrifice of Melchizedek in Genesis 14:18. This happened as a result of the conscious theological reflection on the relationship of the sacrifice of the Church to the sacrifice of the cross.

In the West, Cyprian and Ambrose report as the common understanding of the their churches, that the mystery of eucharistic worship is the offering of Christ himself in which Christ is given the role of Melchizedek. In this milieu the tendency to individualize the sacrificial activity of Christ in the Eucharist can be detected. This tendency eventually led to the conscious idea that, in some sense, each eucharistic celebration contains a new sacrificial act of Christ. Gregory the Great states: "Christ, in the mystery of the holy sacrifice, is offered for us anew" *(iterum)* (*Dial.* 4.58).

This misleading notion was never completely overcome in the Western tradition of eucharistic catechesis down to the end of the nineteenth century. At the outset of the twentieth century the notion of a "virtual new offering" could still be found in some theological textbooks. However, in the course of this century, Catholic theological circles have discarded this concept or, more precisely, transcended this view completely through biblical and patristic studies and through important contributions from the field of dogmatic and speculative theology.

The term "sacrifice" and "oblation" find their counterparts in the Greek church tradition. The term *anaphora,* especially, but also *prosphora,* is used to designate the Eucharist. Here also the emphasis is placed on the mystery of the liturgy as the sacrifice of Christ, or, more accurately, as the commemorative actual presence of the sacrifice of Christ. This Greek concept was grounded on Greek symbolic theology in which the symbol participates in the reality of the prototype. This corresponds to the Platonic idea of the cosmic law of participation of lower realities in higher realities, a participation mediated by the divine light. In the perspective of the Greek Fathers, the Holy Spirit mediates the participation of the divine liturgy in the historical reality on analogy with the divine light of the Platonic system. Hence, in this theology, the danger of awarding to the divine liturgy a kind of repeatable new sacrificial act of Christ was avoided.

Other early names such as *collecta* or *synaxis* indicate that the subject of the liturgy is the whole assembly of Christian people. But since the ninth century, the Greeks have used *leitourgia* almost exclusively. In ecclesiastical terminology this signifies primarily ecclesiastical functions, and only secondarily divine worship. Thus the emphasis fell on the official service which is performed by the hierarchy for the community. A comparable Latin term *summum officium* is found in the Western Church in the late Middle Ages.

In the Latin tradition *missa* was used from the middle of the fifth century in Italy, North Africa, and other places. The original meaning of dismissal from a worship service which entailed a prayer of blessing took on the meaning appropriated to the Eucharist at least by preference. The usage seems to have been influenced by the idea that the Eucharist is the most important source of divine blessings. In this century the term Eucharist has become increasingly popular in Roman Catholic circles, as well as in many other churches of the East and West. It conveys a more "ecumenical" notion, being less tied to one or other ecclesiastical tradition than many of the other traditional terms. In any case the term provides a comprehensive notion that implies, connotes, or can easily include other names.

The term *eucharistia* was employed for the memorial of the death of the Lord at least from the outset of the second century. The textual witness indicates that the term may have derived from the New Testament accounts of the institution of the Lord's Supper which record that Jesus "gave thanks" *(eucharistein)*. Other significant influences on the use of the term need not concern us here. Just as Jesus gave thanks at the Last Supper, so the Christian assembly gave thanks as one aspect of the fulfillment of the command: "Do this in my memorial."

Eucharistia is a Greek word related to *eulogein,* the latter being a translation of the Hebrew *berakah:* blessing on God for his blessings. The root *charis* can refer to a gift bestowed or to a thankful response made to the giver of the gift. *Eucharistia* has the meaning of thanksgiving for the gift: recognition of its coming from the giver. It can also mean the response itself: the intentional giving back of the gift to the giver as a way of maintaining consciousness that the gift is a gift.

In the early Church, the objective side was prominent: the thankful recognition of the gift objectively bestowed. In the third century, Origen explicitly defines the term in this way: "Eucharist is the reception of a good." John Chrysostom, in the fourth century, says: "The best way of securing a kindness is the remembrance of it and thanksgiving *(eucharistia)* for it. Therefore also the . . . mysteries, which . . . are accomplished in worship, are called *eucharistia* because they are the remembrance of many kindnesses."[16]

In the divine liturgy the objective side of the meaning of this term was emphasized: the recognition of the bestowal of a kindness: the blessing derived from the saving acts of God in Christ. The saying of the third-century Eucharistic Prayer of the *Apostolic Tradition* of Hippolytus attests to this: "Recalling therefore his death and resurrection, we offer to you bread and cup, giving thanks . . ." This saying has its counterpart in classical liturgies of both the East and West.

On the other hand, the subjective side of Eucharist was not neglected: the idea of the turning of the liturgical assembly to the divine Giver. In this act the community intentionally gave back itself, but also the gift, to the giver, not because it had no need of the gift but to acknowledge that the gift remains the gift of God of which the community stands in constant need. In a word, the gift is given back in order to be received anew from God.

The sacrificial concept is included in this subjective aspect of Eucharist. The earliest liturgical sources take up this theme. The Eucharistic Prayers both contain sacrificial language and, as we have seen, are called *oblatio* or *anaphora,* and less frequently *prosphora.* In the East *anaphora* was generally employed from the sixth century in Byzantium. This motif of sacrifice is especially prominent in the old Roman Canon and in the Egyptian Liturgy of Mark.

In general, the Eucharistic Prayer over the gifts, symbols of the Church's self-offering, shows that the intention is to recommend the bread and wine to the Father in order that he make of them the once-for-all sacrificial gift of Jesus. Hence the gifts, consecrated and sanctified by acceptance of God, are believed to be the sacraments of the body given and the blood shed of the crucified and risen Jesus Christ. They also, from the second century, are called *eucharistia,* because the consecrated oblation is the objectification of the bestowal of the salvation of God in Christ recalled in the thanksgiving, and also the objectification of the divine acceptance of the subjective thanksgiving of the community of faith accepted by God.

[16] Johannes Betz, "Die Eucharistie als—auch ethische—Umsetzung von Glaubenseinsicht," in *Die Wahrheit tun: Zur Umsetzung ethischer Einsicht.* Festschrift zum 70. Geburtstag von Georg Teichtweier (Würzburg: Echter, 1983) 93–107, at 103–4.

E. MODERN AVERAGE CATHOLIC THEOLOGY OF EUCHARISTIC SACRIFICE

A modern Catholic theology of eucharistic sacrifice cannot be constructed merely by adding to the traditional Catholic scholastic synthesis some proven results of twentieth-century theological research. What can be described as the modern average Catholic theology of eucharistic sacrifice is, in general, a weak synthesis without a future. Some of its glaring defects have already been discussed. Among these defects is its explanation of the relationship between the Eucharist Prayer and the Communion (reception) of the sacraments of the body and blood of Christ: a relationship implied in the early usage of *eucharistia* for both the prayer and the holy food.

In the average Catholic synthesis, the liturgical sacrificial act of Christ and that of the Church is limited to the moment of the conversion of the gifts of the Church which is identified with the moment of the recitation of the words of Christ contained in the narrative of institution. While it is recognized that the sacraments of the body and blood derive from the "sacramental sacrifice," and can be called the "sacrificial sacraments," the ritual act of Holy Communion is not considered to be an essential part of the eucharistic sacrifice. In other words, the sacramental Communion is interpreted as only an "integral"—i.e., not essential—part of the celebration.

In view of the fact that the members of the assembly are also the acting subjects of the Eucharistic Prayer, this average Catholic theology of eucharistic sacrifice logically implies a defective interpretation of the relationship between the Christian assembly and the presiding minister. This is a relationship implied in the subjective aspect of *eucharistia,* as well as in the ancient names of *collecta* or *synaxis* which designate the Christian assembly as the acting subject. In this case, the fundamental relation: Christ—Church—Eucharist is short-circuited by the insertion of the presiding priest between Christ and Church. This conceptualization creates the erroneous impression that the relation Christ—priest—Eucharist is normative and that the Church enters into the transaction through the priest: Christ—priest (Church) —Eucharist. In other words, in the average Catholic view, the presiding priest, because of his relation to Christ the head of the Church who offers himself as head of the Church, necessarily represents the Church of which Christ is head. The community, therefore, is in this view mistakenly seen as entering into the sacrifice of Christ only *through the priest* inasmuch as he acts in specific sacramental identity with Christ, the chief actor of the eucharistic sacrifice. However, if the priest is a substructure of Church, must he not be seen as imbedded in the relation Christ—Church? And therefore, must not the priest's role be explained in terms of a reciprocal relation between Christ and Church? The popular Catholic interpretation, forced on the Latin tradition because of the Western scholastic moment-of-consecration theology, neglects the ecclesiological and supplies an explanation only of the Christological dimension of the Eucharist.

In this mistaken theological outlook which short-circuits the fundamental relation: Christ—Church—Eucharist, the notion of *collecta* or *synaxis* takes on a new meaning. The community is placed vis-à-vis the priest who functions solely as representative of Christ in the central sacrificial act. This results in the erroneous concept of *leitourgia* or *summum officium* as the best description of the dynamics of eucharistic worship, namely, a service of the hierarchy performed on behalf of the Christian community in order to enable it to participate in the visible sacrifice by the spiritual devotion of its members.

Here we have a good example of a conclusion that results from the application of a certain kind of "analytical model." As we mentioned above, the usefulness of such models depends on their correspondence with the objective reality under investigation. In the matter of the interpretation of the representative role of the priest who presides at the Eucharist, the model underlying the average Catholic view is undoubtedly that of the event of the Last Supper. What Jesus did at the Last Supper, at the "first Mass," he now does as the crucified and risen Lord in the Eucharist through his minister. Thus the Eucharist is conceived as derived from the liturgy of the Last Supper or, more precisely, is a continuation of that liturgy in the Church. Hence it is not identified as an act of the Church, but as the act of Christ through his "ministerial priesthood" in the Church for the sake of the Church.

The classical liturgies of the fourth and fifth centuries, from which the liturgies of the traditional churches derive, themselves originate from earlier traditions of the manner of following the command: "Do this in my memorial." The New Testament traditions of the Last Supper, which in some way relate to the historical Last Supper, already reflect the influence of church practice. These traditions so stamp the Christian celebration for all time that it is possible to speak of the echo of the Last Supper of Jesus with his disciples being heard in the classical liturgies. But it is somewhat amiss to speak of the later liturgies as originating in the "liturgy of the Last Supper"; for this leaves the erroneous impression that the Last Supper was, indeed, the first Mass. In fact, before the liturgy of the Eucharist of the Church could be realized, the whole Christ-event had to take place: the death, the resurrection, and glorification of Jesus, and the pentecostal sending of the Holy Spirit to establish the Church and draw its members into the earthly body of Christ.

It must also be mentioned that the average Catholic theological explanation of the relationship of the sacrifice of the cross to the Eucharist is based on very weak biblical grounds when it appeals to the biblical notion of *anamnesis.* The biblical term is applied to the celebration of memorial feasts instituted by Yahweh in order that the participants might recall and share in the blessings of the past saving works experienced by the people of Israel. It is also applied to the Eucharist. But in both cases *anamnesis* is interpreted to mean objective memorial, that is, the liturgical occurrence of the objectivized presence of the past redemptive work of Christ. In other words the foundation event of his death and resurrection which took place in past time and space is conceived as rendered present on the altar at the moment of consecration of the bread and wine.

However, this interpretation is not supported by careful analysis. For the commemorative feasts of the Jewish tradition are not understood to contain the historical saving events which are commemorated, but rather, are considered to be the media by which the participants of the feasts are, as it were, presented to the foundation event that is commemorated. The return consists in the sharing of the blessings analogous to those imparted in the historical event. Thus the strict theological application of the biblical notion of *anamnesis* supports only the idea that the Christian liturgical assembly is, in some sense, represented to the foundation event of the death and resurrection and, as a consequence, enabled by faith to participate in its salutary effects. Moreover, the witness of the liturgy itself, the classical Eucharistic Prayers, do not furnish support for any other understanding of the biblical *anamnesis.* These prayers point in the direction of the representation of the liturgical community to the foundation event of the new covenant.

The inherent weakness of the average modern Catholic understanding of objective anamnesis as applied to the Eucharist is especially made apparent in the attempts to supply a credible theological explanation of how the past historical saving acts of Christ can be rendered objectively present on the altar in a visible sacramental mode of being.

Invariably, what is proposed as a solution only raises further problems for understanding. What precisely is meant by saying that the historical sacrifice of the cross is rendered objectively present on the altar in a visible sacramental mode of being? This is not—and apparently cannot be—satisfactorily answered by an appeal to an authentic tradition, either of the East or the West. Consequently, one is not theologically (or doctrinally) constrained on the grounds of an authentic tradition to seek a credible explanation of the concept of objective anamnesis. Rather, one is free both to evaluate critically the various traditional formulations of the relation of the historical sacrifice of the cross to the eucharistic sacrifice, and to seek out the most satisfactory explanation of this relationship.

Finally, the average modern Catholic theology of the Eucharist displays only a weak integration of trinitarian theology. Most importantly, the theology of the role of the Holy Spirit needs to be thoroughly integrated, and the consequences drawn. In fact, it is the lack of a systematic approach to the role of the Holy Spirit that lies at the basis of the overall weak Western theology of the Eucharist.

F. SALVATION HISTORY-LITURGICAL THEOLOGY OF EUCHARISTIC SACRIFICE

The best access to the more authentic traditional theology of the Eucharist is by way of the classical Eucharistic Prayers when they are viewed from the normative source of eucharistic faith found in the New Testament.

1. *The Eucharistic Prayer*

As already indicated, the classical Eucharistic Prayers have the same basic structure: anamnesis (remembrance) and epiclesis (petition). The narrative of institution can be found in either section. The difference in structure corresponds to two types of Jewish prayer modeled on the Old Testament theology of covenant: the relationship which Yahweh has established with his people as a result of their accepting covenant partnership and its consequences. The Eucharistic Prayers relate especially to those Jewish prayers which contain a reference to some specific past saving act of God that is relevant to the present situation, or include a scriptural text in which God's promise of fidelity takes the form of a direct address. Examples of the latter usage are found in prayers associated with special feasts understood as instituted by Yahweh to be the occasion of a special bestowal of blessings.

In the "anamnetic type" of Eucharistic Prayer, for example the anaphora of St. John Chrysostom (Byz), the anamnesis contains the narrative of institution of the Eucharist. Thus it already takes up the command: "Do this in my memorial." This remembrance is continued in the anamnesis-offering prayer where the community explicitly expresses its obedience in a prayer that recalls the whole Christ-event. The epiclesis of the coming of the Holy Spirit is a petition for the acceptance of the community's obedience which results in the change of the gifts of bread and wine, symbols of the community's self-offering, and the sanctification of the communicants of the body and blood of Christ. Intercessions for others follow as an extension of the epiclesis.

The "epicletic type" is exemplified in the Anaphora of Mark (Alexandrian Mark); the Third Eucharistic Prayer of the Missal of Paul VI; the old Roman Canon (which does not explicitly mention the Holy Spirit in either epiclesis). In this type, the anamnesis is interrupted by the epiclesis which petitions for the advent of the Spirit to sanctify the gifts of the Church. In turn, this epiclesis is interrupted by the resumption of the anamnesis through the recitation of the narrative of institution of the Eucharist and its continuance in the anamnesis-offering prayer. Then the epiclesis for the coming of the Holy Spirit to sanctify the communicants is taken up. Intercessions for others follows as an extension of the epiclesis.

Conclusion

The literary structure of the Eucharistic Prayer shows that it is a unified prayer directed to the Father as the source of all, and to the Son and Holy Spirit. It mirrors the dynamic relation of the partners of the New Covenant in the history of salvation realized fully through Christ in the power of the Spirit. The thankful recognition of the Father's action in Christ (anamnesis) is followed by the petition that the continuing fidelity of the Father to his people be expressed and realized through the sanctifying action of the Holy Spirit by which the communicants are brought to Christ (epiclesis for sanctification of communicants) and by which Christ is brought to the communicants (epiclesis for sanctification of the bread and wine). The extension of the epiclesis in the intercessions is the expression of the Church's desire that all humanity be brought within the sphere of the New Covenant people. The commitment of the Church to the New Covenant is expressed explicitly in the anamnesis-offering prayer.

The *transitus* of the liturgical community to the Father is expressed liturgically in the Eucharistic Prayer. The *transitus* of Christ himself is recalled but is not represented objectively and sacramentally to the assembly in the Eucharistic Prayer, for the Eucharistic Prayer is prayer of the Church. Thus the axiom remains intact: Sacramental celebrations are acts of the Church in which the Church manifests and realizes itself as body of Christ, of which Christ is the head and in which the Holy Spirit is the mediation of the presence of Christ to the Church and the Church to Christ.

The response to the prayer of the Church is represented sacramentally in the sacraments of the body and blood of Christ. Holy Communion enables sacramental communion with Christ as the one who gives himself to the Father for humanity. He gives himself as the "man for others" to draw the believers into personal communion with himself and so into communion with the Father. He does this through the sending of the Spirit as his Spirit to enable the communicants to share in his sentiments of self-offering. In the power of the Holy Spirit the sacramental communion with Christ becomes the medium of spiritual, personal communion with the risen Lord.

In the eucharistic celebration the Holy Spirit is manifested both as the source of the faith in which the Eucharistic Prayer was formulated as memorial of the death of the Lord, and the source of the response of the assembly to the content of this performative form of the act of faith. The Holy Spirit "anoints" the prayer of the Church and "anoints" the participants of the liturgy so that, through the medium of the prayer, Christ comes to the assembly and the assembly to Christ. The Holy Spirit is also the source of the sanctification of the eucharistic gifts of the Church and of the sanctification of the communicants of the sacraments of Christ's body and blood. In this way also the Spirit is seen as the one who brings Christ to the communicants and the communicants to Christ in such a way that spiritual unity between Christ and the communicants and between the communicants themselves is deepened.

2. *Theological Consequences*

The analysis of the classical Eucharistic Prayers shows that their content is a formulation of the covenant response of the liturgical assembly to the Father's fidelity to his covenant with humanity fulfilled in the special missions of the Son and Holy Spirit. The response corresponds to the personal response of faith of the incarnate Son in his humanity for what the Father had done in him for the salvation of the world. It contains [1] the memorial of the past saving acts of the Father in salvation history, culminating in the Christ-event; [2] commitment to the covenant relationship; [3] petition for the divine help to maintain the covenant relationship; [4] petition for the salvation of the world.

a. Function of Ritual Activity

As performative form of the activity of faith of the eucharistic community, the ritual act serves as medium through which the faithful are rendered present in memory to the self-offering of the Son of God in his humanity, which culminated in his Passover from suffering to glory. However, the community is rendered present under the formality, not of passive spectators, but of active participants in Jesus' uniquely acceptable response to what the Father has done in him for the salvation of the world. And this means that responding in faith to the mystery of God in Christ, the community is not only related to Christ's self-offering, but also that the actively present Christ relates his once-for-all self-offering to that of the community of faith. This reciprocal personal relation is grounded on the work of the Holy Spirit who both brings Christ to the faithful and the faithful to Christ.

b. Essence of Active Participation

The active participation of the assembly is realized by the individual believer's degree of agreement with the religious attitudes expressed verbally and gesturally in the ritual act, and which mirror the sacrificial attitudes of Jesus expressed at the Last Supper and in the event of his historical death of the cross.

c. Efficacy of Active Participation

The efficacy of active participation is measured by the "devotion" of the participants. This devotion consists in a dedicated attitude of mind oriented to the active service of the gospel of Jesus Christ impelled by love.

d. The Extent of the Efficacy of Active Participation

The extent of the efficacy of active participation includes the personal deepening of the life of faith of participants, as well as effective intercession for the continuing bestowal of divine blessings on the participants and those for whom intercession is made. Also, it is because a community of faith is gathered to celebrate the memorial of the Lord that it is assured the sanctification of the gifts of the Church by the Holy Spirit and the sanctification of the communicants which alone enables a fruitful sacramental encounter with the eucharistic Christ.

e. The Active Subjects of the Eucharist

The concrete eucharistic assembly physically present and actively engaged by faith is the active subject. This assembly is the local embodiment of the social body of Christ, and represents the universal communion of eucharistic assemblies. Other Christians, not physically present, can participate indirectly in the sense of supporting the eucharistic assembly by their prayer of intercession.

Christ himself is also actively present as head of the Church and high priest of the worship of his earthly Church. Hence it can be said that the eucharistic worship is enacted by the eucharistic community in communion with Jesus Christ, head, priest and bridegroom of his body, priestly people and bride.

f. The Christological Dimension of the Eucharistic Prayer

The eucharistic community enacts its worship *in, with,* and *through* Jesus Christ. This Christological aspect accounts for the acceptability of the worship of the Church and the response of the Father to the intercession of the Church, that is, for the sanctification of the participants and the gifts of the Church, and the effective intercession for those living and dead for whom petition is made.

Worship of the Father in, with, and through Christ: the saying of the old Roman Canon, "Through him, and with him, and in him, is all honor and glory to thee, God the Father almighty, in the unity of the Holy Spirit," takes on a new depth of meaning when the theology of the Holy Spirit's personal mission in the Church is introduced.

"In Christ" answers the question *where* such worship takes place. It takes place in the sphere of personal communion with Christ, grounded on the participation in the one Spirit of Christ, which is the depth dimension signified by membership in the ecclesial community of which Christ is the head and bridegroom. "With Christ" answers the question *how* the worship of the Church relates to, but is really distinguished from, that of Christ. It takes place in an activity really distinguished from that of Christ. Here the image of bridegroom and bride are applicable. "Through Christ" answers the question *about* the dependency of the Church's worship on Christ. It is dependent on Christ who, as risen Lord, is the theandric source of the mission of the Holy Spirit. The Holy Spirit, divine source of the acceptable human worship of the incarnate Son, is sent by Christ from the Father as his Spirit to enable the acceptable worship of the disciples of Christ. It is dependent on Jesus who offered the sole acceptable worship to the Father, and to which the worship of others must be conformed if it is to be accepted: a conformity that is grounded on the inspiration of the Holy Spirit of Christ.

In what sense can it be said that "Christ worships in, with, and through the Church"? Christ associates the Church with his once-for-all sacrifice. This is not to be conceived as a juridical association, but one that is made possible by the Holy Spirit, the same Spirit in Christ and in the assembly of believers. So we can say that Christ worships "in the Church" in the sense that Christ is actively present in the worship of the Church. To say that Christ worships "with the Church" means that his activity is really distinguished from that of the Church but related to it through the Holy Spirit. The idea that Christ worships "through the Church" cannot mean that Christ continues to offer new acts of worship of the Father in the context of the earthly worship of the Church analogous to the categorical acts of worship of his earthly life. This mistaken idea is found in the Latin theological tradition, and has survived up to this century in a less crude form where the idea of an actual oblation of Christ *(oblatio actualis Christi)* is affirmed without contesting the unique character of the sacrificial act of the cross. However, the idea that to every liturgical sacrificial act of the Church there must correspond a separate and renewed act of the glorified Christ misunderstands the meaning of the heavenly liturgy. Christ's eternal sacrificial attitude, as eternally accepted by the Father since Easter, acquires in time, in the action of the Church, a representative visible form.[17] However, it must be asked: Is there an objective sacramental representation of the "eternal sacrificial attitude" of Christ himself in the Eucharistic Prayer? Or does this representation occur only at the distribution of Christ's body and blood? In the latter case, there is certainly a visible representation of the sacrifice of Christ.

What can be said about the phrase: "We offer Christ; Christ offers us"? First of all, there is the witness of patristic literature which attests to the notion that "we offer Christ." Cyprian of Carthage is the first to use this terminology: "The passion of Christ is the sacrifice we offer" (*Epistle* 63.17). This idea is also expressed elsewhere, either implicitly

[17] Karl Rahner and Angelus Häussling, *The Celebration of the Eucharist* (New York: Herder and Herder, 1968) 22–28, at 27, n. 21.

or explicitly, in both the East and the West. However, from the standpoint of systematic theology, this requires explanation. For it cannot be said that we offer Christ himself in a literal sense. Rather, we participate in the self-offering of the whole Christ, head and body. The local eucharistic assembly offers the sacrifice of the whole Christ on the side of (i.e., as) the body of Christ (i.e., it, *as body of Christ,* offers the sacrifice of the whole Christ).

The phrase "Christ offers us" should be explained as meaning that Christ offered himself once-for-all "for us," but certainly not as a substitute for our self-offering made in union with him.

g. The Pneumatological Dimension of the Eucharistic Prayer

The exercise of the priestly worship of the eucharistic community is grounded on its character as a priestly people of God that "participates" in the priestly worship of the one High Priest, Jesus Christ. But this worship takes place in the power of the Holy Spirit.

The Holy Spirit is the ultimate source of the classical Eucharistic Prayers that formulate the faith of the Church. The proximate source of these prayers is the communal experience of the role of the Eucharist in the economy of salvation, formulated by one or more inspired representatives of this faith and recognized as a suitable expression of eucharistic faith. Since the Holy Spirit is the source of eucharistic faith and of its articulation in the classical Eucharistic Prayers, it must be said that the Spirit is the ultimate source of the literary structure and the content of the prayers.

But the Spirit is not only the source of the medium by which the liturgical community is represented to the Passover of Jesus to the Father and by which the Passover of Jesus is represented to the liturgical community. The Holy Spirit, as Spirit of Christ, is the mediation of the personal immediacy of the assembly of the faithful to Christ and of Christ to the faithful because Christ and the believers are personally united in the one Spirit. Moreover, as divine source of the human worship of the Son of Man offered to the Father in faith, the Spirit is also the source of the worship of ordinary human persons conformed to the worship of Christ's humanity. In this sense we can speak of the Spirit of Christ as the source of the participation of the Church in the priesthood and worship of Christ.

In other words, the Spirit is the source of the life of faith, of the life of trust in, and hope in, and love of God. Hence the Spirit is source of acts of the life of faith animated by the religious attitudes conformed to those of Christ. The Spirit who awakens acts of faith is the source of the representation of the believing community to the Passover of Jesus. On the other hand, the Spirit is the source of the representation of the historical saving acts of Christ to the believers. How this should be understood is discussed below.

The Eastern tradition of Eucharistic Prayers explicitly affirms the fact that the Holy Spirit is the source of the sanctification of the eucharistic gifts of the Church and the source of the sanctification of the communicants to the end that they are enabled so to participate in sacramental communion of the body and blood of Christ that there is a deepening of their personal communion with Christ and with those who are in Christ.

The Spirit is also the source of the hierarchically ordered Church, and so the source of the ordained ministry that presides at the Eucharist of the Church as representative of the Church of Christ the head and therefore representative of Christ the head and High Priest of the Eucharist.

h. The Role of the Ordained Presiding Minister of the Eucharist

The pastoral office is an essential structure of the Church, established by the Holy Spirit to serve the ministry of building up the local community of the faithful. The Holy Spirit inspires individuals to offer themselves for this ministry and to employ their natural gifts in the service of leadership. Insofar as these natural gifts are taken up in the life of faith, under the inspiration of the Spirit, they are called charisms. This pastoral ministry is exercised by witness to the faith in word and act: through witness of preaching and teaching, the charitable service of others and through leadership in communal worship.

In presiding at the Eucharist, it is obvious that the deportment of the bearer of office, backed up by his known commitment to the life of faith, constitutes a unique personal contribution to the celebration. Beyond that, the presiding minister of the Eucharist serves as the external agent of communication of the performative form of the eucharistic faith, the Eucharistic Prayer.

It is clear that, from this perspective, the presiding priest acts as representative of the Church's faith and therefore of the faith of the local community. This agrees with the content of the Eucharistic Prayer. But eucharistic worship is an activity of the whole Christ, head and body. Consequently, acting as leader of the community, called by Christ and ordained and commissioned by the Church of

Christ, the presiding priest is related in this ministry to Christ himself who has missioned him, and who is head of the community and high priest of its worship, and who is personally present and active in his worshiping community.

But how is the relation of the presiding priest to be understood? In the East the idea that the priest serves as "icon of Christ" reflects the tendency to view the liturgy as transparency for the deeper mystery content. Here the primacy of vision comes to the foreground. In the Latin tradition more juridical concepts have been used: "in place of Christ," "in the name of Christ." In the tenth-century Romano-Germanic Pontifical with its tendency to employ the term *sacerdos* only for presbyters, and to practically identify the ministry of presbyters with their eucharistic role, three new additions to the rite of ordination of presbyters are found which derive from the North: (1.) the vesting ceremony, (2.) the anointing of hands, (3.) the conferring of chalice and paten with bread and wine. The formula for the *traditio instrumentorum* (handing on of the chalice and paten) reads: "Receive the power to offer sacrifice to God, and to celebrate Mass for the living and dead in the name of the Lord." Here the prayer suggests that the presbyter is acting in the name of the Lord. While medieval rites of ordination do not deal with the relation between Christ and priesthood, liturgical commentaries sustain the theme of symbolic representation of Christ with the title *vicarius Christi* in connection with the power of the priest to celebrate the Eucharist, or in connection with his role in public prayer and in the sacrament of reconciliation. Since the thirteenth century, the term *in persona Christi* is related to the priest's role in the Eucharist. The language of symbolic representation seems to be more congenial to the Latin mentality concerned with the proper ordering of interpersonal relations in society. More recently one finds the use of the Greek term *icon* to describe the relation of the priest to Christ in the Eucharist. But it is not always evident in what sense this is used. In any case, the meaning attached in Greek theology does not correspond to what is meant in our average modern Catholic theology.

The concept "in the person of Christ," as used in modern Catholic theology, as we have seen, means: in specific sacramental identity with Christ. Frequently in this connection one finds such expressions as: "participation in the unique priesthood of Christ."[18] or: Christ

[18] Vatican II, Dogmatic Constitution on the Church, *Lumen gentium* no. 10.

makes presbyters "participate in his consecration and mission."[19] These sayings need interpretation, for no human being, as such, participates in the unique, personal, and incommunicable priesthood of Christ. If misunderstood, such sayings can lead to such exaggerated sayings as: "The priest, therefore, participates in Christ's work permanently and efficaciously in and for the whole Church because he is in his very being identified with Christ."[20]

Clearly this modern concept *in persona Christi* is a development of the Tridentine theology of the relation of the ordained priest to the Eucharist. In Trent's Decree on the Sacrament of Orders, canon 1, the "visible and external priesthood" is said to have the "power of consecrating and offering the true body and blood of the Lord, and of remitting or retaining sins, and not only . . . the ministry of preaching the Gospel . . ."[21] However, this canon was not intended to present a systematic approach to the priesthood of the ordained, but only to affirm functions that were being explicitly denied by some Reformers. Despite that intention, post-Tridentine Catholic theologians did make this canon the basis for a systematic approach. The Second Vatican Council, however, taking a more systematic approach to the subject, gave pride of place to the preaching of the Gospel.[22]

Also relevant to this subject is canon 2 of Trent's Decree on The Most Holy Sacrifice of the Mass.[23] Here it is taught that the Eucharist was instituted at the Last Supper and, at the same time, the ministerial priesthood with the words: "Do this in my memorial," ordering the apostles to "offer his body and blood." The intention was to present the historical event as understood in the tradition. But the council had no intention of resolving the question of the historical moment of the institution of the hierarchical priesthood itself on the basis of critical historical exegesis of Scripture. According to the preamble, the intention was to draw teaching from Scripture, tradition, and the authority of the Church, and to present the convergence of the sources. What we have, therefore, is an example of ecclesiastical exegesis. In other words, chapter 1 of the *doctrina* was not intended to be an accurate historical reconstruction of the events of the Last Supper. More

[19] Vatican II, Decree on the Ministry and Life of Priests, *Presbyterorum ordinis* no. 2.

[20] Donald Wuerl, *The Priesthood: The Catholic Concept Today* [no date] 146.

[21] Trent, Session 23 (1563), *Decretum de sacramento ordinis,* canon 1 (DS 1771).

[22] *Lumen gentium* no. 28.

[23] Trent, Session 22 (1562), *Decretum de ss. Missae sacrificio,* canon 2 (DS 1752).

particularly, the intention was to define the origin of the Eucharist and the relation of the ordained hierarchy to this ministerial priestly service.

In Trent's Decree on Holy Orders, canon 6 states that there is in the Church "a hierarchy instituted by divine ordination, which consists of bishops, presbyters and ministers."[24] While this teaching conforms to the idea of existence of such offices from the beginning of the Church, it does not harmonize with the historical facts. The Second Vatican Council's *Lumen gentium* offers a more realistic view based on a more secure historical consciousness and exegesis of Scripture. Here we read: "Thus the divinely instituted ecclesiastical ministry is exercised in different degrees by those who even from ancient times *(ab antiquo)* have been called bishops, priests, and deacons."[25] Hence in no way does Vatican II affirm that the priesthood was instituted at the Last Supper in the sense understood by Trent.

Regarding Trent's canon 1 of the Decree on Holy Orders mentioned above, the reference to *potestas consecrandi* and *potestas offerendi* calls for some comment. The awarding to the ordained minister the power of consecration conveys the idea that the priest is the acting subject of the consecration of the elements, an activity that is distinguished from the power of offering. The power of consecrating is clearly understood as a ministerial power which is an instrument of the divine act by which the elements are changed into the body and blood of Christ. Thus, in chapter 4 of the Decree on the Eucharist we read that *per consecrationem . . . conversionem fieri.*[26] The idea is that by means of the consecration by the priest, acting as minister of Christ, Christ himself through his humanity, as instrument conjoined to his divinity, and therefore by the divine power common to the persons of the Trinity, converts the bread and wine.

In the twentieth century, the accent on the sanctifying role of the Holy Spirit in the Eucharist has led to a new outlook in official Roman Catholic circles. In the new Eucharistic Prayers of the Missal of Pope Paul VI, the work of conversion of the elements is attributed to the Holy Spirit. Moreover, these prayers tend to present the role of the presiding minister as one who presents the gifts of the Church to the Father in order that they may become "consecrated gifts." The epicle-

[24] DS 1776.

[25] *Lumen gentium* no. 28.

[26] Trent, Session 13 (1551), *Decretum de ss. Eucharistia,* chap. 4 (DS 1642).

sis of the Second Eucharistic Prayer reads in part: "Let your Spirit come upon these gifts to make them holy . . ." The Fourth Eucharistic Prayer has a similar saying: "Father, may this Holy Spirit sanctify these offerings." But the Third Eucharistic Prayer shows a greater emphasis on the role of the presiding priest as one who presents for consecration-sanctification the gifts of the Church: "And so, Father, we bring you these gifts. We ask you to make them holy by the power of your Spirit."

As for the attribution of the power of offering to the presiding priest, canon 1 of Trent's Decree on Holy Orders[27] can accommodate either of the major theories held by Catholic theologians at the Council of Trent: (1.) the coincidence of consecration and offering (Thomistic school), or (2.) consecration by the priest as representative of Christ, and offering of the consecrated species by the priest as representative of the Church (Scotus–Biel school). However, the attribution of this power of offering exclusively to the liturgical leader leaves the way open to continuing a fundamental misunderstanding of the structure of the eucharistic sacrifice. It can give the impression that there is a sacrificial rite, which is the sacramental sacrifice of the one once-for-all sacrifice of the cross in the signs of bread and wine, and which takes place in the Eucharistic Prayer. This approach does not do justice to the relationship and role of the liturgical assembly which also exercises the power of offering in and through the Eucharistic Prayer. In addition, this accent on the power of offering of the presiding priest obscures the relationship between the Eucharistic Prayer and Holy Communion.

i. Relation of Communion to the Sacrifice of Christ

In the *Doctrina de ss. missae sacrificio* of the Council of Trent, chapter 1, *offerre* is used for the ritual offering of body and blood. In chapter 2, the same word *offerre* is also used for the historical self-offering on the cross.[28] As already mentioned elsewhere in this book (pp. 198, 243–44), this mixing up of the terminology led to theories of eucharistic sacrifice in the post-Tridentine period which located a ritual offering of the sacrifice of the cross in the Eucharistic Prayer, and which were based on a pre-Christian concept of sacrifice. But, in fact, the outward form of the representation of the sacrificial gift of Jesus is not found in the Eucharistic Prayer itself, but in the distribution of the consecrated

[27] DS 1771.

[28] Trent, Session 22 (1562), *Decretum de ss. Missae sacrificio,* chap. 1 (DS 1740); chap. 2 (DS 1743).

gifts that takes place in the accomplishment of the meal process. But this (the eucharistic meal) was not considered a sacrificial rite in the common understanding of the term in the history of religions.

The unresolved problem created by the two uses of *offerre* can be resolved only by a new approach which thinks through the relation of the personal self-offering of Jesus and his body the Church and the eucharistic "breaking of bread," that is, the form of the meal, as its efficacious sign.

Biblically speaking, sacrifice and meal are not separable. The meal process is that by which *(modus quo)* the sacrifice of Christ and the Church *(id quod)* is realized liturgically. Hence the notion that the "conversion of the elements" is also the "sacrificial act" needs to be critically evaluated in the light of the normative demands of Scripture. The sacrificial action cannot be limited to an *oblatio* and *immolatio* (to use traditional scholastic language), which happens in the "conversion," while the Communion of the body and blood is relegated to the status of an almost dispensable supplement.

The Council of Trent, in its Decree on the Sacrifice of the Mass, states: "If any one should say that in the Mass a true and proper sacrifice is not offered to God, or that 'is offered' means nothing other than that Christ is given to us to eat, anathema sit."[29] It will be noted here that the canon avoids the separation of the cross from the Mass as would be done by considering the Lord's Supper as a communion service in which only the movement of the divine to the human is recognized. On the other hand, the katabatic aspect is not taken into account in an exclusive way, for that is something that would neither suffice for the event of the cross nor for Christian sacramental existence.

This canon is not closed to the idea that the distribution for eating, as liturgical symbol and as an actual fact, has something to do directly with the sacrifice of Christ. Canon 1 does not speak of this, but the connection is made in chapter 1 of the *doctrina* where it is said that Christ "offered his body and blood under the species of bread and wine to God the Father, and . . . handed . . . to the apostles in order that they receive . . ."[30] In other words, in the interpretation of canon 1, food and sacrifice are not placed in opposition.

[29] "Si quis dixerit, in Missa non offerri Deo verum et proprium sacrificium, aut quod offerri non sit aliud quam nobis Christum ad manducandum dari: an. s."—ibid. (DS 1751).

[30] Ibid. (DS 1740).

The sacramental sharing in the body and blood of Christ makes the community one body and draws it into the fate of the body of Christ. Christ gives himself to the communicants sacramentally and they receive Christ sacramentally. In this way Christ is there to build up the faithful into a spiritual temple, in order that the faithful become changed into the true body of Christ and so become themselves a sacrifice pleasing to God.

The Eucharistic Prayer should be understood as a sacramental symbolic form under which the self-offering of Christ to God and to humanity obtains power over the liturgical assembly. From this point of view, the relation of the cross to the movement of the memorial comes to this: The liturgical assembly is taken up into Christ's self-offering; or, more precisely, is gracefully enabled to participate in the self-offering of Christ. The eucharistic body is not (as traditional teaching would have it) offered as an isolated gift vis-à-vis the community at a "moment of consecration" in the midst of the Eucharistic Prayer in order to entice the community to associate itself with Christ's sacrifice by an act of private devotion.

The Eucharistic Prayer, as prayer of the liturgical assembly, has the orientation from us to the Father. It corresponds to the covenant response of Jesus on the cross to the initiative of the Father in sending the Son for the salvation of the world. On the other hand, the rite of Communion has the orientation from the Father to us. It corresponds to the response of the Father accepting the self-offering of the Son: the sending of the Holy Spirit to quicken the dead body of Jesus. For here, the divine sacrifice, the sacrificial gift Jesus, having been bestowed on the gifts of the Church by the sending of the Spirit to effect the "eucharistic consecration," is given to the communicants in order that they may live. But for this to be realized requires that the communicants accept the gift in faith with its consequences of fidelity to the New Covenant. It requires, in other words, the self-offering of the communicants in obedience and love to the demands of the covenant relationship.

Thus the New Testament concept of sacrifice is mirrored in Holy Communion. This is a reversal of the concept which comes from the history of religions. For sacrifice is not, in the first place, an activity of human beings directed to God and, in the second place, something that reaches its goal in the response of divine acceptance and bestowal of divine blessing on the cultic community. Rather, sacrifice in the New Testament understanding—and thus in its Christian understanding—

is, in the first place, the self-offering of the Father in the gift of his Son, and in the second place the unique response of the Son in his humanity to the Father, and in the third place, the self-offering of believers in union with Christ by which they share in his covenant relation with the Father.

The Holy Spirit brings about the presence of the historical sacrifice of Christ, and acts through it as source of the transmission of the sacrificial attitudes of Christ that enable the liturgical assembly to participate in Christ's self-offering through the medium of the Eucharistic Prayer. The Holy Spirit effects the sanctification of the bread and wine, symbols of the Church's self-offering, making them the sacraments of Christ's body and blood. Likewise the Spirit sanctifies the community so that the communicants communicate spiritually with the Lord whom they encounter sacramentally in the consecrated gifts. In a word the whole liturgy happens "through the power of the Spirit."[31]

The eucharistic sacrifice, just as the historical sacrifice of the cross, is grounded on the initiative of the Father. The whole point of the Eucharist is the participation in Christ's Passover from suffering to glory. This is only possible because of the Father's self-gift in the sending of the Son and the response of the Son in his humanity, and the sanctifying work of the Spirit in the Incarnation and in the life of faith of Jesus.

The believer's eucharistic response is called sacrifice from two points of view. First it is a thanksgiving for, or recognition of, the Father's self-gift of his Son. In the Eucharist the community encounters the whole mystery of Jesus accomplished in his death. The action of the Eucharist stands in a constitutive connection with the redemptive sacrifice of Jesus. It is only possible on the presupposition of his saving death. The Eucharist, in turn, brings to a living presence in the body and blood of the Lord his death and resurrection as center of salvation and of the life of faith. Thus the Eucharist represents, recalls, and applies to the liturgical assembly the event of the cross and resurrection.

Second, the Eucharist has the subjective aspect of the turning back of the community to the Father in which the faithful intentionally offer themselves as the only acceptable subjective response. The radical self-offering of the faithful is the only spiritual response that constitutes an authentic sacrificial act according to the New Testament

[31] Vatican II, Constitution on the Sacred Liturgy, *Sacrosanctum concilium* no. 6.

(Romans 12:1). But it should be noted that the acknowledgment of the Father's gift and the self-offering of the faithful have the goal of eliciting the continual bestowal of the gift and, as far as the self-offering is concerned, the intention is to receive from the Father, the source of all life, the meaning of one's life.

Editor's Epilogue

Edward Kilmartin's manuscript ends at this point. Upon my first acquaintance with it almost four years ago, I assumed that one of my editorial tasks would be to compose an appropriate conclusion. But now, after living closely with this work for the better part of a year, I see the matter differently.

In producing this work, Kilmartin set two major goals, one negative and one positive. His negative goal was to point out and document the inadequacy of the "modern average Catholic theology of eucharistic sacrifice." "Bankrupt" or "has no future" are the blunt terms he uses to describe it. The positive goal, as obvious sequel to the first, was to outline those developments and directions which can lead to a more adequate, more systematic theology of the Eucharist. This was the purpose of his life. But it is also, very clearly, not a goal he thought would be achieved easily or quickly. He repeatedly described it, using the language of the Italian Jesuit liturgical scholar, Cesare Giraudo, as the task of the third theological millennium.

Edward Kilmartin knew well that the ways of the past and the present that do not work as well as they should are much more easily described than the better way of the future for which we are searching. Kilmartin does propose that this better way is to be sought in a more balanced integration of *lex orandi* with *lex credendi,* specifically by attending more carefully to the theological implications of the content and structure of the classical Eucharistic Prayers of the East and the West. And he also proposes that a traditional Catholic theological continuity with the past is to be preserved by seeking a higher understanding of the theology of eucharistic sacrifice. The final section of his last chapter: "Salvation History-Liturgical Theology of Eucharistic Sacrifice" indicates how excitingly mature his synthetic theological vision had become. But he refrains from claiming that here, already, is the Promised Land. He clearly states that he cannot predict what will be the theological way of the third theological millennium. He can only offer us the best map he can. If we can learn by following it, we will be fulfilling the goal of his life, even more so if, in the process, we can develop better maps.

Biblical Index

Index of Councils, Synods, and Papal and Church Documents

Index of Patristic and Liturgical Sources

Index of Names

General Theological Index

97 #2
148 Albert m
194 "megahistorical presence
253 "sacrifice"
255 m
255-256 m(egatime)
257 faith
271 m